The Cambridge Introduction to Satire

In satire, evil, folly, and weakness are held up to ridicule – to the delight of some and the outrage of others. Satire may claim the higher purpose of social critique or moral reform, or it may simply revel in its own transgressive laughter. It exposes frauds, debunks ideals, binds communities, starts arguments, and evokes unconscious fantasies. It has been a central literary genre since ancient times, and has become especially popular and provocative in recent decades. This new introduction to satire takes a historically expansive and theoretically eclectic approach, addressing a range of satirical forms from classical, Renaissance, and Enlightenment texts through contemporary literary fiction, film, television, and digital media. The beginner in need of a clear, readable overview and the scholar seeking to broaden and deepen existing knowledge will both find this a lively, engaging, and reliable guide to satire, its history, and its continuing relevance in the world.

Jonathan Greenberg is Professor of English and Department Chair at Montclair State University and was awarded the Andrew J. Kappel Prize for Literary Criticism in 2007. He is the author of *Modernism, Satire and the Novel* (2012), a Choice Outstanding Academic Title. With Nathan Waddell he co-edited *Brave New World: Contexts and Legacies* (2016). He has also won an Emmy Award for his writing on the classic Nickelodeon cartoon series, Rugrats.

The Cambridge Introduction to Satire

JONATHAN GREENBERG

Montclair State University

CAMBRIDGE
UNIVERSITY PRESS

CAMBRIDGE
UNIVERSITY PRESS

University Printing House, Cambridge CB2 8BS, United Kingdom

One Liberty Plaza, 20th Floor, New York, NY 10006, USA

477 Williamstown Road, Port Melbourne, VIC 3207, Australia

314–321, 3rd Floor, Plot 3, Splendor Forum, Jasola District Centre, New Delhi – 110025, India

79 Anson Road, #06–04/06, Singapore 079906

Cambridge University Press is part of the University of Cambridge.

It furthers the University's mission by disseminating knowledge in the pursuit of education, learning, and research at the highest international levels of excellence.

www.cambridge.org
Information on this title: www.cambridge.org/9781107030183
DOI: 10.1017/9781139343251

First published 2019

Printed and bound in Great Britain by Clays Ltd, Elcograf S.p.A.

A catalogue record for this publication is available from the British Library.

ISBN 978-1-107-03018-3 Hardback
ISBN 978-1-107-68205-4 Paperback

For Megan

Contents

Figures

Abbreviations

For scholarly works from which I quote frequently, I cite the following editions parenthetically using abbreviations and page numbers.

For primary works from which I quote frequently, I use parenthetical references. In most of these cases, parenthetical references indicate page numbers; in other cases, I specify whether they refer to volumes, chapters, cantos, or lines. A list of frequently cited primary works can be found at the back of the book along with a list of films cited.

AC   Frye, Northrop. *Anatomy of Criticism: Four Essays*. Princeton, Princeton University Press, 1957.

AS   Highet, Gilbert. *The Anatomy of Satire*. Princeton, Princeton University Press, 1962.

CS   Quintero, Ruben, ed. *A Companion to Satire: Ancient and Modern*. Malden, MA: Blackwell, 2007.

DI   Bakhtin, Mikhail. *The Dialogic Imagination: Four Essays*. Caryl Emerson and Michael Holquist, trans. Austin, University of Texas Press, 1981.

DSM   Fredric V. Bogel, *The Difference Satire Makes: Rhetoric and Reading from Jonson to Byron*. Ithaca, Cornell University Press, 2001.

FS   Paulson, Ronald. *The Fictions of Satire*. Baltimore, Johns Hopkins University Press, 1967.

LS   Knight, Charles. *The Literature of Satire*. New York, Cambridge University Press, 2004.

PDP   Bakhtin, Mikhail. *Problems in Dostoevsky's Poetics*. Caryl Emerson, trans. Minneapolis, University of Minnesota Press, 1984.

PS   Elliott, Robert C. *The Power of Satire: Magic, Ritual, Art*. Princeton, Princeton University Press, 1962.

PSE   Ashley Marshall. *The Practice of Satire in England, 1658–1770*. Baltimore, Johns Hopkins University Press, 2013.

RHW   Bakhtin, Mikhail. *Rabelais and His World.* Helene Iswolsky trans. Bloomington, Indiana University Press, 1984.

SCR   Griffin, Dustin. *Satire: A Critical Reintroduction.* Lexington, University of Kentucky Press, 1994.

SI   Seidel, Michael. *Satiric Inheritance: Rabelais to Sterne.* Princeton, Princeton University Press, 1979.

SNEE   Paulson, Ronald. *Satire and the Novel in Eighteenth-Century England.* New Haven, Yale University Press, 1967.

SSA   Test, George. *Satire: Spirit and Art.* Tampa, University of South Florida Press, 1991.

STG   Guilhamet, Leon. *Satire and the Transformation of Genre.* Philadelphia, University of Pennsylvania Press, 1987.

The Structure of this Book

This effort at introducing the topic of satire is organized into three large sections. Part I has two chapters. Chapter 1 lays out some basic ideas of what satire is, how it works, and how the understanding of satire among literary critics has evolved. Chapter 2 discusses related terminology in an attempt to familiarize students with frequently used critical categories such as comedy, irony, and parody, and how they have been distinguished from satire. Together, these two chapters aim to offer a serviceable stand-alone introduction to the topic.

Part II commences a historical survey of literary satire, looking at what might be called the traditional canon, though I have sought to expand this canon with texts rediscovered in the last few decades and to update understandings of it with the insights of recent scholarship. Since I view genres as subject to the forces of history, I use both period and genre as organizing principles in an account that is neither strictly chronological nor strictly genre-based. In each chapter I offer an overview followed by a series of readings. While intensive close-reading is not possible due to considerations of space, I do aim for what might be called a "middle-distance-reading" that covers a range of texts but with enough detail and nuance to help readers launch their own sustained analyses. Chapter 3 surveys classical satire, focusing on Athenian Old Comedy, Roman verse satire, and ancient Menippean satire. Chapter 4 examines the Renaissance and early modern period across genres, looking at prose, poetry, and drama. Chapter 5 looks at varieties of prose satire in the Enlightenment, while Chapter 6 covers verse satire in the same historical era, but extends its account through the Romantic era, and glances at some modern examples.

Part III focuses on satire roughly from the mid-eighteenth century to the present, satire that is too often ignored in introductory texts like this. A brief transition frames the critical issues surrounding satire and the novel, and satiric novels are the focus of Chapters 7, 8, and 9. Rather than offer a single chronology of novelistic satire, I identify three different kinds of satiric novel, and provide a historical account of each one. As in the earlier periods,

I assume that formal or generic questions intersect with historical ones. Because introductory courses are likely to vary widely in the novels that they read, I generally treat a greater number of texts in these chapters through shorter readings. Chapter 10 then takes a broad look at satire in popular culture, analyzing satire in a wide variety of forms including journalism, cartoons, light verse, songs, cinema, and television. An epilogue examines the 2015 murders of the French satirists who worked at the magazine *Charlie Hebdo*, and the questions posed by their satire and the public discussion about it.

I should say a few words about my selection of texts. For the most part, I have limited my focus to the English-language tradition I know best. However, in the earlier periods a few key texts – *Gargantua and Pantagruel, Don Quixote, Candide,* and of course the seminal classical authors – are simply too important, and too much in conversation with Anglophone works, to ignore. In the later sections, I occasionally nod to well-known or otherwise significant non-English texts as appropriate. A book like this can always include more, and none of the generous colleagues who read drafts of this work failed to make valuable suggestions of material to add. I hope that as readers draw up their own lists of satires that deserve more critical attention, the analysis I offer here will be of some value.

Acknowledgments

Ray Ryan of Cambridge University Press first suggested that I undertake this book. I am grateful for his belief in me and in the book, for his advice and support, and for his willingness to allow this project the time it demanded. Nicholas Nace read the entire manuscript – much of it more than once – and offered brilliant and detailed commentary throughout, improving it immeasurably. I doubt there is a scholar of his generation as deeply or as widely read in the field of satire. Naomi Liebler provided crucial help on early modern satire and even more crucial pep-talks at various stages along the way. Many other friends and colleagues lent their expertise by reading and commenting on individual chapters: Joe Ansolabehere, Lee Behlman, David Galef, Keith Leslie Johnson, Naomi Liebler (again), David Sedley, Miranda Sherwin, Art Simon, and Robert Weisbuch. On certain specialized questions I consulted Oscar Alcantara, Jessica Burstein, Maria DiBattista, Jeff Gonzalez, David Greenberg, Judith Greenberg, Faye Hammill, Jeff Miller, and Adam Rzepka. And David Currell, Maria DiBattista (again), and Simon Dickie shared unpublished work that helped me to think through questions about satire and the epic, Anita Loos, and picaresque fiction. My graduate assistants Janine Butler and Dayna Arcurio helped with the initial proposal for this book; a few years later, the irreplaceable Giana Milazzo contributed smart, thorough, lucid research that must have saved me hundreds of hours of work. The New York Public Library provided research space and support; at Montclair State University, the entire staff of Sprague Library, particularly those helping with interlibrary loans, deserves special mention. A sabbatical granted by Montclair State University allowed me time to complete this book, and Dean Robert Friedman of the College of Humanities and Social Sciences provided assistance for some key expenses.

My parents, Robert and Maida Greenberg, continue to be an inexhaustible source of love and support. My children, Hank and Maggie, enrich my life every day; in them, I am happy to say, the satiric spirit runs strong. Above all, Megan Blumenreich has been a kind, patient, generous, wise, loving, funny, and utterly invaluable companion through the disquietingly long time it has taken to complete this work. I can't thank her enough.

Part I

Chapter 1

What Is Satire?

Satire: a poem in which wickedness or folly is censured.

— Dr. Samuel Johnson[1]

Satire: the act of being a wise-ass and saying it's for a higher purpose.

— *The Onion Book of Known Knowledge*[2]

Three Episodes

Sometime in the summer of 1674, John Wilmot, the Earl of Rochester, driven by a malice born of sexual rejection and betrayal, hatched a hasty plan to destroy the friendship of three noblewomen. He visited an old crone reputed for her magical powers, a character straight out of *Macbeth*, and, in exchange for the promise of enshrining her name forever in his poetry, secured from her a magical gift, an enormous dildo "long and large as Hector's lance" (83.81). Hastening to the resort town of Bath, Rochester presented the oversized sex toy to the three women, with instructions that it should be given "to the Lady most deserving" (83.87), setting off a bitter feud among them. A truce was attained only with the intervention of a clergyman – and then, apparently, only after he himself had sex with all three women.

Such is the raunchy parody of the *Iliad*'s "Judgment of Paris" as told in heroic couplets by a Restoration-era poet, most likely Rochester himself.[3] An early example of the mock-epic form, the untitled 154-line poem was, according to the scholar Harold Love, probably written as "an act of revenge" in an ongoing feud between Rochester's lover, the Duchess of Portsmouth, and Queen Catherine, whose partisans are depicted as insatiable sex fiends; a handwritten copy of the poem may have been delivered to the women along with an actual dildo. This playful take on the erotic practices, real or imagined, of the Carolean court depends upon an old trope: the "tradition of misogynistic dildo" poems goes back at least to the first or second century CE. But Rochester executes the joke deftly, and his opening pair of questions –

> Say Heav'n-born Muse, for only thou canst tell,
> How discord dire, between two Widows fell?
> What made the Fair one, and her well-shaped Mother,
> Duty forget and pious Nature smother?   (81.1–4)

– likely served as a model for Alexander Pope in his famous poem *The Rape of the Lock*.[4] Rochester's poem certainly shares with Pope's mock epic a fusion of classical parody and thinly veiled references to contemporary acquaintances.

Throughout his short career, Rochester's combination of racy material and verbal dexterity, along with his personal reputation as a rake, won him great recognition, and Andrew Marvell is reported to have called him the leading satirist of his age.[5] But Rochester's penchant for provocation also got him into trouble. The young courtier turned his wit on the king himself, depicting, in another poem, a sovereign in thrall to his sexual cravings:

> For princes' pricks, like to buffoons at court,
> Do govern us, because they make us sport.
> His was the sauciest that e'er did swive,
> The proudest, peremptory prick alive:
> Though safety, religion, life lay on't,
> 'Twould break through all to make its way to c – t.   (86.A14–19)

As a court poet of the Restoration, Rochester did not publish most of his work through the printing press. His poems were copied longhand and intended to be read aloud at court to an audience that was happy or at least willing to be scandalized, provoked, or insulted.[6] Unfortunately, however, during a party, Rochester – perhaps driven by some self-destructive impulse, perhaps simply drunk – mistakenly placed a copy of this poem in the king's pocket. According to one account (a scenario that could easily belong to a tired sitcom), the king had asked to see a different poem and Rochester confused the two manuscripts. Although the king was known for his good-humored indulgence of the earl's antics, this time the attacks, according to one contemporary observer, "touch[ed] too severely upon the King,"[7] dangerously equating political and sexual misrule. In the face of Charles's wrath, or perhaps that of his offended mistress, the Duchess of Portsmouth, Rochester was forced to flee the royal court.[8]

On Valentine's Day, 1989, the Booker and Whitbread Prize-winning novelist Salman Rushdie was sentenced to death by Iran's spiritual leader, the Ayatollah Khomeini, for having written a novel that included among its several storylines a fictional speculation on the life of Muhammad. The novel's title, *The Satanic Verses*, refers specifically to a tale from the "collections of *hadith* or traditions about the life of the Prophet" in which Muhammad, or as Rushdie calls him, Mahound, initially recited certain Qu'ranic verses that accepted the legitimacy of three rival goddesses of Allah, but later recanted these same verses when he recognized them to have been inspired by the devil, Shaitan.[9] As depicted in Rushdie's novel, Mahound's decision is largely a political calculation made to secure an alliance with local non-Muslim authorities. The prophet urges his disciples to accept the three pagan goddesses as a pragmatic concession that will further the growth of his upstart faith:

> You all know what has been happening. Our failure to win converts. The people will not give up their gods . . . Angels and devils . . . Shaitan and Gibreel. We all, already, accept their existence, halfway between God and man. Abu Simbel asks that we admit just three more to this great company. Just three, and, he indicates, all Jahilia's souls will be ours.[10]

The novel had originated during Rushdie's undergraduate years at King's College, Cambridge, where, inspired by his own father's speculations on the historicity of the Qu'ran, he delved into Arabic and Western scholarship about the life of the prophet; twenty years later his research gave rise to an exuberant, multilayered, and fantastical work of fiction that offended the devout in many ways. In addition to its speculations on the composition of the satanic verses, the novel represents a scribe named Salman the Persian taking creative license in writing down the prophet's recitation, the prostitutes of Mecca playfully adopting the names of Muhammad's twelve wives, and a malignant, turbaned, and Khomeini-esque imam living in exile in Kensington while plotting a return home.

In all likelihood, neither Khomeini nor those who backed his *fatwa* had actually read Rushdie's book, but their condemnations spurred demonstrations, riots, and violence worldwide, including the murder of the novel's Japanese translator, and the near-murder of its Norwegian publisher and its Italian translator. Bookstores were firebombed, paperback publication delayed, political debate unleashed. Writers ranging from Jacques Derrida to Bob Woodward to Nuruddin Farah defended Rushdie's right to free speech and the artistic value of his novel; many upheld what Rushdie later called the great "antireligious literary tradition of Boccaccio, Chaucer, Rabelais, Aretino and Balzac."[11] Yet indignant moralists on both the left (Jimmy Carter, John le Carré) and the right (Kingsley Amis, George Steiner) blamed the victim, scolding Rushdie for exercising his artistic and political freedom in a provocative and offensive manner. Rushdie went into hiding for over a decade as the British government worked to have the edict lifted, and only in 2000 was he permitted to relinquish his security detail in the UK. The death threat remains in effect today; state-run Iranian media have recently raised the bounty.

In November 2012, Pete Wells, a *New York Times* restaurant critic, reviewed a new Times Square restaurant called Guy's American Kitchen & Bar, owned and run by Guy Fieri, a popular television chef with platinum-bleached hair, a furry brown goatee, and copious tattooing who had shot to fame after winning a Food Network reality show competition. Wells's review began, innocently but atypically for the genre, by posing questions directly to the restaurateur: "Guy Fieri, have you eaten at your new restaurant in Times Square? Have you pulled up one of the 500 seats at Guy's American Kitchen & Bar and ordered a meal? Did you eat the food? Did it live up to your expectations?"[12] But while the first paragraph displayed a mild insolence restrained by professional decorum, the second threw off any pretense of good manners as it inquired into the state of Fieri's "mind" and "soul":

> Did panic grip your soul as you stared into the whirling hypno wheel of the menu, where adjectives and nouns spin in a crazy vortex? When you saw the burger described as "Guy's Pat LaFrieda custom blend, all-natural Creekstone Farm Black Angus beef patty, LTOP (lettuce, tomato, onion + pickle), SMC (super-melty-cheese) and a slathering of Donkey Sauce on garlic-buttered brioche," did your mind touch the void for a minute?

And so the review continued, piling high the rhetorical questions, not only inquiring about the delinquent service and greasy food, but also skewering Fieri the author – attacking his language, the crazy, spinning "adjectives and nouns" of menus and marketing. At the same time Wells conjured comic-grotesque images of bodily functions that rendered the food wholly unappetizing: "When we hear the words Donkey Sauce," he asked, "which part of the donkey are we supposed to think about?"

Within two days, the review had gone viral on the Internet, reaching 45,000 Facebook shares. Fieri took to a morning television show to defend his restaurant and to accuse Wells of snobbery and self-promotion. Fellow TV personalities such as the drawling self-help therapist "Dr. Phil" joined the counter-attack while the *Times*'s public editor defended the scathing review. Pundits in print and digital media interpreted the conflict in all kinds of ways: as a culture war flare-up between the reviewer's blue-state elitism and the TV chef's red-state populism; as an emblem of a new digital media world in which "snark" and controversy are rewarded with clicks, hits, tweets, likes, and shares; as a case study in camp aesthetics in which an attack on a cynical marketing ploy was largely misread as an attack on innocence; even as a sociocultural protest, "a giant fuck you to the whole food network celebrity chef culture."[13]

A bawdy Restoration poem, a multi-plot postcolonial novel, a snarky restaurant-review-turned-Internet-meme: what do they have in common? All three texts enact some judgment or attack – on the sexual habits of Charles II, on the authority of canonical interpretations of the Qu'ran, on the culinary skills of a popular TV chef. All the texts seem to refer to real-world, historical people, even when those people are disguised or somehow transmuted into fictional entities. All these judgments, moreover, rely upon transgression as well as aggression: Rochester insults the king with vulgar language; Rushdie violates both the religious stricture against questioning the divine authorship of the Qu'ran and the Western liberal one against maligning anyone's religious beliefs; Wells crosses lines of decency, fair play, or etiquette, exceeding what seems the proper evaluative function of a review.

Yet none of these writings is *merely* a work of aggression or transgression. They all shape their judgments into an artistic form and blend attack with entertainment. Rochester's satire on the king is as notable for its playful representation of the monarch's sex life as for any cogent political critique. As his invocation of medieval and Renaissance satirists suggests, Rushdie's story of the satanic verses is a rebellious but imaginative exploration of the nature of artistic and spiritual inspiration, and he sets his inquiry within a narrative structure that deliberately confuses present and past, natural and supernatural, consciousness and dream, reality and delusion. Wells's rant, in its own small way, explodes the genre of the restaurant review, and in its strict adherence to the interrogative mood it joins a tradition of literary forms like the villanelle or lipogram that force creativity upon the author through the imposition of arbitrary constraints.[14] The artistry produces pleasure, even laughter. Imagination and wit render the object of attack amusing or ridiculous.

Finally, all of these works provoke real-world controversy. They intervene in the world's business. The "incidents" surrounding these texts involve not only the writer and the apparent target, but also other readers, actual and notional. Even the episode about which we know the least – Rochester's accidental disclosure of his satire to King Charles – likely caused problems for the poet not merely because the king didn't like to be insulted, but because he didn't want the insulting poems to circulate at court. The Wells–Fieri fracas, by most measures a trivial event, merited time on a popular morning news show and commentary from the public editor of America's leading newspaper. The Rushdie controversy – if that word is strong enough to describe it – remains, thirty years later, a major cultural and political reference point. The debate that surrounded it has come to represent a fundamental clash of values that, Rushdie has maintained, can now be seen as a prologue to the destruction of the Twin Towers, not to mention the terrorist killings that followed the publication of satirical cartoons in France's *Charlie Hebdo* magazine in 2015. In all these cases, something playful became serious.

Rochester's poems, Rushdie's novel, and Wells's review are all examples of satire. Whether this claim strikes you as obvious or tendentious may depend upon your own experience as a reader and a student of satire – what you think "satire" means. For some scholars, satire is primarily a historical *genre*, narrowly defined, that reached its heights of accomplishment during the early Roman Empire and Enlightenment-era Europe. As Harry Levin has written, "It is generally agreed that English satire enjoyed its heyday during the first half of the eighteenth century; it declined ... with the emergence of mere sentimental and romantic touchstones."[15] For much of the last century, this idea of satire prevailed among literary critics, and for some good reasons. Beginning in the late eighteenth century, the lyric emerged as the dominant form of poetry and the novel the dominant form of prose fiction. Few new works of literature today formally resemble the satires of eighteenth-century figures like Alexander Pope and Jonathan Swift, and those that do are often relegated to minor status as parodies, entertainments, or light humor. Yet Levin's description of a genre of literature that belongs mainly to the past bears little resemblance to what non-scholars usually mean when they talk about satire. In common usage, people apply the term to a vast range of literature and other kinds of cultural production – music, visual art, journalism, film, video, performance, even customs, rituals, and other activities – that they read, witness, and participate in regularly. Any analysis of satire that ignores this everyday usage of the word will exclude a huge body of material in which satiric attitudes and behaviors survive prominently and vitally in the present. In this wider conception, satire is often referred to as a *mode*, or even, for one recent critic, a *practice* (PSE).

In seeking to outline what satire is and has been, in the rest of this chapter I offer not a narrow definition of satire but a broad discussion. I begin with the "ordinary language" assumption that satire is *whatever it is that we call satire.* Common usage, in other words, should guide us more than the pedantic diktats of critics. I first address the distinctions between satire as genre, mode, and practice. I then describe the still-influential understanding of satire that coalesced in the 1950s and 1960s as morally purposive literature that deploys wit, irony, fantasy, and humor. But as literary studies have changed, this view has been challenged, and I therefore review the major arguments against that old model. I fill out the analysis with examination of other features often associated with satire, and, finally, I discern some ways that satires can be described or grouped in order to help the reader find new lines of connection.

Genre, Mode, Practice

The first distinction to be made in analyzing satire is between satire as a *genre* and satire as a *mode* – or between the *form* and the *tone* of satire (*FS* 4). Throughout much of history, the word "satire" referred to a particular kind of *poem*. In his *Dictionary* of 1755, Samuel Johnson defined satire as a "poem in which wickedness or folly is censured." The ancient Roman poets who wrote satire and the eighteenth-century English writers who took those Roman poets as models used the term explicitly in the titles of their works. Even a later figure such as Thomas Hardy called his 1914 collection of poems *Satires of Circumstance*. Writers may have used different genre names to describe their poems – Horace's *sermones* or talks, Pope's epistles and essays – but the resemblances in form, style, content, and tone remain strong enough that scholars classify these poems as satires. These works constitute what George Test has called "a special kind of poetry," *formal verse satire* (*SSA* 10). Conventional wisdom holds that in English-language literature the years from John Dryden to Samuel Johnson – or, more liberally, from John Donne to Lord Byron – constitute the era in which formal verse satire attained its greatest cultural centrality and aesthetic achievement.

But in addition to formal verse satire, there exists a second genre of satire, one that has come to be called *Menippean satire*, after the Greek philosopher Menippus of the third century BCE, whose writings are lost but whose influence survives through the work of Marcus Terentius Varro and Lucian of Samosata. Although Menippean satire shares characteristics with verse satire, it is generally understood as a prose form, or a combination of prose and verse, marked by what the ancients called a "seriocomic" tone. Whereas Horace, Juvenal, and Persius are the major figures in Roman verse satire, the classical authors Varro, Lucian, Seneca, Petronius, and Apuleius exemplify the Menippean genre. Like formal verse satire, Menippean satire re-emerges forcefully in early modern Europe; some writers are famous for satires in both prose and verse. Menippean satire has generated its own body of scholarship and debate. Some argue for a wide definition, while others urge restraint, arguing that term has been abused.[16] Some claim that it should be considered discrete from formal verse satire, while others see the genres as overlapping. Some claim that it has been absorbed in modern times by the novel, while a few insist that the novel and the Menippean satire must be considered separate genres. In almost all accounts, however, ancient and early modern Menippean satire is recognized as an important precursor to contemporary satiric fiction.

Even when satire is understood as a genre (or two), it is often understood as a genre that resists or complicates the very idea of genre. Satire combines, inhabits, or transforms other genres. It mixes subject matter, linguistic registers, and literary traditions. Satire, moreover, exists in ironic or secondary relation to "higher" genres, and it negates the authority of epic, saga, and myth (*SI* 63). Some critics go so far as to claim that the "appropriation of other forms is unique to satire and one of its chief identifying characteristics" (*STG* 13). Satire indeed often appears as a mock form: a mock epic, a mock encomium, a mockumentary. The word *mock* can mean either to imitate or to ridicule via imitation, and both of these connotations adhere to our understanding of satire as a genre that mocks other genres.

For most readers today, however, satire cannot be limited to these genres at all. Much drama is satiric. Whether or not the work of Aristophanes is best described as satire or comedy – scholars call it "Old Comedy" to distinguish it from the later phases of Greek comedy that focus more exclusively on domestic life – it possesses many satiric elements and has deeply influenced satirists ancient and modern. The plays of Ben Jonson and Molière offer early modern examples of satiric drama, and audiences have found satire in Oscar Wilde's comedies of manners, in the social critiques of Henrik Ibsen and George Bernard Shaw, in the ironic method and political purpose of Bertolt Brecht's "epic theater." And anyone who sees *The Book of Mormon* on stage, or *Last Week Tonight* on TV, or *Saturday Night Live* on her iPhone will recognize that satire applies meaningfully to a much broader range of culture, performance, and media than even the three major genres of literature. One way to widen our understanding of satire, then, would be to recognize, as I do in this book, the many satiric subgenres: city comedies, mock epics, picaresque novels, mockumentaries, modest proposals, and more.

To appreciate the full range of satiric literature, we need to consider satire not as a *genre* but as a *mode*. A mode, according to Alastair Fowler, is a looser sort of category than a genre, lacking the strong structural and formal markers of a genre but still sending "distinct signals" to a reader.[17] Because it is more nebulous than a genre, we often describe a mode with an adjective rather than a noun: *satiric* rather than *satire*. For Charles Knight, satire is "not a genre" but rather "pre-generic." It is "an exploiter of other genres," but also a "frame of mind," a "skeptical attitude towards life" (*LS* 4). In a previous book, I have called satire a "sensibility," since it implies a way of seeing the world – something short of a fully worked-out philosophical position, but something more than a mere feeling or mood.[18]

But even the idea of satire as a mode has its problems: it can restrict criticism to the formal analysis of a text that is understood to be a self-contained artifact. If, like Ashley Marshall, however, we think of satire as a *practice*, we recognize it as an action or behavior that takes place in a specific historical context. The idea of satire as practice has not been explicitly theorized in the way that satire as a genre or mode has been, but many thinkers point the way to how it might be done. Drawing on speech-act theory, Linda Hutcheon says that "irony happens" – it requires a particular context of expectation and interpretation in order to be received as irony– and the same insight can be extended to satire.[19] Steven Jones notes that because satire is among the most "culturally embedded" kinds of literature, "to read satire" is always "to contextualize" it within specific historical parameters.[20] Drawing on theorists such as Jürgen Habermas and Michael Warner, we might further recognize satire as an intervention in a public arena of discourse, an activity that brings people together (and pushes others away) to create a "public" or a dissenting "counterpublic."[21] Satire circulates through a culture, accruing new shades of meaning and eliciting new public responses. Finally, satire might be understood as an assertion of what Pierre Bourdieu called cultural capital. By distinguishing good from bad, satire distinguishes *us*: in delineating what we as writers or readers accept and reject, it positions us within a social "field" according to our tastes, judgments, and behaviors.[22]

Definition and Its Difficulties

Satire's ambiguous status as genre, mode, and practice already suggests some of the difficulty that besets any effort at defining it. Even the etymology of the word is duplicitous. It derives from the Latin *satura*, part of the phrase *lanx satura*, meaning a mixed platter of fruit or nuts. It presumably refers to the varied and miscellaneous nature of Roman verse satire. But in part due to a fourth-century work of criticism by the grammarian Diomedes, the word *satire* became confused with the Greek word *satyr*, and a kind of literature became associated with a Greek mythological creature and the ancient Greek "satyr plays" named for it. Rough, crude, and sexually aggressive, the satyr came to seem an apt figure for the rough, crude, and verbally aggressive satirist.[23] Although the false etymology was debunked by Isaac Casaubon in 1605, the erroneous association persisted because its assumptions about satiric aggression seemed logical, and early modern poets often called their verses "satyres."

But defining satire risks a greater danger than etymological confusion. It risks pedantry and irrelevance, and can become mired in fussy quibbling. It is therefore not surprising that, as Dustin Griffin observes, "since the 1960s there has been something of a retreat from large-scale theoretical claims about 'the nature of satire'" (*SCR* 31). Critics and students alike have put the definitional questions to one side and simply gone ahead with the work of analysis. After all, maybe not all satires in all periods and cultures work the same way or do the same things. Moreover, as Griffin points out, some of the most famous proclamations about satire tend to be quoted out of their original contexts and converted into rules and definitions, even though they originate as specific claims made in response to specific questions (*SCR* 37–39). Unwittingly, scholars fashion ironbound rules from casual or ironic remarks. For these reasons, a rigid definition of satire may be less useful than the description of a set of what Wittgenstein called "family resemblances." Kathryn Hume urges scholars to "conceptualize satire and the satiric as a family defined by a bundle of features. No single feature need be present, just a substantial number of them."[24] Such a policy gives up the goal of determining categories once and for all, and allows a flexible treatment attuned to the variety of works that appear to different readers as satire.

Yet even such a flexible approach requires some discernment of family traits. What are the notable family features of satire? Modern critics have generally begun with two basic criteria. In Northrop Frye's 1957 formulation, "Satire demands at least a token fantasy, a content which the reader recognizes as grotesque, and at least an implicit moral standard" (*AC* 224).[25] Minimally, satire requires a *fantasy* (specified as grotesque), and a *moral standard* (possibly implicit). But Frye's two-part model easily expands, so that George Test can distinguish four essential elements – *aggression, judgment, play, laughter* – with Test's first two criteria corresponding roughly to Frye's moral standard and the second two to Frye's grotesque fantasy (*SSA* 15). Another foundational theorist, Gilbert Highet, lists five elements – *topicality, exaggeration, shock, informality, dark or grotesque humor* – and then stipulates that the emotion evoked must be a "blend of amusement and contempt" (*AS* 21). Edward Rosenheim requires three elements: attack, "a manifest fiction," and reference to "historical particulars."[26] For Kathryn Hume, the list grows to a clunky and perhaps redundant nine: *attack, humor or wit, self-display, exaggeration, moral or existential truth, mockery, inquiry,* a *moral ideal,* and a *reformative aim.*[27] Clearly, these terms are heterogeneous, slippery, and prone to multiplication. How can we put them together?

The Canonical Model

An influential effort to form a coherent model of satire took place in the 1950s and 1960s. The work of several scholars – including Frye, Maynard Mack, Alvin Kernan, Robert C. Elliott, and Ronald Paulson – coalesced into a description of satire that I will call canonical. (It is sometimes referred to as "New Critical," but not all of its assumptions were New Critical.) The canonical model holds that satire is purposeful, "directed toward a preconceived end."[28] Satire's purpose is to exercise moral judgment. It condemns human failings, what Johnson called "wickedness or folly" ("knaves and fools"). It calls attention to individual or collective evil, and, explicitly or implicitly, urges the reader or viewer to participate in the censure of that evil. Satire therefore relies on the concepts of *laus et vituperatio,* praise and blame; by praising and blaming it neatly separates the world into good and bad. The British satirist Wyndham Lewis announced his aesthetic credo in the 1914 journal *Blast* with just this formulation, "blessing" and "blasting" those people, institutions, and phenomena that he liked and didn't like (*PS* 224) (Figure 1). And because issuing praise or blame – toward a person, a group, a practice – implies a norm against which that person, group, or practice is measured, even satire that appears wholly negative is thought to imply a higher standard of behavior. Likewise, a statement of praise can implicitly censure those who do not conform to the standard set by the object of praise (*STG* 21–22). As Ezra Pound put it, "Satire reminds one that certain things are not worth while."[29]

In addition to judging people against a moral norm, satire, according to the canonical model, requires a motive and a mechanism. Satire does not just identify vice and folly but aims to reform or punish them. Readers or viewers of satire discern vice or folly in others and are roused to indignation, brought into alliance with the satirist against a common target. Or if readers see themselves in the target of the satire, they are shamed into reform. Satire thus draws upon norms that are widely shared, and its meaning is fundamentally stable. The enforcement of stable moral norms makes satire culturally conservative, as the satirist speaks on behalf of age-old truths in the face of a decadent modern world. Satire is therefore a public mode or genre: it aims to apply its norms to a community, a nation, or even all of humanity.[30] The canonical model thus tends to locate satire in particular societies and time periods, particularly the eighteenth century. W.H. Auden sums up this old view: "Satire flourishes in a homogeneous society where satirist and audience share the same views as to how normal people can be expected to behave, and in times of relative stability and contentment."[31]

(a)

BLAST

The Post Office   Frank Brangwyn   Robertson Nicol

Rev. Pennyfeather   Galloway Kyle
(Bells)   (Cluster of Grapes)

Bishop of London and all his posterity

Galsworthy   Dean Inge   Croce   Matthews

Rev. Meyer   Seymour Hicks

Lionel Cust   C. B. Fry   Bergson   Abdul Bahai

Hawtrey   Edward Elgar   Sardlea

Filson Young   Marie Corelli   Geddes

Codliver Oil   St. Loe Strachey   Lyceum Club

Rhabindraneth Tagore   Lord Glenconner of Glen

Weiniger   Norman Angel   Ad. Mahon

Mr. and Mrs. Dearmer   Beecham   Ella
A. C. Benson   (Pills, Opera, Thomas) Sydney Webb

British Academy   Messrs. Chapell

Countess of Warwick   George Edwards

Willie Ferraro   Captain Cook   R. J. Campbell

Clan Thesiger   Martin Harvey   William Archer

George Grossmith   R. H. Benson

Annie Besant   Chenil   Clan Meynell

Father Vaughan   Joseph Holbrooke   Clan Strachey

(b)

BLESS

Bridget   Berrwolf   Bearline   Cranmer Byng
Frieder Graham   The Pope   Maria de Tomaso
Captain Kemp   Munroe   Gaby   Jenkins
R. B. Cuningham Grahame   Barker
(not his brother)   (John and Granville)
Mrs. Wil Finnimore   Madame Strindberg   Carson
Salvation Army   Lord Howard de Walden
Capt. Craig   Charlotte Corday   Cromwell
Mrs. Duval   Mary Robertson   Lillie Lenton
Frank Rutter   Castor Oil   James Joyce
Leveridge   Lydia Yavorska   Preb. Carlyle   Jenny
Mon. le compte de Gabulis   Smithers   Dick Burge
33 Church Street   Sievier   Gertie Millar
Norman Wallis   Miss Fowler   Sir Joseph Lyons
Martin Wolff   Watt   Mrs. Hepburn
Alfree   Tommy   Captain Kendell   Young Ahearn
Wilfred Walter   Kate Lechmere   Henry Newbolt
Lady Aberconway   Frank Harris   Hamel
Gilbert Canaan   Sir James Mathew Barry
Mrs. Belloc Lowdnes   W. L. George   Rayner
George Robey   George Mozart   Harry Weldon
Chaliapine   George Hirst   Graham White
Hucks   Salmet   Shirley Kellogg   Bandsman Rice
Petty Officer Curran   Applegarth   Konody
Colin Bell   Lewis Hind   LEFRANC
Hubert   Commercial Process Co.

Figure 1 Wyndham Lewis, "Blast" and "Bless." From *Blast*, Issue 1, June 20, 1914. By permission the Wyndham Lewis Memorial Trust, a registered charity. Photograph courtesy of the Modernist Journals Project, Brown University and University of Tulsa.

Lewis offers a modern variation on the old satiric theme of *laus et vituperatio*, or praise and blame.

Yet the shared moral standard – along with the stable meaning and the aim of punishment or reform – is only one side of satire. The canonical model has another component. In the prologue to Ben Jonson's play *Volpone*, the chorus explains the playwright's intentions: "In all his poems still hath been this measure, / To mix profit with your pleasure" (49). This combination of profit and pleasure was a central Renaissance formula for all literature, derived from Horace's dictum in *Ars Poetica* that poetry should mix the useful with the sweet (*"miscuit utile dulci"*). Indeed, from Horace's two functions of literature it is a short skip to John Dryden's influential discussion in his 1693 "Discourse Concerning the Original and Progress of Satire," and from there to Frye's two-pronged definition.[32] Comedy writer-turned-US Senator Al Franken put it plainly when he titled his 2005 book *The Truth (with Jokes)*. Despite the jokes, however, the moral purpose of satire remains primary; wit, humor, irony, parody, caricature, grotesquerie are merely satire's "methods" – sugar added to help the medicine go down. And because satire's overriding purpose has been seen as one of moral judgment or attack, the humor most closely affiliated with satire is that which Freud calls "tendentious": the targeted laughter of ridicule and mockery.

Revising the Canonical Model

The canonical model has many virtues. It shifted academic criticism of satire from what Fredric Bogel calls a "preformalist" historicism to literary analysis, and it gave critical shape and weight to what had been vague intuitions and assumptions (*DSM* 5). But over the last half-century, waves of literary theory have challenged and complicated the old consensus. Most crucially, scholars have become more skeptical about characterizing satire as a necessarily moral mode. Even if satire does exert judgment and rely on norms, not every norm is a moral one. Guy Fieri's restaurant may be awful, but can pretzel chicken tenders, no matter how grease-laden, be immoral? Satire may just as easily take aim at social or intellectual failings as ethical ones.[33] As Charles Knight points out, "ugliness, clumsiness, foolishness, bad taste, [and] stupidity" are generally not thought to be forms of immorality (*LS* 5). For Robert Hume, the critical shibboleth of a "high moral norm" has survived only because of intellectual inertia and cannot withstand a detailed examination "the nitty-gritty daily actualities" of satiric practice.[34] To be sure, some famous eighteenth-century satirists claimed moral motives: Pope said that satire "heals with Morals what it hurts with Wit" (262), Swift that he wrote "with a moral View designed / To cure the Vices of Mankind" (634).[35] But the expression of moral purpose is often no more than a convenient theme, a cliché that offers an occasion for satiric observation or performance (*SCR* 37). P.K. Elkin noted back in 1973 that the moral justifications of early eighteenth-century satirists were often little more than "handy sticks with which to beat off their assailants."[36]

Even when a moral purpose can be discovered, this purpose rarely spurs reform. Swift's Lemuel Gulliver observes with mock surprise that his countrymen's behavior has failed to change despite the popularity of his *Travels*: "Behold, after above six months warning, I cannot learn that my book has produced one single effect according to my intentions." He continues:

> I desired you would let me know, by a letter, when party and faction were extinguished; judges learned and upright; pleaders honest and modest, with some tincture of common sense, and Smithfield blazing with pyramids of law books; the young nobility's education entirely changed; the physicians banished; the female *Yahoos* abounding in virtue, honour, truth, and good sense; courts and levees of great ministers thoroughly weeded and swept; wit, merit, and learning rewarded.   (255)

Satire, despite its "plainly deducible" lessons, brings about no magical, instantaneous reform. Indeed, Swift observes elsewhere, readers have an uncanny ability to deflect satiric criticism away from themselves and onto others: "Satire is a sort of glass, wherein beholders do generally discover everybody's face but their own" (95).

In Woody Allen's *Manhattan*, Ike Davis offers a slightly different reason for doubting satire's power. Having learned of an imminent neo-Nazi march, Ike proposes that he and some friends "get some bricks and baseball bats and really explain things to 'em." A woman instead suggests reading a "devastating satirical piece on that on the op-ed page of the *Times*," but Ike dismisses the vaunted power of satire:

IKE: Well, a satirical piece in the *Times* is one thing, but bricks and baseball bats really gets right to the point down there.

HELEN: Oh, but really biting satire is always better than physical force.

IKE: No, physical force is always better with Nazis ... It's hard to satirize a guy with shiny boots on.[37]

Satiric commentary seems wholly inadequate in the face of the murderous hatred of neo-Nazis, just as it proves inadequate to the flood of corruption and vice that plagued Gulliver's England.

The most powerful criticism of the old model, however, is that the focus on moral norms overstabilizes satire, eliminating its volatility, misrepresenting its emotional dynamics, and occluding our understanding of it. The invocation of a moral purpose may be not just a lazy critical assumption or a worn generic convention but a dishonest pretext. In *The Onion*'s definition – "the act of being a wise-ass and saying it's for a higher purpose" – satire relies on its moral claim as an excuse to engage in irreverent behavior. The reformative purpose of satire becomes what Michael Seidel calls "a preserving fiction, a mere saving of appearances" (*SI* 3). Kenneth Burke viewed satire as founded on an act of projection in which "the satirist attacks *in others* the weaknesses and temptations that are really *within himself*," displacing his forbidden desires onto a target whom he can punish.[38] Justified and emboldened by the pretext of improving public morals, a writer or reader can enjoy the scolding and ridiculing of satiric targets, the vicarious participation in violations and vices. Much satire in fact degrades its targets far beyond the needs of moral reform; it appears animated by what William Hazlitt called "the pleasure of hating," a primitive pleasure we experience "at being restored . . . to freedom and lawless unrestrained impulses."[39] Thus in the 1930s, Wyndham Lewis attempted to separate satire and morality entirely, arguing that "the best satire is non-moral" – that it does not let moral compunction restrain the more fundamental impulses of the artist.[40]

As changes in the wider field of literary studies have eroded the belief that satire promotes moral norms, so other features of the canonical model have come into question. Deconstruction has dismantled old assumptions about the stability of satiric irony and the formal unity of literary works. Psychoanalysis has challenged our confidence in the transparency and consistency of human motives, and instilled in readers a suspicion of high moral claims. Mikhail Bakhtin's analyses of language, culture, and genre have offered an understanding of satire as anti-authoritarian and emancipatory. Feminism and cultural studies have recovered much satiric writing that failed to fit the formulas of Dryden, Pope, and Swift. Scholars of the eighteenth century have rejected the idea of the so-called Augustan Age as a stable time of shared values; we now see (contra W.H. Auden) that satire thrives not in times of stability but in times of conflict and strife. Habermas, Warner, and Bourdieu might help us recognize how satire operates and circulates in a dynamic social field. The result has been that not only has satire's moral basis come into question, but so have many of the other tenets of the canonical model. These critical changes and challenges inform the following discussion of other satirical elements that have sometimes been recognized but not always emphasized in satire criticism.

Provocation, Fantasy, Performance

Once the moral purpose of satire is dislodged from its position of primacy, other motives for satire become more visible. For Griffin, satire can be seen not only to judge, attack, and blame, but also to inquire, provoke, and explore (*SCR* 39ff.). Consider the controversy over *The Satanic Verses*. One can interpret the novel as a targeted judgment against authoritarian religious codes, but it is better described as a broad inquiry or exploration into the process of inspiration, both religious and artistic. The prophet Mahound is shown to be enmeshed in history and politics, but his decisions, though calculating, are not cynical, and Rushdie takes seriously the possibility of divine inspiration. Similarly, a hypercanonical satire such as *Gulliver's Travels* has given rise to conflicting interpretations regarding the norms that it might endorse, but virtually all readers agree that its fantastical scenarios inquire into serious questions about human nature and society. Swift's own motive, if we can take him at his word, was "to vex the world rather than divert it" (676), suggesting a contrarian provocation. Satire can often open philosophical, moral, and political questions more successfully than it can resolve them.

Another element of satire is what Frye called its fantasy content. Satire relies on techniques like exaggeration, deformation, caricature, and distortion, which push satiric representations beyond a threshold of realism. Characters, scenes, images, and events are taken to extremes. Satire depicts improbable events like Lucius's transformation into a donkey in Apuleius's *The Golden Ass* and Slim Pickens riding a nuclear warhead like a bronco in *Dr. Strangelove* (Figure 2). Satiric fantasies can appear humorous, as when Rabelais's giant Gargantua combs cannonballs out of his hair, but they can also give shape to disturbing fears and desires. Paul Beatty's novel *The Sellout* imagines a contemporary African-American gentleman farmer who re-establishes segregation and slavery. In Sherman Alexie's caustic poem "Evolution," a character named Buffalo Bill opens a pawn shop on an Indian reservation, "right across the border from the liquor store."[41] The Indians rush to sell him their possessions, including treasured artifacts, so they can buy alcohol. When they run out of possessions, the poem's imagery assumes a grotesque cast: "The Indians / pawn their hands, saving the thumbs for last, they pawn / their skeletons." In literalizing the Indians' symbolic self-mutilation, Alexie censures both the white man (the knave) for his wickedness and the Indian (the fool) for his folly, and he expresses this censure in the stark surreal language of the unconscious. The history of satire is full of such fantasies, which express primitive fears of being abandoned, killed, eaten, or dismembered. Among the common motifs of satire are

Figure 2 Slim Pickens as Major "King" Kong riding a very phallic nuclear warhead in Stanley Kubrick's *Dr. Strangelove or: How I Learned to Stop Worrying and Love the Bomb*. © 1963, renewed 1991 Columbia Pictures Industries, Inc. All Rights Reserved. Courtesy of Columbia Pictures.

Kubrick furnishes one of cinema's most vivid examples of satire's use of garish, fantastical imagery to dramatize unconscious fears and wishes.

excremental imagery, mob violence, cannibalism, and human transformations into beasts.

But the wildness of satiric dreams and nightmares exists in tension with satiric realism. Satire shows us dimensions of human experience generally closed off to the higher genres – the messy functioning of the body, the ignoble desires of the soul, the hard truths about society's corruption. Realism and satire share the functions of truth-telling and exposure, examining the world closely and unflinchingly.[42] They authorize their representations with a claim to show things as they are; they disclose what official, sanitized accounts keep hidden. As Horace writes, satire removes "the glossy skin" behind which people "conceal / their ugliness" (2.1.64–65). Wyndham Lewis argued that satire is an external method of art that approaches its object with a cold and clear vision; it sides with the ugly rather than the beautiful, and its goal is "to bring human life more into contempt each day."[43] Satire ironizes, debunks, burlesques, and redescribes. It subjects lofty ideals and grand theories to the test of real-life experience. When Byron considers why young Don Juan associates the boundlessness of the heavens with his lover's eyes, he rejects a spiritual motive for a biological one: "If *you* think 'twas philosophy that this did, / I can't help thinking puberty assisted" (1.93). Mohsin Hamid, tracing the course of his protagonist's life, casts the prospect of a financially secure old age in a satiric light: "in the race between death and destitution, you can look forward to the former emerging victorious."[44]

Many elements of satire are playful: humor, wit, exaggeration. The canonical model of satire relegates play to secondary status, a means of illustrating norms. Yet the indulgence of play can just as easily be seen as satire's real "purpose," and the moral justification or judgment as merely a "method" of launching that play. Satiric joking and play afford a rebellious release from authority, including the authority of reason. Rochester's poetry offers a good example. It affords a transgressive frisson in its discussion of sexual behavior, but it is not pornographic. Instead, Rochester takes his fantastical conceits and over-the-top raunchiness to a point that they become ludicrous, granting the reader "a dispensation from reticences which are normally activated when we mean to be taken 'seriously.'"[45]

The novelist Dawn Powell wrote that "The enjoyment of satire is that of nine-pins – seeing the ball strike truly and the pins go down."[46] She identifies not only the aggressive satisfaction of hitting a target, but also an appreciation of the execution of the ball well thrown, the authorial skill that makes satire succeed. As the poet Lady Mary Wortley Montagu said, satire must possess not only the "rage" but also "the talent of abuse" (28). The heroic couplets of Pope and the *ottava rima* stanzas of Byron dazzle with their intricate verbal virtuosity. Novelists like Will Self or Gary Shteyngart create alternate worlds that astonish us in their imaginative fecundity. The critic Stanley Fish has remarked that reading a great sentence is akin to watching an astonishing sports highlight: both are "performances of a certain skill at the highest level," for which our "admiration" includes "a rueful recognition that you couldn't do it yourself."[47] In formulating incisive, original turns of phrase, wits like Oscar Wilde and Dorothy Parker call attention to their inimitable talents. Freud notes that "the motive force for the production of innocent jokes is not infrequently an ambitious urge to show one's cleverness," and he links this motive with "exhibitionism in the sexual field."[48] This narcissistic exhibitionism makes satire a highly performative mode in which the satirist wins our admiration.

Satire, finally, is also distinctive among literary modes in the feelings that it engages. It draws upon negative emotions such as anger, indignation, disgust, sadism, contempt, and aloofness. It produces similar feelings in readers – unless it elicits shame, unease, or anxiety. Yet even here it is hard to generalize. Satiric voices and tones vary, and some satires seem predominantly playful or even jovial: an important strain of satire running from Aristophanes through Rabelais to Mel Brooks is dominated by hearty laughter and revels in humanity's imperfections. But often satire works against the evocation of compassion. It works as a check on runaway or unmerited sympathy, an antidote to sentimentality, an emotional astringent. It offers a hard-headed caution against overlooking human baseness. Yet even bitter and bleak satire can harbor covert idealism or romanticism, and as satiric works grow in complexity, they can make room for tenderness and compassion alongside disgust, contempt, and indignation.

The Real World

A final characteristic of satire is that it makes reference to the real world. Satire speaks about specific individuals and situations. The controversies described at the beginning of this chapter – over Rochester's poem, Rushdie's novel, Wells's review – only occur because satire refers, or is taken to refer, to real people. Satire's disruptive force depends upon this referentiality. Horace praises the Greek playwrights of Old Comedy for their outspokenness in naming names: "If any person deserved to be publicly exposed for being / a crook and a thief, an adulterer or a cut-throat, or for being notorious / in some other way, they used to speak right out and brand him" (1.4.3–5). From Aristophanes' attacks on Socrates to Dryden's on Thomas Shadwell to Twain's on Belgium's King Leopold, satire goes after living figures, even though it may assume a veil of fiction. In his novel *Black No More*, George Schuyler insults virtually all of the major African-American leaders of the time: W.E.B. DuBois becomes Shakespeare Agamemnon Beard, who writes editorials "denouncing the Caucasians whom he secretly admired and lauding the greatness of the Negroes whom he alternately pitied and despised"; James Weldon Johnson becomes Napoleon Wellington Jackson, who "sought to prove conclusively that the plantation shouts of Southern Negro peons were superior to any of Beethoven's symphonies"; Marcus Garvey becomes Santop Licorice, who advocates that blacks return to Africa even though he himself "had not the slightest intention of going so far from the fleshpots."[49] Schuyler's comic renditions of his intellectual enemies indict a black intelligentsia that he saw as self-important and hypocritical. But referentiality also gives satire another appeal, a charge of pleasure in guessing who is really being targeted, or even in being targeted oneself. Evelyn Waugh marveled that his acquaintances were always eager to claim themselves as prototypes for his most unsavory characters.[50]

But what exactly is the relationship between a character represented in satire and the real-world person on whom that representation is based? Can we say that Schuyler's Shakespeare Agamemnon Beard "is" W.E.B. DuBois? The Socrates of *Clouds* cannot be exactly the same Socrates that we find in Plato's dialogues; we recognize him as a literary character, not a historically valid representation of the philosopher who lived in the fifth century BCE. Sir Philip Sidney asserted that the poet "never lieth" – that literary statements are devoid of truth-claims altogether – and this has long been a defense for satirists who deny that they attack individuals. But it can also function as a screen behind which the author can hide, especially when her satire might upset the powerful and bring retribution upon herself. Thus in the eighteenth century, the referentiality of satire counted as a mark against it since it indicated a base motive of personal animus rather than a noble one of moral reform. Critics of the time distinguished "lampoon," which attacked individuals, from "satire," which focused on general targets. Finally, the referentiality of satire might be seen, like the invocation of a moral purpose, as a mere rhetorical convention, important because it fulfills expectations of the genre. Puzzling over real-life references might turn out to be as fruitless as "searching for the real god invoked by an epic poet" (*DSM* 10).

Related to referentiality is the topicality of satire, the capacity of literature to treat people and issues that are of pressing public interest at the time of the writing. By naming names, or by not-so-subtly disguising them, satire – in contrast to epic or tragedy – tethers itself to its immediate, present-day context. Yet as years pass and audiences change, the timely nature of satire becomes problematic, and references to people and debates widely understood at the time of initial publication or performance can become obscure. What does it mean for the significance of satire if we believe that its meaning depends upon references that can only be understood by the expert, or by the student with a mass of footnotes – many of which turn out to be infuriatingly useless, such as these notes to my edition of Horace's *Satires*?:

> 109. Albius and Baius: unknown.
> 112. Scetanus: unknown.
> 114. Trebonius: unknown.[51]

We no longer even know whether these names belong to real individuals or whether they are stock characters. This question of how to interpret the topical elements of satire magnifies a question present in all literary interpretation, the question of historical context. How much knowledge is needed to understand and interpret a work? With too little historical mooring, we don't understand jokes, we fail to make necessary inferences, we can misread wildly. Yet great works resonate because of insight and power that transcends the topical. We don't need to know that *Jonathan Wild* is intended as a commentary on Prime Minister Robert Walpole in order to grasp Fielding's point about the incompatibility of moral decency and worldly success; the "sex strike" in Aristophanes' *Lysistrata* is compelling as an exercise of female power even if Athenian audiences would have viewed the very notion as absurd. No easy rules or resolutions are available here: some satires are so strongly rooted in their moments that only specialists read them today, while others seem astonishingly relevant to the present. And of course most topical satire – which we find everywhere on TV, in the newspapers, on the Internet – has no pretensions of making it into the Norton Anthology: it is content to make a fleeting impact in the immediate present.

Kinds of Satires

If this heterogeneous list of features tells us anything, it is that satires are not all alike. Indeed, the vast variety of satiric works makes analysis a special challenge. Satire can be found throughout the history of literature, across national and cultural boundaries, in varied genres and media, and there are many relatively self-evident ways one can separate and classify satiric works: by historical eras, by national traditions, by major genres, and media. But kinship also exists across eras, nations, genres, and media, and the lines of those kinships are worth tracing. Moreover, because satire often contains paradoxical or contradictory elements, it is useful to think of satire not simply in terms of discrete characteristics but in terms of *tensions*. Some of these tensions have already emerged in our discussion – satire ranges, for example, between fantasy and realism, and between the timely and the timeless.

No aspect of satire is more contested than its politics. The canonical model holds that satire is inherently conservative, since it directs its ridicule against those who deviate from traditional, communal norms. But the transgressive, anti-authoritarian impulses of satire can just as easily make it appear a progressive force that criticizes the powerful and fosters rebellion against the status quo. In his translation of Swift's epitaph, Yeats wrote of the great satirist that he "Served human liberty."[52] In the wake of the killings of cartoonists at the French satirical magazine *Charlie Hebdo*, the historian Simon Schama tweeted a defense of satire that aligned it with freedom and dissent: "Satire was the father of true political freedom, born in the 18th century; the scourge of bigots and tyrants. Sing its praises."[53] In Derek Walcott's poem "The Spoiler's Return," the great satirists of the past are described as "all those whose anger for the poor on earth / made them weep with a laughter beyond mirth."[54] It would in fact be reductive to claim satire for a single political stance. There are satires directed against both left and right, new and old, authorities and dissidents. They attack women and men, elites and the populace, the rich, the poor, and the bourgeoisie. Rather than viewing satire as simply conservative or liberal then, it might be better to note a tension within satire between enforcing norms and violating them, between *restraint* and *license*.

As literary study has turned its attention to social categories such as race, gender, and class, readers have come to see that the perceived political stance of a work of literature depends upon the position of an individual or community within a wider social field. Where you stand can shape how you judge the politics of a given work. As Freud recognized, some "benevolence or neutrality" is necessary for a joke to function, and the same is true of satire.[55] Someone who identifies with a social group under satiric attack will receive the satire differently from the person who identifies with the satirist. When satire deliberately sets out to transgress – when *South Park* represents Saddam Hussein and Satan as gay lovers, when *The Onion*'s Twitter feed calls nine-year-old Oscar nominee Quvenzhané Wallis "kind of a cunt" – the result might not appear as satire at all. In short, satiric attack and critique can operate from a position of relative power or weakness. Indeed, even determining who occupies a position of power may be contested. To judge the politics of a work of satire, you must attend to the context in which it is produced and received, and contexts are notoriously prone to shifting. And because some satires may seem more prone to shifting meanings and contradictory interpretations, another useful tension to highlight is that between *stability* and *instability*.

Satires often vary in tone, mood, and attitude. Charles Knight justifiably links satire to a skeptical frame of mind, yet satire can also appear passionately committed to certain beliefs, even if those beliefs are negative or critical ones. Hence another tension to discern is between *engagement* and *detachment*. Satire that is engaged in its moment tends to produce intense or "hot" feelings like anger, scorn, indignation, or aggression; detachment allows for cooler emotions such as aloofness, amusement, or resignation. Similarly, we call some satires light or gentle, suggesting that the stakes of their critique are relatively low, or that their implicit vision of the world is ultimately tolerant and forgiving, and these satires sometimes shade toward the comic. In contrast, dark or harsh satires imply a bleaker vision, a less charitable view of human failings, a more pessimistic appraisal of the dangers described; they approach the tragic. A related distinction is that between wild or unruly satire and more polite or decorous satire. The physical and linguistic excesses of Rabelais seem to know no limits, while the restraint and dry irony of a writer like Austen make her barbs sting all the more sharply.

Critics have found a number of recurring satiric character "types and stereotypes" (*SSA* 204ff.). Fools and naïfs unwittingly expose the flaws of their societies, even as they serve as the butt of jokes; clowns are more deliberate in soliciting laughter, yet can turn their merriment to the ends of critique. Imps, tricksters, and rogues might play dumb, but usually know better, using their savvy for personal gain or for the exposure of other people's failings. Iconoclasts challenge received pieties directly and angrily, while dandies mount their rebellion through aloofness and the cultivation of personal style. Misanthropes find so much fault with the world that they reject humanity altogether. Villains function satirically when they become so charismatic that they cause us to question our own ethical identifications. Satiric plots, meanwhile, are often circular, regressive, digressive, static, pessimistic, or unresolved, offering, as in Samuel Johnson's *Rasselas,* conclusions in which nothing is concluded.

Finally, there is the subject matter of satire. There exist some particularly famous traditions and themes of satire – anti-war satires, anti-religious satires, misogynistic satires against women – but the persistence of these themes probably attests more to the presence of certain perennial struggles than to the suitability of satire for some topics over others. In everyday talk, we often describe and informally classify satires according to the targets that they attack, or – since it can be unclear who or what is under attack – for the arenas they explore. Philosophical or intellectual satires depict bad ideas. Aristophanes attacks Socrates in *Clouds*; Voltaire goes after Leibniz, in the guise of Dr. Pangloss, in *Candide*; Swift's Academy of Lagado satirizes the absurdities of a science that, having lost touch with the real world, attempts to extract sunbeams from cucumbers and turn feces back into food. Social satires ranging from *The Rape of the Lock* to the academic novels of David Lodge take aim at the manners of a society, often zeroing in on a given socioeconomic class. Satire can also expand to take on far-ranging and amorphous institutions and systems, such as we see in Dickens's satire of Chancery Court in *Bleak House* or in the movie *Network*'s representation of the television news industry. Even though satire has no single political position, there are lots of political satires and political leaders are favorite targets Aristophanes' mockery of Cleon; Shelley's invective against the "old, mad, blind, despised, and dying king," George III;[56] Charlie Chaplin's send-up of Hitler in *The Great Dictator*; Rushdie's caricature of Muhammad Zia ul-Haq in *Shame*. Literary satires, in the form of parodies and spoofs, take other texts and genres as their primary objects. *Don Quixote* tilts at tales of knight-errantry; *Austin Powers* shakes and stirs James Bond.

Finally, "universal" or "cosmic" satire attacks the human condition itself. Italo Calvino, after expressing his reservations about satire, remarks:

> Most certainly I admire satire, and feel homuncular in comparison, whenever the charge of derisive fury is taken to the utmost limits, leaving the threshold of the particular to call the whole human race to account, as in Swift and Gogol, who border on the tragic vision of life.[57]

The Earl of Rochester wrote satires not only about the sex lives of King Charles II and his mistresses, but also about philosophical topics, as in his "Satyr against Reason and Mankind." Rochester's speaker scorns his human condition, professing that he'd rather "be a dog, a monkey, or a bear; / Or any thing but that vain animal / Who is so proud of being Rational" (57.5–7). Upending the age-old claim that reason sets man above the other animals, the speaker declares that it leads him into a life of error that he recognizes only when it is too late:

> Then old Age and Experience, hand in hand,
> Lead him to death, and make him understand,
> After a search so painful and so long,
> That all his life he has been in the wrong.
> Huddled in dirt the reasoning engine lies,
> Who was so proud, so witty and so wise.   (58.25–30§)

Calling the whole human race to account, Rochester's satire provides a bleak picture of human existence itself as a series of futile errors that leads to neither happiness nor wisdom.

Chapter 2

What Isn't Satire?

Satire is angry and optimistic ... Comedy is good-tempered and pessimistic.

— *W.H. Auden*

Irony is used in some satire, not in all; some irony is satiric, much is not.

— *Wayne Booth*

Satire is a lesson, parody is a game.

— *Vladimir Nabokov*[1]

What isn't satire? Where does the domain of satire come to an end? Anyone exploring the boundaries of the satiric inevitably finds herself invoking all sorts of related critical categories, themselves important in the history and theory of literature, which may contrast, overlap, or be frequently conflated with satire. Terms such as "comedy," "irony," and "parody," like satire itself, are broad and varied in their meanings, and the student using them must honor the range of ordinary usage while retaining the precision needed for clarity. This chapter therefore takes up key terms related to satire, with the aim of yielding practical value for the student and the scholar. Some of these terms (comedy, irony, parody, and the mock form) receive extended treatment; those with more specialized meanings get discussed more briefly.

Comedy

Today satire is widely thought of as a particular *kind* of comedy – a purposive, critical, or tendentious kind – and handbooks on comedy often include a chapter dedicated to satire, as if comedy were the genus and satire the species.[2] Terms such as "stand-up comedy," "situation comedy," "romantic comedy," "screwball comedy," and "sketch comedy" only begin to suggest the vast range of comedic forms saturating popular culture, compared to which satire looks like a highly specialized practice. Thus while it might be claimed that all comedy is at heart satiric, since all comedy has targets or victims – some

Malvolio who suffers so that others can laugh – for most readers at least some comedy is non-satiric. Critics often designate this non-satiric comedy with phrases like "the purely comic" (*PSE* 32). Such a notion suggests that satire is something potentially distinct from comedy but which frequently mixes or overlaps with it. Where, then, do they overlap and where do they remain discrete?

One way to distinguish comedy from satire is the perceived *threat-level* of the object represented. Leon Guilhamet finds the technique of reduction at the heart of both comedy and satire, but argues that if the target of an attack is perceived "as harmful or destructive," then the work is satiric, whereas if it is perceived as harmless or trivial, the work is comic. This criterion won't satisfy everyone: it denies the label of satire to works such as *Gargantua and Pantagruel* and *Tristram Shandy*, and presumably the novels of Kingsley Amis and the films of the Marx Brothers (*STG* 7–8). Still, it resonates with critical intuitions about satire's underlying seriousness and sense of purpose. But while common sense might suggest that certain targets are inherently more threatening than others, the "threat-level" can depend on a writer's *representation* of an object as much as the nature of the object itself. Serial murder seems to be a serious evil, yet the Ealing comedy *Kind Hearts and Coronets* treats it as an inconsequential game and uses it at the basis for light, farcical comedy. Conversely, the social absurdities of Anita Loos's *Gentlemen Prefer Blondes* seem benign, but they open onto a deep indictment of the economic and sexual rules structuring her society.

Slightly different from Guilhamet's distinction is Ruby Cohn's claim that comedy makes the reader laugh *with* its object, while satire makes us laugh *at* it. This dichotomy goes back to the ancient Greeks, who distinguished between liberal and illiberal jests, the first of which "gives pleasure to all," the second of which singles out individual or collective "victims."[3] James Wood similarly differentiates a "comedy of forgiveness" from a "comedy of correction." The first is the signature mode of the novel as a genre, while the second is an older mode, found in the ancient Greeks and the Hebrew Bible, and characteristic of satire.[4] Cohn and Wood distinguish not the seriousness of the threat but the level of sympathy shown toward the represented object. Unlike satire, comedy is marked by sympathy, forgiveness, and inclusion.

Maybe the most obvious criterion for separating comedy and satire is the presence of laughter. Comedy is funny. In contrast, at least some satires do not aim to be funny. Indeed, the view that satire is funny may be a relatively recent one. Passages in Juvenal read as pure denunciation. Dryden's *Absalom and Achitophel* appears as polemical and witty, but its *gravitas* makes it feel closer to the epic than to the comic. Orwell's *Nineteen Eighty-Four* contains grim ironies but no jokes or punchlines. Many modern satirical novels such as Nathanael West's *The Day of the Locust* induce at most only a muted or anxious laughter – the kind of laughs that Samuel Beckett called "laughs that strictly speaking are not laughs but modes of ululation" and which he taxonomized as "the bitter, the hollow, and the mirthless."[5] Comedy, in short, has a different pattern of *affect* from satire. Satire induces negative feelings (indignation, revulsion, unease); comedy, positive ones (mirth or glee). Of course, all of these distinctions are easier to draw in theory than in practice. Many works laugh both *at* and *with*, display both scorn and sympathy, elicit both outrage and amusement. Judgments about which emotions dominate the experience of a text will vary with context and reader.

A final way to distinguish comedy from satire is on the basis of plot. Northrop Frye invented four archetypal "narrative categories" which he whimsically aligned with the four seasons. Comedy, with a narrative of birth and growth, he aligned with spring; romance, based in quests and adventures, with summer; tragedy, characterized by decline, with autumn; satire and irony, which proffer cold, hard realities, with winter. These categories emphasize narrative closure. A comic plot "moves toward a happy ending," offering resolution, reconciliation, and wish-fulfillment (*AC* 167). Comedy reintegrates alienated heroes, punishes or rehabilitates antagonists, stages marriages and reunions, remedies material struggles. Society proves flexible enough to change for the better. But satiric plots reject such reconciliation. The protagonist remains alienated from society – physically, emotionally, morally. Swift's Gulliver withdraws to his horses in their stables, unable to endure sitting at dinner with his family. Evelyn Waugh's *Vile Bodies* concludes with a chapter ironically called "Happy Ending" in which the hero sits surrounded by carnage "in the biggest battlefield in the history of the world" while a drunk major beds a lost prostitute in the back of a disabled limousine.[6] By such a standard, novels such as *Pride and Prejudice* or *At Swim Two-Birds* are comedies, despite the presence of sharp judgments and cruel humor. *Huckleberry Finn*, meanwhile, occupies an ambiguous position: happily, at the novel's close, Jim finds freedom and Huck safety, yet Huck, still wary of attempts to "sivilize" him, vows to light out for his own freedom once again, and the larger social evil of slavery remains intact.

All of these distinctions – regarding target, sympathy, affect, closure – ultimately suggest that how we categorize a work relies on interpretive judgments about the underlying attitude that it displays toward a community, a society, or even human existence itself. Because comedy laughs with, and tells stories of reconciliation, it usually seems a lighter, more optimistic mode;

since satire laughs at, and tells stories of continued antagonism, it appears darker and more oppositional. According to such criteria, the ending of Anthony Burgess's novel *A Clockwork Orange* is comic because it shows the reconciliation to society of the criminal narrator Alex, who outgrows his vicious impulses; the ending to Stanley Kubrick's film adaptation, however, is satiric, since Alex's free will is restored only so that he can once again indulge his "ultra-violent" desires. Yet W.H. Auden (quoted above) reaches exactly the opposite conclusion: for him, comic stories of reconciliation suggest an underlying pessimism because they imply that we must accept a flawed world, while the irresolution of satire implies a stubborn idealistic resistance that refuses to surrender the desire for change. For Auden, the smiling face of comedy ratifies the norms of an existing society while the grimace of satire protests them.

Ultimately, we should be wary of sweeping claims in either direction. Where some may find in comedy what Herbert Marcuse called an affirmative culture that eases our compliance to an unjust system, others locate utopian hope in comedy's simple articulation of wish-fulfillment. For some, laughter liberates, but for others such laughter is a subtle means of discipline and control. As Slavoj Žižek insists, "beneath the clownish mask there is a mastery of . . . power functioning with ruthless efficiency."[7] In the final analysis, both comedy and satire are best seen as "transideological" or "multiaccented,"[8] and only through acts of interpretation can we determine what politics accompany their representations.

Irony

The overlap between irony and satire is so great that in certain circumstances they function as synonyms. Alvin Kernan claims that it is "nearly impossible to think of satire without thinking of irony."[9] Indisputably, the satiric feeling of certain texts derives directly from their irony. William Blake's poem "The Little Black Boy" presents an African-born child speaker who envies the white skin and privileges of an "English child" whom he describes as "white as an angel." The black boy's mother comforts him with the promise of an afterlife, yet her consolatory fable leads the boy to imagine a heaven that possesses the same racial hierarchy as earth:

> I'll shade him from the heat till he can bear
> To lean in joy upon our father's knee.
> And then I'll stand and stroke his silver hair,
> And be like him and he will then love me.[10]

Even though the boy can imagine himself free from his black skin and therefore superficially "like" the white boy, he cannot imagine himself free from his role of serving the angelic white boy – or worse, free from his desire for the white boy's love. He remains inculcated with the ideology of white supremacy. "The Little Black Boy" is an ironic poem in the way it reveals a gulf between the boy's understanding of his situation and the reader's. What makes this irony feel especially satiric is that it relates to a broader social issue (racism and its psychological effects) and raises indignation at the racial–religious ideology of eighteenth-century Britain. (Notably, the satiric tone does not preclude sympathy; the poem elicits a painful compassion for the child's desire to be loved.) Without such irony, Blake could denounce the evil of racism, but the poem would not feel satiric; irony-free satire, if we can imagine such a thing, would lie at the edges of the satiric terrain, in the area of what Frye calls "sheer invective or name-calling" (*AC* 223).

In other cases, however, irony and satire are not so neatly synonymous, in part because of irony's own fraught critical history. In the mid-twentieth century, New Criticism expanded the term to cover any tension or ambiguity in meaning, nearly equating irony with literature itself. For others, irony has been elevated to the status of an entire worldview. As such, it is associated with youth culture or intellectuals, misunderstood as mere indifference, and disparaged as failure of moral seriousness. In the mid-1990s David Foster Wallace fretted about the prevalence of ironic attitudes in TV and advertising, worrying that the critical irony of postmodern fiction had degenerated into mass-market attitudinizing.[11] (The argument is a version of Peter Sloterdijk's claim that a politically indifferent "cynicism" has, since the 1960s, replaced an oppositional "kynicism."[12]) More sanctimonious judgments against irony were offered after the attacks of September 11, 2001, when American journalists declared and then applauded a "death of irony." Yet the decade that followed saw a resurgence of irony-laden political satire in popular culture, proving the moralists wrong.

Still, even positive appraisals of an ironic worldview often share the detractors' association of irony with detachment. Richard Rorty describes "ironism" as an ability or tendency to "redescribe" one set of values in the vocabulary of another, to recognize the partiality and contingency of any set of beliefs.[13] Matthew Stratton shares Rorty's positive assessment of irony, but disagrees that irony is of little use in fostering political solidarity; for him irony is not "a withdrawal from praxis" but the basis of "an activist literary politics" that can unsettle "too-tractable and too-ideological publics."[14] Linda Hutcheon observes that irony can often be a strategy for disempowered individuals or social groups to offer an indirect "counterdiscourse" that challenges authoritative norms.[15]

The persistent view of irony as a critical, skeptical, or even cynical world-view that stands aloof from commitment or engagement points to another ambiguity in understanding satire. For although satirists, like ironists, are sometimes attacked for believing in nothing, a different view of satire – or perhaps a view of a different kind of satire – finds in satire a passionate commitment to underlying principles. The critic James English distinguishes satire from irony in his reading of Joseph Conrad's *The Secret Agent*. English opposes two different ways of interpreting the novel: as a pointed and political *satiric* attack directed specifically at the revolutionary anarchists whom the novel caricatures as hypocritical, ineffectual, fat, and lazy; and as an *ironic* work that holds all political positions at arm's length. For English, satire is politically engaged in a way that irony is not.[16]

The most widespread meaning of irony, however, describes not a world-view but a rhetorical trope or device. Literary criticism distinguishes at least three common kinds of irony: verbal irony in which "what seems to be and what is are in some way opposed";[17] dramatic irony, in which a character's words or actions are more meaningful to the audience than to herself; and cosmic irony – common in tragedy – in which a character's efforts to avoid a certain outcome unintentionally bring it about. All three rely on an implicit difference or doubleness of meaning.[18] Irony understood in this fashion is so central to satire that Alvin Kernan calls it a "master-trope." Many satiric genres – mock epics, dystopias, beast fables – represent "large-scale ironic techniques," ironic contrasts built into the very premise of a work:

> The satirist never seems to attack directly but always pretends not to be doing what in fact he is doing. He praises what he loathes, speaks with enthusiasm of Utopias which he proves to be wastelands, creates pleasant little tales about the beasts and never seems to notice that his animals are reductions of human beings, solemnly dresses his contemporaries in epic robes far too large for them, and confidently puts Achilles' spear in hands which cannot hold it.[19]

George Test, following this lead, argues that many of the devices or techniques predominant in satire, such as mock epic and parody, are most accurately categorized as varieties of irony (*SSA* 160ff.).

Wayne Booth distinguishes between *stable* and *unstable* ironies, the first of which allows a reader to recover a determinate meaning, the second of which does not. Satire, Booth argues, mainly relies on stable ironies. (His distinction is similar to English's contrast between the stability of "satire" and the open-ness of "irony.") For Booth, a work such as Jonathan Swift's "A Modest Proposal" provides enough clues to its complex combination of ironic statements that a reader can confidently recover an intended meaning. Any educated reader realizes that Swift cannot endorse his speaker's proposal for eating babies, and that he even smuggles in explicit recommendations for alleviating the poverty of the Irish. For Booth, stable ironies like this are intended, covert, and finite. They are intended in that someone deliberately creates the irony; covert in that the intended meaning is not the explicit, superficial one; and finite in that they do not invite endless questioning or further ironization of the intended meaning. Booth argues, finally, that stable irony is by far the most common form of irony prior to the twentieth century.[20]

Booth's argument provides a useful check on runaway interpretation, but many literary theorists and philosophers of language reject it because it too stringently limits the play of language. Especially when we move from short, "local" utterances to larger works of literature, irony – even satiric irony – produces shades of meaning and ambiguity, and its indirect methods can be contradictory, confusing, and inconclusive. Among the most trenchant critics of Booth has been Hutcheon, who insists on the irreducible complexity of ironic discourse, the possibility that irony can "misfire," and the inherent volatility of the ironic discourse or gesture: "The one thing irony would not seem to be is what it is usually claimed to be: a simple antiphrastic substitution of the unsaid . . . for its opposite, the said." Rather, the ironic meaning consists in the interplay between the two meanings. Hutcheon asserts that if irony were as stable as Booth claims, the "political problems" it poses "would be relatively straightforward."[21] To this claim Darryl Dickson-Carr adds that since meanings depend on interpretive contexts, "differences between or among cultures destabilize ironies": texts can mean different things for different "discursive communities."[22]

Parody

A parody is work that imitates another work in a humorous or playful way. One might say that parody represents other texts or other artworks, whereas satire represents the world itself. Yet texts are part of the world, and so in *parodying* texts writers often thereby *satirize* the ideas, values, or attitudes embodied in them. For this reason the categories overlap: parody is often cited as a "technique" of satire or even as a subtype, and the act of parody can double as an act of satire. A related distinction is offered in this chapter's epigraph from Nabokov: "Satire is a lesson, parody a game." The quip opposes the serious purpose of satire to the unserious play of parody. Yet this distinction is equally delicate, since satire, as we've seen, is playful as well as purposeful, and the games of parody can turn out to offer lessons.

There are subgenres of parody. Simon Dentith discriminates between a "general" parody of a genre (sometimes called a spoof) and a "specific" parody of a single writer or text. Genres become susceptible to parody when their conventions become highly distinctive and codified, often as a result of popular success. Cervantes's *Don Quixote* parodies chivalric romances, Jane Austen's *Northanger Abbey* the Gothic novel, Mel Brooks's *Blazing Saddles* the Western. Similarly, specific parody tends to latch on to an author with a highly mannered or familiar voice, as in Max Beerbohm's parody of Henry James, John Updike's parody of Jack Kerouac, or the many famous parodies of Ernest Hemingway – by James Thurber, E.B. White, and thousands of others who for years submitted entries to an annual "Bad Hemingway" competition sponsored by Harry's Bar and Grill in Los Angeles.[23]

Both kinds of parody thrive in popular culture – the song parodies of Weird Al Yankovic, the allusions to classic cinema in *The Simpsons*, the reworking of James Bond in Dos Equis beer commercials featuring The Most Interesting Man in the World, or *Saturday Night Live* sketches such as Ana Gasteyer and Molly Shannon spoofing public radio hosts in their monotone enthusiasm for Alec Baldwin's "Schweddy Balls." As parody infuses sketches, commercials, commentaries, Internet memes, and ever-briefer forms, it approaches mere reference or citation. Dentith therefore identifies, in addition to "general" and "specific" parody, a third type that he calls "glancing parodic allusions." Unlike a "fully developed formal parody," such allusive parodic language is multidirectional, offering a refraction of many different voices and discourses with degrees of mockery or exaggeration. Dickens, for example, generates a "multitudinous recycling of the diverse languages of mid-nineteenth cen-tury English," keyed not to any specific text but to the whole linguistic environment in which he lived.[24]

Parody works by exaggerating stylistic traits enough to push them into the realm of the comic. It requires "oscillation between similarity to and differ-ence from a target": it maintains some elements of an original while altering others for the sake of contrast.[25] (Some parodies, like the impersonations of stand-up comedians, give pleasure because of the fidelity of the imitation rather than the exaggeration of any idiosyncratic traits.) Often a parodist will deploy a parodied style in conjunction with dissonant content so as to jar the reader into an awareness of the artificial nature of the style itself. Wendy Cope's "A Nursery Rhyme" written in the style of Wordsworth offers an excellent example:

I walked towards him on the stony track
And, pausing for a while between two crags,
I asked him, "Have you wool upon your back?"
Thus he bespake, "Enough to fill three bags."[26]

Mild archaisms (the two syllables given to "walked," the absurd "bespake"), combined with the bucolic setting and the subtle touch of the speaker's contemplative pause, clash with the out-of-place nursery-rhyme trope of the talking farm animal. The mannerism of the style becomes suddenly visible when applied to the ill-fitting content of the nursery rhyme.

Critics disagree whether parody implies a satiric attack on the imitated text. For Gerard Genette, parody must not be polemical, while for Gilbert Highet, it must be (*AS* 68).[27] One of the great modern parodists, Max Beerbohm, denied any malice in his efforts, claiming them to be motivated solely by admiration. Yet one should be wary of such disavowals. Parody renders the parodied object no longer unique, lowering it in the esteem of the reader, even if momentarily (*AS* 68). Thus Fredric Bogel argues that parody can simultaneously serve as an act of both "hostility and tribute," qualities that are "not definitively demarcated" (*DSM* 73).

We can try, however, to isolate the game-like element that Nabokov recognized. Much of the pleasure of parody comes from the reader's vicarious participation in the virtuosity of the parodist. Like a comedian doing impressions, the parodist entertains with the ability to replicate what had seemed unique. The parodist appropriates the glory of the parodied writer, diminishing the singularity of the imitated while showing off the talent of the imitator. As the phenomenon of the Bad Hemingway contest illustrates, parody is a test, an exhibition of skill, and an implicit competition. The reader, meanwhile, is rewarded for recognizing the mannerisms singled out by the parodist. Parody thus functions as oblique literary criticism, since in directing attention to eccentric elements of a style, it helps to demystify that style. But as parody becomes more purely a game of imitation and recognition, it tends toward the light and the highbrow – "catnip for bookworms" in Louis Menand's phrase.[28] In its lightest varieties, it doesn't undermine the enjoyment of this game with the disturbing social critique or transgressive thematic material that satire trades in. Parody of this sort may retain a satiric tinge, but belongs more firmly to the category of humor or light verse with its modest aspirations.[29]

Yet game-playing and virtuosic display can sometimes carry polemical thrust. *Blazing Saddles* attacks the manifest-destiny ideology that canonical Westerns promulgated. When Gene Wilder's Deputy Jim explains the racism of the townspeople of Rock Ridge, he recites patriotic clichés that he immediately debunks: "You've got to remember that these are just simple farmers. These are people of the land. The common clay of the new West. You know ... Morons."[30] Stella Gibbons's *Cold Comfort Farm*, by imitating D.H. Lawrence's attribution of primal sexual urges to the landscape, indicts Lawrence's romanticism, which valorizes a violent, regressive sexuality. And Kenneth Koch, in parodying William Carlos Williams's "This Is Just to Say," uses his precursor's tercets and second-person address to amplify the bad logic and masculine egotism of the earlier poem:

> I gave away the money that you had been saving to live on for the next
>   ten years.
> The man who asked for it was shabby
> and the firm March wind on the porch was so juicy and cold.[31]

The adjectives "firm" and "juicy" make sense only in reference to the stolen plums of Williams's poem, while the skewed choice of "shabby" suggests that Koch is slipping into Williamsese, underscoring the older poet's fetishization of poverty and simplicity. By parodying stylistic tics, Koch's poem satirizes not only Williams's attitude of male entitlement but also the way that his aesthetic of plain-spokenness masks the indulgence of his own appetites.

In these examples the parodic processes of imitation and deformation mock not only stylistic eccentricities but also the ideological freight that the eccentricities carry. Such acts of parody are in fact possible, Pierre Bourdieu notes, because culture itself is dynamic, always riven by competing aesthetic values. New works or performances cannot help but deploy an element of parody when they imitate or invoke canonical works, since they necessarily resituate the old work in a new context. Avant-gardes can thus mobilize parody to recontextualize past works and challenge orthodox values. At the same time, even the unintentional "simple *repetition* of a work from the past in a radically transformed field of [interpretive possibilities] produces an entirely automatic *effect of parody*."[32] An overly faithful repetition or imitation of past works will still unwittingly parody its precursor, because the context of production and reception is never stable. Every text is thus like the version of *Don Quixote* written by Borges's Pierre Menard; the most perfect imitation calls attention to the changes that have occurred in the work's sociohistorical context.

Yet it is not always so easy to determine what it is that a parody satirizes. Marcel Duchamp's "LHOOQ," a postcard reproduction of the Mona Lisa on

L. H. O. O. Q.

Figure 3 Marcel Duchamp (1887–1968) "L.H.O.O.Q. Mona Lisa," 1919 (replica from 1930). © Association Marcel Duchamp/ADAGP, Paris/ Artists Rights Society (ARS), New York 2017. Photo credit: Philippe Migeat © CNAC/MNAM/Dist. RMN-Grand Palais/ Art Resource, NY. A parody of the Mona Lisa? A satire on the commodification of art?

which the artist has drawn a mustache and beard (Figure 3), does not mock da Vinci per se so much as it uses various contrasts – between high and low, between the original artwork and the mass-produced souvenir, between the veneration of the museum-goer and the disrespect of the hand-drawn graffito – to provoke reflection on the role of high art in modern society. The letters of the title, when pronounced in French, sound like "*Elle a chaud au cul*" ("She is hot in the ass"), offering a further sneer at the masterwork – although it is not easy to say whether Duchamp himself is doing the sneering. Is LHOOQ a parody of the Mona Lisa? A satire on the traditions of art? Gilbert Highet sniffed that Duchamp was not satirizing high art but "merely insulting it" (*AS* 68), but he was actually mounting a bold challenge to the cultural norms governing how art is viewed, canonized, interpreted, and commodified.

Mock Forms

Sometimes satire appropriates another genre in a way that uses the prior form less as a target of attack or even respectful imitation than as a handy framework to give shape to satiric content. These works are called "mock forms." Whether a mock form is precisely the same as a general parody is ultimately less important than the recognition of the centrality of mock forms to satire. The variety of mock forms is virtually limitless. *The Daily Show* and *Last Week Tonight* are mock news programs, *Zelig* and *This Is Spinal Tap* mockumentary films, Swift's "A Modest Proposal" a mock political pamphlet, Djuna Barnes's *Ladies' Almanack* a mock almanac, Jane Collier's *An Essay on the Art of Ingeniously Tormenting* a mock conduct book, Mohsin Hamid's *How to Get Filthy Rich in Rising Asia* a mock advice manual, Borges's "Pierre Menard" a mock academic review, Sam Lipsyte's *Home Land* a series of mock letters to a mock alumni newsletter. For at least some critics, this sort of imitation of precursor forms is not merely a common but an essential component of satire. Charles Knight maintains, "Close to the essence of satire as a genre is its powerful tendency to disguise as independent speech acts, whether formally recognized literary genres ... sub-literary genres ... or non-literary speech" (*LS* 32; *STG* 13). From its beginnings, satire exists in a revisionary relationship to more serious or authoritative genres, and the irony and play of satire derive at least in part from this revisionary stance.

Mock forms may satirize the imitated form and its implicit values. Recently dominant satiric genres such as the mockumentary, the mock interview, and the mock newspaper undermine the claims to seriousness and the implicit authority of the non-fictional forms that they repurpose. But the converse is also true: mock forms may use the imitated genre "as a standard of excellence" by which some other target is deemed corrupt or ridiculous. Pope's target in *The Rape of the Lock* is usually understood to be not the epic poems such as *The Aeneid* or *Paradise Lost* to which he profusely alludes, but the flirtation rituals and sexual politics of the upper classes in his own day – a modern morality which appears debased in comparison to the noble behavior of ages past (*FS* 6). Oliver Jensen's 1957 "Gettysburg Address as Delivered by Eisenhower" (if you don't know it, Google it) uses the grandeur of the past (Lincoln's oratory) to call attention to the ills of the present (Eisenhower's bland corporate speech).[33]

Yet even this choice of options – between attacking the past and attacking the present – is too simple. As Bogel maintains, the contrast that the mock form appears to offer actually masks an underlying confusion: "What the mock-epics, mock-pastorals, and mock-georgics of writers like Swift, Gay, and Pope suggest, surely, is that such distinctions [between ancient and modern, great and small] are far from clear and secure." Mock forms are "not mere exercises in sardonic subtraction but new kinds of text" (*DSM* 22). The appropriation of an aesthetic form creates cognitive tension between the content that the reader expects and the content she encounters, resulting in surprise, discomfort, frisson, or amusement. And the less accustomed we are to seeing a form reinvented in a fictional, comic, or otherwise non-serious mode, the greater the dissonance. A novel in the form of "a series of footnotes to a vast obscure unfinished manuscript," as Nabokov described his own *Pale Fire*, foregrounds its tense relation to its parent-form, whereas a fictional diary or autobiography is so familiar a thing that it fails to register as inherently parodic or satiric.

The most well-known mock form is the mock epic (also called mock heroic), whose earliest instance is *The Battle of Frogs and Mice* (or "Batrachomyomachia"), a fifth-century BCE Greek poem modeled on Homer's *Iliad*, written "in a strong and melodious hexameter verse, full of traditional epithets and lofty words and bardic turns of phrase" (*AS* 80). Canonical examples include Dryden's *Mac Flecknoe* and Pope's *The Rape of the Lock*. But the mock epic is not only a discrete subgenre; it can also be a satiric technique. It can function locally as well as globally. It occurs whenever a satirist uses heroic language to treat unheroic events. When, in the opening monologue of Ben Jonson's *Volpone*, the title character prays to his hoard and compares the gleam of his gold to the first glow of light in the creation of the universe, he is elevating money to the level of the divine, calling attention to his (unheroic) greed.

Novels too can use mock-epic technique. In Sinclair Lewis's *Babbitt*, the technique renders the mundane event of parking a car grandiose, reflecting George Babbitt's inflated view of himself and pride in his machine:

> Epochal as starting the car was the drama of parking it before he entered his office. As he turned the corner from Oberlin Avenue round the corner into Third Street, N.E., he peered ahead for a space in the line of parked cars. He angrily just missed a space as a rival driver slid into it. Ahead, another car was leaving the curb, and Babbitt slowed up, holding out his hand to the cars pressing on him from behind, agitatedly motioning an old woman to go ahead, avoiding a truck which bore down on him from one side. With front wheels nicking the wrought-steel bumper of the car in front, he stopped, feverishly cramped his steering-wheel, slid back into the vacant space and, with eighteen inches of room,

maneuvered to bring the car level with the curb. It was a virile adventure
masterfully executed. (27)

Lewis shows how Babbitt unconsciously transforms his sedentary white-collar
routines into heroic trials of the body, mocking the entitlement, impatience,
and self-deception that shape Babbitt's bourgeois code of masculinity.

Related to the mock epic is burlesque or travesty, which performs the
converse operation, treating gods, heroes, or leaders in laughably degrading
ways to puncture the aura that surrounds them. In Apuleius's *The Golden Ass*,
the goddess Venus appears as a shrewish mother-in-law, jealous and con-
temptuous of her daughter-in-law Psyche, berating her son Cupid and lowering herself from the realm of the divine to the domestic.[34] Monty Python
deploys a gentle burlesque in *Monty Python and the Holy Grail* when the
knights of the round table, lacking horses, are forced to simulate the sound of
hoofbeats by clacking coconuts together, or in *The Life of Brian* when Brian,
having denied that he is the Messiah, is told by his followers that "Only the
true Messiah denies his divinity":

BRIAN: What?! Well what sort of chance does that give me? All right,
          I am the Messiah!
CROWD: He is! He is the Messiah!
BRIAN: Now ... fuck off!
          [silence]
ARTHUR: How shall we fuck off, O Lord?[35]

In *Don Quixote*, Don Quixote himself represents the mock-heroic principle
and Sancho Panza the burlesque: the hidalgo Alonzo Quijano puffs himself up
to assume the stature of a heroic knight-errant, while his squire deflates the
puffery with plainspoken skepticism and common sense (*AS* 106–107).

The first two books of *Gulliver's Travels* suggest the same split. The
Lilliputians are comic because they think their tiny world is a grand one, as
we see in the official description of their six-inch-tall emperor:

> Most mighty Emperor of Lilliput, delight and terror of the universe,
> whose dominions extend five thousand *blustrugs* (about twelve miles in
> circumference) to the extremities of the globe; monarch of all monarchs,
> taller than the sons of men; whose feet press down to the centre, and
> whose head strikes against the sun; at whose nod the princes of the earth
> shake their knees; pleasant as the spring, comfortable as the summer,
> fruitful as autumn, dreadful as winter. (36)

This is all funny because the reader never forgets that this mighty emperor can fit in an ordinary person's shirt pocket. But in Gulliver's next voyage, the gigantic Brobdingnagians in turn demonstrate that the human-scaled world of Gulliver and the reader is itself Lilliputian. Here mock epic and burlesque work together, adding irony to irony.

Caricature and Cartoon

Two terms from visual art pertain to satire. Caricature refers to drawings of human figures that exaggerate some features and simplify others, creating a comic but often grotesque impression. In colloquial usage, caricature can thus mean something very close to satire, and the history of the concept accompanies the career of satire. The Italian word *caricatura* originates in the Renaissance; fittingly, the word enters the English language in the eighteenth century, when literary satire was in the ascendant and William Hogarth was publishing caricatures in popular periodicals that offered sharp political and social critique. According to one art historian, "it was Hogarth who converted caricature from a fashionable divertissement into an art form and an expression of the age."[36] With Hogarth and his successors – James Gillray, Thomas Rowlandson, George Cruikshank – the art of caricature becomes firmly associated with satirical attacks on historically specific targets. But caricature can also be gentle, playful, and benign. Like parody, caricature often appeals because of its fanciful qualities and aesthetic virtuosity in fusing likeness and exaggeration. It showcases the artist's grace or inventiveness, especially in that minimalist variety which seeks to do its work with as few strokes as possible, thereby conveying an attitude of diffident talent.[37]

A related concept, cartoon, derives from the word *carta*, paper. Originally it referred merely to "a drawing on stout paper, made as a design for a painting," and entered the English language in the seventeenth century. Not until the mid-nineteenth, however, did it acquire the connotation of comic drawing,[38] at about the time that the British magazine *Punch* (founded 1841) helped to popularize the form, and just before the American political cartoonist Thomas Nast invented lasting icons like the Republican Party's elephant and the modern American image of Santa Claus. The emergence of the modern cartoon is thus linked to its flourishing in nineteenth-century print culture, and different kinds of cartooning – not all of them satirical – develop in the twentieth century with the emergence of new periodical genres and new media. In the 1890s newspapers began to feature comic strips, a genre that in the 1930s spawned the modern comic book, which quickly expanded beyond "comic" stories. Beginning in the 1920s, the *New Yorker* cartoon, offering gentle social satire, addressed itself to an educated upper-middlebrow readership; in the 1950s *Mad* magazine's parodies of pop-culture phenomena inspired many a future satirist; in the 1960s, the satirical *Private Eye* succeeded the gentler *Punch* as the leading comic magazine in the UK. With the birth of film animation, the cartoon came to name a popular genre of film comedy, one that soon spread to TV. The cartoon's capacity for visual exaggeration and reduction lies behind the historical association of animation and the comic, and accounts for the continued affinity between animation and satire in TV shows like *The Simpsons* and *South Park*.

Both terms, caricature and cartoon, are often extended to cover certain literary representations of human character – perhaps because of the non-etymological phonic similarity of *character* and *caricature*. In verse and on stage, satire and comedy famously deal with gluttons, misers, fops, and other stock types. These are examples of what E.M. Forster called "flat" characters, those who "in their purest form ... are constructed round a single idea or quality."[39] The isolation, exaggeration, and repetition of a key trait make a character immediately recognizable to the reader, who then collaborates in the ridicule. For this reason, flat characters are central to the comic novel. Jane Austen can with a few deft strokes – and here the virtuosity of the caricaturist is evident – make a character contemptible: Mr. Rushworth in *Mansfield Park* shows his stupid narcissism as he repeatedly crows about the "four and twenty speeches" he must learn for a performance; Mr. Collins in *Pride and Prejudice* repeatedly intones the empty phrase that marriage will make him "the happiest of men."

In Dickens, Forster notes, nearly every character "can be summed up in a sentence."[40] Through repeated catch-phrases, speech patterns, and physical mannerisms, Dickens bestows on his fictional people a memorable consistency that slides into mechanical rigidity, making them, as one modern critic says, "mere collections of humors or tics."[41] Character can become so flat that it merely names a social role, like the magnates at the Merdles' dinner party in *Little Dorrit*: Treasury, Bar, Admiralty, Bishop, Horse Guards. Yet Forster insists that Dickens's characters possess a "wonderful feeling of human depth," a "vitality" that makes them "vibrate a little" in spite of their flatness.[42] Their exaggerated, theatrical quality actually animates them.

Forster notes that Dickens derives his method of characterization from the early modern comedy of humors, whose foremost practitioner was Ben Jonson. William Hazlitt, writing in 1818, disparages Jonson's flat characters as "machines, governed by mere routine": "A cant phrase, an odd gesture, an old-fashioned regimental uniform, a wooden leg, a tobacco-box, or a hacked sword, are the standing topics by which he embodies his characters to the imagination."[43] But over a century later Wyndham Lewis defends Jonson on the grounds that Hazlitt has failed to understand or appreciate the methods of satire: "Is it not just because they are such *machines, governed by routine* ... that the satirist, in the first instance, has considered them suitable for satire?"[44] In rejecting Hazlitt's Romantic preference for Shakespeare over Jonson, Lewis scorns the humanistic overestimation of individuality and freedom. Reducing character to involuntary compulsions, he debunks human pretentions to exceptionality and autonomy.

Allegory and Fable

Angus Fletcher describes allegory as a mode that "says one thing and means another." This description makes allegory sound almost exactly like irony, and allegory resembles irony in demanding interpretation beyond a "surface" meaning. Thus for Fletcher allegory is fundamentally a "process of encoding our speech," a process that turns out to be present in an "extraordinary variety of literary kinds." Yet allegory's doubleness is of a certain sort. Allegory's "deeper" truth takes the form of an abstraction, often about moral, religious, or political principles: a person or object stands for a quality or an idea. Furthermore, at least since Coleridge, allegory has been distinguished from symbol because of the artificial and rigid nature of the correspondence between the object and the idea that it represents. This strict one-to-one correspondence makes allegory a sharply didactic mode; the expression of a truth becomes the *raison d'etre* for the artwork. It also helps to illuminate the overlap between allegory and satire, which can share both a project and a method: allegory is "the chief weapon of satire," and allegory often assumes a "satirical function."[45]

A fable is a short allegorical story. According to one scholar, "Fables' ... plots always generate explicit morals – interpretations that turn the preceding stories into convincing figures for home truths." Consequently, the fable implies "a stable set of symbolic conventions ... in which concrete examples instill socially relevant precepts."[46] A subgenre of the fable is the beast fable or animal fable, which, as Frank Palmeri notes, is "not about animals, but rather transpose[s] human and social relations onto the animal world in order to narrate and comment on human behavior."[47] The beast fable has a long association with satire due to the combination of its didacticism and its fantasy content.[48] As a character of Aldous Huxley comments, "The fabulists were right ... when they took beasts to illustrate their tractates of human morality. Animals resemble men with all the truthfulness of a caricature."[49] The use of animal characters as stand-ins for humans, along with the fable's short length, emphasize its pedagogical function and suit it for child readers, in stories ranging from Aesop's fables in sixth century BCE Greece through European medieval tales of Reynard the Fox and Br'er Rabbit of African-American folklore. But the power and appeal of such tales make the beast fable equally hospitable for satire directed at adult readers: Chaucer's "Nun's Priest's Tale," Jonson's *Volpone*, Orwell's *Animal Farm*. Many other well-known satirical works – Aristophanes' *Birds* and *Frogs*, Swift's *Gulliver's Travels*, many of the stories of Kafka, Art Speigelman's *Maus* – also draw on the tradition of the beast fable, but complicate it significantly. Since Darwin's discovery of evolution, animal stories have tended to frame the human relation to the non-human animal as the result of a common evolutionary history that suggests human beings' own animal nature, rather than in the iconic use of animals as allegorical distillations of particular human qualities. Indeed, the conclusion of *Animal Farm* itself, in which the pigs become indistinguishable from the humans they have overthrown, can be read as strictly allegorical ("meet the new boss, same as the old boss"), but it also enacts a breakdown of allegory itself, showing a collapse of the categories, animal and human, on which the allegory depends.

Epigram

The shortest satiric form is the epigram. A brief, witty statement, usually written in the present tense or imperative mood and offering a universal truth or a piece of general wisdom, the epigram need not be satiric, but often is; one seventeenth-century poet defined it as "satyre reduc'd to an epitome."[50] While proverbs, maxims, adages, aperçus, and aphorisms also lay claim to universal truths, the (satiric) epigram likes to subvert proverbial wisdom, to undercut widely held beliefs and establish a rival truth-claim. In poetic form epigrams usually are couplets or quatrains, sometimes longer, often with short three- or four-beat lines. They draw their force from their brevity, abstractness, and quotability. The poet Martial is the most famous ancient practitioner; later periods see memorable epigrams from Ben Jonson, François de la Rochefoucault, Pope, Swift, Friedrich Nietzsche, Mark Twain, Karl Krauss, H.L. Mencken, and Dorothy Parker. Maybe the most distinguished of all is Oscar Wilde, whom Parker honored with a self-referential quatrain:

> If, with the literate, I am
> Impelled to try an epigram,
> I never seek to take the credit;
> We all assume that Oscar said it.   (220)

Comic epigrams like this can appear, like parodies and caricatures, light, jokey, and disposable. Yet the very ephemerality and quotability of the quip, especially the spoken quip, can bestow on it an ability to circulate and, paradoxically, to endure.

The epigram also shares with Roman verse satire and biblical proverbs a capacity to distill wisdom that one can or should live by. William Blake's "Proverbs of Hell" belong to this tradition:

> Drive your cart and your plow over the bones of the dead.
> The road of excess leads to the palace of wisdom.
> Prudence is a rich ugly old maid courted by Incapacity.
> He who desires but acts not, breeds pestilence.
> The cut worm forgives the plow.[51]

These are Proverbs of Hell because they question the wisdom of orthodox Christian morality. Denying the values of restraint, reverence, and prudence, they usurp the authority of the short present-tense generalization to challenge a dominant ideology. (Many of Blake's epigrams share with allegory and fable the techniques of personifying abstract terms and illustrating principles with examples from the animal world.) They are not precisely comic but they are ironic, and they achieve their impact by an implicit contrast to expectations.

The epigram, finally, can function as a piece of a larger satiric form. Satiric definitions are one subclass of epigram. Such definitions can be compiled in satiric dictionaries such as Fielding's *Modern Glossary*, Flaubert's *Dictionnaire des Idées Reçues*, and Ambrose Bierce's *Devil's Dictionary*, which constitute a notable if minor subgenre that dates back at least to the "Social Dictionary" of the fourteenth-century Persian satirist Ubayd Zakani.[52] The heroic couplet, especially as practiced by the Augustan satirists, appears particularly hospitable to the epigram. Dryden begins *Mac Flecknoe*, for example, with a generalization that establishes the plot for his poem: "All human things are subject to decay / And when Fate summons, Monarchs must obey" (1–2). Characters in the plays of Wilde or the novels of Ivy Compton-Burnett sometimes speak in almost nothing but epigrams. An epigram can also play a part in a novel, and some of fiction's most memorable first sentences are derived from the form and satirical tone of the epigram, as in *Pride and Prejudice*: "It is a truth universally acknowledged, that a single man in possession of a good fortune must be in want of a wife." The fact that works such as *Mac Flecknoe* and *Pride and Prejudice* begin with epigrams suggest that the form is not always a device for closure, but one that announces a theme, and opens space for satiric elaboration (*SCR* 113).

Invective

Among its minor characters, Salman Rushdie's *The Satanic Verses* portrays a seventh-century Arab poet named Baal who "make[s] a living by writing assassination songs." This "young lampoonist," trained in "the skills of rhymed malice," is the most gifted of many poets who compose "vicious satires, vitriolic odes commissioned by one chief against another, by one tribe against its neighbor." Baal himself describes the "poet's work": "To name the unnamable, to point at frauds, to take sides, start arguments, shape the world and stop it from going to sleep." To which the narrator adds: "And if rivers of blood flow from the cuts his verses inflict, then they will nourish him. He is the satirist."[53]

This idea of satire as assassination song has been elaborated by the scholar Robert Elliott. In Arabian culture, Elliott notes, the satirist was a leader in battle whose satirical assaults were considered a deadly weapon. Even earlier, the ancient Greek poet Archilochus is alleged to have unleashed such furious "rhymed malice" at a would-be bride and her father that both victims were driven to hang themselves. In Irish mythology the satirist Athirne was said to have composed lethal verses attacking Luaine, fiancée of King Conchobar (*PS* 31). According to Harold Love, the roots of Restoration satire, which frequently took the form of personal attack, lie in ancient "folk poetry" and in the rustic traditions of British skimmington, charivari, or "rough music" – communal rituals of mockery and shaming meant to target "simple violations of the moral code."[54] Rushdie's novel invokes the roots of satire in direct, public insult, as do other modern satires such as Flann O'Brien's *At Swim-Two-Birds* and Ishmael Reed's *Mumbo Jumbo,* whose plots draw, respectively, on Irish and Haitian traditions of magic and witchcraft.

Invective thus retains the power, as Rushdie says, to name names, point out frauds, start arguments, and draw blood. This power renders satire dangerous and suspect. The Augustans tried to lift satire above such suspicions by distinguishing it from lampoon. Satire, they claimed, serves the public by attacking vices in general, while lampoon, which attacks individuals, only furthers personal vendettas. Yet it is not so easy to determine how personal an attack is. In one poem Mary Wortley Montagu only refers to Alexander Pope as an "imitator of Horace," but her readers would have had no doubt as to her target. When she likens him to a porcupine shooting a quill, she alludes to his diminutive, hunchbacked physique – calling him an "angry little Monster" (76) – and hints at sexual impotence by calling his phallic quills "harmless" (74) and "unwounding" (78). The line between satire and lampoon here looks very shaky.

Invective is everywhere in modern culture. Fused to wit or artful expression, it becomes satiric, and certain reviewers and pundits who specialize in witty invective are best understood as a class of satirist. Consider Christopher Hitchens's 1995 Juvenalian diatribe against Mother Theresa, whose espousal of misogynistic, homophobic doctrine is overlooked in her public hagiography:

> Given how much this Church allows the fanatical Mother Teresa to preach, it might be added that the call to go forth and multiply, and to take no thought for the morrow, sounds grotesque when uttered by an elderly virgin whose chief claim to reverence is that she ministers to the inevitable losers in this very lottery.[55]

In today's art world, William Powhida attacks pop-art superstar Jeff Koons in "Dear Jeff Koons" as the "blue chip luxury asset producing darling of new money oligarchs"[56] in an artwork that borrows from the literary form of the letter – recalling the court of Charles II when handwritten satiric poems were taped to the doors of their targets as "court graffiti" (Figure 4). Some poets, such as Ezra Pound, seem to write their best when giving vent to outrage – in Pound's case, over the wasted young lives of World War I: "There died a myriad, / And of the best, among them, / For an old bitch gone in the teeth, / For a botched civilization."[57] The irony here inheres in the events described, a gap between the quality of the men lost and the worthiness of the cause they fought for, and the invective takes on a satiric cast because of its strong sociopolitical content. Vice and folly – "bitch" and "botch" – are equally lambasted.

Invective can assume a ritual function. Anthropologists have identified ritual contests of insults in many different cultures, and ritual invective has been identified in the medieval Scottish tradition of flyting, in the friendly obscenity that Bakhtin calls "billingsgate," and in the African-American oral tradition of the dozens, described by music historian Elijah Wald as "exhibitions of masculine nobility and rhetorical skill, learned, adapted, polished, and appreciated as theater."[58] Roasts and similar functions represent another form of such rituals, as does the genre of stand-up performance called "insult comedy," exemplified by Don Rickles, and more recently by Robert Smigel's foul-mouthed puppet, Triumph the Insult Comic Dog. Such ritualized insults and obscenities constitute, as Griffin notes, both satiric play and satiric display. They contain or sublimate (but do not fully eradicate) satire's wounding power, while showcasing the improvisatory prowess of the speaker (*SCR* 88ff.).

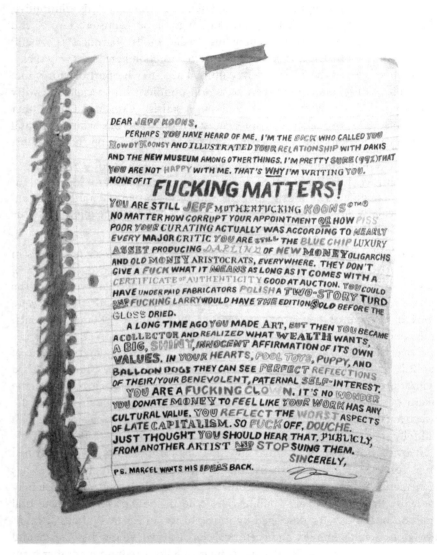

Figure 4 William Powhida, "Dear Jeff Koons" 2011. Graphite, colored pencil and watercolor on paper. Reprinted by kind permission of the artist. Powhida playfully draws on the proximity of satire and invective.

Black Humor

Black humor – joking about suffering, cruelty, and death – is often seen as a characteristic mode of the twentieth century. The Surrealist André Breton, who compiled an *Anthology of Black Humor* in the 1930s, saw black humor as "the opposite of joviality, wit, or sarcasm," and described its manner as "macabre," "ironic," and "absurd."[59] It is, in Breton's words, "the mortal enemy of sentimentality," and offends middlebrow, middle-class sensibility in order to critique it. Breton's canon of black humorists comprises admired fellow-travelers from both the present and the past. He cites "the midnight sunbursts" of the film comedians W.C. Fields and the Marx Brothers, and crowns Jonathan Swift as "the true initiator" of the mode. Nonetheless, Breton insists upon the difference between black humor and satire: "Satiric and moralistic intentions exert a degrading influence on almost every work of the past that, in some way, has been inspired by that kind of humor."[60] For Breton, as for many after him, black humor eschews the narrow moralism of satire, embracing instead its perversity and violence; in the words of comic novelist Bruce Jay Friedman, black humor explores "darker waters out beyond satire."[61]

In the 1960s "black humor" became a catch-all descriptor for an array of cultural products and performances – novels, stand-up routines, films, magazines, cartoons – seen as transgressive, outrageous, and anti-authoritarian. Auschwitz and Hiroshima appeared as the most prominent historical reference points, as artists, writers, and performers recognized both the possibility of sudden mass death and the human capacity to engineer such annihilation. Analyses of black humor gravitated toward the then-fashionable existentialist jargon of the "absurdity" of existence, but the phenomenon itself often spoke to specific social conditions: governmental, economic, and environmental changes seemed to be transforming not only society also but individual subjectivity. And while standard accounts cite McCarthy-era repression and conformity as a spur to this countercultural black humor, it was the postwar loosening of constraints that allowed greater expression of heterodox attitudes and beliefs.[62]

Sick humor was another popular term of the time, one that was linked to a Jewish cultural strain of joking, seen in the work of comedians such as Mort Sahl and Lenny Bruce, and in the fiction of Philip Roth. Such comic performances ranged from irreverent clowning to pointed political critique, and were shared by non-Jews like Thomas Pynchon, Terry Southern, and Kurt Vonnegut. A crucial theoretical formulation of such comic stances comes from Freud's essay "On Humour," where he discusses the Jewish tradition of "gallows humor." Freud gives the example of a man who, being led to his execution on a Monday morning, remarks, "Well this week's beginning nicely!" Such gallows humor is "rebellious," writes Freud, because of "the ego's victorious assertion of its own invulnerability."[63] It denies the reality of imminent death and asserts the pleasure principle in the face of it. Thus while the rebelliousness of 1960s humor came to include other kinds of transgression – against social strictures, sexual taboos, political authorities – the spirit of postwar black humor is most pithily captured by the subtitle to Stanley Kubrick's film *Dr. Strangelove: Or How I Learned to Stop Worrying and Love the Bomb*. Potential annihilation becomes occasion for a celebratory, farcical comedy that warns about destruction but denies its seriousness with laughter.

Camp

The aesthetic category of camp is rarely discussed as satire. The term came to critical prominence through a passage in Christopher Isherwood's 1954 novel, *The World in the Evening*, which in turn gave rise to Susan Sontag's foundational analysis in her 1964 essay "Notes on Camp." The consensus of critics since then has been that camp entails extremity, theatricality, artifice, and exaggeration. In Sontag's formulation, it is an aesthetic that emphasizes style or stylization rather than beauty per se. But in addition to its enthusiasm for the mannered style, camp also involves irony, parody, humor, and detachment – what Sontag calls the "off," "things-being-what-they-are-not," "everything in quotation marks," "Being-as-Playing-a-Role." This irony gives camp a double vision: on the one hand it offers an appreciation or celebration of that which is melodramatic, operatic, and sentimental, but on the other it requires a detachment from the perceived intentions of the artwork that allows a critical recognition of the artwork's aesthetic failure. Camp is a sensibility, a taste, a way of seeing, as much as a quality that inheres in an object.

Just as black humor is seen to display a Jewish sensibility but is hardly limited to Jewish producers and consumers, so camp is usually seen as a gay sensibility but one that can be shared by others. The objects of camp taste are often those that make visible bourgeois, heterosexual tastes as manifested in mass culture. The most obvious examples Sontag offers are big-breasted or big-muscled old-time movie stars (Jayne Mansfield, Steve Reeve), or, even more explicitly, "stag films seen without lust."[64] Camp, in other words, exposes heterosexual desire as constructed, scripted, and artificial. Its persistence in gay culture suggests that it serves a social or sometimes clandestine political function as a variety of irony that constructs what Wayne Booth calls "amiable communities" – or, even better, what Michael Warner called "counterpublics" – groups of strangers bound together by a text in their skeptical regard for mainstream tastes and values.[65]

The history of camp that Sontag offers suggests affinities between camp and satire. For Sontag camp originates in the eighteenth century "because of that period's extraordinary feeling for artifice, for surface, for symmetry" (she counts Pope an early practitioner), and reaches maturity with late Victorian aestheticism and its heirs – Oscar Wilde, Aubrey Beardsley, Max Beerbohm, Ronald Firbank, Ivy Compton-Burnett.[66] But camp in the twentieth century evolves away from the "high" aestheticism of Wilde. Whereas Wilde displays a revulsion from the vulgar, camp enjoys it, while still maintaining its position of superiority. Hence for Sontag and many after her, camp's purest form is not "deliberate" camp, but rather "naïve" or unintentional camp – camp that exists in those artifacts of mass culture which aspire to aesthetic grandeur but fail. Camp of this variety fails to recognize that the standards to which it aspires are outmoded, and thus becomes unwitting self-parody.

Is camp then a kind of satire? Some critics explicitly oppose the two, seeing camp as amoral and frivolous, and satire as morally tendentious. Isherwood denied the aggressive element in camp, "You're not making fun *of* it; you're making fun *out* of it," and Sontag says that camp is neither "bitter" nor "polemical."[67] Yet a more psychologically sophisticated account recognizes camp as form of satire, one through which "an out-group . . . announces its status as an in-group . . . Behind the manifest ludic element are the twin aggressive and sexual drives, though they may be disowned."[68] The play element in camp masks but does not eradicate a satiric attack. In this way, camp may resemble many other forms of light humor, comedy, caricature, or parody, in which an innocent dimension may seem to predominate but beneath whose playful surface lurks the aggression of satire.

Part II

Chapter 3

Classical Origins

"The ugliest man who ever came to Troy": so Homer in the *Iliad* describes the soldier often claimed as the inaugural satirist of the Western tradition, the club-footed, hunch-backed, chicken-necked Thersites (*PS* 130; *SI* 4–5), who in Book Two of the epic mocks Agamemnon's leadership and is in turn rebuked and beaten by Odysseus ("You and your ranting slander – you're the outrage"), bringing mirth to the dispirited troops.[1] Despised and ridiculed by the epic's warrior-heroes, the little man is a dissident truth-teller who challenges the authority of kings and debunks the value of military glory. His satiric voice, although violently silenced, undercuts the values of the epic from within the epic. Yet his ugliness also bespeaks a deep ambivalence about satire: an ugly message seems to belong in the mouth of an ugly messenger.

But Thersites is only one ancient prototype of the satirist. A second is the sixth-century BCE poet Archilochus, who according to legend wrote verses that so cruelly shamed his would-be bride and her father that they were driven to suicide. Conceived as personal invective rather than political critique, the satire in Archilochus's lines – called iambics after their meter – constitutes a powerful verbal weapon that draws upon a primitive belief in the magical practice of cursing (*PS* 4). This model of satire emphasizes not political dissent from below, but an aggressive and uncanny form of verbal violence.

Yet a third source for satire is the Greek diatribe, a loose, improvisatory genre practiced by Bion of Borysthenes (fourth–third centuries BCE), whom Horace praised for the "black salt" of his caustic humor. The diatribe, in turn, stems from the dialogues of Socrates, a conversational form that prompts a free-flowing ethical inquiry which offers an alternative to dogmatic or systematic philosophy.[2] Later writers from Lucian to Oscar Wilde to Don DeLillo use variations of the dialogue to showcase their wit as they juxtapose competing philosophical views. Satire in this vein is witty, open, and inquiring.

A fourth and final satiric progenitor is the pre-Socratic Democritus, known as "the laughing philosopher" (*LS* 1–3). Democritus's atomist theory, which takes a materialist view of the universe, proves amenable to satire because it de-idealizes the world, understanding the cosmos as simply the sum of blind physical forces. Seeing through our false accounts of both the physical and the moral world, Democritus adopts the stance of an amused observer of human folly. Later satirists take him as a model: Rabelais is called the "French Democritus" for his laughter at human folly, Robert Burton adopts the persona of "Democritus Junior" to enunciate the view that all the world is mad, and Samuel Johnson calls for the laughing philosopher's return, that he might bring his "cheerful wisdom and instructive mirth" to a corrupt England (50). Here satire is conceived less as a particular form or technique than as an emotional and philosophical way of looking at life.

Whether as ugly and despised political critic, abusive voice of shame, improvisatory conversationalist, or amused observer of folly, the figure of the satirist thus has ample precedent among the Greeks. Of course, early manifestations of the satiric are hardly limited to the Greco-Roman world. The Hebrew Bible's prophetic writings, especially those that denounce or lament corruption, give rise to the genre of the jeremiad, and biblical wisdom literature directly informs the satire of writers such as Erasmus, Johnson, and Blake. More broadly, biblical narratives frequently stage scenes in which moral outrage and instruction operate through ridicule, and the laughter of Yahweh is invariably a derisive, mocking laughter.[3] Outside of the West, many ancient cultures produced writings and stories resembling what we now call satiric literature. But in the classical world, satiric literature coalesced into three particularly enduring forms: in drama, the Old Comedy of Aristophanes; in poetry, the formal verse satire of Horace and Juvenal; and in prose and mixed forms, the category of Menippean satire.

Aristophanes: Imagination's Happy Home

The greatest of the Athenian comic dramatists, Aristophanes brings together all of the satiric strands just described: criticizing political authority, attacking individual enemies, mixing high and low registers of language, laughing at human folly. According to one critic, his influence touches "every single tradition of comic theatre and humour in the West," including "personal satire, philosophical satire, mimicry, parody, puns, *double entendre*, Saturnalian role inversion, Rabelaisian and Bakhtinian carnival, drag acts and cross-dressing, stand-up, bawd and scatology, slapstick, farce, and knock-about"; she further notes his impact on Arab culture and throughout the Mediterranean world.[4] He is believed to have written forty-four plays (four attributions are likely spurious), of which eleven survive as the only extant examples of the genre called Old Comedy. Old Comedy's attention to issues of public concern distinguish it from the later New Comedy of Menander; it was also distinct from the genre of the satyr plays, which treated epic and tragic themes parodically. Aristophanes' plays addressed highly topical political and social issues, and many of the details of his historical context are lost to us, yet in spite of their topicality they consistently transcend the moment of their original performance and resonate forcefully in the present.

Aristotle relates in his *Poetics* that comic drama descended from "phallic songs," presumably fertility rites. (The word *komos* means a band of revelers, and *komoidia* the revelers' song.) Early in the fifth century, some decades after the tragedies were first performed, comedies began to be staged before audiences of thousands at yearly celebrations honoring Dionysus. These communal festivals included sacrifices and processions and were attended by a large portion of the citizenry. All Athenian drama therefore performed a social function, yet Old Comedy in particular directly addressed issues of immediate concern to the body politic: war, education, political rhetoric, the legal system. Aristophanes names individual citizens and often singles them out for criticism, as in his attacks on Socrates in *Clouds* and Euripides in *Frogs*; the statesman Cleon, depicted in several plays as a rabble-rouser, may have brought legal action against the playwright for slander. Alongside these pointed personal jabs, the plays teem with low comic episodes of slapstick and obscenity, and the actors' costumes, featuring large phalluses, enhanced the opportunities for crude sexual jokes. All of these elements endow the plays with a liberating quality, granting a freedom to laugh at serious issues and important people.

But for all his exuberance and outrageousness, Aristophanes is about more than verbal abuse and dick jokes. His genius and his continuing appeal lie in the quality of his imagination, still startling in its inventive power. Jeffrey Henderson summarizes the formula. Typically in his plays a hero or heroine "who typifies a class of citizens who feel frustrated or victimized" will conceive "a fantastic scheme" executed through a series of comic episodes and conflicts; he or she eventually brings about "a triumph of wish-fulfillment over reality," leading to a celebratory conclusion in which order is restored but improved, and opponents are won over or banished.[5] Aristophanes, in short, reinvents the imagined society, showing an alternate universe that serves as both an object of laughter and a critique of the real world. Even at this early stage in the history of satire, Aristophanes exploits one of the fundamental paradoxes of the mode, through which fantasy critiques reality but is itself ironized through its own fantastical impossibility. The invention of the city of Cloudcuckooland in *Birds*, what Euelpides calls "imagination's happy home," might indeed be seen as an emblem of Aristophanic creativity itself: a city for the birds impossibly built of bricks between earth and sky, it is both an alternative to Athens and a rival to Olympus. It is a polis intended to be free from the wearying troubles plaguing Athenian life, but one whose subjects – the birds – are manipulated by the protagonist Pisthetairos in quintessentially Athenian fashion. As William Arrowsmith suggests, the fantastical city-state displays the worst of Athenian imperial grandiosity, yet simultaneously stands as a demand for Athenian renewal via the removal of "informers, sponges, charlatans, sophists, bureaucracy, and abuses."[6] The play thus initiates an ongoing dialogical movement between realist critique and fantastic escape, a movement that satire undertakes whenever it creates a world that stands as an alternative to the here-and-now.

Aristophanes' fertile imagination deploys a style of extreme unpredictability and discontinuity. The plays move suddenly but easily from slapstick to song, frivolity to exhortation, vulgarity to lyricism. As Michael Silk notes, they enact a "celebration, even glorification, of the richness and variety of language," and they possess less a single style than an assemblage of styles, a verbal "mobility" that draws upon "the audience's own sociolinguistic experience." Aristophanes shifts poetic meters, imitates dialects and jargons, tosses off puns and jawbreaking comic compound coinages.[7] He is especially famous for this last feature: examples include "Cloudcuckooland" itself as well as the longest word in the ancient Greek language, the 173-letter, 79-syllable word in *Assemblywomen* that names a bird-fish-and-meat stew.

Because modern readers – and Aristophanes has always had readers as well as audiences – naturally warm to the freedom of Aristophanic laughter, it is important to stress that debate surrounds the political interpretation of his plays. He is often seen as a conservative whose satiric judgment supports positions favorable to the upper classes and entrenched order, and who discerns dangers to the polis in demagoguery, the participation of the masses on juries, and the newfangled ideas of Socrates and Euripides. Some scholars, however, contend that the comic genre, developing alongside democratic institutions, performed an inherently liberalizing function by giving public voice to political criticism and thus legitimizing dissent.[8] Still others steer us away from all political certainties, reminding us that comedians go for the available joke, pander to the audience, bow to the exigencies of genre, and enshroud didactic pronouncements in hazy irony. The ambiguous politics of mockery are fully on display in Aristophanes: he can ridicule a particular target in service of a narrow aim, but can also promote the ridiculous as a liberating end in itself.

Figure 5 Aubrey Beardsley (1872–1898), "Lysistrata Defending the Acropolis." © Victoria and Albert Museum, London.
The late-Victorian illustrator Beardsley found inspiration in the ribaldry of Attic Old Comedy.

Lysistrata, which depicts a sex strike by the women of Greece in protest of the Peloponnesian War, is among the most popular of Aristophanes' plays today, and it is regularly cited in news stories about real-life female sex-strikes around the globe aimed at bringing warmongering men to heel. The play, both then and now, is a call for peace: at the time of its first performance, the Peloponnesian War had been going on for two decades at immense social, political, and economic cost to Athens. The heroine, Lysistrata, fed up with war, summons the women of all the Greek city-states, including Athens's enemy Sparta. Speaking with a vulgarity that would have jolted the audience, she enjoins the women to withhold sex from their husbands until the men agree to make peace:

> If we sat around at home all made up, and walked past them wearing only our see-through underwear and with our pubes plucked in a neat triangle, and our husbands got hard and hankered to ball us, but we didn't go near them and kept away, they'd sue for peace, and pretty quick, you can count on that! (51)

At the same time, she organizes Athens's older women to seize the city's treasury at the Acropolis to cut off the money for the war – a 411 BCE version of Occupy Wall Street. After much battling between the sexes and broad comedy about gigantic unrelieved erections, the men capitulate. Athens and Sparta make peace, mapping out a treaty on the body of a naked girl, and the play concludes with a celebration of peace, sex, and love.

To what degree can the play be understood as a proto-feminist or proto-pacifist statement? A strictly historical understanding will note that Athenian women did not vote or participate in public life, and that the comedy of the play's conception lies in the very idea that women could assume a role in shaping decisions of the polis. The notion of women running the government would have been far stranger and funnier to the Greeks than it is to us today, and one might argue that *Lysistrata* is no more a feminist manifesto than *Birds* is a call for animal rights. The play brims with sexist jokes that stereotype women as horny, adulterous, devious, and drunk. As for pacifism, a call for peace with Sparta and solidarity among Greek peoples does not imply a broader ethical opposition to war itself. Still, the play inaugurates the rejection of war as one of satire's most enduring topics.

Yet even if we check the inclination to interpret the play according to modern-day values, we can still see why its treatment of sex and gender relations, and of war and peace, resonates across history. Despite the stereotypes, the play reduces men and women alike to their sexual desires, and – like the *Seinfeld* episode "The Contest" where the characters vie to see who can refrain from masturbation the longest – it shows sexual desire as a universal human trait, comic in its irrepressibility. The opening scenes' frank acknowledgment of masturbation, the discussion of sexual positions in the women's oath of solidarity, the attention the women pay to each other's bodies, and the explicit, vulgar language may trade on gender stereotypes, but they also place a positive value on libido. However undignified the lustful human being appears, sex is allied in the play with love and peace. "Men get no pleasure in sex when they have to force you" (51), Lysistrata tells her conspirators, and sexual instincts ultimately prove more powerful and more admirable than the aggressive instincts that drive the war.[9] And just as love triumphs over war, so women hold out longer than men. In the episode of Myrrhine and Cinesias, it is the wife Myrrhine who proves to be the master of her domain, tantalizing her desperate husband in high comic fashion.

Even if the idea of women running the polis was to the Greeks inherently absurd, this absurdity cannot eradicate the political force of Lysistrata's appeal. Merely to place a woman at the center of a comedy was a bold choice, and to render her uniquely free from satire a bolder one. Her name, which means "disbander of armies," may have suggested the name of the priestess of Athena, Lysimache, or "disbander of battles," lending the fictional character prestige through association with one of the few women who held a public role in Athenian life.[10] Nor are her arguments absurd, despite their comic veneer. She makes analogies between the domestic and the public spheres of life, likening the "complicated international mess" of the war to a tangled ball of yarn that a woman knows how to untangle. She then compares the process of good government to the art of weaving a cloak:

> Imagine the polis as a fleece just shorn. First, put it in a bath and wash out all the sheep-dung; spread it on a pallet and beat out the riff-raff with a stick and pluck out the thorns; as for those who clump and knot themselves together to snag government positions, card them out and pluck off their heads.

Corrupt politicians must be removed from the wool, and the final product, "a fine new cloak for the people" (65), must include those groups – foreigners, debtors, and colonial subjects (though notably not women) – excluded from Athenian democracy. She also lists the ways in which women bear the burdens of war: wives sleep alone; virgins lose the chance to marry; mothers endure the death of sons in battle. When the Spartan ambassadors arrive, Lysistrata asserts: "I am a woman, but I've still got a mind ... and because I've listened many a time to the conversations of my father and the older men I'm pretty well educated too" (83). These are not ludicrous comic claims.

The older men are the most unequivocal target of the play's satire. During the Peloponnesian War, elders called *probouloi* had been appointed to make decisions outside of the Assembly, altering the democratic process of Athenian government, and the attacks on them suggest attacks on a war-hungry leadership unrepresentative of the populace. The leader of the *probouloi* displays a fear of female power:

> If any man among us gives these women the tiniest thing to grab onto, there's no limit to what their nimble hands will do. Why, they'll even be building frigates and launching naval attacks ... And if they turn to horsemanship, you can scratch our cavalry: there's nothing like a woman when it comes to mounting and riding; even riding hard she won't slip off. (67)

The risqué, misogynistic jokes indict the speaker, revealing a connection between a repressive patriarchy and the fear of an emasculating female sexuality. After the women defeat the *probouloi* at the Acropolis, the magistrate is draped in Lysistrata's veil, literally travestied or cross-dressed. Here we see the subtext of the play's fanciful conceit: female power effects an inversion that is funny, frightening, and exciting all at once.

But even as it stages these conflicts and inversions, the play also reassuringly suggests that the conflicts of the world – the war with Sparta and the discontent within Athens – are manageable.[11] The "battle" between the men and women at the Acropolis is merely name-calling and a water-fight; the murderous threats of the *probouloi* are never carried out. (In contrast, other plays do end in provocation or violence; in *Clouds*, Socrates' "Thinkateria" is set on fire.) The drafting of a treaty with Sparta on the naked body of a young woman named "Reconciliation" is played entirely for laughs, with pun after pun comparing legs, buttocks, and genitals to geographical locations, as the slack-jawed, sex-starved men are so busy ogling her that they readily accept Lysistrata's terms. The play is not a practical plan for an actual treaty, but rather an imaginative, utopian, and even impossible fantasy of peace.[12] When peace is made, sexual order is restored. The divided chorus of men and women unites and renounces the satiric ridicule that would have been expected from a choral speech at this moment: "We don't intend to say anything / the least bit slanderous about / any citizen, you gentlemen out there [in the audience], / but quite the opposite: to say and do / only what's nice" (81). When men and women, and Athens and Sparta, make peace, the need for satire vanishes. Satiric ridicule and slander are byproducts of social antagonism – antagonism which the play itself heals, if only at the level of the imagination.

Roman Verse Satire: Scouring the City

The Old Comedy of Aristophanes and his contemporaries is often cited by the Roman satiric poets as both influence and ideal. The poet Persius praises Aristophanes as the *senex praegrandis*, or colossal old man, for his forthright, acerbic wit: "If you've caught the spirit of brave Cratinus / or are pale from devotion to angry Eupolis and the Grand Old Man, / if you've an ear for a concentrated brew, then look at this. / I want a reader with his ears well steamed by that comic vinegar" (1.123–26). The parabases of Old Comedy, in which the chorus directly addresses the audience, may even have served as a direct formal source for verse satire (*STG* 24; *FS* 42). Yet for all its influence on the satiric tradition, Aristophanes' drama was called comedy. The word satire did not exist in Greek and it did not come to describe literary works until the poet Ennius used the Latin word *saturae* to name his works: *satur* means "full," and the term is assumed to refer to a full plate (*lanx satura*). For Ennius (whose works are mostly lost) *satura* might have been merely a catch-all term, like "miscellany" or "picked-up pieces," but under his successor, Lucilius, the word acquired the association with sharp-tongued social criticism that it retained for Horace, Persius, and Juvenal.

These three figures, and especially Horace and Juvenal, are the canonical Roman verse satirists, and they all consciously work in the genre and use the hexameter line established by Lucilius, the champion of republican *libertas*, or free speech, in the second century BCE. Yet even as formal verse satire becomes established as a particular genre of poetry, it remains a hard one to define. Its subject matter is multifarious. "All human endeavors," Juvenal claims, "men's prayers, / fears, angers, pleasures, joys and pursuits, these make / the mixed mash of my verse" (1.85–86). As Mary Claire Randolph wrote years ago, *satura* includes "miniature dramas, sententious proverbs and quotable maxims, beast fables (often reduced to animal metaphors), brief sermons, sharp diatribes, series of vignettes, swiftly sketched but painstakingly built-up satiric 'characters' or portraits, figure processions, little fictions and apologues, visions, and apostrophes to abstractions."[13] The form tends to be a monologue or dialogue, but subgenres abound: Horace's two books of satires include a travel narrative, a symposium or dinner-party, a parodic underworld dialogue between figures of legend, and a reworking of Aesop's fable of the country mouse and the city mouse, all rendered in comic fashion. Even as verse satire is formalized as a genre, then, it retains some of the disjunctive variety of Aristophanic comedy.

Horace and Juvenal are traditionally upheld as a contrast in styles, two opposing models of voice and attitude. Horace's dominant persona is the amused critic of foolish excess – comic, urbane, lighthearted, "presenting the truth with a laugh" in the way that teachers give children cookies "to coax them into learning their ABCs" (1.1.25–26). Juvenal is famous for his rage. "Indignation will drive me / to verse" (1.79–80), he claims as he denounces the vices of a decadent metropolis. Whether in Dryden's 1693 contrast between the "comical satire" of Horace and the "tragical satire" of Juvenal (96), or in Gilbert Highet's 1962 distinction between the Horatian reformer who aspires to cure human folly and the Juvenalian misanthrope who aims "to wound, to punish, to destroy" (*AS* 235), the opposition between the two has endured. Yet it is also reductive: Horace can scold and Juvenal can laugh.[14] Juvenal's later satires sometimes relinquish their indignation for a more Democritean or Horatian tone, while his much-quoted claim to be at the mercy of an uncontrollable satiric impulse – "It is difficult not to write satire" (1.30) – is actually one he derives from Horace's Satire 2.1. But the Horatian/Juvenalian distinction has endured for its value as a theoretical discrimination between tonalities – between, for example, the severity of Jane Austen's *Mansfield Park* and the sly grace of *Pride and Prejudice*, or between the strident contempt of George Carlin and the irreverent vulnerability of Richard Pryor. A satiric vision can shade into comedy or tragedy, into optimism or pessimism. Its affect can vary, too, from Juvenalian heat to Horatian cool, from disgusted immersion to amused distance. Wry Horace speaks in an anti-heroic voice, while Juvenal approaches heroic registers in his rhetorical fervor.

Horace sets out his aesthetic standards for satire by distinguishing himself from Lucilius. While he praises his predecessor for "scouring the city with caustic wit" (1.10) and "remov[ing] the glossy skin / in which people were parading before the eyes of the world and concealing / their ugliness" (2.1.63–65), he also says of Lucilius, "As he flowed muddily on, there were things you'd want to remove" (1.4.11), and argues for a style with greater refinement, brevity, and humor, one that can vary between the light banter of a "clever talker" and the higher diction of an "orator or poet" (1.10.12–13). His motives – at least his professed ones – are gentle; he claims that the point of his pen "will never attack a living soul, unless provoked" (2.1.40). Thus although he applauds Lucilius for his boldness and *libertas*, Horace hints that this *libertas* owes something to Liber, the god of wine, that free speech resembles drunken rambling.[15] In contrast, Horace presents himself as restrained and measured, a pose that provoked Dryden to call him "a well-mannered court slave" (87). This restraint may result from his precarious social standing as the son of a freedman, his explicit need for the patronage of Maecenas, or, especially in the second book, the politically delicate climate when he wrote, as the Republic was transforming into the Empire and the Lucilian ideal of open and bold speech was fading.[16]

Whatever its psychological or political causes, Horace's easy, colloquial style suits the standard of reasonableness that informs the moral wisdom he dispenses. He advocates for moderation and common sense. He mocks the miser as irrational rather than cruel; taking money from a big pile, Horace says, is no different from drawing from a little one: "it's as if you needed only a jug or a glass of water / and said 'I'd sooner draw it from a big river than from this / piddling stream'" (1.1.54–56). Yet the other extreme, profligacy, is no better: "Things have a certain proportion ... there are definite limits" (1.1.106). He articulates the principle that he will later, in his Odes, call a "golden mean." In eating and sex he similarly counsels a "middle way," one that fools seem unable to find (1.2.28). *Satura*, the genre of the full plate, is etymologically related to *satis*, meaning "enough," and for Horace satire is about knowing when one is full and respecting natural limits.[17]

Horace presents his wisdom as not only reasonable but also pragmatic. He rejects systematic philosophy, rigid moralism, and Stoic dogma, preferring the authority of common sense, tradition, and the teachings of his father. The question of whether "our motives [are] idealistic or selfish" (2.6.75) runs throughout his satires, and he usually judges in favor of self-interest. He rejects stinginess because it leads your relatives to long for your death, and adultery because you might be beaten, blackmailed, raped, or castrated (1.2.41–46). Sexual morals come down to a simple, "I like sex to be there and easy to get" (1.2.119).

Horace's pragmatism and reasonableness are set within what Niall Rudd calls a "dialectical framework" in which the speaker "hears objections" and "makes concessions."[18] He turns the tables on himself, especially in Book 2, by having characters such as his slave Davus sermonize to him, pointing out his own failings. He reveals his own comic follies, as when, on a trip to Brindisi accompanying Maecenas, he calls himself "an utter fool" for waiting up for a girl who never shows, leaving him sexually frustrated (1.5.82). He emphasizes his humble origins as the son of a former slave.[19] Even his own cognomen, Flaccus, becomes the occasion for a limp penis joke, as he worries that his "Floppy" satire might not "penetrate" the emperor's ear (2.1.18). In moments like this, the persona is almost that of a schlemiel. Yet for all his self-effacement, Horace makes sure to implicate his reader too. "What are you laughing at? Change the name and you are the subject / of the story," he says to his interlocutor in his programmatic first satire (1.1.69–70). His insistence on implicating his reader, indeed, anticipates Swift's claim that satire is a glass in which we discover everybody's face but our own: "Before examining your own faults you smear ointment / on your bloodshot eyes, but when it comes to your friends' foibles / your sight is as sharp as an eagle's" (1.3.25–27).

All kinds of slippery ironies thus pervade the self-presentations of Horace's speakers. How seriously should we take the attitudes and beliefs they put forward? Charles Knight discerns five discrete ways in which Horace's verbal "performances" are laced with irony, ranging from the use of an interlocutor explicitly critical of Horace to the instabilities of "shifting" first-person speakers identified more closely with the poet himself (*LS* 158). More radically, Kirk Freudenberg has suggested that the Horatian persona is deliberately rendered as a bumbler whose "wisdom" is so buffoonish as to be funny – along the lines, maybe, of the fatherly advice that Homer Simpson dispenses: "Kids, you tried your best and you failed miserably. The lesson is never try."[20] The audience recognizes such advice as comically bad, but it can contain a kernel of pragmatic value.[21] Ultimately, however we might value particular nuggets of advice, Horace's persona remains amiable, amused, restrained, and sly.

Over a century later, Juvenal's satire takes up "themes well worthy of Horace's pen" (1.51). In his first satire, he explains his choice of genre as a rejection of the worn-out epic, whose clichéd stories are declaimed in the homes of wealthy patrons, and whose "rubbish" echoes among the sycamore trees (1.13). Unlike the tired and irrelevant epic, which dwells upon the past, satire treats the present, and for Juvenal, that present demands satiric treatment:

> When a flabby eunuch marries, when well-born girls go crazy
> for pig-sticking up-country, bare-breasted, spear in fist;
> when the barber who rasped away at my youthful beard has risen
> to challenge good society with his millions; when Crispinus –
> that Delta-bred house-slave, silt washed down by the Nile –
> now hitches his shoulders under Tyrian purple, airs
> a thin gold ring in summer on his sweaty finger
> ("My dear, I couldn't *bear* to wear my *heavier* jewels") –
> it's harder *not* to be writing satires.   (1.22–30)

Roman decadence leaves him no choice but to write.

Juvenal's scene is the urban core of "down-town Rome" (3.5), a crowded, dirty, dangerous place, filled with foreigners, homosexuals, adulterers, nymphomaniacs, blackmailers, flatterers, skinflint landlords, corrupt politicians, and bad poets. Here husbands pimp out wives, "schoolboys are adulterers" (1.78), the courts offer no justice. Decaying buildings, crowded streets, drunken thugs, and sudden fires all threaten the vulnerable citizen. Social climbers borrow recklessly to keep up with neighbors and trample the poor in their haste to curry favor with rich. This view of modern decadence – xenophobic, homophobic, misogynistic – is fundamentally conservative, painting contemporary immorality as a falling-off from an ancient, virtuous past. It identifies vice with social, economic, and sexual mobility, diagnosing a failure of people and things to remain in their "proper" places.[22] Rome becomes a place of paradox and contradiction, where success is to be gained by "swearing black is white" in the manner of the Greek sophists. Hence in Satire 3 Juvenal's friend and surrogate Umbricius announces he is leaving the city for the country because in the city nothing is as it seems. Rome, paradoxically, is no longer Roman, controlled as it is "by a junta / Of Greek-born secret agents" (3.119–120) who possess no core self but only enact a series of roles: "schoolmaster, rhetorician, surveyor, artist, masseur, / diviner, tightrope-walker, magician, or quack" (3.76–77). Homosexuals likewise disrupt "natural" categories: a former priest of Mars is "decked out in bridal frills" and "a wealthy, well-born man [is] married off to a man" (2.125, 129). Reality itself is a mirage of shifting appearances, and proper values are so hard to discern that the speaker of Satire 10 finds "few indeed there are can distinguish / true good from its opposite, or manage to dissipate / the thick mist of error" (10.2–4). This is the confusing, burgeoning metropolis of the Empire, filled with immigrants from subjugated lands, teeming with economic activity, mixing everything together without appreciable order.[23] Juvenal even suggests that material comfort is an evil because it leads to decadence. Without war to keep men strong or poverty to keep women chaste, Rome suffers "the ills of long peace" in which "luxury, a more deadly / incubus than warfare, avenges the world we subdued" (6.292–293).

The voice that dominates Juvenal's sixteen satires is one of outrage and disgust. Whereas Horace criticizes Lucilius for stylistic excess, Juvenal imagines his republican predecessor as a noble warrior, a member of the equestrian class rushing into battle against vice: "when fiery Lucilius rages with Satire's naked sword / His hearers go red; their conscience freezes with their crimes" (1.165–166). Influenced strongly by the barbed epigrams of Martial, Juvenal's voice is blustery and declamatory. His outrage, communicated through "rhetorical questions, exclamations, apostrophes, and ellipsis," is carefully constructed to appear a spontaneous eruption onto the page, an involuntary explosion of righteousness far removed from Horatian restraint.[24] Even though Juvenal rejects the epic genre, then, the thundering satirist risks, in his grandiloquence, the same bombast that he criticizes in others.

With Juvenal's blustering tone comes an aesthetic of grotesquerie and exaggeration. If he offers a gritty realism that shows the underside of Roman life, this is still a "realism" of outlandish caricatures. We see sybarites and sycophants at dinner parties and poetry readings, drunkards and libertines in taverns and whorehouses. He shows us a glutton consuming an entire roast boar (1.141), a "queer brotherhood" where mascara-wearing "initiates" drink "wine / from a big glass phallus" (2.84, 94–95), a dinner where the rich eat imported mullet while the poor are fed a sewage-bloated pike from the Tiber that has been "a long-term *habitué* / of those cesspools underlying the slums of the Subura" (5.105–106). At night oversexed drunken women "reel from their litters, here they relieve themselves, / pumping out their piss in long bursts, on the Goddess's statue" before "they ride each other in turn," while the next morning a hapless husband splashes through his wife's urine (6.309–311). These depictions of bodily functions offer nothing of the gleeful liberation that characterizes Aristophanes' risqué description of acrobatic sexual positions, or even the goofy comedy of Horace's chats with his penis, but rather are pervaded with disgust.

We seem to be worlds away from Horatian subtlety here, yet a central interpretive question in reading Juvenal, as in reading Horace, remains that of the persona (*SCR* 75–77). Might Juvenal's strident persona be exaggeratedly strident, so as to serve as both a voice and a target of satire? Might the noble zealotry admired by Dryden deliberately offer an example of moralistic fury taken to excess? Might Juvenal's persona exemplify the self-indicting speaker, a familiar satiric trope seen in figures ranging from Jane Austen's Lady Susan to William Faulkner's Jason Compson to Robert Coover's Richard Nixon?

Perhaps, if Homer Simpson's faux fatherly advice might suggest a way to read Horace's irony, *South Park*'s Cartman might provide a handle on Juvenal's. Bemoaning the newly multiracial demographic of Colorado, Cartman bursts into a song lamenting "too many minorities in my waterpark." Most viewers will recognize Cartman's racism as a clear target of the show's satire, but his funny expression of his feelings licenses an uncomfortable participation in the racist sentiments: "There's no place for me to sit anymore, / And the lines just keep getting crazier. / There are Mexicans all around me. / The lazy river has never been lazier."[25] In similar fashion, Juvenal's satire mobilizes resentment and outrage at all sorts of groups, even while it takes positions a reader would recognize as extreme. As William Anderson argues, Juvenal's attack on a changing society is simple, stubborn, and childish.[26]

After all, anyone who wallows in filth to the extent that Juvenal does must harbor *some* secret appetite for the sewage-bloated river-pike – or for the urine-polluted swimming pools of exurban Colorado. He must feel some vicarious thrill in depicting the orgies and debaucheries he purports to be so repulsed by. When Juvenal asks, in high dudgeon, "when has there been so abundant a crop of vices?" (1.87), he reminds us that for the satirist vice is fruitful. No vice, no poetry. Like Shakespeare's fever longing for that which nurses the disease, Juvenal's febrile tirades sustain themselves on this rich, fermenting crop of Roman debauchery. His familiarity with decadence is indeed suspiciously intimate, extending to the details of secret gay orgiastic rites. He appears to have seen all this up close and personal.

Thus Juvenal the outraged moralist makes us wary of outraged moralism. He begins Satire 2 by turning the critique onto those sermonizers and hypocrites who invoke "high moral discourse" and "affect ancestral peasant virtues" (2.2, 3). The "false moralists" (2.35) who claim to know what's best for us turn out to be category-defying transvestites, scorned women who pass as men until exposed by a doctor who has been called in to lance their hemorrhoids (2.12–13). Similarly, when the speaker grumbles, "Here's no restraint of speech, no decent table-manners" (2.110), the reader must ask how is it that the strident Juvenal, of all people, is calling for manners and restraint. Like a man screaming for quiet, then, Juvenal sometimes hits such a pitch that we begin to doubt his reliability as a witness to Roman decadence. Ranting about the various sins of women, he seems to recognize momentarily how ludicrous he sounds, stopping his tirade to asking the reader directly, "Do you think this is melodrama? / Am I making this whole thing up?" (6.634–635). Juvenal thus masters the art of condemning Roman vices and enjoying them at the same time. For this reason Juvenal doubles his persona in Satire 3, creating both "Umbricius" and "Juvenal," in order to have it both ways. After rehearsing a litany of complaints about modern Rome, Umbricius flees the city in disgust while Juvenal remains to harvest the crop of vices and transform them into the satiric poems that, at the end of the conversation, Umbricius promises to read.

Menippean Satire: Plenty of Food for Laughter

In addition to formal verse satire there exists, in the words of the Roman grammarian Quintilian, "another and even older type of satire," one written in a combination of prose and verse.[27] This genre has come to be known as "Menippean satire," a term employed by the Roman author Varro (first century BCE) to describe his own writings, which were modeled on those of the Greek Cynic Menippus (third century BCE). For Varro "Menippean Satires" serves merely as a title; the phrase does not name a genre until the Belgian humanist Justus Lipsius so deploys it in the late sixteenth century.[28] It was in the Renaissance that the theory of satire fully acknowledged the importance of this category. In the words of the French scholar Pierre Pithou:

> Everyone who has been educated in literature knows well that the word "satire" signifies not only a poem of slanderous material written to reprimand someone for his public or private vices . . . but also all sorts of writings, filled with different matters and arguments, an interlarded mixture of prose and verse.[29]

Like many taxonomic terms, therefore, "Menippean satire" is applied retro-actively, and today the canon of ancient Menippean satire has come to include Lucian's dialogues, Seneca's *Apocolocyntosis*, Petronius's *Satyricon*, and Apuleius's *The Golden Ass*. Although the prose–verse mixture remains an essential criterion for many, it is largely a narrative form, often linking disparate episodes in an imaginary voyage or picaresque adventure. (In the late seventeenth century, Dryden called his poems *Absalom and Achitophel* and *Mac Flecknoe* Menippean satires, presumably because they were narrative poems (67).) The comic dialogue is a favorite form of Lucian, and parodic versions of other classical genres, such as the symposium and the romance, crowd under the Menippean umbrella. Dustin Griffin helpfully identifies three "branches" of the Menippean family tree: "a tradition of fantastic narrative," "a tradition of wild and parodic display of learning," and "a tradition of dialogue and symposium" (*SCR* 33). In the ancient world such satires were considered part of the tradition of what the Greeks called *spoudogeloion*, the seriocomic. Thus Lucian introduces his fantastical narrative "A True Story" by urging his reader to take a respite from heavy, "serious works" and to take up "light, pleasant reading which, instead of merely entertaining, furnishes some intellectual fare as well" (14). Old Comedy, with its playful treatment of serious matters, was a significant influence on the Menippean writers, offering both a "linguistic model" of mixed speech registers and "a source for tales of the triumph of simple common sense" over dogma and charlatanry. Yet whereas Old Comedy offers authoritative *parabases* and resolves its plots with happy reconciliations, Menippean satire offers no single authoritative view and tends to conclude uncertainly, without any statement or dramatization of positive values.[30]

The influence of these ancient jocoserious texts extends into the Renaissance, the Enlightenment, and beyond. Major prose satires by Erasmus, More, Rabelais, Swift, Baron Munchausen, Lewis Carroll, Samuel Butler, and others owe a great debt to ancient Menippean satire. Still, significant debate remains as to how broadly the genre should be defined: influential mid-twentieth-century treatments from Northrop Frye and Mikhail Bakhtin have led to liberal application of the label, while more recent critics such as Howard Weinbrot warn against laxness, complaining that Menippean satire has become "the genre that ate the world."[31] In any event, it is clear that the Menippean lineage survives within the history of the novel, particularly in those misfit, oddball, digressive varieties that descend from Laurence Sterne's *Tristram Shandy*.

For Frye, Menippean satire is one of the basic forms of narrative fiction, and its defining characteristic is not its seriocomic tone but rather its intellectual focus. It "deals less with people as such than with mental attitudes," making its characters "mouthpieces" for ideas. As intellectual rather than social or moral satire, it mocks "pedants, bigots, cranks, parvenus, virtuosi, enthusiasts, rapacious and incompetent professional men of all kinds" (*AC* 309). For Bakhtin, in marked contrast, the essence of what he calls the *menippea* is a playful spirit of "joyful relativity." At different moments in the ancient world, "a number of genres coalesce ... constituting a special realm of literature," the carnivalesque, in which the serious, the rational, and the doctrinaire are undercut by a pervasive comic, parodic, and ironic presentation. Deriving an "indestructible vitality" from popular and folkloric roots, the carnivalesque is anti-dogmatic, anti-authoritarian, anti-hierarchical; it laughingly overturns all ideas, powerful figures, and forms of discourse that aim to monopolize the truth (*PDP* 106–107). The *menippea* provide "one of the main carriers and channels for the carnival sense of the world in literature" (*PDP* 113).

Bakhtin elaborates fourteen characteristics of the genre, but his unwieldy list might be condensed into a shorter list of four. The most basic element Bakhtin refers to as "freedom" – a freedom from conventions of both plot and thought (*PDP* 114). This freedom, built into the comic nature of the genre, relies on heterogeneity of language and style. Menippean satire mixes poetry and prose; it juxtaposes a variety of voices in dialogue; it blends Greek and Roman traditions; it makes liberal use of "inserted" genres and tales, and of widely digressive episodes. Above all, it parodies or travesties existing genres, playing off against works of epic, tragedy, oratory, dialogue, romance, and even formal verse satire. In Petronius's *Satyricon*, for example, the "Cena Trimalchionis" episode functions as a mock-symposium in which the ideas put forward by varied speakers are often comically confused and jumbled. The content of Menippean satire, furthermore, is just as "free" as the style – free from the constraints of logic and seriousness, from the decorum governing the high genres of epic and tragedy, from the verisimilitude of a realistic plot.

Thus a second trait, linked to this comic freedom, is "experimental fantasticality" (*PDP* 116). Menippean satire rejects realist logic and takes the reader on voyages to fictional lands, or to heaven or hell, as in Seneca's *Apocolocyntosis* – a parodic account of the apotheosis of the Emperor Claudius, his judgment in heaven, and his banishment to Hades. The genre can enact magical transformations such as that of Lucius into a donkey in *The Golden Ass*, or the metamorphosis of man into wolf that Niceros relates at the table of Trimalchio. This fantasticality often parodies the more improbable episodes from historical and epic narratives. The narrator of Lucian's "A True Story" sails with the reader across seas of ice and milk, and through the skies to the moon; he visits the innards of a 150-mile-long whale and the fabled Isle of the Blest. At one point, his ship whipped into the sky by a storm, he sails past Cloudcuckooland, discovering Aristophanes' fantastical creation to be real. The author tips his hat to his comic predecessor: "I was minded of how people had foolishly been skeptical of what the playwright Aristophanes had written; he was a wise man who told the truth" (27). Lucian has told us that his story will be full of lies, but in the case of Aristophanes, the lies of fiction contain truth.

Yet while Menippean satire casually throws off the demands of verisimilitude, it also deploys a low comic realism, what Bakhtin calls "slum naturalism" (*PDP* 114). It visits brothels, inns, lodging houses, taverns, thieves' dens, and marketplaces, observing a variety of social types, recording vulgar and blasphemous language, showing the body in its base material functions of eating, drinking, eliminating, and copulating. Apuleius's ingenious device for displaying this slum naturalism is the transformation of his protagonist Lucius into a donkey. In his new body the narrator witnesses aspects of other people's private lives that would be off-limits to him as a man. He witnesses crimes and debaucheries, serving as a voyeur or spy on behalf of the reader. Often the content slides from the crude and the bawdy into the grotesque, as when Lucius the ass is almost forced to copulate with an insatiable woman. Drawing on the genre of comic folktale known as the Milesian tale, this low realist impulse engages the "open" present rather than the closed-off "absolute" past of legend or epic. The past and the genres that sanctify it are viewed critically, parodically, even cynically. So although realism may seem to work against fantasy, both aspects of Menippean satire debunk the sacred, the ideal, and the culturally authoritative.

A final characteristic of the genre is what Bakhtin calls "the testing of an idea, of a truth" (*PDP* 114). Here Bakhtin's view finally dovetails with Frye's understanding of the genre as intellectual satire in which ludicrous ideas are placed in the mouths of one-dimensional characters. For Bakhtin, Frye's pedants and charlatans contribute to a structure in which "ultimate philosophical positions are put to the test" and bad ideas discredited. The philosophical and ethical concerns that run through Horace and Juvenal – the questions of how to live and what to value – coexist with the most ludicrous treatment of them. The rejection of scholarly authorities in Menippean satire can signify anything from mere scoffing at intellectual pretensions to a more developed philosophical skepticism toward all human claims to knowledge.[32] For example, in Lucian's *Dialogues of the Dead*, death is seen as a great leveler, reducing all human strivings to idle vanities, much as in Juvenal's Satire 10. Lucian, however, provides no Juvenalian conclusion counseling a tranquil life of virtue and a simple desire for a sound mind in a sound body; he leaves the reader with no clear positive value aside from the scoffing of Menippus. Lucian upholds neither Horace's ideals of moderation and rural retreat, nor Juvenal's nostalgia for republican virtue, but only a "mocking, cynical, normless Menippean world."[33]

The works of Menippus and Varro exist only in fragments, but Lucian, an Assyrian-born author of the second century CE, continues their tradition, and Menippus himself appears in many of Lucian's dialogues. Called the "father of the family of Scoffers" by the seventeenth-century writer Izaak Walton,[34] Lucian relentlessly debunks claims to authority and idealism. He burlesques the gods and goddess of traditional religion by reducing their behavior to base motives of lust, vanity, jealousy, and vindictiveness. (Here Lucian again picks up a theme from Aristophanes' *Birds*, in which the Olympians are represented as selfish tyrants who care only that the birds are intercepting the sacrifices men send up from earth.) *A True History* exposes Herodotus and other historians as liars and embellishers, while a second-century prophet named Alexander is discredited as a quack in a biography whose comic ruthlessness anticipates Christopher Hitchens's gleefully vitriolic portrait of Mother Theresa. Philosophers, with their pretensions to knowledge, are frauds in the manner of Voltaire's Pangloss. In the dialogue "IcaroMenippus," the moon, Selene, complains of them in language that may recall the anti-intellectualism of Aristophanes' attacks on Socrates:

> There is a class which has recently become conspicuous among men; they are idle, quarrelsome, vain, irritable, lickerish, silly, puffed up, arrogant, and, in [the] Homeric phrase, vain cumberers of the earth. These men have divided themselves into bands, each dwelling in a separate word-maze of its own construction, and call themselves Stoics, Epicureans, Peripatetics, and more farcical names yet.[35]

In "Philosophies for Sale," the philosophers and their ideas are represented as slaves on the auction block, peddling abstruse ideas without practical values, while in "A True Story," a visit to Elysium shows Socrates doing little but chasing after boys.

Thus, as Ronald Paulson writes, "Lucian is always seeking new viewpoints from which to see man's folly ... [and] pretensions" (*FS* 33). Trips to the underworld force characters to recognize the transience of earthly glories. When Menippus visits, Hermes points him toward the beautiful figures of myth and legend such as Helen and Leda, but Menippus replies that he can only see "bones and skulls without any flesh on them" (205). When the dead prepare to cross the river Styx, they are stripped naked; they must leave behind their robes and crowns, their treasures and wealth, their trophies and statues. The beautiful must shed their long hair and rosy cheeks, the strong their muscles, the famous their names and reputations. Conversely, journeys to the heavens allow a lofty, disinterested perspective – what was called *catascopia* – on the petty, Lilliputian world of men. From the heights of heaven, Menippus notes, "the whole of Greece ... might measure some four inches." He explains:

> You must often have seen a community of ants, some of them a seething mass, some going abroad, others coming back to town. One is
> a scavenger, another a bustling porter loaded with a bit of bean-pod or half a wheat grain. They no doubt have, on their modest myrmecic [ant-like] scale, their architects and politicians, their magistrates and composers and philosophers. At any rate, what men and cities suggested to me was just so many ant-hills.[36]

Such an Olympian perspective could evoke a cold nihilism, yet there is in Lucian a levity, a light-hearted "genial and easygoing" tone joined to silly Aristophanic fantastication.[37] In the fabulous creatures he invents in "A True Story," he gleefully throws off the laws of physics, chemistry, and biology, imagining all kinds of exotic anatomies and bizarre methods of copulation and reproduction. This combination of intellectual seriousness and childlike joking finds a rough contemporary parallel in the way that Monty Python inquires into the meaning of life. Their "Galaxy Song" remakes *catascopia* for a post-Einsteinian world:

> Just remember that you're standing on a planet that's evolving
> And revolving at nine hundred miles an hour
> That's orbiting at nineteen miles a second, so it's reckoned,
> A sun that is the source of all our power.
> The sun and you and me and all the stars that we can see
> Are moving at a million miles a day
> In an outer spiral arm, at forty thousand miles an hour
> Of the galaxy we call the milky way.[38]

Thus while Menippus comes to recognize "the absurdity and meanness and insecurity that pervade all human objects, such as wealth, office, power," he retains a sense of humor, finding in the parade of human folly "plenty of food for laughter."[39]

Like Apuleius's *The Golden Ass*, Petronius's *Satyricon* is a longer narrative, sometimes called a Roman novel, which anticipates the modern picaresque novel with its traveling hero and episodic adventures. Written during the rule of the Emperor Nero, and surviving in fragmentary form, it is popularly understood as a satiric representation of the decadence of imperial Rome. Its longest surviving episode, the "Cena Trimalchionis" (based in part on Horace's Satire 2.8) describes an ostentatious banquet hosted by an obscenely rich former slave, Trimalchio, an emblem of the aesthetic gaucherie and moral grotesquerie of the Roman one percent. (F. Scott Fitzgerald nearly named his novel about the *nouveau-riche* Jay Gatsby *Trimalchio*, while T.S. Eliot opens his own poem of modern decadence, *The Waste Land*, with an epigraph from that chapter in the *Satyricon*.[40]) Petronius's narrative includes still-disturbing scenes of child rape and sadism as well as more amusing scenes of voyeurism, vulgarity, violence, and all kinds of sexual libertinism. In the fragment that stands as the conclusion to the work, the poet Eumolpus, masquerading as a decrepit millionaire in a scheme to swindle some legacy-hunters, insists that those who want to inherit his wealth must promise to eat his dead body, adding "some seasoning to disguise the taste" (147). He connects the consumption of his body with the legacy-hunters' venal pursuit of his wealth. The literal cannibalism, like that of Swift's Anglo-Irish landlords in "A Modest Proposal," represents a grotesque moral cannibalism.

But while at moments like this the *Satyricon* presents "a morally collapsing world from which there seems no exit,"[41] the absence of any clear authorial commentary on this decadence (combined with the gaps in the surviving manuscript) makes the work notoriously difficult to interpret. The narrator Encolpius, like Apuleius's Lucius, struggles to make sense of the events that unfold about him; like Gulliver and Candide after him, his obtuseness allows him to be both the target of satire and its "unwitting vehicle."[42] Therefore although Encolpius's rebuke to moralistic "Catos" might appear as a defense of the satire's bawdy content – "My honest tongue recounts how men behave. / For mating and love's pleasures all will vouch; / Who vetoes love's hot passion on warm couch?" (134) – it can equally be seen as hollow self-justification. And if the *Satyricon*, especially the "Cena Trimalchionis," is taken to be a judgment on the excesses of the Emperor Nero – Petronius served as *elegantiae arbiter*, or arbiter of taste, in Nero's court – then vice and folly would seem to be represented specifically for the purpose of moral censure. Of course it is rarely a simple either/or in satire, and moral indignation and voyeuristic excitement are old bedfellows.

In addition to its moral satire, the *Satyricon* performs a kind of literary satire through its relation to other texts. The overarching story parodies the contemporaneous narratives known as Greek romances, but substitutes the homosexual couple of Encolpius and his slave Giton for the heterosexual couples of its predecessors. The high romantic rhetoric that Encolpius spouts as he loses and regains his lover becomes "double-voiced" as clichéd comic bombast.[43] The epic genre is also parodied; whereas Homer's Odysseus has incurred the epic wrath of Poseidon, Encolpius has angered Priapus, a minor fertility god known for his persistent erection, and is consequently cursed with impotence. (Thus the title *Satyricon* refers not to satire or *satura* but to *satyroi*, satyrs.) Direct parodies of the epic poets Virgil and Lucan come from the pompous versifier Eumolpus, whose unsolicited recitations provoke passers-by to throw rocks at him. The parody deflates the seriousness of high genres, and the authority of literary tradition proves as fatuous as the invocations of morality and education that characters sporadically offer.

The *Satyricon* presents an uncertain world of extreme mutability, in which fickle Fortune suddenly turns slaves into millionaires and vice versa, in which the rhetoric of love masks the transient urgings of lust, in which characters don disguises and act out roles in their efforts to create or stage new selves.[44] They stage these selves through displays of wealth, taste, manners, education, and knowledge, and in this attention to self-display, the *Satyricon* brings moral satire to a meeting point with social satire. For Erich Auerbach, Petronius's precise "fixation of the social milieu" establishes a new realism in Western literature, and a similar claim might be made about his development of a satiric mode newly attentive to the everyday habits that establish social standing.[45] Anticipating the comedy of manners as practiced by novelists like Jane Austen and Evelyn Waugh, the *Satyricon* judges and mocks its characters according to criteria of taste and sophistication. Yet while it satirizes snobbery and social climbing in its representation of new wealth, bad taste, and sexual excess, it simultaneously displays, through its very engagement in satiric judgment, its own investments in these ostensibly disavowed categories. We participate in snobbery and pretention even as we deride them.[46] The *Satyricon* might appear to offer sharp judgments, but it leaves us as readers on unsteady ground, never fully certain whether we are the perpetrators of the satire or its victims.

Chapter 4

Renaissance Satire: Rogues, Clowns, Fools, Satyrs

In the account of the critic Mikhail Bakhtin, three literary types embody the laughter of the Renaissance: the rogue with his "level-headed, cheery, and clever wit," the clown with his "parodies and taunts," and the fool with his "simpleminded incomprehension" (*DI* 162). All three offer laughter as an antidote to the deficiencies of "straightforward genres, languages, styles, voices" (*DI* 59), and all three expose "all that is vulgar and falsely stereotyped in human relationships" (*DI* 162). The rogue, living on the margins of society, describes its laws and customs but scorns its authority. The clown preserves "the right to be other in this world," and reveals, through his jesting and teasing, "the underside and the falseness of every situation" (*DI* 159). The fool, in his stupidity and folly, may be a target of satire, but he acts as a source of wisdom who calls attention to the more profound folly of those around him. Through these two-faced characters, a double-edged laughter emerges, one which dismantles false beliefs and hierarchies in order to establish a "new, whole, and harmonious" worldview (*DI* 168).

These familiar Renaissance characters go by other names as well: the simpleton, the naïf, the knave, the *pícaro*, the trickster, even the madman (*folie* is French for madness), but one additional name deserves mention: the satyr. As Alvin Kernan has detailed, the mythological figure of the satyr became a prototype for the Renaissance verse satirist, who reveals his rude, mischievous, and lustful nature in "harsh meters, coarse language, and frank descriptions of the most unattractive kinds of vice."[1] Even when he claims to enforce moral and social norms, the satyr does so from a position dangerously close to the deviants he excoriates. The satyr-satirist may not always appear as cheery or good-natured as Bakhtin's rogue, clown, and fool, but he shares with them a liminal position on the edge of the socially acceptable.

The greatest satire of the Renaissance was allied to the cultural movement now called humanism. Humanism placed new value on social reform, secularism, individual dignity, and *studia humanitatis* (the study of humanity). It rejected hidebound medieval scholasticism and turned for its models to the literature of Greece and Rome.[2] This rediscovery of ancient culture included renewed attention to Roman satire, and humanist satirists deliberately pat-terned their work on Horace, Persius, Juvenal, Lucian, and others. Yet the sources of Renaissance satire were not exclusively classical. Satiric elements such as bawdy comedy, social critique, moral preaching, and fantastical allegory can be found in native medieval genres such as fable, sermon, and complaint. The rise of vernacular literature in writers like Boccaccio and Chaucer supplied an earthy comic realism. And the festive, anti-hierarchical ethos of the carnivalesque drew from roots in medieval folk practices includ-ing parodic liturgies, religious feasts, comic theater, and the social and linguistic mixing that took place in the market square.

As it draws on many sources, so satiric writing in the Renaissance adopts many forms. Short comic tales and picaresque adventures, beginning with the anonymous *Lazarillo de Tormes* (1554) in Spain and Thomas Nashe's *The Unfortunate Traveler* (1594) in England, depict and analyze society in its socioeconomic diversity. Menippean satire thrives in the subgenre of the anatomy, a comically expansive survey of a given topic that exhibits scholarly learning gone haywire; examples include Sir John Harrington's *Metamorphosis of Ajax* (1596), Nashe's *Lenten Stuff* (1599), and Robert Burton's *Anatomy of Melancholy* (1621), as well as large portions of Rabelais's *Gargantua and Pantagruel* (SCR 33).[3] And as more satire is written, so literary theory begins to study it: Thomas Lodge and George Puttenham in England and Isaac Casaubon, Joseph Scaliger, and Daniel Heinsius on the Continent trace its origins, discern its characteristics, classify its subtypes, and debate the merits of its practitioners. Amid this plethora of satiric forms, however, four stand out as notably influential: the mock discourses of Erasmus and Thomas More, the vernacular fictions of Rabelais and Cervantes, the English verse satire of the 1590s, and the genre of drama called city comedy, exemplified in the work of Ben Jonson.

Renaissance Humanism: Erasmus and More

In the early decades of the sixteenth century, two strange short books appeared almost simultaneously: Desiderius Erasmus's *Praise of Folly* (1511) and Thomas More's *Utopia* (1516). Written in Latin, both books engaged profound moral and philosophical questions through peculiar, whimsical literary forms – a mock encomium and a fictional travel narrative.[4] The writers were good friends; Erasmus wrote *Praise of Folly* at More's house in London, dedicated the book to him, and later published *Utopia* for More on the Continent. Erasmus's Latin title, *Moriae Encomium*,

Figure 6 "Social Ship of Mechanics." Author, Sebastian Brant, 1458–1521. Artist, Albrecht Dürer, 1471–1528. By permission of University of Houston Digital Library. Renaissance humanists frequently direct their satire against a fundamental madness in human behavior.

even puns on the similarity of More's name to the Greek word for fool: it can be roughly translated as *Praise of More*. Both men were central figures in the northern European humanist movement, and both books owe a clear debt to what More calls "the witty persiflage of Lucian" (69) – a writer whose works the men had translated together. Indeed, in Lucian's seriocomic style they found an ideal mode through which they could unite wisdom derived from classical learning, a progressive critique of European institutions, and a witty spirit of play.

Praise of Folly and *Utopia* share a project of surveying the contemporary world and finding in it a parade of fools. Here Erasmus and More are themselves anticipated by the Italian humanist Leon Battista Alberti's *Momus* (*c.* 1450), a dialogue among the gods that satirizes philosophers' intellectual pretentions and courtiers' social follies, and most immediately by the German theologian Sebastian Brant's *Ship of Fools* (1494), which depicts, in a series of poetic caricatures, an array of madmen sailing for a false paradise (Figure 6) – a text that begins to break down the sharp distinction between vernacular farce and satire with serious didactic aims.[5] (Chaucer's *Canterbury Tales* might also be seen as a satiric procession.[6]) Both *Folly* and *Utopia* are also works of *fictive discourse*. They stake out philosophical positions provisionally, ironically, and playfully, veiling their meanings and speaking through the voices of others. And both create possibilities for later satirists. Erasmus's mock encomium looks forward to satiric forms that pretend to be non-ironic discourse – mock policy proposals of Defoe and Swift, Jane Collier's mock conduct book, Stephen Colbert's mock praise for George W. Bush at the 2006 White House Correspondents' Dinner. Its central trope of blame-by-praise recurs in Panurge's praise of debt in Rabelais's *Third Book*, Pope's praise for Dulness in the *Dunciad*, even H.L. Mencken's praise for William Jennings Bryan's intellectual simplicity. Meanwhile, More's imaginary voyage launches a different subgenre, the literary utopia, whose descendants run from Jonathan Swift's *Gulliver's Travels* (1726), to Samuel Butler's *Erewhon* (1872) and H.G. Wells's *The Time Machine* (1895), through the dystopian novels and movies that proliferate today.

Praise of Folly purports to be an act of self-praise spoken by the goddess Stultitia (Stupidity or Folly), who claims to "confer benefits on all men" (11). Through her self-praise, she condemns and exposes the folly of the human race. Erasmus's very premise, the project of praising folly, is of course a paradox: how can it be wise to behave unwisely? The complexity of this paradox takes him well beyond the ambitions of ancient mock encomia that humorously lauded unworthy objects such as insects or illnesses. Erasmus, through Folly's shifting arguments and repeated reversals, opens a *mise en abyme* of wisdom and foolishness so dizzying that Folly herself becomes confused about which word to use:

> What is this life ... if you remove pleasure from it? You applaud. Well, I know none of you is so wise, or so silly rather – but perhaps I'd better say so wise – as not to agree with me on that point. (13)

Folly's claim to govern human affairs includes at least two distinct assertions: a descriptive one, that all the world *is* foolish, and a prescriptive one, that because folly brings happiness, all the world *should be* foolish. The slippage between these claims forces the reader continually to reassess Folly's meanings. Through these puzzles and paradoxes, Walter Kaiser claims, Erasmus "invented a new kind of irony," one which mocks but in the same gesture mocks its own mockery, so thoroughly undercutting itself that the reader can find no secure landing space.[7]

In the twists and turns of her oration, Folly assumes various stances. Especially in the first parts of her discourse, her claims for her own virtues can be compelling, as when she speaks about the happiness of children who in their obliviousness are unburdened by the cares of adulthood. "Folly" here means a blissful ignorance of oppressive truths about human suffering. (Almost two and a half centuries later, Thomas Gray would write of his lost youth, "[W]here ignorance is bliss, / 'Tis folly to be wise.") Likewise, the goddess, borrowing from Horace's Satire 1.3, argues that she is essential to love: "When a man kisses his girlfriend on her mole, when another is delighted with his mistress's misshapen nose, when a father says his cross-eyed son has a lively expression – what I ask you is that if not pure folly?" (20–21). Like Horace, Folly promotes moderation, valuing natural pleasures such as drinking, joking, sex, and song (*STG* 32), and Erasmus reconciles Christianity with the classical Epicureanism of Horace and Lucretius.[8]

At other moments, however, Folly's praise looks like condemnation. She anatomizes human pursuits, revealing what Samuel Johnson would later call the vanity of human wishes. Folly discovers folly everywhere: in pointless activities like hunting, gambling, alchemy, and superstition; in vain desires for military glory and worldly fame; in particular groups of people who qualify as fools, including doctors, lawyers, actors, and – disconcertingly – women. Scholastic theologians, a favorite targets of humanists, are fools because they get lost in arcane debates:

> Whether divine generation occurred at a particular point in time? Whether several filiations co-existed in Christ? Is it thinkable that God the Father hated Christ? Could God assume the shape of a woman, of a devil, of an ass, of a pumpkin, or a piece of flint?   (57)

Just as the pedantry of the theologians is criticized, so is the materialism of the clergy. If the popes were truly to live by Christ's teaching, "Off they would go, all those riches, honors, powers, triumphs, appointments, dispensations, special levies and indulgences; away with the troops of horses, mules, flunkies, and all the pleasures that go with them!" (70).

But in the final section of her oration, Folly shifts strategies once more, citing scripture to argue that "the entire Christian religion seems to bear a certain natural affinity to folly" (82). Again the reader must adjust her understanding of the ironies at play, and of the word folly itself. Erasmus seems now to condone folly, which no longer connotes the pursuit of worldly rewards but rather names the (apparent) madness of the pious who disdain such rewards. The irony here is structural: the superficially foolish Christian ideal rebukes by contrast the truly foolish contemporary materialism.

As the technique of Erasmus's satire varies, so does the tone. In his preface Erasmus, like Lucian at the start of his *True History*, urges the serious to take "a little time off for play" (4), and Folly herself sometimes adopts Lucian's *catascopia*, smiling at the behavior of mortals from her Olympian height. She delights in the "theater" of human pettiness, and compares her view to that of Menippus, whose lunar perch allows him to see human activity as

> a swarm of flies or gnats, all struggling, fighting, and betraying one another, robbing, playing, lusting, birthing, sickening, and dying. You'd never believe what tumults and tragedies could be set in motion by this puny homunculus who is destined to disappear so quickly.   (50)

This Lucianic distance is fused to a Horatian style that moves briskly from example to example, showing men and women unable to find a golden mean: "One man rushes headlong to spend every last penny he possesses, another hoards his coppers like a miser. Here's a candidate for public office who canvasses high and low for votes; his counterpart dozes by the fireside" (50). Yet as her oration progresses, Folly's description of princes and courtiers, priests and popes, begins to ring with Juvenalian indignation. Sensing this, she pulls up short: "But it's no part of my present business to arraign the lives of popes and priests, lest I seem to be composing a satire rather than encomium" (73). With a wink to the reader, Erasmus reveals his satirical purpose.

In his preface, Erasmus rejected charges that his satire will be too biting like Old Comedy, and promises that "unlike Juvenal" he has "made no effort to rake in the sewer of hidden crimes" (5). But by the end of his satire he has abandoned the pretense that he will attack only folly, and not vice. Indeed in Folly's account the two look very much alike. Yet the paradoxes of folly are so tightly spiraled, so dizzyingly recursive, that to read *Praise of Folly* as simple denunciation is to grant it a monolithic wisdom that it everywhere disavows. Here Folly's gender becomes crucial. As a woman, Folly claims, by virtue of her sex, an immunity from the demands of reason. Of course this is a masculinist Renaissance stereotype, but by disarming herself, by surrendering phallic power, Folly frustrates any attempt to pin her down. As J.M. Coetzee puts it, Folly claims "the position of not having to take a position."[9]

More's *Utopia* is a philosophical dialogue, a travel narrative, and a parody of both. It blends these elements into a minor but influential genre of its own, the literary utopia. Indeed it creates, all at once, a genre, a word (*utopia*), and a political concept. It draws on descriptions of the ideal commonwealth in Plato's *Republic* and Augustine's *City of God*, while its more strictly literary progenitors include Lucian's *True History* (with its visit to the Isle of the Blest), medieval poems about the Land of Cockayne (a peasants' fantasyland set in the Atlantic where food and sex are limitless), and the pagan myth of a Golden Age of Saturn (a time of peace and plenty before Zeus's reign). But the most immediate historical source for More's imagination is the European discovery of the Americas, known through the accounts of explorers like Amerigo Vespucci. The New World exerted a powerful pull on the European imagination, introducing it to new nations, peoples, cultures, and customs, suggesting more things in heaven and earth than Western philosophy had dreamt. The literary genre of utopia thus appears at the moment when both European imperialism and modern political theory are being born.

Utopia describes an imaginary island nation (the name means Nowhere) where people live in happiness, free from the conflicts that plague contemporary Europe. More does not play this new world for big laughs, as Aristophanes does Cloudcuckooland, but deploys blank irony and social critique. As Fredric Jameson says, More's satire takes the form not of ridicule directed at "unrealistic and fanciful" schemes for social perfection but rather of a "passionate and prophetic onslaught on current conditions and on the wickedness and stupidity of human beings in the fallen world of the here and now."[10] More carries out his satire by creating what is – to use the phrase with which Joseph Hall later named his own satiric fiction – *mundus alter et idem*, a world other and the same. Any utopia, by its mere existence, serves as a rebuke to the here-and-now; the perfection of Utopia satirizes by implicit contrast the ills of Europe.[11]

The book purports to relate a description of the customs and beliefs of Utopia that More has heard from a Portuguese traveler named Raphael Hythlodaeus ("Nonsense-peddler"). But this account isn't given until *Utopia*'s Book II; Book I presents a conversation between More ("Morus," Latin for "fool") and Hythlodaeus that centers on conditions in Europe. The division of the work into two "books," one focused on the Old World, one on the New, makes visible a dialectical quality that pervades the work: *Utopia* describes two worlds; it presents a dialogue between a trickster and his dupe; it is playful and serious. These doublings leave gaps for irony and uncertainty, forcing much like *Praise of Folly* – a constant movement of the mind rather than an easy certainty.

In Book I, Hythlodaeus offers a sharp recitation of social evils including income inequality, the greed and corruption of the rich, the destructive effects of land enclosure, and the incessant war-mongering of European rulers. His method is Socratic; he poses hypotheticals and coaxes answers out of More to advance his argument. But he is also a Horatian reformer, rejecting Stoic severity and excessive punishment. "A good part of the world," he observes with dismay, "seem to imitate bad schoolmasters, who would rather whip their pupils than teach them" (16).

Book II describes Utopia itself: its geography, government, agriculture, and labor practices; its customs regarding meals, alcohol, dress, recreation, travel; its beliefs regarding education, religion, politics. Each one of the Utopian practices offers a satirical rebuke to Europe, through open or implicit comparison. Undergirding all of the reforms is the elimination of private property, which marvelously eradicates all vice and suffering: "There is plenty of everything, and no reason to fear that anyone will claim more than he needs. Why would anyone be suspected of asking for more than is needed, when everyone knows there will never be any shortage?" (50). In an economy of plenty, the evils that spring from scarcity disappear. And although the Utopians are not Christian, their theistic Epicurean philosophy proves compatible with northern humanism's blend of classical wisdom and early Christian precept.[12]

More's satire works through a variety of techniques. He offers moments of more-or-less straightforward denunciation, as in Hythlodaeus's final condemnation of the European socioeconomic order as a "conspiracy of the rich" (95). He uses fable when he imports from Lucian's *Nigrinus* the story of the Anemolian ambassadors who visit Utopia wearing their showiest clothing and jewelry in an effort to impress their hosts, yet turn out to be the objects of laughter since they are wearing "all the articles which in Utopia are used to punish slaves, shame wrongdoers, or entertain infants" (56). But his most pervasive trope is to observe that the Utopians regard modern European customs as contrary to nature and reason. They consider it lunacy to "be pleased by empty, ceremonial honors" (62). Those who cherish jewels are considered "mad," as are misers (familiar from Horace) "who pile up money not because they want to do anything with the heap, but so they can sit and look at it" (63). Gambling and hunting, self-mortification and asceticism, fortune-telling and divination – all are considered "mad" or "crazy" or "ridiculous" in Utopia. More thus shares with Erasmus a view of European social and political life as, in Stephen Greenblatt's phrase, "fundamentally insane."[13]

There are, however, ironies that disrupt any simple equation of the Utopian life with More's own prescriptions, including Morus's final remark that he cannot agree with Hythlodaeus on everything. Surely some aspects of the utopian state will unsettle today's readers, as they sometimes unsettle Morus himself. The culture is thoroughly standardized, with little opportunity for self-expression or self-definition. Conformity is enforced by a society of surveillance which allows "no chance to loaf or any pretext for evading work"; because the Utopians "live in the full view of all, they are bound to be either working at their usual trades or enjoying their leisure in a respectable way" (53). As Greenblatt observes, getting rid of private property eradicates greed, deception, and anxiety, but it also squelches the development of the private self, of "modern individuality" per se.[14] Still another problem arises with the Utopians' indignation against vice, which rises to a violent, genocidal pitch; in the event of war, they never worry about the deaths of the mercenary Zapoletes "for they think they would deserve very well of all mankind if they could exterminate from the face of the earth that entire disgusting and vicious race" (81). A reader, having been urged to find Utopian attitudes more natural and rational than her own, might pull up short. What has happened to this nation so compassionate it will not slaughter its own livestock? Here More alights on the contradiction within the very idea of utopia that will eventually give rise to the twentieth-century dystopias of Huxley, Orwell, and Atwood: great violence or repression seems always necessary to achieve utopia. As Walter Benjamin said, every document of civilization is also a document of barbarism.[15]

Whether or not More endorses the Utopian lifestyle as a program of reform, his fantasy creates a provisional realm for provocation and exploration. He relativizes European beliefs and practices, redescribing the natural and necessary as cultural and contingent. Folly is just a function of perspective and training. More's Utopians, like Erasmus's Stultitia, give us a picture of a Europe whose inhabitants are so confused that they mistake wisdom for folly and folly for wisdom.

Renaissance Laughter: Rabelais and Cervantes

The slim learned volumes of Erasmus and More, with their shifting elusive ironies, open pathways for early modern satire to attack the specific historical abuses of religious and secular authorities and to explore broad philosophical topics such as knowledge, wisdom, justice, and freedom. Yet two of their most significant successors create markedly different books: monumental prose fictions teeming with unlikely happenings and robust laughter, populated with outsized, iconic characters. François Rabelais's *Gargantua and Pantagruel* (written as four books, 1532–1552, with a posthumous, likely spurious fifth, 1564) and Miguel de Cervantes's *Don Quixote* (two books, 1605, 1615) are sprawling narratives stuffed with comic and satiric motifs and incidents. Both authors build upon the satiric humanist legacies of Erasmus and More, but they turn from Latin to the vernacular and integrate the classical heritage with popular prose traditions such as the bawdy comedy of Boccaccio. While the Horatian combination of instruction and delight remains a guiding rubric, the sheer size of these works tilts the balance toward delight, since few readers, then or now, have the patience for a thousand pages of moral instruction.

Erasmus's ideas and writing gained immediate popularity throughout Europe, and his influence on all of Renaissance literature is vast. Rabelais acknowledges his debt to Erasmian humanism directly in a 1532 letter to the sage of Rotterdam, whom he lauds as his intellectual "father and mother." Cervantes, born eleven years after Erasmus's death, studied under a Spanish Erasmian, Juan López de Hoyos, absorbing his humanist influence despite the Inquisition's 1559 ban on *Praise of Folly*.[16] Both writers express More's influence as well. Rabelais's Pantagruel is the king of a comic version of Utopia, and Gargantua establishes the Abbey of Thélème, which offers a "utopian counterculture" that, in contrast to the monasteries of Europe, offers true freedom.[17] Don Quixote's squire Sancho Panza is granted his dream of governing his own utopia, the "island" of Barataria, and he proves to be a wise and decent ruler until practical jokers make it impossible to rule and (like More's Hythlodaeus) he renounces politics to "return to [his] old liberty" (2.53.808).

Both books take up Erasmus's paradox of foolish wisdom. Rabelais's Panurge (especially in the *Third Book*) and Cervantes's Quixote and Sancho are figures of the wise fool. For some critics the authors' sympathy for these fools, and their charitable view of human fallibility, push us out of the satiric terrain entirely and into the comic (*STG* 58–59). Yet the ubiquity of comic folly in Rabelais and Cervantes does not preclude satiric judgment. Their representation of human error exposes false orthodoxies, outworn customs, and self-serving hypocrisies. Both books, in addition, embody Bakhtin's carnivalesque, with its celebration of the body and its inversion of social hierarchies. *Praise of Folly* and *Utopia* contain hints of carnivalesque comedy: More's Utopians fashion their chamberpots out of precious metals and literally shit on their vast stores of silver and gold; Erasmus's Folly notes that it is not the head or the heart but the penis, "so stupid and ridiculous that it can't be named without raising a snicker," which is "the sacred fount from which all things draw their existence" (12–13). But such motifs, used sparingly in Erasmus and More, mark virtually every page of Rabelais, whose oeuvre, Bakhtin maintains, "is an encyclopedia of folk culture" (*RHW* 58). These motifs are prevalent in *Don Quixote* too, most obviously surrounding the figure of Sancho whose belly (*panza* in Spanish), appetite, thirst, and "abundant defecation" may not rise to Gargantuan scale, but still offer "a bodily and popular corrective to individual idealistic and spiritual pretense" (*RHW* 22).

Rabelais's "Pantagrueliad" tells of the lives of two giants, a father, Gargantua, and his son, Pantagruel, their births, their educations, and their

(mock) heroic quests and adventures in war. Episodic, expansive, and digressive, it allows for humorous disquisitions on religious, philosophical, and
political questions. Episodes treat a huge variety of comic material: battles
where enemies are drowned in the giants' urine, the miraculous revival of
a decapitated comrade, travels to imaginary islands inhabited by bizarre
Lucianic creatures. Rabelais's humanist agenda undergirds satiric sequences
that mock scholastic dogma, doctrinaire thinking, churchly corruption, and
religious superstitions. The educations of both Gargantua and Pantagruel, for
example, suggest the virtues of the classical curriculum and the deficiencies of
the scholastics; the valor of Gargantua's companion Friar John is contrasted to
the laziness and cowardice of the average monk; practices such as pilgrimages
and the sale of indulgences are directly ridiculed. Some figures appear to be
strongly allegorical: the rapacious landowner Picrochole probably represents
the Holy Roman Emperor, Charles V, while the pompous ignoramus Janotus
de Bragmardo has been seen as a stand-in for the conservative Sorbonne
theologian Noël Béda.[18] Yet for all their historical pointedness, these satiric
attacks transcend their particular targets, and offer a broad indictment of
dogmatism and ignorance. Drawing on classical learning, but orienting its
wisdom toward the future, Rabelais's work advocates freedom, rationality,
and benevolence.

These values coexist easily with the joyous celebration of the body that
Bakhtin describes, which offers a satiric corrective to sexual repression,
excessive intellectuality, and false morality. The grotesque body is everywhere
in Rabelais, beginning with the gigantic protagonists themselves, whose
physical excessiveness allows for comic episodes such as when the narrator
gets lost in Pantagruel's mouth, or when Gargantua accidentally eats six
religious pilgrims with his salad. Gargantua's birth through his mother's left
ear offers a playful reinvention of human biology and a scatological parody of
the Christian miracle of the virgin birth. Another memorable example occurs
when the young Gargantua needs to wipe his butt. After experimenting with
a velvet scarf, a lace bonnet, satin earmuffs, a cat, various herbs, linen sheets,
curtains, cushions, scarves, hay, straw, bags, baskets, hats, and much else, he
declares to his father:

> I affirm and maintain that there is no bottom-wiper like a downy
> young goose, provided that you hold its head between your legs.
> Believe me on my honor, for you can feel in your bumhole
> a mirifical voluptuousness, as much from the softness of its down as
> from the temperate heat of the young goose which is readily
> communicated to the arse-gut. (2.12.249–250)

Pantagruel, proud father, finds in these experiments a precociousness akin to that of the young Alexander the Great. Here, as elsewhere in the text, the verbal play works against aversive feelings like indignation or disgust.[19] The elaborate linguistic presentation sublimates the infant's pleasure in playing with excrement; the high rhetoric contrasts comically with the low subject matter but it also provides an intellectualized alternative to the actual physical mess. Nowhere can one detect the antipathy that characterizes the representation of bodily functions in an ancient satirist like Juvenal or in modern ones like Thomas Pynchon and Will Self.

Indeed the excesses of Rabelais are excesses of language as much as of the body, and one of Rabelais's most famous bequests to satiric fiction is his signature device of the comic list or catalogue, a device taken up by Swift, Sterne, Joyce, and Pynchon, among others. Often Rabelais's lists can run on for pages without any context or explanation, mixing various and unlikely items, taxing the reader's attention through the mere accumulation of terms but rewarding her (as in the list of wiping devices) with hilarious surprises. The technique of accretion shares an expansive tendency with both Aristophanes' compound neologisms and the encyclopedism of the entire Pantagrueliad. The list has a flattening effect too, eliminating any organizational principle other than mere sequence. It thus dissolves logic and narrative in "an irrational celebration of the diversity and plenitude of words themselves."[20] In fact, the Rabelaisian list, and more broadly, the general profusion of language in his work, disrupts basic ideas of reading.

Pantagruel's companion Panurge adds a dimension of comic but often cruelly violent mischief. In "Pantagruel," Panurge plays the role of rogue or clown more than the fool, although like many rogues he sometimes finds himself on the wrong end of schemes and pranks. (The rogue or trickster has his own roots in medieval European culture, in the folkloric character Till Eulenspiegel and in Reynard the Fox, the protagonist of medieval beast fables.) Panurge's abundant resources for mischief and subversion find an apt symbol in the cloak he wears, and from which he produces, like Harpo Marx, an endless supply of objects that he uses to commit pranks upon the unwitting: small knives to cut purses, fleas and lice to throw upon the collars of young women, hooks and pins to attach men and women to each other in crowds, flowers fashioned into phalluses that he attaches to the hoods of unsuspecting maidens. Panurge is, then, not just a trickster but, with his insatiable sexual appetite, a *satyr*. His pranks and jests are directed at not only the pompous and the proud but also the prudish. In one famous episode he revenges himself on a stuffy noblewoman who refuses his sexual propositions by extracting "materia medica" from a bitch in heat and scattering it on the woman during a church service. All the dogs of Paris besiege her, urinating all around her and even on her head. The comedy is unquestionably sadistic, and even Rabelais's narrator himself declares the joke to be "the most horrible trick in the world" (1.14) – distancing himself from the misogyny of the character, and perhaps condemning the reader for his silent complicity. Panurge is thus a paradoxical figure: mischievous, subversive, iconoclastic, and even satanic, he licenses immoral pleasures while disturbing the moralistic and the complacent.[21]

Rabelais himself articulates positive ideals. A letter Gargantua writes to his son praises the rise of humanism, describes a wide-ranging curriculum that includes classical languages, history, music, science, and moral philosophy, and urges simple Christian virtues (1.8). But this letter is immediately followed by the appearance of Panurge, a juxtaposition that shows how Rabelais's "satire, despite its humanistic pedigree, [is] capable of criticizing the very humanism that had engendered its revival."[22] Thus the elaboration of a new morality almost always takes second place in Rabelais to the demolition of false authorities and the creation of open space for laughter and play. As he notes in the prologue to Book Two, Rabelais follows Horace in hoping that his books smell of wine rather than of midnight oil, of festive pleasure rather than of bookish labor. Even when he offers direct attacks on monks and theologians, Rabelais demonstrates for us how to "live joyfully" – enjoying and inhabiting the object that he mocks, reveling in the extravagance of his parodies. Like Aristophanes, Rabelais possesses a comic exuberance so powerful that it appears as a value in itself. In throwing off constraints, Rabelais valorizes excess of the body, of appetite, of language.

Rabelais's giants are a playful fiction, metaphors for human possibility, and would have been understood by his readers as a delightfully entertaining invention. But at least one Renaissance reader believed in giants. "In the matter of giants," declares Cervantes's Don Quixote, "there are different opinions as to whether or not they ever existed in the world, but Holy Scripture, which cannot deviate an iota from the truth, shows us that they did by telling us the history of that huge Philistine Goliath" (2.1.467). Despite the mischievous reference to biblical precedent, Quixote's belief in giants is a comic idea, symptomatic of a larger delusion: unable to distinguish the improbably enchanted medieval world of knight-errantry from the mundane reality of the modern, Alonso Quijano transforms himself into a wandering knight, Don Quixote of La Mancha. He turns his nag into a heroic steed, a barber's basin into his helmet, a local peasant into his squire, a farm girl into his lady, flocks of sheep into armies, inns into castles, windmills into giants. It is a fertile premise, producing a potentially limitless series of comic mistakes – heroic forays that result in pratfalls, beatings, and bludgeonings. When Quixote watches a puppet show, his failure to distinguish representation from reality leads him to destroy the show: "He unsheathed his sword, leaped next to the stage, and with swift and never before seen fury began to rain down blows on the crowd of Moorish puppets, knocking down some, beheading others, ruining this one, destroying that one" (2.26.632). Even better, the chaos he sows only furnishes him with further evidence for the reality of his illusions. After destroying the puppet theater, Quixote proudly boasts of his achievement: "if I had not been there, just think what would have happened to the worthy Don Gaiferos and the beauteous Melisendra" (2.26.633). The brilliance of the scene comes from the narcissistic stubbornness of the knight's belief in his own heroism; his self-love – what Erasmus called Philautia – is so powerful that he becomes impervious to persuasion.

How satiric is *Don Quixote*? The hero has been read at various points in history as "a rogue and a burlesque figure, then as a vehicle for satire, later as an amiable humorist, and finally as a pathetic idealist."[23] Cervantes's professed aim was to attack the chivalric romances that corrupt Alonzo Quijano's mind, "to undermine the authority and wide acceptance that books of chivalry have in the world and among the public" (1.Pr.8). Such tales were seen as encouraging folly and even tyranny; Erasmus himself cautioned against reading them.[24] Yet in reading an ironist like Cervantes we must be wary of accepting his narrator's pompous assertions. At the end of the novel he avows that his "only desire has been to have people reject and despise the false and nonsensical histories of the books of chivalry," yet it is Quixote's loss of belief in those books that has ended the hero's life.

Whether we view the knight as noble or stupid, Cervantes's extended parody of the romances suggests that the inflexible heroic values of old are out of place in modern Spain, and the knight-errant's quest is but a series of errors. What demolishes the chivalric illusion – what smiles away Spain's chivalry, in Byron's phrase – is a low realism that marks a different strain of satire from the fantastication that Rabelais indulges. Sancho Panza, with his simple wants and earthy wisdom, gives voice to this worldview, warning Quixote that the windmills he attacks are not really giants. Reality triumphs over illusion in the gritty details of painful but funny beatings that Quixote and Sancho take; as Milan Kundera notes, Homer never wonders whether Achilles and Ajax still have all their teeth after a battle, but we see Cervantes's hero spit out his broken molars.[25]

Yet *Don Quixote* is more than a parody of romances and heroic quests. It is also a parody of history and of narrative itself, in the tradition of Lucian's *True History* with its mockery of Herodotus and the outlandish claims of historians

(*SI* 60–64). Cervantes dismantles the conventions by which fictional narratives avow their historical truth. Early on, the narrative breaks off in the middle of a swordfight, and the narrator claims that the record is incomplete. But he then miraculously discovers in a Toledo marketplace an Arabic manuscript that picks up the story just where it broke off. The author of this manuscript is a historian named Cide Hamete Benengeli (Mr. Hamid Eggplant) who, Cervantes warns, cannot be trusted because he is an Arab: "In this account I know there will be found everything that could be rightly desired in the most pleasant history, and if something of value is missing from it, in my opinion the fault lies with the dog who was its author rather than with any defect in its subject" (1.8.69). Here Cervantes capitalizes on a real historical prejudice: the decision to make his narrator an Arab, like Erasmus's decision to make his speaker a woman, ironizes any authoritative judgment or even factual account. The narrator's distrust of his source –much like Quixote's belief in sorcerers – allows him to substitute the contents of his mind for the evidence of his senses. Hamete Benengeli, like Rabelais's narrator Alcofribas Nasier, thus adds to the narrative a comic overlay that feels less a pointed attack on chivalric values than an irreverent subversion of the authority granted to the discourse of history. This destabilization of narrative authority follows an Erasmian strategy of undermining orthodoxy without establishing an orthodoxy of one's own.[26] At the same time it acknowledges and even celebrates the remarkable powers of the human imagination.

Carlos Fuentes notes that Quixote's reading is his madness, his *lectura* his *locura*.[27] This trope of reading as madness gives rise to a great line of literary descendants: Swift's Grub Street Hack reading the moderns, Fielding's Parson Adams reading the classics, Charlotte Lennox's Arabella reading French romances, Jane Austen's Catherine Morland reading Gothic fiction, Nabokov's Charles Kinbote reading John Shade, Borges's Pierre Menard reading Cervantes himself. In Michel Foucault's history of madness, getting lost in the world of fiction represents more than a benign game of parody:

> In appearance, this is nothing but the simple-minded critique of novels, of fantasy, but just under the surface lies an enormous anxiety concerning the relationships, in a work of art, between the real and the imaginary, and perhaps also concerning the confused communication between fantastic invention and the fascinations of delirium.[28]

It is the brilliance of *Don Quixote* that we can read it as both a warning against the "fascinations of delirium" and an advertisement for them (Figure 7).

Cervantes's most remarkable invention may be the way that Quixote, in his madness, makes the world around him as mad as he is. In Book Two, Quixote

Figure 7 Francisco Goya (1746–1828), "Don Quixote Beset by Monsters," *c.* 1812–1820. By permission of the British Museum, London. Goya draws out the darkness latent in the vision of his countryman Cervantes, highlighting what Michel Foucault called "the fascinations of delirium."

and Sancho discover that, thanks to the publication of Book One, they have become famous (2.2.472). Yet while Quixote thinks himself a hero of a romance, the world sees him as the hero of a satire. The characters in Book Two, especially the Duke and Duchess, stage all kinds of absurd scenarios so that they can better enjoy Quixote's folly.[29] But in doing so they grant his delusion a reality. And so, like Peithetairos and Euelpides of *Birds*, the knight establishes a Cloudcuckooland built on air, a universe of knight-errantry that seems – almost – to function. The Duke and Duchess's elaborate arrangements make them just "as mad as the deceived": "The duke and duchess came very close to seeming like fools since they went to such lengths to deceive two fools" (2.70.914). Quixote's folly in Book Two exposes both the cruelty of his deceivers and their own folly: they are also mad readers – mad readers of Cervantes's first book. And to the degree that we believe in the reality of Quixote and laugh at his follies, we too become mad readers. As the Bachelor

Sanson Carrasco says, *"stultorum infinitus est numerus"*: the number of fools is infinite (2.3.479).

Cervantes's relentless Erasmian ironies multiply perspectives on the world without resolving them, suggesting a reality too complex to reduce to any monolithic view. Readers will continue to debate the meaning of the text, but even here Cervantes anticipates his critics, whom he describes through the point of view of Sancho: "As for your grace's valor, courtesy, deeds, and undertakings . . . there are different opinions. Some say, 'Crazy, but amusing'; others, 'Brave, but unfortunate'; and others, 'Courteous, but insolent'; and they go on and on so much in this vein that they don't leave an untouched bone in your grace's body or mine" (2.2.472).

Donne and Elizabethan Verse Satire

The fictive discourses of Erasmus and More and the overflowing prose fictions of Rabelais and Cervantes display the proclivity of Renaissance humanism for comic-satiric forms. But the early modern period also saw the specific revival of formal verse satire. In England, this new verse satire borrowed tropes and structures directly from Horace, Persius, and Juvenal, although it also reshaped its classical inheritance as it developed, discovering new subgenres and responding to new concerns. The revival begins in the 1590s, with the appearance of works by several young poets, mostly born in the 1570s, including Joseph Hall, John Marston, Everard Guilpin, and John Donne. In Hall's *Virgidemiarum* ("a gathering of beatings": from *virga*, meaning rod or switch, and *demia*, meaning harvest), the poet, with a masculine swagger, dubs himself the first English satirist:

> I first adventure, with fool-hardy might
> To tread the steps of perilous despite:
> I first adventure, follow me who list,
> And be the second English Satirist.[30]

Although Hall is presumptuous in claiming priority over his peers, he is justified in asserting the novelty of a genre and style that soon found wide readership.[31] Satiric poetry in English did not begin in the 1590s; many older examples can be found. The anonymous "goliards" of the twelfth and thirteenth centuries wrote irreverent comic verses that praised drinking and mocked Church leadership. In the fourteenth century Langland's *Piers Plowman* offered a "plain, unlettered, commonsensical rustic" as an exemplary satiric persona.[32] Chaucer, called "the English Ennius" (241) by Dryden, is full of bawdy joking mixed with social and moral criticism.[33] Yet the young poets of the 1590s represented a "new type of satirist," Alvin Kernan has argued, one who "expressed the values of the Renaissance rather than of the medieval world."[34] For all his subtle ironies and comic energy, Chaucer's persona is still that of "the plain, guileless, humble man," whereas the verse satirists of the 1590s proudly showcased their education, wit, and worldliness.[35]

The themes of this new verse satire are anticipated in Elizabethan stage comedy and various prose forms (picaresques, anatomies, pamphlets), but the poets of the 1590s set themselves apart by their self-conscious identification as writers of satire, and by their deliberate turn to classical examples. This move was, in part, a bid for cultural capital; the Roman poets bestowed an imprimatur that allowed their English imitators to disavow association with both the sensationalistic prose writings of "downwardly mobile hacks" such as Thomas Nashe and Robert Greene and also the "outmoded and blunt" native tradition of homiletic complaint.[36] The new verse satirists were university educated and steeped in Latin poetry, and they came to London's Inns of Court as law students seeking professional and social advancement.[37] Young, brash, and witty, they held higher social standing than their prose rivals, and class-based snobbery may have contributed to what Lawrence Manley calls their sharp "assertion of literary and social difference" and "pointed disdain of popular and professional writing."[38]

Whatever its social benefits, classical verse satire fitted the needs of the late Elizabethan poets and shaped their style. Juvenal proved the most congenial model, that of the outraged, outspoken observer of urban moral rot. The Elizabethans echoed Juvenal's claim that the decadence around him compelled the writing of satire. In Marston's words, "grim Reproof, stern Hate of villainy, / inspire and guide a Satyr's poesy."[39] Juvenal's lurid descriptions of vice, his bombastic rhetoric, and his high moral pitch provided a formula to address anxieties that seemed strikingly apposite to a burgeoning London: urbanization, population growth, social mobility, economic upheaval. Essential to this new Juvenalian stance was aggression. In the much-quoted opening of Hall's Satire 3:

> The Satire should be like the porcupine,
> That shoots sharp quills out in each angry line,
> And wounds the blushing cheek, and fiery eye,
> Of him that hears and readeth guiltily.[40]

The very titles of the satirists' collections announced the violence of their ambitions: "*The Scourge of Villanie, The Whipping of the Satyre, The Letting of*

Humours Blood, The Scourge of Folly, Abuses Stript and Whipt, A Strappado for the Divell."[41] In unleashing this violence, the Elizabethans donned the mask of the satyr: the goatish creature of myth was seen to embody a rough, masculine, unflinching honesty. And because the satyr takes pleasure in castigating vice, he indulges his own sadism at the same time that he roots out moral filth.

The basic irony here – that satire savors the crimes it upbraids – is one we saw in Juvenal, and it did not escape the poets themselves. Donne is the most sophisticated of his generation in examining the contradictions of the satirist's overly aggressive moral policework. He recognizes that satirical representations of sin might impede rather than promote reform, and he compares the moral effect of the royal court to that of the pornographic engravings by Marcantonio Raimondo that illustrated the works of the Italian satirist Pietro Aretino:

> Aretine's pictures have made few chaste;
> No more can princes' courts, though there be few
> Better pictures of vice, teach me virtue.   (4.70–72)

The idea of the satirist as a creature who feeds on vice reaches an extreme in Thomas Middleton's prose satire *The Blacke Booke* (1604), whose satyr-satirist figure is the cloven-footed Lucifer himself, reveling in the stew of iniquity he finds on earth.[42] This trope of the satanic satirist ultimately supplants the pagan satyr, surfacing in both prose and verse in Alain-René Lesage's *The Devil on Two Sticks* (1707), William Combe's *The Diabioliad* (1777), and devil-tours-Earth poems by Romantic poets including Southey and Coleridge ("The Devil's Thoughts," 1799), Shelley ("The Devil's Walk," 1812), and Byron ("The Devil's Drive," 1812). Later prose writers, including Melville, Twain, Bulgakov, and Rushdie, continue the tradition, using satanic characters to play the role of "the attorney for the other side."[43]

Donne draws upon and revises all three major Roman precursors, Horace, Persius, and Juvenal.[44] Like Horace, his manner is dialectical and self-questioning and his voice chatty and prone to rumination; he borrows Horace's trope of a helpless speaker waylaid by an insufferable blowhard; he advocates a golden mean. The complexity of his style and his religious preoccupations, meanwhile, recall Persius. And there is plenty of Juvenalian outrage in his monologues, evoked through raw, grotesque images. He depicts plagiarizing poets as scavenging animals:

> But he is worst, who (beggarly) doth chaw
> Others' wits' fruits, and in his ravenous maw

> Rankly digested, doth those things out-spew
> As his own things;

Yet with characteristic metaphysical wit, Donne then revises his conceit:

> and they are his own, 'tis true,
> For if one eat my meat, though it be known
> The meat was mine, th'excrement is his own.   (2.25–30)

He indicts sycophantic suitors who curry favor with powerful officeholders, and depicts the entire social structure as one of predatory consumption: "the world [is] a man, in which, officers / Are the devouring stomach, and suitors / th'excrements, which they void" (5.17–19). And with one stroke he can condemn both the depravity of court life and the lurid curiosity of the gossip who describes it: "Who wastes in meat, in clothes, in horse, he notes; / Who lovés whores, who boyés, and who goats" (4.127–128).

Donne's urban environment teems with a familiar cast of early modern caricatures – foppish courtiers, corrupt judges, avaricious lawyers, ragged whores, bombastic soldiers, usuring Jews, tyrannical politicians. And while these types embody the timeless vices of the seven deadly sins, the London milieu is a distinctly modern one which registers the pressures of a rapidly changing society. For Donne, as for Juvenal, those who move between established categories are especially suspect, like the courtier of Satire 4:

> A thing more strange, than on the Nile's slime, the Sun
> E'er bred, or all which into Noah's Ark came:
> A thing, which would have posed Adam to name;
> Stranger than seven antiquaries' studies,
> Than Afric's Monsters, Guyana's rarities.   (4.18–22)

Even the vices of this new world flout the old classifications, as the Mosaic commandments cannot account for modern mutations of perversion: "strange sins canonists could hardly tell / In which commandments' large receipt they dwell" (2.37–38).

Peopled with such freaks and criminals, the public scene of Elizabethan satire is, as Kernan says, one of "disorderly profusion," and the satirist often a helpless observer.[45] But the ranging, improvisatory quality of the genre allows it to capture the variety, abundance, and chaos of the city, which becomes a setting for chance encounters.[46] In this unpredictable space, the satirist becomes vulnerable to risky libidinal attachments and losses. In Satire 1, the homosocial bond between the speaker and the "fondling motley humorist" (1.1) is figured as marriage, and their urban cruising assumes an erotic charge. The humorist, who has a roving eye for every fashionable figure in the street, eventually abandons the speaker, only to return with faux remorse when he himself is rejected. This gentle account of erotic risk is transposed into a darker key in Satire 4, where the speaker's companion exposes him not just to rejection but also to disease:

> hearing him, I found
> That as burnt venomed lechers do grow sound
> By giving others their sores, I might grow
> Guilty, and he free.   (4.133–136)

The bravado of the invective-spewing satirist appears here as a reaction formation to an underlying vulnerability, and the speaker's withdrawal into the world of his own study, or his own self, often becomes his safest option – as Swift's Gulliver will later retreat to his stables, or Pope to his Twickenham grotto, or Austen's Mr. Bennet to his library.

Donne's London, governed by changing fashions, is ultimately character-ized by a fakery so thorough that civilization becomes a hollow simulacrum; the world is like a "waxen garden" full of "gay painted things, which no sap, nor / Taste have in them" (4.169, 172–173).[47] Donne's efforts to navigate these shifty surfaces leave him despairing or self-questioning. Satire 2 ends with the speaker's recognition of his words' powerlessness, while the speaker of Satire 4 asks the all-seeing sun whether any place on earth could be as wretched as the royal court:

> Thou which since yesterday hast been
> Almost about the whole world, hast thou seen,
> O Sun, in all thy journey, vanity
> Such as swells the bladder of our court?   (4.165–168)

The satire boom of the 1590s, however, was short-lived. On June 1, 1599, the Archbishop of Canterbury and the Bishop of London issued the "Bishops' Ban," an edict which ordered the destruction of certain writings and decreed "That noe Satyres or Epigramms be printed hereafter."[48] We can only spec-ulate as to the reasons for the ban. The popularity of the new satiric verse may have suggested the genre's potential for political subversion and thus led to its demise. Richard McCabe concludes that with the queen ailing and the gov-ernment's future unclear, "the authorities must have decided that satire had gone far enough."[49] Although enforcement of the ban turned out to be inconsistent, when joined to changes in the political culture under James I, it probably encouraged satirists to redirect poetic satire either into libels, pamphlets, and other popular forms, or onto the stage, where satiric mono-logues could be tailored to the voices of various characters.[50]

City Comedy: Jonson's *Volpone*

It was on the stage that early modern England saw its most memorable satire. During the same years that Cervantes was composing *Don Quixote* in Spain, England witnessed the plays of Shakespeare and the greatest age in the history of the theater. But although Shakespeare's comedies can contain satiric elements, it is in the subgenre called "city comedy" that Elizabethan and Jacobean dramatic satire takes its most unalloyed form. The term "city comedy" has been applied to plays by Thomas Dekker, Thomas Middleton, John Marston, George Chapman, and others (including some works by Shakespeare), but its preeminent practitioner is Ben Jonson.

Jonson situates his work firmly in a classical tradition that includes Greek and Roman satire. Dryden called him a "learned plagiary" of the ancients, noting, "You track him every where in their Snow" ("An Essay" 43). Jonson alludes freely to Horace and Juvenal, Lucian and Petronius, as well as to the humanists More, Erasmus, and Rabelais. In his play *The Poetaster* he represents himself as Horace, uttering lines directly translated from Satires 1.9 and 2.1, and styling himself a judicious critic who offers "sharp, yet modest rhymes / That spare men's persons, and but tax their crimes" (3.5.133–134), a defense later echoed by many satirists.[51] Horace's combination of wisdom and irony, his tone of urbanity and decorum, and his ear for spoken idiolects clearly inform Jonson's style and his values.[52] Yet the Horatian is not Jonson's only vein of satire. In *Every Man Out of His Humour* the character Asper vows "with an armed and resolved hand, / [to] strip the ragged follies of the time / Naked as at their birth," striking a violent, Juvenalian tone more typical of the Elizabethans.[53] Elsewhere Jonson invokes "Archilochus's fury" and commends the "bold satire" of Juvenal, Persius, and Aristophanes for its "sharper wit."[54] Finally, Lucian, known to Jonson through Erasmus, serves the playwright as a source of material and, along with Erasmus himself, as a model of a "Protean artist whose personality is disguised by, and expressed through, the creation of characters" and who consequently becomes "a teasing manipulator of his public's responses."[55]

In addition to these classical sources, Jonson's satire is influenced by medieval and Renaissance popular traditions. Verse satire and religious invective ("complaint") provide him with themes and rhetoric, while he gathers material from the widely read Elizabethan "cony-catching" pamphlets of Thomas Nashe, Robert Greene, and others, which describe the tricks of urban rogues in admonitory, sensational narratives.[56] He draws upon the Italian popular tradition of the *commedia dell'arte,* loosely scripted comic performances enacted by touring companies which deployed recurrent types such as the clown Arlecchino (Harlequin), the sadistic Pulcinella (Punch), and the aged miser Pantalone. Finally, his most famous work, *Volpone*, fashions itself as a beast fable, a genre which thrived in medieval folk culture. The characters in Jonson's play are human, but are named allegorically for animals, and Volpone (the fox) alludes to both Aesop's fable of the Fox and Crow and the medieval tales of Reynard (*FS* 80).

These traditions come together in Jonson's characters, plots, and settings. Jonson's characters typically possess a single, exaggerated trait. Sometimes called comedies of humors, his plays invoke a medieval physiology of bodily fluids (or humors), which were believed, when out of balance, to make people eccentric. As Asper puts it: "when some one peculiar quality / Doth so possess a man, that it doth draw / All his affects, his spirits, and his powers, / In their confluctions, all to run one way."[57] His plots, meanwhile, make use of the phenomenon that Robert Elliott called the "satirist satirized" – dramatic characters who act as satirists in exposing the vice and folly of others, yet simultaneously serve as objects of authorial judgment (*PS* 98). This sort of irony is not wholly new: the elusive personae of the verse satirists, the uncomprehending fools of Erasmus and More, and duplicitous characters from folk narratives such as Reynard all create space for authorial irony. But in the drama, the distance between the author and the character is stark and absolute. Indeed, by one account, it was Jonson's turn to the drama of Aristophanes that provided him with a structural model that could address the social conflicts of urban life: morally ambiguous protagonists like Peithetairos and Euelpides of *Birds* can critique Athenian society while remaining satiric targets themselves.[58] And because the Elizabethans generally conceived of the satirist as a coarse, outspoken figure, this dramatic distance allows an author to have the satirist in the text do his dirty work of attacking others while himself maintaining a safe distance.

The urban location of Jonson's plays, finally, allows them to speak with directness to the rapidly evolving social, economic, and political conditions of his day. Aristophanic comedy focused on the Athenian polis; Juvenal's verse satire depicted the Roman imperial center as a hotbed of vice. Jonson's Prologue to *The Alchemist* places that play firmly in this tradition of contemporary urban satire: "Our scene is London, 'cause we would make known, / No country's mirth is better than our own: / No clime breeds better matter for your whore, / Bawd, squire, impostor, many persons more" (191). Expunging "material appropriate to romance, fairy tale, sentimental legend or patriotic chronicle," city comedy relishes the immorality of the modern urban scene, even as it holds it up for censure. The setting is disenchanted and modern, unlike the festive, quasi-pastoral mode of much Shakespearean comedy. Reflecting the social changes associated with urbanization, the rise of capitalism, and the demise of the old feudal order, city comedies thus analyze and indict their own historical moment.[59] They depict a society in flux, represented in characters who make money in new and often unethical ways, seeking to alter their socioeconomic status as they negotiate a world of uncertain moral codes. Thus Jonson's *moral* satire, purporting to take as its object timeless sins like greed and lust, constitutes a *social* critique of the conditions that produce new behaviors, anxieties, and values.

Volpone can illustrate how the dramatic form complicates satiric formulas and offers social and psychological analysis in the guise of a putatively timeless moral satire. The title character, a greedy miser with no heir, and his servant or "zany," Mosca, scheme to multiply Volpone's fortune by hoodwinking equally avaricious legacy-hunters – their "gulls" – who themselves jockey to be named Volpone's heir. (The theme of legacy-hunting will be familiar to the reader of Horace Satire 2.5 or the final fragment of the *Satyricon*.) The play's dedicatory epistle and verse prologue establish familiar Horatian terms for understanding satire. In the epistle Jonson declares that one must be a virtuous man to be a good poet, distinguishes his work from the "ribaldry, profanation, [and] blasphemy" of "poetasters," and quotes Horace's Satire 2.1 in his defense (42, 43). In the prologue, the speaker differentiates Jonson's decorous satire from the ill-mannered "railing" of others, and insists that the author has drained the "gall and copperas" from his ink, leaving "only a little salt" – Horace's term for therapeutically abrasive wit (49, 40). Like Horace telling the truth with a laugh, Jonson aims "To mix profit with your pleasure" (49).

But who exactly will profit from the play? The audience's moral profit coexists uneasily with the playwright's financial profit – a double meaning that few will overlook in a story about a miser first seen worshipping a hoard of gold. Even as it lays out a justification for satire, the play undercuts it, making us doubt the morality of Volpone's pleasures and our own: the delight taken in acquisition, the sadistic joy of "punishing" the legacy-hunters. Using a villain as a satiric agent plays havoc with any neat dichotomy between the playwright's moral authority and the vice and folly of the world he analyzes. We favor Volpone and Mosca over their gulls less because of their contorted Horatian justifications for their actions than because we admire their intelligence and charisma and participate in their delightfully clever ruses. The audience is caught between the pleasure of watching the con artist operate and its awareness of his moral baseness.

The awareness of Volpone's immorality becomes even more acute when Volpone and Mosca pursue new, less deserving targets – the morally upright

Celia and Bonario. As Volpone's driving motive shifts from calculating greed to uncontrolled lust, the moral innocence of the new victims gives the lie to Volpone's earlier self-justifications. The complex layering of Jonson's irony now fully emerges. When Volpone, savoring how Corbaccio's greed has made him susceptible to deception, observes, "What a rare punishment / Is avarice to itself!" (67), he locates an irony in Corbaccio's self-defeating behavior. But with this same statement the playwright does the character one better – a dramatic irony – since Volpone is also speaking unknowingly of his own avarice, which will soon constitute *his* rare punishment.

Ultimately some rough justice prevails, yet it prevails not because of the health of the legal system but because the greedy Volpone and Mosca turn on each other.[60] The contrivance of this turn of events, combined with the shallow and conventional "goodness" of Bonario and Celia, makes the moral economy of the play brittle. The good are vindicated and the bad punished mainly to let us believe that our enjoyment of the play contains a degree of moral "profit." During the trial in Act Four, Voltore tries to persuade the judges that Bonario is a liar, despite his good reputation: "So much more full of danger is his vice / That can beguile so, under shade of virtue" (132). This disingenuous claim serves as a key to the entire play, through which Jonson beguiles his own judges – the audience – under shade of virtue.

In other words, even as it manipulates our moral sentiments, *Volpone* problematizes the judgment of right and wrong. The court scenes, in their staging of witnessing and judging, belong to a larger meta-theatrical motif in which audiences of various kinds hear speeches and make judgments; the judges' bench, the actors' stage, and the charlatan's bank all function in the play as what Swift will, a hundred years later in *A Tale of a Tub*, call "oratorical machines" designed to raise the individual above the crowd (27). Just as Aristophanes' birds appeal directly to the audience in the parabasis, comparing the political judgment of a democratic electorate to the spectators' judgment of the play in which they are represented, so *Volpone* implies a homology between the legal judgment of the *avocatori* and the aesthetic judgment of the audience. In almost every scene Mosca and Volpone stage elaborate scenarios – Volpone as lead actor, Mosca increasingly as writer-director – to bilk the legacy-hunters, to seduce Celia, to vindicate themselves. In short, they stage plots to catch other characters in their vices or follies, just as the Duke and Duchess of *Don Quixote* rearrange their world to showcase the folly of the knight, or as Hamlet turns producer in order to catch the conscience of Claudius. This is what satirist-playwrights do: they engineer dramatic scenarios that will reveal the truth of a character hidden beneath deceptive surfaces. Audiences participate in both judging and being judged, and their consciences too are caught.

The restoration of order at the play's conclusion does not, therefore, assure us of the workings of the benign hand of justice, but rather placates us so that we can savor vicariously the pleasures of deception and acquisition, of disguise and performance. Even Volpone seems not to take his own final punishment too seriously. In what might be described as his Groucho Marx moment, as he is about to be led away to justice he turns to the audience and declares, "This is called mortifying of a Fox" (170). More literary critic here than criminal, Volpone, in addressing the spectators, reasserts his role as stage-manager, delighted by the conclusion to the evening's entertainment.

The real "profit" that the play mixes with pleasure, then, is not the audience's moral profit but Jonson's financial profit. Yet we, like him, "glory more / in the cunning purchase of [his] wealth / Than in the glad possession" (52); we enjoy the activity of scheming, which offers an endlessly stimulating erotics of deception and disguise. A denizen of a new proto-capitalist society, Volpone in acquiring profit also provides pleasure via his ability to assume "many shapes" – a talent for self-reinvention that he shares with the sexually insatiable Olympians whom he describes to Celia (114). Mosca similarly relishes his own polymorphousness, which he links to the skin-shedding, shape-shifting, devilish figure of the serpent: "I could skip / Out of my skin, now, like a subtle snake, / I am so limber" (96).

This capacity for self-reinvention is in turn linked to the modern city and a sea change in the social order. Staged in a burgeoning London whose middle class had never been wealthier, set in a Venice on the borders of Christian Europe and hospitable to sexual, economic, and social boundary-crossings, *Volpone* presents a world in which new flows of money render traditional feudal norms of rank and status unstable, in which Mosca and the gulls alike seek social promotion through the acquisition of wealth, in which Volpone, like a financier, parlays his hoard into even greater riches.[61] Traditional family and class structures are thrown off – Volpone, like Quixote, is childless. Ideals of marital fidelity and patrilineal inheritance are easily monetized, as Corvino and Corbaccio casually barter wives and children for a shot at Volpone's gold. Opportunities to remake oneself and opportunities to enrich oneself look very much alike.

The world of Jonson's city comedy is thus one that shares assumptions with "Nick Machiavel" (121) in which analysis of social and political conditions moves, as it were, beyond good and evil.[62] Even as it aims to offer a moral judgment against timeless vices such as greed, lust, and jealousy, Jonson's city comedy offers an analysis of conditions particular to a new social order in which what Hobbes would soon call "the war of all against all" seems quite close to the surface. The clash of old and new values is perhaps nowhere more visible than the moment when Celia protests Corvino's command that she lie with Volpone. Celia invokes Corvino's own honor, to which he replies (with an echo of Falstaff): "Honour! tut, a breath. / There's no such thing in nature; a mere term / Invented to awe fools" (108). It would be going too far to suggest that Jonson himself disdains Celia's faith in "heaven and saints" (109) in favor of Corvino's cynical nominalism. Yet Corvino's easy dissolution of a concept like honor is emblematic. His new values are part of an emerging social order that Celia's older Christian morality can do little to resist.

Chapter 5

Enlightenment Satire: The Prose Tradition

In traditional literary histories, English-language satire produces its greatest works in the late seventeenth century and the early eighteenth. A half-century after the death of Ben Jonson, John Dryden oversees the rise of the era, and his 1693 "Discourse" on satire enunciates its aesthetic principles. Jonathan Swift, Alexander Pope, and their circle occupy the pinnacle: the 1720s see the publication of Swift's *Gulliver's Travels*, Pope's *Dunciad*, and John Gay's *Beggar's Opera* – major works in fiction, poetry, and drama written by three close friends. By mid-century, Samuel Johnson is presiding over satire's decline, as the novel and a poetry of sensibility turn away from satiric values. In this account, Enlightenment satire in Britain belongs first of all to the coterie of Swift and Pope – sometimes called "Tory Satirists" because of their politics, "Augustans" because of their admiration for the writers of the early Roman Empire, or "Scriblerians" because of their collaborative work on the memoirs of the fictitious Martin Scriblerus. These men were conservatives, the story goes, partisans of the ancients over the moderns, proponents of neoclassical values of order, decorum, and refined wit. In writing satire they relied on a set of shared norms whose violations could be easily recognized and ridiculed.

No doubt this picture retains some value. Swift and Pope remain towering figures in the history of satire, and although labels such as "Tory Satirists," "Scriblerians," and "Augustans" have been challenged, they were in many ways conservatives, insistent that only a traditional notion of virtue could regenerate a corrupt social body.[1] Yet in a wider sense, our picture of Enlightenment satire has been transformed. The conservatism of the canonical figures now appears complex, even paradoxical. Swift's *Tale of a Tub* and Pope's *Dunciad* may attack modernity for its bad ideas and bad literature, but in parodying their targets, they reproduce rather than eradicate a chaotic modern world.[2] More broadly still, the old roll call of great names can no longer be said to represent the immense variety of the period's literature. Prose narratives by women such as Delarivier Manley's *New Atalantis* (1709) and Eliza Haywood's *Memoirs of a Certain Island Adjacent to the Kingdom of*

Utopia (1725), previously cordoned off from the rolls of satire as "amatory fiction," "secret histories," or *chronicles scandaleuses*, are now seen to deploy Menippean tropes such as island utopias and dialogues among the gods. Manley in fact described her coded account of sexual intrigues in Queen Anne's government (which led to her arrest for seditious libel) as a "Varronian satire," and it includes many features that place it in this tradition: classical allusions, displays of erudition, digressive and interpolated tales, a mixture of prose and verse, topical political attacks, and condemnation of luxury and promiscuity.[3] Furthermore, cheaply printed popular forms such as broadsides and lampoons are now seen as important features of the satiric landscape; according to Ashley Marshall, the most influential satire of the late seventeenth century was not a mock-heroic poem by Dryden or Samuel Butler but a ballad – Thomas Wharton's 1688 anti-Irish broadside, *Lillibullero* (*PSE* 118). The era also launched a century-long vogue for graphic satire, in the work of William Hogarth and his late century inheritors Thomas Rowlandson and James Gillray. Satirical prints, both social and political in content, decorated middle-class homes, while "violent personal vendettas" were expressed "in prints and counter-prints."[4] Acknowledging this variety of writers, works, and contexts enlarges our picture of the era, but it makes generalizing about it far more difficult.

One development indispensable to the flourishing of satire in the era is what Jürgen Habermas called the rise of the public sphere. After the uneasy resolution of the civil war and religious strife of the seventeenth century, England experienced a combination of developments – economic, religious, political, educational – that transformed the context in which satire was written and read. The close of the seventeenth century saw the establishment of a Bill of Rights, the elimination of censorship, the first modern cabinet government, and the founding of the Bank of England. As late as the reign of Charles II, much satire had been published scribally, but as the new century dawned, satire took to print. A growing reading public made writing profitable, and Britain witnessed a proliferation of printed material – books, newspapers, periodicals, and pamphlets, readily available in the thriving metropolis of London. The rise of Parliament and partisan politics meant, moreover, that statesmen had to appeal continually, through this medium of print, to a public that exerted new influence over political affairs. In coffeehouses and salons, literate citizens exchanged ideas, adding a rich layer of debate to the print conversation.[5] The theaters, between their re-opening in 1660 and the restrictive Licensing Act of 1737, offered a public space for often highly political satire by (among others) Aphra Behn, Thomas Otway, William Wycherly, John Gay, and Henry Fielding. As J. Paul Hunter writes, "the world of print had joined the world of conversation, gossip, and rumor in a singular devotion to issues of the moment."[6]

Satire found a natural home in a public sphere saturated with polemic. The first daily newspapers appeared in these years, as did the influential journals *The Tatler* and *The Spectator,* offering a mix of news and opinion. This climate, writes Catherine Gallagher, produced "an unprecedented politicization of authorship," as literary works were read in the context of partisan debates and "political controversy was virtually the only road to making either a name or a living as a writer."[7] For example, Gay's *Beggar's Opera* and Fielding's *Jonathan Wild,* which depict a colorful underworld of criminals and prostitutes, were readily understood as coded Tory attacks on the Whig minister Robert Walpole. In short, even "literary" satire was immersed in, and emerged out of, the political and cultural debates of the day. Thus, while the long eighteenth century might seem a stable era in comparison to the previous century with its bloody revolutions, it was yet a turbulent time, full of political contest, religious controversy, changing morality, even new understandings of human nature.

Modest Proposals: Defoe and Swift

The subgenre of the satiric pamphlet illustrates how satire of the time was enmeshed in a discourse that was topical, political, and journalistic. Short, unbound, and inexpensive, pamphlets were easy to produce and distribute, like the tweets, comments, and posts that fill our own blogosphere. Elizabethans such as Thomas Dekker, Thomas Nashe, and Robert Greene had written satirical pamphlets, but the form proliferated in the early eighteenth century, which produced its two most famous examples: Daniel Defoe's *The Shortest-Way with the Dissenters* (1702) and Jonathan Swift's *A Modest Proposal* (1729). These two ironic suggestions for policy reforms, both of which engage charged political issues, represent a new variety of mock argument. These proposals, of course, only purport to be modest: they soft-peddle extreme ideas, couching violence in euphemism. They intimate the possibility of a harmonious utopian future, but the worlds they conjure are horrific dystopias.

Defoe, one of England's foundational novelists and a prolific journalist, wrote *The Shortest-Way* in response to an attack on the religious liberty of those Protestants, called "Dissenters," who did not belong to the Church of England. In 1702, with Queen Anne succeeding King William III, a bill was proposed in Parliament that would make it harder for Dissenters to serve in public office. (The bill would have ended the practice known as occasional conformity by which Dissenters could occasionally take Anglican communion to qualify as Anglican for the purposes of holding office.) To stoke opposition to the bill, Defoe published *The Shortest-Way*, in which he impersonates the voice of hardline Anglican preachers, called "high-flyers," such as Henry Sacheverell and Charles Leslie; in this voice he calls for the eradication of Dissenters from England. He did not range far from his source material: Leslie himself had published pamphlets called *A Short and Easie Way with Deists* and *A Short and Easie Method with Jews.*[8] Defoe published the pamphlet anonymously but was unmasked, and the ensuing controversy upset both sides – Dissenters alarmed at the violence of the proposal, Anglicans angry at being duped. Defoe was convicted of seditious libel and sentenced to stand in the pillory.

The pamphlet poses interpretive difficulties, the most fundamental of which is discerning exactly what is being proposed. Defoe's speaker calls for harsh measures to "extirpate" Dissenters, but he leaves uncertain whether he is calling for execution, exile, or merely the prosecution of leaders:

> 'Tis cruelty to kill a snake or a toad in cold blood, but the poison of their nature makes it a charity to our neighbours, to destroy those creatures, not for any personal injury received, but for prevention; not for the evil they have done, but the evil they may do. (95)

The passage is ambiguous: is killing a snake a metaphor for murdering a Dissenter, or merely for any method of rooting out dissent? Time and again the speaker appears to propose violence, only to make a tactical retreat. Such vague intimations lend the pamphlet a menacing quality: the threat of brutality lurks behind a façade of reason but never fully emerges.[9] Extremist rhetoric, Defoe shows us, can assume mild and alluring guises.

Defoe may have intended to mock the tone and arguments of his enemies, or he may have meant to pass himself off as an Anglican in order to alarm Dissenters into action (*PSE* 157). Either way, the satiric force of *The Shortest-Way* derives from its deconstruction of two key differences: the difference between particular and universal interests, and the difference between justice and violence. In the Aesopian fable with which the pamphlet opens, a cock, roosting on the ground among horses, urges the larger animals to remain still "for fear we should tread upon one another" (88). What the cock claims as a collective or universal interest is merely his own particular wish for self-preservation; by analogy, the Dissenters' putatively principled call for toleration is redescribed as self-interest by the speaker, who maintains that when the Dissenters held power they showed no "mercy" or "forbearance" (89) to Anglicans.

As the speaker redescribes the universal as particular, so he rewrites violence as justice. A little violence now, he insists, will make future violence unnecessary. Cruelty in the present is renamed as kindness toward the future: "How many millions of future souls, we save from infection and delusion, if the present race of Poisoned Spirits were purged from the face of the land" (96). Conversely, a failure of nerve today will only lead to greater violence tomorrow should the "merciless" and "uncharitable" Dissenters be allowed to flourish. Sparing the Dissenters amounts to a "foolish pity" that "will be more barbarous to our own children and dear posterity" (95) than taking immediate action. Mercy thus becomes weakness, brutality strength, and the difference between justice and violence one of mere perspective: "Justice is always Violence to the party offending" (89). Paul Alkon calls this paradoxical rhetoric "newspeak,"[10] and indeed Defoe participates in a long-standing satiric critique of double-talk that runs from Juvenal to Orwell.

Defoe does not endorse this newspeak, but he does highlight paradoxes that pervade not merely the Tory rhetoric he imitates but also the entire Augustan public sphere. The ease with which one's own interests can be represented as universal, or with which one's own violence can be described as mercy-by-other-means, derives from a partisan context in which principles are always being reduced to tactical interests in disguise, and tactics are always being justified casuistically in the name of higher principles. Swift will make the same point in *Gulliver's Travels* where Lilliput and Blefuscu feud over which end of an egg to break, as will Voltaire with the parallel behavior of the warring Abares and Bulgars in *Candide*: diametrically opposed political stances can appear remarkably symmetrical. Even as Defoe decries the violent threats of his enemies, then, he exposes underlying paradoxes in the nature of public debate.

Swift's even more famous proposal differs in notable ways from Defoe's. The idea Swift puts forth – eating babies as a remedy for Irish poverty and hunger – diverges far more radically from the norms of his era, and his wry comic tone contrasts sharply with Defoe's strident denunciation. But if the tone is more moderate, the irony is ultimately more obvious, and, unlike Defoe, Swift calls direct attention to his actual views, most obviously in the long paragraph near the end of his essay that mentions (even as it dismisses) a litany of more mundane and more truly "modest" reforms. Along with other clues, this paragraph serves to "anchor" Swift's discourse, pointing us to a non-ironic meaning. Such rhetorical mooring has led Wayne Booth to uphold *A Modest Proposal* as a model of "stable irony" whose meaning is unequivocal.[11] Swift is not the Modest Proposer, and he expects us to see that.

But recognizing that Swift doesn't himself endorse cannibalism ultimately tells us little about the peculiar power of his satire, and reducing his meaning to a non-ironic set of pragmatic reforms is at best a first step toward analysis. Swift's wizardry lies in the rhetoric by which he amuses, bewilders, and reassures the reader all at once. Central to his accomplishment is his crafting of a speaking persona that achieves memorable distinctiveness. Swift realizes this persona in part by floating incidental biographical details, in part through his tone of self-assurance and suave reasonableness. (Defoe's speaker in contrast is a flat political type woodenly reiterating talking points.) Swift's Proposer attains an aura of rationality by addressing the question of mass hunger in purely economic terms, throwing statistics at us and offering a solution that is, in the jargon of today's idiot bureaucrats, "data-driven." This focus on the numbers diverts us from noticing the extent to which any recognizable idea of morality is absent from his argument.

This cold, Spock-like utilitarianism, which views human beings as resources and starvation as a problem of balancing the books, underwrites the Proposer's repeated swerves into the discourse of animal husbandry – his casual references to numbers of "Breeders" and to "a Child just dropt from its Dam." And once human beings are reduced to livestock, the Proposer can blithely invoke not only the discourse of breeding but also that of haute cuisine:

> I have been assured by a very knowing *American* of my acquaintance in *London*; that a young healthy Child, well Nursed, is, at a Year old, a most delicious, nourishing, and wholesome Food; whether *Stewed, Roasted, Baked,* or *Boiled*; and, I make no doubt, that it will equally serve in a *Fricasie,* or *Ragoust.*   (297)

Swift puts the reader in the position of the gourmand, identifying with the eater rather than the eaten: "I rather recommend buying the Children alive, and dressing them hot from the Knife, as we do *roasting Pigs*" (298).

In proposing these outrages, Swift commits an astounding imaginative transgression. Simply put, *A Modest Proposal* presents as reasonable the primitive fantasy of consuming human flesh. Swift's gambit is not merely an attention-getting stunt but rather the risky occupation of an obscene stance that reveals the awful appeal of the horror he proposes. Claude Rawson is right to insist that the piece is not "the compassionate protest against injustice that later readers sometimes take it to be," for although hints of compassion occur in the Proposer's representation of the abject condition of the Irish poor, his discourse also exhibits a strong disdain for the Irish themselves, and moralistically harps upon Irish failures in child-rearing and sexual restraint. The desire to be rid of poverty, as Rawson notes, slides easily but uncomfortably into a desire to be rid of the poor themselves. While on one level Swift is taking up the cause of the Irish, on another he participates in the long English tradition of viewing the Irish as subhuman, capable of cannibalism and deserving of being cannibalized.[12]

This obscene subtext unnerves even the reader who grasps the easier ironies of the piece. Swift's mock discourse, although different in tone and rhetoric from Defoe's, similarly serves both to analyze and to undermine the kind of public debate that thrived in eighteenth-century England. Just as Defoe's title would be understood in the context of non-fictional pamphlets, so Swift's was read by a public that would have been familiar with "serious" proposals to remedy poverty such as *An Essay or Modest Proposal, of a Way to increase the Number of People, and consequently the Strength of this Kingdom* (1693), a *Modest Proposal for the More Certain and yet more Easie Provision for the Poor* (1696).[13] By inhabiting the form and exploding it from the inside, Swiftian satire, as Christian Thorne argues, "constitutes a generalized attack on the conventions of public discourse and debate" because it destabilizes the very ability of the public sphere "to test truth claims." Through its reasonableness, it shows how rational argument fails to lead to morally acceptable conclusions.[14] Even as it emerges from a climate in which fierce polemics are the norm, the mock pamphlet, mobilizing a wild subtextual fantasy, exposes the limitations of the public sphere itself. Rather than offering another form of argument, such satire renders argument itself untenable.

The Contrarian Spirit: Mandeville and Collier

The battles of the books occasioned by (and productive of) satire did not arise only from political pamphlets. Two works, one addressing economic theory, the other domestic relations, illustrate the tendency of eighteenth-century satire to attack cherished pieties. Bernard Mandeville's *The Fable of the Bees* (1714) makes no policy recommendations, genuine or counterfeit, and treats political questions only on a philosophical level. Yet it provoked criticism from preachers, poets, and moralists, earning a jab from Pope in *The Dunciad* and an indictment from a 1723 grand jury for disparaging "Religion and Virtue."[15] It began as a short poem published anonymously in 1705 called *The Grumbling of the Hive*, and over the next two decades Mandeville supplemented it with prose explication, articulating a political, moral, and economic theory.

The Fable is a modest proposal in reverse. Mandeville offers an animal fable, an allegory of English society as a prosperous hive of bees. Despite their prosperity, the bees bemoan the dishonesty in their ranks, rousing the indignation of Jove, who rids "The bawling Hive of Fraud" (70). But when fraud is banished, the economy crashes. Greed turns out to have been good. Whereas *A Modest Proposal* puts forth an unthinkable reform as a remedy for a dire crisis, Mandeville proposes a wholly unobjectionable reform – the eradication of vice – for what turns out to be a specious crisis. With a "be careful what you wish for" irony, he reveals to his readers the unforeseen consequences of their desire. Mandeville thus "expose[s] the Unreasonableness and Folly" of his fellow man, especially of moralists who are "always murmuring at and exclaiming against those Vices and Inconveniences" while still enjoying their benefits (55).

But Mandeville has a narrower target too: the philosophy known as benevolism or optimism, promoted by the Third Earl of Shaftesbury, which argued that a natural human propensity for virtue leads to individual and collective happiness. Against Shaftesbury, Mandeville puts forth two points. First, what are normally condemned as "Private Vices" actually lead to "Public Benefits": "[Man's] vilest and most hateful Qualities are the most necessary Accomplishments to fit him for the largest ... the happiest and most flourishing Societies" (53). Luxury, avarice, and prodigality spur productivity, trade, and wealth. Even criminals like house-breakers and pick-pockets create jobs for locksmiths, lawyers, jailers, and judges. Thus Virtue is "Made Friends with Vice" (68).

Beyond this economic argument, Mandeville offers a moral one. Those qualities that we call "Moral Virtues," he claims, are merely perversions of fundamentally amoral passions, "the Political Offspring which Flattery begot upon Pride" (88). Flattery and Self-Love, those handmaidens of Erasmus's Folly, are the driving force behind all human endeavors. Mandeville cheerfully redefines our noblest qualities as self-interest in disguise. Military honor means "nothing else but the good Opinion of others" (98), while sexual modesty is a social custom, not a virtue at all: "Was there virtue in modesty, it would be of the same force in the dark as it is in the light, which it is not" (107). Like the Swift of "Verses on the Death of Dr. Swift," Mandeville takes an impish pleasure at contradicting the moral assumptions of his society.[16]

Mandeville fuses this perverse contrarianism with the familiar satiric stance of the disinterested truth-teller. Whereas the "short-sighted vulgar" cannot "see further than one link" in a chain of cause and effect, Mandeville claims a longer view: "those who ... [gaze] on the prospect of concatenated events may, in a hundred places, see good spring up and pullulate from evil, as naturally as chickens do from eggs" (123). This Lucianic *catascopia*, in turn, enables laughter at folly, and Mandeville repeatedly observes how "silly" the human species is. He laughs at how people hide, even from themselves, the instinct of lust:

> Can any man be so serious as to abstain from laughter when he considers that for so much deceit and insincerity practiced upon ourselves as well as others, we have no other recompense than the vain satisfaction of making our species appear more exalted and remote from that of other animals than it really is? (168)

Mandeville concludes his poem with a "moral" that urges the reader to "leave Complaints" because "Fools only strive / To make a Great an honest Hive." To enjoy both status and virtue – what Fielding in *Jonathan Wild* distinguishes as "greatness" and "goodness" – "is a vain / *Eutopia* seated in the Brain" (76). In contrast to Thomas More, Mandeville believes that designing plans for Eutopia (here with spelled with *eu*, indicating a "good" place) is fruitless speculation. To be sure, Mandeville shares a lot with More. Both stress the role of arbitrary custom in shaping behavior; both regard pride as a funda-mental human motive. As More scoffs at the garish robes of the Anemolian ambassadors, Mandeville laughs at man's fondness for fine clothes, wonder-ing why he should pride himself on "what is robbed from so innocent and defenceless an animal as a sheep" (151). Mandeville even praises the Morean idea of a commonwealth guided by Horatian values of moderation and temperance. Yet the differences between them are crucial. More laments the stubbornness of pride, but Mandeville acknowledges its ineradicability and seeks to manage it profitably. More scorns self-display, but Mandeville accepts it as an effort to seek recognition from others. Finally, while Mandeville acknowledges the appeal of the Utopian rejection of modernity, he – in contrast to More – decisively severs traditional ideas of virtue from socio-economic prosperity. A humble life demands the renunciation of modern comforts, and Mandeville knows that his countrymen have no desire to do so.

The satire of Jane Collier's *An Essay on the Art of Ingeniously Tormenting* (1753) operates not in the philosophical realm but in the domestic, but it shares with Mandeville a contrarian comic spirit and a skepticism toward pieties about human goodness. It imitates the eighteenth-century form of the conduct book, a genre written for young women instructing them in proper behavior. But instead of enunciating rules for virtue, Collier offers a how-to guide for petty cruelty, assembling "in one small pocket volume" (6) the best advice for tormenting one's spouse, children, servants, and friends. In offering this mock advice, Collier elaborates on the immediate example of Swift, whose

Directions to Servants (1745) ostensibly prescribes good manners but actually catalogues the myriad offenses of butlers, footmen, and maids. Swift's work captures both the haughty frustration of the master whose directives are ignored and the passive-aggressive resourcefulness of the servant who can exercise power only through small acts of defiance. (In Philadelphia, in 1750, Benjamin Franklin had published "Rules for Making Oneself a Disagreeable Companion.") In the same way, Collier is able through her ironic discourse to condemn the little, nameless, unremembered acts of malice that pervade domestic life while also tempting the reader with the allure of such mean-spirited power.

As a woman satirist, Collier challenges patriarchal norms simply through the act of writing satire; wit was considered dangerous and associated with loose sexual morals. By analyzing women's indirect methods of wielding power, moreover, Collier opens their experiences for a satiric treatment far different from the misogynistic mansplaining of Juvenal and Pope. In training its eye on domestic, erotic, and social relations, Collier's satire also possesses a kinship with the emerging genre of the novel. While not a novel itself (its genre is closer to the anatomy), *The Art* repeatedly turns to contemporary novels for illustration, indicating that the new genre was already a favored vehicle for satirical analysis of the domestic.

Collier favors not the "common and vulgar" (18) methods of tormenting such as unadulterated abuse, but the more "delicate strokes" (52) through which the tormenter can inflict misery yet retain the appearance of kindness. Essential to these more subtle methods are sudden reversals of temper, aimed at keeping the victim nervously off-balance. Collier's Tormenter-speaker relishes no-win situations in which the victim can be harassed no matter what course she takes:

> Always scold at her, if she is the least undressed or dirty; and say you cannot bear such beasts about you. If she is clean and well-dressed, tell her, that you suppose she dresses out for the fellows; for the wenches of this age are so forward, that the men can hardly be quiet for them.   (19)

Skilled tormenting thus proceeds through a combination of mixed signals, guilt trips, passive aggression, and general mind-fucks.

Collier's irony, much like Erasmus's, can be tricky. Sometimes the reader can simply reverse Collier's meaning. When Collier says that it "is much better to select out one or two" servants than to torment them all (14), the reader understands "much better" to mean "much crueler" – but also "much more fun." The Tormenter's prescription is Collier's description: a catalogue of already existing practices. Yet by disguising her blame as the Tormenter's praise, and by inducing the reader to laugh with her, Collier makes the reader complicit in her sadism and leaves her caught between enjoyment and disavowal.

Collier moreover seems to endorse at least some of the attitudes of the Tormenter-narrator. Like Mandeville, she redescribes virtue as self-interest, speaking hard truths about human fallibility: "To see one's dearest friend get the start of one in anything, is too much for such friendship to bear" (73). This jaded view of human nature allows the Tormenter to dismiss as insipid those benevolent but boring people who have no taste for cruelty. Her musings on children, meanwhile, recall *A Modest Proposal*:

> To make away with the troublesome and expensive brats, I allow, would be the desirable thing: but the question is, how to effect this without subjecting yourself to that punishment which the law has thought proper to affix to such sort of jokes. Whipping and starving, with some caution, might do the business.   (37)

This breezy disdain for the inconveniences of the law assumes the reader's agreement and brings her into a select circle of those who know better.

The domestic world Collier represents, then, is not so different from the world of con-artists and gulls presented in *Volpone* or *The Beggar's Opera*. The Tormenter even deploys the vocabulary of rogues, cautioning her reader that it is important to select the perfect "dupe," and to draw her in with "specious bait" of false virtue (60). As in *Volpone*, the art of trickery is the art of acting, and the Tormenter uses language of staging, feigning, pretending, and performing. She counsels her reader to keep her emotions always in check for the purpose of feigning anger as needed; the best exemplars of the art of tormenting are "not the openly cruel and hard-hearted, but rather the specious pretenders to goodness, who, under an outcry about benevolence, hide the most malevolent hearts" (63).

Ultimately Collier discloses a view of domestic relations that is all about what *Seinfeld*'s George Costanza called "having hand" in a relationship. The book reduces all human motives to the single end of self-aggrandizement. It is funny to see power relations played out in petty domestic vignettes, but Collier also presents a bleak sense of the real struggles for power that take place in the drawing room, the kitchen, the bedroom. And while depicting this cruelty may morally rebuke those who practice it, Collier is fundamentally suspicious of moralism, which throughout *The Art* proves to be a cover for sadism. The art of tormenting thus turns out to be the art of satire itself. Although "the most expert practitioners ... frequently declare, when they whip, cut, and slash the body, or when they tease, vex, and torment the mind that 'tis done for the good of the person that suffers," Collier concedes that cruelty is an end in itself, "exercised for its own sake" (7). Tormenters, like satirists, hide their malevolent hearts behind a pretense of goodness.

Gulliver's Travels: A Lusus Naturae

"Here is a book come out that all our people of taste run mad about," wrote Mary Wortley Montagu of Jonathan Swift's *Gulliver's Travels* soon after its anonymous London publication in October 1726.[17] An immediate bestseller, this account of four voyages "into several remote nations of the world" was reprinted twice before the end of the year and translated into Dutch, French, and German before the end of the next. It spawned a series of poems by Pope, a kind of sequel by John Arbuthnot, and various "keys" to the book's allegorical references – all part of a stream of what Gulliver, in a (fictional) 1735 letter, refers to as "Libels, and Keys, and Reflections, and Second Parts" (255). *Gulliver's Travels* continues to puzzle and please: a satire at once moral, social, textual, intellectual, and existential, it balances the darkness of its vision with a buoyant sense of play; and although the book is probably the most famous satire in English literature, major critics have questioned whether it even is satire.[18]

What kind of book is *Gulliver's Travels* then? The best term may be that with which the King of Brobdingnag classified Gulliver himself – a *lusus naturae*, a freak of nature. It is a parody of the era's travel narratives such as William Dampier's non-fictional *New Voyage Round the World* (1697) and Daniel Defoe's fictional *Robinson Crusoe* (1719), which fed a hunger for stories of newly discovered lands, alien peoples, life-threatening adventures, and exotic cultural practices. It is also a send-up of the Protestant conversion stories promulgated through these tales of travel. It draws on Lucian's imaginary voyages, which in spoofing Herodotus and Homer counsel skepticism about the outlandish claims of travelers. It presents a utopia, and, like More, Swift uses imaginary nations to provide perspective on his own. Yet it is a dystopia as well: a lesser-known and more broadly comic precursor is Joseph Hall's *Mundus Alter et Idem* (*c.* 1605), whose narrator makes sea voyages to four imaginary lands – Crapulia (land of gluttons), Viraginia (of viragoes), Moronia (of morons), and Lavernia (of thieves) – and which exaggerates English vices and follies rather than offering an ideal alternative. *Gulliver's Travels* in fact combines More's strategy of negation and Hall's strategy of exaggeration. Swift's alien lands can serve, like Utopia, as a model, as when the Lilliputians educate girls along with boys, but they can also magnify the faults he finds at home, as in the ludicrous projects of the Academy of Lagado or the repulsive carnality of the Yahoos.

Gulliver's Travels is also in places a Socratic dialogue; the wise questioning of Gulliver's "masters" elicits an awareness of truths about England, Europe, and human nature. The fourth voyage draws on the beast fable, questioning the place of the human animal in the natural order. The third voyage, primarily an intellectual satire, conforms most closely to the anatomy; as in *A Tale of a Tub*, Swift attacks the bad new ideas of modern thought, presenting fools like the scientist seeking to extract sunbeams from cucumbers, the mathematicians so divorced from practical concerns that they can't build a house with a single right angle, or the intellectuals so lost in thought that they need to be hit with inflated bladders to recall them to the real world. In Glubbdubdrib, Gulliver conducts a Lucianic dialogue of the dead, while the immortal and decrepit Struldbrugs recall Juvenal's Tenth Satire with its reminder of the perils of aging. Finally, Swift's tale is a political allegory, spoofing skirmishes between Whigs and Tories, England and France, and various personalities at Queen Anne's court.

Swift's satire hangs upon his supple if not fully consistent use of his narrator. Gulliver's name suggests a gull or fool, and he develops the satiric tradition of the naïve narrator who understands less than the author and the reader; his incomprehension allows us to see what he doesn't. But Gulliver is not always a fool, and sometimes seems nobler and wiser than those whom he visits. (By and large, in Parts One and Three Gulliver appears as superior to the others in the world, while in Parts Two and Four he is inferior.) He rarely learns from experience, and when, at the end of his last voyage, he finally does learn, we question the value of his newfound wisdom, which leads him to walk with an equine trot, to shun his own wife and children, and to spend hours in the stables talking to his horses (4.11.244). If he is naive at the beginning of his travels, he is mad by the end.

The encounter between two cultures, coupled with the perspective of Gulliver's innocent eye, allows Swift to practice the technique that the Russian Formalist critics called defamiliarization. He makes us see familiar things anew by describing them as though they are seen for the first time. When Gulliver endeavors to explain his society, his own simple language makes European beliefs, customs, or inventions appear strange. His account of lawyers, for example, dispenses with nuance and euphemism:

> I said there was a Society of Men among us, bred up from their Youth in the Art of proving, by Words multiplyed for the Purpose that White is Black, and Black is White, according as they are paid. To this Society all the rest of the People are Slaves. (4.5.210)

Swift can make defamiliarization a game with the reader, as when the Lilliputians inventory Gulliver's pockets and describe its contents – a giant-sized comb, pistol, knife, razor, and so on – while the reader silently attempts to guess the objects described (1.2.28–31). But defamiliarization acquires its strongest force when it compels the reader to re-examine beliefs and customs. Gulliver's straight-faced descriptions of politicians, war, weaponry, religious sectarianism, sexual courtship, luxury goods, and class structure expose the corruption of his society even when he professes to praise it.

In other cases the technique is reversed, and Gulliver's hosts do the work of defamiliarizing. Gulliver's master observes in the Yahoos behavior whose "modern" parallels we easily discern:

> [I]n most Herds there was a sort of ruling *Yahoo* ... who was always more *deformed* in Body, and *mischievous in Disposition*, than any of the rest. That this *Leader* had usually a Favourite as *like himself* as he could get, whose Employment was to *lick his Master's Feet and Posteriors, and drive the Female* Yahoos *to his Kennel*; for which he was now and then rewarded with a piece of Ass's Flesh. (4.7.221)

Satire here is a language game, an effort to find new ways to present phenomena by peeling away outworn accounts.

Among the most memorable tropes of *Gulliver's Travels* is its play with size and scale, a conceit that Swift derives from Rabelais. In Part One, Gulliver's great height affords him a Lucianic *catascopia*, as he looks down with amusement and derision on the Lilliputians, who prove petty not only in their size but also in their morals and their self-importance. Swift makes wry jokes that underscore the paltriness of human pretension and achievement such as when Gulliver describes the Lilliputian emperor as "taller by almost the breadth of my Nail, than any of his Court" (1.2.24). The technique carries over into descriptions of Lilliputian politics and religion: the Rope-Dancing that serves as a metaphor for the way that nimble politicians skilled in political game-playing retain power (1.3.32); the political parties whose disagreements are reduced to the mere one-fourteenth of an inch that differentiates the height of the heels of their shoes (1.4.40); the Lilliput–Blefuscu rivalry, responsible for thousands of deaths, which derives from a difference of opinion over which end of an egg to break (1.4.41).

In Part One Gulliver's great height allows him to condescend to the Lilliputians, but the situation is reversed in Part Two, where Gulliver finds himself the object of mirth for the great Brobdingnagians. Puffed up by his experience in Lilliput, admired for his surpassing strength (as well as his awe-inspiring "fire hose"), he is now humiliated, forced to battle for his life with wasps, flies, rats, and birds, bullied by an enormous, cruel palace dwarf. Gulliver's superior stance in Part One is rewritten as a grandiose and ephemeral fantasy of power, a misguided belief in his own Pantagruelian benevolence. In particular Gulliver's pride and patriotism suffer. He boasts to the King about his "beloved Country," but receives in reply only a burst of laughter and an expression of amused contempt. The King of Brobdingnag now becomes the satiric mocker of human pretense while Gulliver appears as idiotically jingoistic, blushing "with Indignation" as he listens to his homeland described as a land of "diminutive Insects" (2.3.89).

The manipulation of scale in the first two voyages also permits Swift to indulge a play with big and small that taps into primitive childhood fears and fantasies about one's relationship to the gigantic world of adults, as well as nostalgia for the pleasures of children's games and toys.[19] These shifts and contrasts in size indulge an exploration of the body and its functions, and indeed the book is rife with scatological humor. The female body in particular repulses Gulliver. He confesses his disgust at the sight of a Brobdingnagian woman's six-foot-high "monstrous breast": "The Nipple was about half the Bigness of my Head, and the Hew both of that and the Dug, so varified with Spots, Pimples, and Freckles, that nothing could appear more nauseous." Gulliver tentatively extends this disgust to the beautiful "English ladies" at home, noting that they "appear so beautiful to us, only because they are of our own size, and their Defects not to be seen but through a Magnifying Glass" (2.1.77). Gulliver's view of the undressed Brobdingnadian maids takes this revulsion further, as he describes their "coarse and uneven" skin, gigantic moles with hairs "thicker than Pack-threads," and hogsheads of urine discharged. Gulliver alludes to his possible service as a sex toy, and his affectation of delicacy goes just far enough to provoke the reader's curiosity:

> The handsomest among these Maids of Honour, a pleasant, frolicsome Girl of sixteen, would sometimes set me astride upon one of her Nipples, with many other Tricks, wherein the Reader will excuse me for not being over particular. (2.5.99)

His revulsion from the female body continues in Part Four, where he recoils first from the advances of the female Yahoo and later from the embraces of his own wife.

Part Four raises the broadest and most universal questions – what kind of creatures are we as human beings, what is our place in the natural order, are we ruled by reason or passion – questions stoked by ongoing imperial conquests and curiosity about racial and cultural differences. Whether you take the Yahoos to represent all human beings in a state of nature or only non-

Europeans, they are loathsome, and Gulliver's loathing extends from them to their European kin. Hence the charge of misanthropy is frequently brought against both Swift and Gulliver, a charge that Swift himself legitimates when he writes to Pope that the book is built upon a "foundation of Misanthropy" (854). The King of Brobdingnag voices similar misanthropy when he describes recent English history with a Rabelaisian list, calling it "a heap of conspiracies, rebellions, murders, massacres, revolutions, banishments, the very worst effects that avarice, faction, hypocrisy, perfidiousness, cruelty, rage, madness, hatred, envy, lust, malice, and ambition, could produce," and judging – with Democritean amusement rather than Juvenalian disgust – "the bulk of [Gulliver's countrymen] to be the most pernicious race of little odious vermin that nature ever suffered to crawl upon the surface of the earth" (2.6.110–111). It is in the Country of the Houyhnhnms, however, that the critique of the human species is most insistent. At times the entire section seems little more than a long acid recitation of human vices.

The question as to whether Gulliver's hatred of his species is warranted by Swift has divided critics into what are sometimes called "hard" and "soft" schools of interpretation.[20] The hard school sees the rational Houyhnhnms as Swift's ideal and their society as genuinely utopian; the soft sees the Houyhnhnms themselves as a satiric target and Don Pedro de Mendez as a preferred model of human decency. A hard interpretation notes that Swift casts human motives as base, animalistic, self-interested, and prideful, while a soft interpretation counters that Gulliver's final withdrawal to his stables is a sign of his own madness rather than the world's.

As for the Houyhnhnms, although they are wiser, less vicious, happier, and more peaceful than the human race, they are not above Swift's irony, and their admirable rationality, like that of More's Utopians, approves of genocide. As Gulliver lives among them, his contempt for the Yahoos permits ever-greater disregard for their claim to life, even as he acknowledges that they are indeed human. Initially we see the subjugated Yahoos used, horse-like, to drag sledges. Soon Gulliver uses their bodies – first their hair (4.2), then their skins (4.3) – to make traps and clothes and shoes. By the end of the voyage the Houyhnhnms are debating "Whether the *Yahoo* should be exterminated from the Face of the Earth" (4.9.228). Ultimately they opt for mass castration, a solution that ironically they have learned from Gulliver's account of how horses are treated in England. Gulliver is voted off the island, departing in a homemade canoe rigged with a sail of Yahoo – that is, human – skins, which Gulliver describes with straight-faced black humor reminiscent of *A Modest Proposal*: "I made use of the youngest I could get, the older being too tough and thick" (4.10.237). Swift again imagines the horrors of ethnic cleansing with a sober and rational state of mind.[21] The troubling paradoxes of *Gulliver's Travels* are thus summarized in Swift's remark to Pope that "the chief end" of his labor "is to vex the world rather than divert it" (676).

The Oriental Tale: Johnson and Voltaire

In the decades following *Gulliver's Travels*, prose satire finds a lasting home in the genre of the novel. The subgenre of the picaresque, made popular by Henry Fielding and Tobias Smollett, weaves together social observation, low comedy, and gritty realism. Laurence Sterne develops the wildly digressive tradition of Rabelais and Swift into a recursive, self-conscious novelistic tradition that satirizes narrative itself. Some decades later Jane Austen perfects a highly focused, finely understated comedy of domestic manners. But in the same years that the novel is on the rise, another fictional form flourishes, the oriental tale. Filled with fabulous adventures set in "the East" – a vaguely defined space which could range from Turkey and Arabia to China and Japan – the oriental tale capitalizes on the popularity of new translations of *The Arabian Nights* (1704–1717). It does not emphasize psychological nuance, character growth, or attention to the domestic, but incorporates fantasy, didacticism, comedy, adventure, travel, and pornography. It is often a philosophical tale, raising far-reaching social and ethical questions, revamping the folktale for modern concerns, and using transcultural perspectives to critique European practices in ways far more self-critical and far less imperialistic than contemporary treatments of orientalist discourse generally understand. *Gulliver's Travels* contains hints of the genre (Swift includes Japan among the many invented remote nations that Gulliver visits), and even "A Modest Proposal" cites George Psalmanazar's fraudulent 1704 account of Taiwanese cannibalism as a transcultural precedent for eating Irish babies. In France, Montesquieu's *Persian Letters* (1721) deploys many of the genre's tropes for intellectual and social satire by observing and critiquing French customs, law, and religion through the perspective of two visiting Persian noblemen, producing a "stereoscopic vision" that transcends the epistemologies of either the West or the East alone. Readers of the eighteenth century, of course, would hardly have distinguished realistic "novels" from fantastical "tales," but rather moved freely among stories variously called adventures, histories, lives, narratives, fables, and journals.[22]

Two mid-century satiric fictions owe a debt to this understudied tradition. Published in 1759, both Samuel Johnson's *Rasselas* and Voltaire's *Candide* survey mankind – perhaps not quite "from China to Peru," but from

Suriname to Crimea and Abyssinia to Persia. Both stories feature an innocent abroad who traverses seas and continents in search of wisdom, accompanied by a sage and a female companion. As in *Gulliver's Travels*, naiveté and even stupidity make the known world appear strange; in pointing out the world's follies, the heroes Rasselas and Candide resemble the simple child who observes the nakedness of the emperor and doesn't know to keep his mouth shut. In the word of Johnson's friend and biographer, James Boswell, "the proposition illustrated by both these works [is] the same, namely, that in our present state there is more evil than good." Still, there are stark differences between the fundamentally religious Johnson and the fervently anti-clerical Voltaire. Johnson's sallies can be so gentle that some question whether they are satire, while, as one critic puts it, "Voltaire's snowballs have rocks in them."[23]

Like his Juvenalian poem "The Vanity of Human Wishes," Johnson's *History of Rasselas, the Prince of Abissinia* offers a panorama of human activity as it inquires into what constitutes the happiest "choice of life." Yet from the beginning, happiness is a paradox. In order to seek the source of happiness, Rasselas and his sister Nekayah must leave the Happy Valley of their childhood, since the Valley's Edenic satisfaction of every material need leaves them spiritually restless. But the episodes that follow, in which Rasselas conducts various "experiments upon life" (17.101), offer more folly than wisdom and more regret than satisfaction. Characters seek happiness in hedonism, pastoral retreat, wealth, power, and longevity, but none finds it. Johnson's tale, which he called a "moral fable," thus comes across as sober, bracing, and severe. Yet *Rasselas* has its comic moments too, and Johnson's "sentimental solemnity," as Paul Fussell notes, cohabits with "broadly ironic and farcical details."[24] Rasselas meets a "mechanic" who, Dedalus-like, has manufactured wings in an attempt to fly, but the man's grandiose ambition culminates in a comic flop:

> on a morning appointed, the maker appeared furnished for flight on a little promontory: he waved his pinions a while to gather air, then leaped from his stand, and in an instant dropped into the lake. His wings, which were of no use in the air, sustained him in the water, and the prince drew him to land, half dead with terror and vexation. (6.83)

This crash-landing, worthy of Wile E. Coyote, literalizes the gravitational pull of satire, which brings human aspirations and pretentions down to earth.

The main characters can be fools too. Rasselas's behavior and his questions about the world can be comically naïve, and Johnson is surely smiling at the young hero when he philosophizes on human nature to an audience of goats in the Happy Valley, or when his meditations become too self-absorbed: "he passed four months in resolving to lose no more time in idle resolves" (4.80). The sage Imlac can sound like a narcissistic pedant, and his disquisition on aesthetics concludes when Rasselas cuts off his pontificating: "Imlac now felt the enthusiastic fit, and was proceeding to aggrandize his own profession, when the prince cried out, 'Enough! Thou hast convinced me, that no human being can ever be a poet'" (11.90–91).

Yet Johnson's treatment of folly edges away from the harshly judgmental mode of Swift. W. Jackson Bate has called Johnson's mode "satire manqué" because "ridicule, anger, satiric protest are always in the process of turning into something else."[25] Some of Johnson's characters, such as the mechanic, or the mad astronomer who thinks he can control the weather, surely resemble Swiftian lunatics like the "projectors" of Laputa. But Johnson corrects or educates such folly, balancing reduction and ridicule with compassion and even apology. Like Don Quixote, Rasselas is a fool who wins a measure of sympathy, and Johnson recognizes human failings and self-deceptions as universal and inescapable.

Like *Don Quixote* too, *Rasselas* embodies a warning against the power of the imagination, a faculty of the mind that often looks to Johnson like delusion itself. The opening sentence cautions against heeding "the whispers of fancy," and pursuing "the phantoms of hope." Much later, Imlac interprets the Egyptian pyramids as a "monument to the insufficiency of human enjoyments" since they were built "only in compliance with that hunger of imagination which preys incessantly upon life" (32.123). The madness of the astronomer is likewise viewed as a consequence of having "indulge[d] the power of fiction" to excess: "All power of fancy over reason is a degree of insanity" (44.141).

Yet for all its stern warnings, this moral fable is not wholly didactic, and Johnson balances his wisdom with skepticism toward wisdom. Johnson offers wise-sounding pithy generalizations, but when Rasselas learns to be wary "of the emptiness of rhetorical sound, and the inefficacy of polished periods and studied sentences" (18.104), we sense that Johnson is directing his wariness at his own powers of rhetoric. Rasselas's entire quest for meaning itself is ironized, since too much contemplation of life can lead to a neglect of living. As Imlac says:

> The causes of good and evil … are so various and uncertain, so often entangled with each other, so diversified by various relations, and so much subject to accidents which cannot be foreseen, that he who would fix his condition upon incontestable reasons of preference, must live and die inquiring and deliberating. (16.101)

Fittingly, *Rasselas* ends with a "conclusion in which nothing is concluded." The final decision to return to Abyssinia signals a circular quest, even if the high-sounding resolutions of the characters point to new projects. Imlac and the astronomer, meanwhile, can only resolve to drift "along the stream of life without directing their course to any particular port" (49.153). Wisdom and experience have been gained, but they are subject to revision and provide no foolproof recipe for happiness. In *Rasselas*, excessive contemplation leads to obsession, solipsism, and madness. Johnson's contemporary David Hume distinguished between the natural and the philosophic man, noting that when he is mired in philosophical doubt, the way out of the muddle is not further contemplation but rather dinner, backgammon, and conversation with friends.[26] In this spirit, Johnson shows that however much Rasselas and his companions may ruminate upon the choice of life, their human nature compels them eventually to cease ruminating and live.

Candide shares much with *Rasselas*: the structure of its plot, the roles of its characters, its generally pessimistic view of human nature and human society. The tone of the book, however, is harsher, the judgment angrier, the pacing swifter, and the comedy bigger, cruder, and crueler. Johnson's sage Imlac becomes the windbag Pangloss, while the chaste princess Nekayah is replaced by the oversexed Cunegonde (whose name puns on French words for "cunt" and "gonad"). Unlike Johnson's Happy Valley, the Eden out of which Candide and Cunegonde are cast is a shabby excuse for a royal court, and on their quest for wisdom the travelers suffer repeated rapes, beatings, even murders. While *Rasselas* provides a mode of satire based in ethical inquiry, *Candide* offers satire based in attack.

The most famous target of Voltaire's satire is the philosophy of Gottfried Wilhelm von Leibniz, whose treatise *Theodicy* (1710) describes the world as "the best of all possible worlds" since it has been created by a benevolent deity. For Voltaire, atrocities of both human and natural origin – decades of bloody warfare, the Spanish Inquisition, the devastating Lisbon earthquake of 1755 – have rendered this view absurd. But while Leibniz, caricatured as Pangloss, is the book's most visible target, Voltaire refutes not just the man but also his combination of philosophical optimism and causal determinism. Voltaire's satire thus extends to other thinkers as well, including Shaftesbury (Mandeville's prime target) and Pope, who puts forth his own theodicy in "An Essay on Man" (1734). Pope argues that the world only appears to hold evil because human perspective is limited:

> All Nature is but Art, unknown to thee;
> All Chance, Direction, which thou canst not see;

> All Discord, Harmony not understood;
> All partial Evil, universal Good.   (1.289–292)

But Pangloss's judgments reduce to absurdity Pope's conclusion that "One truth is clear, whatever is, is right." Pangloss, moreover, inverts cause and effect, confusing the accidental with the necessary:

> [T]hings cannot be otherwise than they are, for since everything is made to serve an end, everything necessarily serves the best end. Observe: noses were made to support spectacles, hence we have spectacles. Legs, as anyone can plainly see, were made to be breeched, and so we have breeches.   (1.2)

He takes up a position in the Lucianic–Swiftian tradition of foolish thinkers who are out of touch with reality, too wrapped up in their own ideas to notice the world around them. And Pangloss's reasoning is not just illogical; it is harmful. He explains away horrors as necessary and therefore good. When the virtuous Anabaptist Jacques falls into the ocean, Candide wants to rescue him, "But the philosopher Pangloss prevented him by proving that the bay of Lisbon had been formed expressly for this Anabaptist to drown in" (5.9). Pangloss's slogans – "all is for the best," "things could not possibly be otherwise" – are drenched in irony.

The swift pace of *Candide*'s storytelling, with its absurdly coincidental reunions and cartoonish regeneration of characters who appeared to have been murdered, undercuts any pretense to realism. But as Erich Auerbach noted years ago, the style, plotting, and tempo have a philosophical meaning as well; like the caricatures that stand in for human beings, these plot devices constitute a simplification of the world. Voltaire "arranges reality so he can use it for his purposes," distilling the complexity of life down to an intense draught of unadulterated misery.[27] Yet while some might say that Voltaire rigs the game against Leibniz, for the satirically minded reader *Candide* is no more a distortion of reality than is the opposite view of the world that minimizes evil by finding divine purpose in every atrocity. Moreover, the breakneck pace and cartoon logic are cause for laughter, demonstrating a wild invention and uninhibited cruelty that transcends didactic aims. Voltaire is unleashing his own sadism, not simply critiquing the sadism of others.

Nor is Voltaire's satire merely an attack on a particular philosophical view. He loves to redescribe treasured ideals with cold, dry irony. When Candide is conscripted into the Bulgar army, he sees that military "heroism" means nothing more than raping and butchering others. After he attempts to desert, he learns that "liberty" means only a choice between two punishments, "to be flogged thirty-six times by the entire regiment or to receive summarily a dozen bullets in the brain" (2.4). Love, too, suffers ironic redescription; when Pangloss shows up "covered in pustules, his eyes … sunken, the end of his nose rotted off, his mouth twisted, [and] his teeth black," the philosopher attributes his condition not to syphilis but to "love": "love, the consolation of the human race, the preservative of the universe, the soul of all sensitive beings, love, gentle love" (4.7). And in England, justice is reduced to an illogical paradox: Candide is told that an admiral who has lost a military battle is being killed because "he didn't kill enough people" (23.55).

Contra Leibniz, then, the "best" of all possible worlds turns out to be full of purposeless horror, cruelty, and suffering. Some of this misery is due to natural causes like earthquakes and diseases, but much is the work of human beings: rapes, murders, wars, torture, theft, cannibalism. In the middle of the tale the characters therefore depart for New World as if to suggest that people have so badly screwed up the old world that a fresh start is necessary. Voltaire's satire in these chapters tacks to the method of *Utopia*, showing us alien customs in the New World in order to relativize European practices. The most obvious example is Candide's interlude in the utopian city of Eldorado, which like Swift's Island of the Houyhnhnms suffers from no petty religious disagreements and requires no courts or prisons.

Like Rasselas and Gulliver, however, Candide cannot remain in utopia, although he leaves for utterly selfish reasons: "If we stay here, we shall be just like everybody else, whereas if we go back to our own world, taking back with us a dozen sheep loaded with Eldorado pebbles, we shall be richer than all the kings put together" (18.38). With the return to Europe, the parade of evils and absurdities resumes, but the satire increasingly becomes social as well as philosophical, as Voltaire describes eighteenth-century quarrels over aesthetic values and literary taste. The new target is urban sophistication, and Martin describes Paris as "a chaos, a mob, in which everyone is seeking pleasure and where hardly anyone finds it" (21.45). Candide's experience at the theater introduces him to a snobbish critic who "hates successful [plays and books] as eunuchs hate successful lovers" (22.48), while in Venice Lord Pococurante's sensibility finds fault with virtually all great literature so that his only pleasure consists in criticism – he takes "pleasure in having no pleasure" (25.63). These characters reflect a new Enlightenment concern with taste and education as cultural capital, expressed through an insider's knowledge of what to like and what to dislike. Exemplars of bad taste are, like the vulgarians of Petronius, satirized to restore social hierarchy, yet so too are the over-refined who turn literary judgment into status-mongering.

Like *Rasselas*, *Candide* concludes inconclusively. The final dictum of the old Turkish man, that we must cultivate our garden, may be the best advice in the book, but it is modest and ambiguous. In counseling a retreat from public life similar to that offered by More's Hythlodaeus, it promises only to keep at bay "three great evils" – boredom, vice, and poverty. Candide repeats it less as a full-throated endorsement than as a way to shut up the prattling Pangloss. Like the return of Rasselas and his companions to Abyssinia, Candide's withdrawal to his farm suggests a philosophical surrender in the face of insoluble big questions. The dervish whom Candide and his companions consult about man's place on earth dismisses them impatiently, asking, "When his highness sends a ship to Egypt does he worry whether the mice on board are comfortable?" (30.73) before slamming the door in their faces. Voltaire does the same to his reader. The Enlightenment spirit of inquiry proves wearying, and leaves us with resignation rather than illumination. Yet if *Candide* ultimately tells us little about what's right in the world, it none-theless revels – unflinchingly, energetically, delightedly – in telling us what's wrong.

Chapter 6

Verse Satire from Rochester to Byron

It has been claimed that no span of English literary history has been so dominated by one genre as verse satire dominated the century from 1660 to 1760.[1] However, just as the old unitary narrative of this era's prose satire has begun to dissolve, so has the old account of its poetry centered on Dryden, Pope, and Swift. In her recent study, Ashley Marshall divides the era into quarter-centuries and even decades during which she discerns widely varying styles and forms. Many names not included in the Norton Anthology write verse satire in these years, and many satires are published without any authors' names at all. Some poems call themselves satires, but the genre also includes epistles, verse essays, epigrams, fables, and imitations. Horace and Juvenal, available to English poets in a stream of new translations, are powerful influences, but poetic satire also departs from Roman models. Dryden has been said to inaugurate a new standard of decorum, but the tone of the century's satire can be comic and silly, harsh and personal, or earnest and moralistic. Nor are poetic careers monolithic: Marshall, for example, argues that "early Swift" of the 1700s, with his openly propagandistic aims and his proclivity for parodic impersonation, has more in common with the Whig provocateurs he opposed such as Arthur Maynwaring and John Tutchin than he does with his Tory friends Pope and Gay (*PSE* 181). The era's formal verse satire, in short, displays remarkable variety. Defoe's *True-Born Englishman* (1701) and Swift's *Satirical Elegy on the Death of a Late Famous General* (1722) are openly political. Pope's *Epistle to Burlington* (1731) attacks new money and bad taste. Gay's *Trivia* (1716) views the modern cityscape through mock-georgic; Ebenezer Cooke's *The Sot-Weed Factor* (1708) laughs at the struggles of an obtuse tobacco merchant in the American colonies. Satire even turns on the satiric temper of the times, in Richard Blackmore's *Satyr against Wit* (1700).

The dominant metrical form of verse satire is the heroic couplet, the end-stopped iambic pentameter pair of rhymed lines. As its name indicates, it was initially associated with high genres like the epic. It emerged when Renaissance poets standardized Chaucer's ten-syllable line with an iambic meter and a system of pauses – a caesura in the middle of each line, a grammatical stop at the end.[2] These pauses divide the couplet into four half-lines, providing structure and balance. Different reasons have been offered for the couplet's proliferation in the long eighteenth century: its equilibrium fit the public, discursive aims of the era's poetry; its binary structure matched the polarized politics of the time; its easy detachability permitted the formulation of witty maxims.[3] But whatever the reasons, its structure enables the poet to present clear comparisons and contrasts. Key rhetorical devices – parallelism, antithesis, chiasmus – forge connections between different half-lines. These connections can occur on the levels of sound, syntax, or meaning, and any given connection can be one of either similarity or difference.

This recognition of the heroic couplet's ability to balance binaries should not, however, reduce it to an expression of sobriety and moderation. As historians have ceased to regard the eighteenth century as a stable, harmonious era, students of prosody have ceased to view the couplet as an inherently staid and stately form. Instead they emphasize its appetitive, exploratory nature, noting how its elaborate combinations of similarities and differences create dynamism and complexity.[4] Like the fateful scissors of Pope's *Rape of the Lock*, the sharp edges of the heroic couplet join in order to divide.

Rochester and the Court Wits

The revival of verse satire based on classical models actually begins, as we saw, in the 1590s. After the Bishops' Ban of 1599, however, satire tends toward forms such as libels and pamphlets, while the satiric poetry published in the early 1600s mostly drops the combative Juvenalian mode for the safer native tradition of homiletic complaint.[5] In the politically turbulent mid-century, satire becomes highly politicized. Verse satire in these years is dominated less by classical models than by "low" cultural forms such as street ballads, anthems, comic invective, and army-camp entertainments: "poetry cast for the street and the ale-house."[6] In a country sharply divided between Puritans and Anglicans, between parliamentarians and royalists, satiric songs re-route the camaraderie of the drinking song for political propaganda, fostering a feeling of "all-togetherness" that can be directed against a political foe. These songs, squibs, and doggerel verses constitute "lethal satire in disguise as imitation folk-poetry."[7] The us-against-them politics of such poetry shifts satire away from a critique of social types to allow for polemical, topical, and ad hominem libels or lampoons, while also cultivating techniques of parody and mimicry that influence later writers such as Butler, Dryden, Pope, and Swift.

But verse satire really gets going during the Restoration years. Robert Hume insists that, in the history of satire, the reign of Charles II (1660–1685) should be viewed as a discrete period in which satire is still marked by the divisions of the mid-century, and its main functions are "political combat and personal abuse."[8] The comedy of the newly reopened Restoration theaters incorporates bawdy joking and lampoons directed at individuals, and any notion of Augustan "decorum" can hardly apply to the raunchy, gossipy, and abusive satire of the Carolean years. Among the most popular poems of these years is Samuel Butler's long narrative *Hudibras*, which uses tetrameters ("Hudibrastics") rather than heroic pentameters and imitates Cervantes rather than Juvenal or Horace. Butler's knight Hudibras and his squire Ralpho, based on Quixote and Sancho, mock the low-church sects of Presbyterians and Independents, and the poem presents Puritan beliefs as outdated in the manner of the old chivalric tales.[9] On the other side of the religious–political divide, Andrew Marvell's *Last Instructions to a Painter* portrays Charles II's court as rife with sexual decadence (which it was) and attacks Charles's management of the recent war against the Dutch. John Oldham's anti-Catholic *Satires on Jesuits*, meanwhile, revives the hot-tempered style of the Elizabethan years, putting self-incriminating monologues into the mouths of nefarious Jesuit speakers who conspire against Protestant England.

But the signature verse satire of the Restoration came from within the court of Charles II. There a "loose fraternity" of aristocrats called the "Court Wits,"[10] including the Duke of Buckingham, the Earl of Dorset, Sir George Etherege, and Sir Charles Sedley, famous for their "exploits in taverns and boudoirs," wrote the bawdy, often obscene poetry that Harold Love has called "clandestine satire." Published scribally, recited orally, or printed in secret, clandestine satire existed at the beginning of the seventeenth century in the courts of James I and Charles I, but in the court of Charles II it reaches new heights (or depths), functioning as "an instrument of factional warfare within [the royal] court" as writer-courtiers compete for political power, social status, and sexual conquests.[11] The explicit sexuality of this poetry is part of the era's backlash against the severity of the Puritan interregnum, and the poetry overlaps in tone and content with the risqué comedies of Restoration playwrights such as William Wycherley. To judge the Court Wits merely as "cynics, skeptics, libertines, Epicureans, pagans, and atheists" may be unfair, but they clearly disdain the old religious and moral codes.[12]

The leading poet of this circle was John Wilmot, Earl of Rochester. His popular reputation is that of a rake, due to the explicitness of his poetry and the scandals of his personal life. A 1679 satire by the Earl of Mulgrave and John Dryden describes him as "thought to have a tail and cloven feet" and "Mean in each motion, lewd in ev'ry limb."[13] What contemporaries considered lewd, however, readers today are more likely to find misogynistic: time and again Rochester describes women as "whores" and "cunts," sexually omnivorous and cruelly fickle. Yet while his attention to genitals and fluids can seem crude or adolescent, the ludic quality of his poetry can (as in Rabelais) mitigate the offensiveness, and Rochester balances vulgar content with graceful prosody and a tone that can even attain elegance.[14]

Many of Rochester's long poems are written in iambic couplets and continue Roman traditions of formal verse satire, while many more deploy ballad and lyric forms with satiric content. "A Ramble in St. James's Park" features the kind of public space seen in Donne, where classes and social types mix profligately, here in a Hefneresque grotto:

> Unto this all-sin-shelt'ring grove,
> Whores of the bulk and the alcove,
> Great Ladies, chamber-maids, and drudges,
> The rag-picker, and heiress trudges;
> Car-men, divines, great Lords, and tailors,
> Prentices, poets, pimps and gaolers,
> Foot-men, fine fops, do here arrive
> And here promiscuously they swive [fuck].   (77.25–32)

Rough tetrameters and comic feminine rhymes ("Had she picked out to rub her arse on / Some stiff-pricked clown or well-hung parson" (78.91–92)) give the poem a casual feel suitable to the subgenre of the ramble, in which a man explores the city seeking alcohol and women. But when the speaker is forsaken by his lover Corinna for three (!) rivals, frivolous lewdness turns to furious cursing in the tradition of Archilochus: "May stinking vapours choke your womb" (79.133). The female body, Corinna's "devouring cunt" (79.119), becomes, like the park itself, a site of indiscriminate mixing.[15] The woman thus represents the risky, haphazard exchanges of urban modernity, while the emotional arc of the poem, with its teasing opening and intensifying rage, produces a rhythm in which satiric outburst substitutes for sexual release, and compensates for erotic rejection.

"A Letter from Artemiza in the Town to Chloe in the Country" offers a more refined rehearsal of such attacks on hypersexual women and the risks of erotic attachment. The subgenre of the letter or epistle goes back to Horace, but Rochester's poem also looks forward to novelists like Smollett and Austen, whose characters use letters to share the gossip of town and country.[16] Artemiza offers Chloe an account of a "Fine Lady" – a caricature of a fashionable London woman – who in turn relates a moral exemplum about (another) Corinna. All three women – Artemiza, the Lady, Corinna – describe or embody the flawed values of the city, where love is "debauched by ill-bred customs" (64.39), and women choose the "action" of sex over the "passion" of love (65.63). Woman appears as both wise and impertinent, a "mixed thing" (67.148) given only a portion of sense. As such, she resembles the Fine Lady's pet monkey, a "dirty chatt'ring monster" (67.141), whose position near the borders of the human anticipates the Yahoos of *Gulliver's Travels.*

Dealing with such mixtures of wisdom and impertinence, the reader must scrutinize the morals and maxims drawn on every level of the poem. The life of the ruined Corinna first appears as a simple *"memento mori* to the rest" (69.202), but she evolves into a villain who manipulates a naïve fool from the country to be her lover. Yet a residual compassion shifts our judgment from Corinna to the larger sexual ideology that compels her to behave as she does. Artemiza's characterization of love as "That cordial drop Heav'n in our Cup has thrown, / To make the nauseous draught of Life go down" (64.44–45), with the sexual innunendo of "drop" and "cup," must be understood as the sentiment of a speaker made cynical by town life, moralizing as she gossips. Thus, whether you read the poem as a misogynistic Juvenalian satire or a rebuke to the male fool, its final anecdote paints a grim picture. Artemiza drily presents the demise of all the characters as the handiwork of an ironically providential "Nature" who "Wisely provides kind-keeping fools, no doubt, / To patch up vices men of wit wear out" (70.254–255). Woman's redemption is achieved only by man's ruin.

For all their ribaldry, Rochester's satires attain a philosophical depth. A reader of Hobbes and Lucretius, Rochester was drawn to the new materialist philosophy of his age. The rhyming tercets of "Upon Nothing" narrate a mock cosmogony in which the concept of "nothing" evolves from a name for an ontological void – "thou elder brother even to shade" (46.1) – to a synonym for myriad social evils:

> The great man's gratitude to his best friend
> Kings' promises, whores' vows – towards thee they bend,
> Flow swiftly into thee, and in thee ever end.   (48.49–51)

In its rapid spiral from theological parody to political and social satire, the poem links the origin of the universe to the petty deceptions of daily life.

The greatest of Rochester's philosophical satires is "A Satyr against Reason and Mankind." Modeled on the eighth satire of Rochester's French contemporary Nicolas Boileau, the poem uses the comparison of man and animal to investigate human nature. What are these "strange prodigious creatures" (57.2) called men? Are we made in the image of God? Do we sit "above" the animals in a great cosmological chain of being, or are we merely one more kind of beast? Even the gesture of asking such questions is called into question, for the speaker reasons against reason – a faculty whose possession only puffs up human pride: "This supernatural gift that makes a mite / Think he's the image of the infinite" (59.76–77). Reason separates us from body, action, and pleasure. The opening sequence, an allegory of human aspiration, concludes by observing that man's "wisdom did his happiness destroy / Aiming to know that world he should enjoy" (58.33–34).

In the tradition of classical satire, Rochester's speaker expatiates on abstract propositions with anecdotes, and shares the stage with an interlocutor. But the interlocutor, a moralistic churchman, raises our suspicions when he leaps on the bandwagon to condemn "this jibing, jingling knack called wit" (58.49) and sententiously proclaims the nobility of his species: "Blest glorious Man! To whom alone kind Heaven / An everlasting soul has freely given" (58.60–61). In response, the speaker is forced to distinguish his own "right reason," which acknowledges the needs of the body, from the preacher's (false) reason, which denies them. The speaker's most blistering satire then erupts in the final section, a quasi-Hobbesian argument that man can extricate himself from a state of all against all only by preying on his fellow man. Like Mandeville decades later, Rochester reduces the noblest human qualities to perversions of survival instincts – "honesty's against all common sense; / Men must be knaves, 'tis in their own defence" (61.159–160); like Swift in *Gulliver's Travels*, he views man's pittance of reason as a feeble adaptation that equips him but poorly for survival.

The Mock Heroic

The late seventeenth century sees the emergence of a major new subgenre, the mock heroic. Sometimes called the mock epic, it is defined by the use of epic style, tropes, and allusions in the treatment of a modern, unheroic, or trivial subject. Parodies of heroic genres have an ancient history, but the mock heroic as a distinct literary genre can be dated from Nicolas Boileau's *Le Lutrin* ("The Lectern") in 1674, after which it quickly becomes ubiquitous.[17] Yet mock heroic is not easy to analyze. Even among the most canonical works, there exists a variety of form and technique, with tonal possibilities that range from epic grandeur to slapstick comedy. Nor is there consensus as to its relation to the epic proper. Some argue that the mock heroic evokes the epic as a lost standard of excellence, some that it attacks the style and values of the epic,[18] some that it merely inhabits the epic as a convenient host form.

Dryden suggests in his "Discourse" that satire should be a lofty genre: he praises Boileau's fusion of satiric "venom" with epic "sublimity" (107) and Juvenal's noble zeal for "Roman Liberty" (108).[19] His own *Absalom and Achitophel* (1681), moreover, demonstrates how close satire can hew to an epic style and theme. It tells the biblical story of King David and his son Absalom, but correlates the mythical characters and events to the Popish Plot and the Exclusion Crisis. (In the Popish Plot, Protestant opponents of King Charles II falsely alleged a plot by Charles's Catholic brother James to assassinate the monarch and assume the throne. In the Exclusion Crisis, Parliament sought to exclude James from succession to the throne and establish a claim for the Duke of Monmouth.) The poem is thus epic, allegory, and political commentary all at once: David stands for Charles, Absalom for his illegitimate son Monmouth, and Achitophel for his enemy the Earl of Shaftesbury.

Yet for all its epic ambitions, *Absalom* is a partisan political poem, one written "in passionate support of the king in the midst of a dangerous political crisis" (*PSE* 291). Despite the artistry, Dryden's aims were propagandistic, his satire directed at individuals. And while his defense of Charles does not spare the king, the thrust of the attack is against Monmouth and his supporters. The technique is caricature. Zimri, who represents the Duke of Buckingham, displays a fluid, "various" nature that embodies the fickle populace, "Stiff in Opinions, always in the wrong; / . . . everything by starts, and nothing long" (545, 547–548). Shimei, who represents the Sheriff of London, is corrupt and hypocritical:

> *Shimei*, whose Youth did early Promise bring
> Of Zeal to God, and Hatred to his King;
> Did wisely from Expensive Sins refrain,
> And never broke the Sabbath but for Gain:
> Nor ever was he known an Oath to vent,
> Or Curse, unless against the Government.   (585–590)

Over and over, Dryden sets up the reader with the language of praise, then undercuts it with an appended phrase: "*and* hatred to his king," "*but* for gain," "*unless* against the government." Most elegant of all is the understated "expensive": the word alliterates gracefully with the rest of the line but its presence overturns the entire meaning.

The poem's villain is Achitophel, whom Dryden associates with Milton's Satan, another gifted rhetorician.[20] As in Milton's epic, the reader must sniff out the fallacies in the characters' arguments – first those of Achitophel and later those of Absalom as well. When Absalom is seduced to revolt, the alert reader will detect the bad logic disclosed by the satanic oxymoron of "godlike sin":[21]

> I find, I find my mounting Spirits Bold,
> And *David*'s Part disdains my Mothers mold.
> Why am I Scanted by a Niggard Birth?
> My Soul Disclaims the Kindred of her Earth:
> And made for empire, Whispers me within;
> Desire of Greatness is a Godlike Sin.   (367–372)

Achitophel similarly turns the truth upside-down. He fallaciously compares Absalom to the "Saviour" (240) and King David to Lucifer, "the Prince of Angels" (274). Through such gnarled logic, Dryden discredits the rebels and exposes the paradoxes of their politics. On a broader level, then, the target becomes political rhetoric itself – an Orwellian doublespeak or oxymoron in which "peace itself is War in Masquerade" (752). Indeed, the very idea of the revolt of a son against a father is a satiric inversion, as is Monmouth's ambition to inherit the throne while the king still lives (*SI* 146).

Lawful sexuality thus proves necessary for legitimate inheritance. The alternative to the lawful is "Nature's state; where all have Right to all" (794). Rochester offered a Hobbesian redescription of altruism as self-interest; here that Hobbesianism is placed in the mouth of the unreliable Achitophel, who urges Absalom not to be dissuaded from revolt by David's paternal love, which he demeans as "Nature's trick to Propagate her Kind" (424). But "Nature's trick" loses out to God's law, which affirms David's/Charles's legitimacy: "Once more the Godlike David was Restor'd, / And willing Nations knew their Lawfull Lord" (1030–1031). *Lord*, linked by alliteration to *Lawfull*, refers both to God and to the Godlike David; linked by end-rhyme to *Restor'd*, it buttresses the claim to legitimacy by recalling the Restoration of the monarchy in 1660. After satiric inversions and satanic fallacies, the poem concludes with epic hierarchy winning out over mock-epic misrule.

The tone of Dryden's *Mac Flecknoe: Or a Satyr upon the True-Blew-Protestant Poet, T.S.* (1682) is strikingly different. It is filled with slapstick gags, fat jokes, and bathroom humor, and its target is not the ominous threat of rebellion against King Charles, but the bad poetry of Thomas Shadwell, the all-but-named "T.S." of the title, presented as the successor to the almost-as-bad poet Richard Flecknoe. (About thirty years earlier, Marvell had satirized

Flecknoe in "Flecknoe, an English Priest at Rome.") Yet like *Absalom, Mac Flecknoe* is a story of succession and inheritance, and like *Absalom* it borrows from the epic in style and content. Epic conventions – the coronation, the vision of the empire to come – are invoked, but they are too grand for the subject, and the heroic veneer creates comic incongruities. *Mac Flecknoe* is cruder and wilder in its lampooning than *Absalom*, and its 217 lines reduce the epic adventure to a mere sketch.

The poem's basic joke is blame-by-praise, often through the simple substitution of an antonym for an expected word. Flecknoe, we learn, "In Prose and verse, was own'd, without dispute / Through all the Realms of *Non-Sense*, absolute" (6–7). Flecknoe's panegyric thus becomes Dryden's satire:

> Then thus, continu'd he, my Son advance
> Still in new Impudence, new Ignorance.
> Success let other teach, learn thou from me
> Pangs without birth, and fruitless Industry.   (145–148)

The success of this strung-out joke depends entirely on the deliberate misuse of the heroic style: the stateliness of the couplets steadily imparts an aura of grandeur that, ever-renewed, can be ever-undercut.

Dryden joins these ironies to comedy of the body. Shadwell is not only fat – "his goodly Fabrick fills the eye" (25) – but, through the abbreviation of his name, identified with shit:

> From dusty shops neglected Authors come,
> Martyrs of Pies, and Reliques of the Bum.
> Much *Heywood, Shirly, Ogleby* there lay,
> But loads of *Sh* – – almost choakt the way.   (100–103)

Shadwell's poetry, and that of his ilk, is best used to line a pie plate or serve as toilet paper. In a sense, then, *Mac Flecknoe* is an oblique *ars poetica*, a guide to good writing, and it sorts out worthy and unworthy poets. Thus Shadwell's "inoffensive Satyrs never bite" (200), and he is too weak to handle the deadly weaponry of Archilochean "Iambicks," resorting instead to the vapid word-games of "Anagram" (204) and "Acrostick" (206).

Flecknoe's final indignity – disappearing mid-sentence through a trap-door – mocks the slapstick gags that Shadwell himself used in his stage comedies. His passage downward through an excremental chute, accompanied by the upward passage of "wind" (215), confirms the mock heroic as a genre for the low comedy of cartooning and lampooning. Bad writing is identified with sexual and excremental pollution, and Dryden himself takes "polluted joys" (71) in identifying the poetry of Shadwell with physical filth and noxious gas.

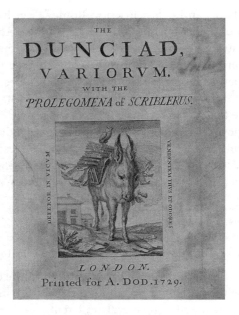

THE

DUNCIAD,

VARIORVM.

WITH THE

PROLEGOMENA of *SCRIBLERUS.*

LONDON.
Printed for A. DOD.1729.

Figure 8 Frontispiece, *The Dunciad Variorum*, 1729. The New York Public Library Digital Collections, Henry W. and Albert A. Berg Collection of English and American Literature. The frontispiece to Pope's *Dunciad Variorum* shows an ass bearing a heavy stack of printed matter. In the poem, the explosion of print has become an existential threat to the polity.

The same combination of celebration and revulsion animates Alexander Pope's *The Dunciad* (Figure 8). First published in 1728, reissued the next year with an elaborate mock-scholarly apparatus as *The Dunciad Variorum*, published yet again in 1743 with a fourth book, *The Dunciad* pushes the themes and techniques of *Mac Flecknoe* as far as they can go. Like *Mac Flecknoe*, the poem describes, in a style modeled on Virgil and Milton, the coronation of a king of bad poetry (Lewis Theobald in the earlier version, Colley Cibber in the later). Pope's attack on literary enemies opens onto an indictment of an entire culture. In the *Dunciad Variorum*, Pope's fictional editor, Martinus Scriblerus, describes the explosion of commercial publishing that had occurred in the half-century since Dryden's poem, creating a permissive and dangerous world in which "Paper ... became so cheap, and printers so numerous, that a deluge of authors cover'd the land." These authors "would forthwith publish slanders unpunish'd, the authors being anonymous" (344). The explosion of print has become an existential threat to the polity.

As in *Mac Flecknoe*, all this bad writing is associated with human waste. The ceremonial games that accompany Cibber's coronation include a diving contest that takes place in Fleet Ditch, a sewer which "with disemboguing streams, / Rolls the large tribute of dead dogs to Thames" (2.271–272). The bookseller Edmund Curll gains strength through a gift of feces from the goddess of sewage:

> Renew'd by ordure's sympathetic force,
> As oil'd with magic juices for the course,
> Vig'rous he rises; from th' effluvia strong;
> Imbibes new life, and scours and stinks along[.]   (2.103–106)

Through it all, the narrative never drops its heroic pretensions.

Pope's targets include Eliza Haywood, Daniel Defoe, Bernard Mandeville, and scores of others. Most are Whigs; all are part of the new Grub Street world of commercial publishing. Their grotesque writings rush out from a cave located, fittingly, near the throne of Folly, the Erasmian goddess:

> Hence Miscellanies spring, the weekly boast
> Of Curll's chaste press, and Lintot's rubric post:
> Hence hymning Tyburn's elegiac lines,
> Hence Journals, Medleys, Merc'ries, Magazines;
> Sepulchral Lies, our holy walls to grace,
> And New-year Odes, and all the Grub-street race.   (1.39–44)

In opposition to these Grub Street writers, critics, and booksellers, Pope hails his friend Jonathan Swift, the poem's dedicatee, whom he compares to Rabelais and Cervantes (1.21–22).

The disorder of Grub Street is representative of an emerging capitalist world marked by confusion, change, and waste; and through the goddess Dulness, queen and mother of the modern horde of hacks, Pope codes the sewage-filled city and the noisy public sphere as female.[22] Dulness's body, like London, is excessively generative, producing a flood of rejectamenta: "A motley mixture! in long wigs, in bags, / In silks, in crapes, in Garters, and in rags" (2.21–22). As social hierarchies are confused so are literary categories: "Tragedy and Comedy embrace" while "Farce and Epic [be]get a jumbled race" (1.69–70). There is of course irony in the fact that this condemnation comes from the author of a hybrid mock heroic said to be the first modern commercial author: Pope participates in the very scene he disavows (*DSM* 23).

Dulness, for her part, brings into being long lists of non-entities, reminiscent of Rochester's "Upon Nothing":

> the Fool's Paradise, the Statesman's Scheme,
> The air-built Castle, and the golden Dream,
> The Maid's romantic wish, the Chemist's flame,
> And Poet's vision of eternal Fame.   (3.9–12)

Like the South Sea Bubble of 1720 driven by empty credit, the Empire of Dulness is built on air.[23] Her final restoration seems a dark parody of *Absalom and Achitopel*'s affirmation of Charles II: "Lo! thy dread Empire, CHAOS! is restor'd / Light dies before thy uncreating word" (4.653–654). Her imperial expansion is a regression, and Pope's bad writers produce only misbirths. Fittingly, her reign concludes with a vision of annihilation in which "Universal Darkness buries All" (4. 656). But perhaps the bleakest moment of the poem (so jubilant in its ridicule) is a moment of *catascopia* where we discern that for most of human existence ignorance has ruled. "Science" (meaning knowledge in general) has only illumined a narrow portion of the globe for a tiny span of years:

> How little, mark! that portion of the ball,
> Where, faint at best, the beams of Science fall:
> Soon as they dawn, from Hyperborean skies
> Embodied dark, what clouds of Vandals rise!   (3.83–86)

Pope gives content to the existential nothingness of Rochester; dullness becomes the "embodied dark" of barbarism.

Absalom and Achitophel, then, shadows the epic; *Mac Flecknoe* and *The Dunciad* invert it. The most famous mock-heroic poem, *The Rape of the Lock*, miniaturizes it, turning it into a comedy of manners. The poem still deploys the conventions and language of the epic: Ariel echoes Milton's Satan; Belinda, Virgil's Dido; Clarissa, Homer's Sarpedon. But rather than savaging the filthy chaos of "the Grub Street race," the poem drolly tweaks the refined world of London's upper classes. The story is based on a real act of hair-theft that sparked a feud between two prominent Catholic families; Pope's professed aim was "to make a jest of it, and laugh them together again."[24] The initial audience, in other words, was an elite in-group, and the poem feels like a private drawing-room performance rather than a bold sally into a tempestuous public sphere. From the invocation to the apotheosis, Pope carefully fits his epic apparatus to a delicate social setting. Indeed, Pope's couplets, with their intricacy and sheen, appear as exquisite *objets d'art* in their own right, fully of a piece with this glittering, opulent world.

Pope does provide glimpses of a world beyond the romantic concerns of its *beau-monde*, and it is a dark world in which animal appetites win out over justice for the poor: "The hungry Judges soon the Sentence sign, / And Wretches hang that Jury-men may Dine" (3.21–22). There are similar dangers permeating Hampton Court, where polite chatter masks a deadly game of jockeying for sexual opportunity and social status: "One speaks the Glory of the *British Queen*, / And one describes a charming *Indian Screen*. / A third interprets Motions, Looks, and Eyes; / At ev'ry Word a Reputation dies" (3.13–16). Words here are as lethal as the curses of Archilochus, and they provide a dark and dangerous backdrop to the light and frothy action of the poem.

But while words in *The Rape of the Lock* can kill, they can also entertain. Pope's famous periphrases – his use of inflated language to describe the ordinary – make the mock heroic into a parlor game. Much as Swift challenges the reader to figure out the objects in Gulliver's pockets from the Lilliputians' descriptions, so Pope uses the epic style to tease the reader. When he writes, "From silver Spouts the grateful Liquors glide, / And *China*'s Earth receives the smoking Tyde" (3.109–110), he is describing only the pouring of tea into a porcelain cup. The puzzling union of a tortoise and an elephant turns out to be the placement of tortoise-shell and ivory combs in the heroine's hair.

What the poem most thoroughly redescribes, of course, are the mysteries of female beauty and the vagaries of female affection, "the moving Toyshop of their Heart" (1.100). Rituals of dress and make-up, "the sacred Rites of Pride" (1.128), are normally kept hidden from the male gaze, but now "stand displayed" (1.121). To represent the social forces that produce normative femininity, Pope added in 1714 the poem's supernatural "machinery" – the sylphs, gnomes, sprites, and salamanders. These small-time versions of the Greco-Roman gods create the nymph as an object of desire, while schooling her in sexual modesty. How do young women learn the arts of flirtation?

> 'Tis [Gnomes] that early taint the Female Soul,
> Instruct the Eyes of young *Coquettes* to roll,
> Teach Infant-Cheeks a bidden Blush to know,
> And little Hearts to flutter at a *Beau*.   (1.87–90)

What protects maidens from predatory rakes?

> 'Tis but their *Sylph*, the wise Celestials know,
> Tho' *Honour* is the Word with Men below.   (1.77–78)

For *Volpone*'s Corvino honor is but a breath; here honor names an equally airy social code.

Another satiric trope of the poem is zeugma, which uses one verb in two senses to yoke disparate elements. Pope uses it to link the lightness of the characters' social concerns with the heavy moral issues at stake in their flirtations. Below, the verbs *stain* and *lose* each take two direct objects very different in value:

> Whether the Nymph shall break *Diana*'s Law,
> Or some frail *China* Jar receive a Flaw,
> Or stain her Honour, or her new Brocade,
> Forget her Pray'rs, or miss a Masquerade,
> Or lose her Heart, or Necklace, at a Ball;
> Or whether Heav'n has doom'd that *Shock* must fall.   (2.105–110)

"Dire" moral losses and "trivial" material ones – stained honor and a stained brocade, a lost heart and a lost necklace – stand side by side, as if to say that Belinda cannot tell the difference. Yet even as it makes its moral point, the passage also teases us with risqué, proto-Freudian symbolism: a "jar" is a curvy, feminine receptacle; the loss of virginity entails a "stain"; the "Shock" (of hair) who sits in Belinda's lap may suggest something else furry concealed beneath (*SI* 229–230).[25] The reader's moral judgment and voyeurism are evoked simultaneously.

Belinda again fails to make the right distinctions when she tries to draw a moral from the rape of her hair. When she first laments her fate, she wins approval for her desire to withdraw from the public eye. But the reader's sympathy dissolves into scandalized laughter with the inadvertent double entendre that ends her speech:

> Oh hadst thou, Cruel! been content to seize
> Hairs less in sight, or any Hairs but these!   (4.175–176)

The value of beauty has supplanted the value of sexual virtue, as Belinda seems to prefer a real rape to a bad hair day.

Critics debate whether Pope blames Belinda for withholding herself sexually from the Baron, or, alternatively, for nurturing a secret desire for the Baron or another lover. Likewise they disagree over how much authority to vest in Clarissa's speech, which was added, as a note to a 1736 edition claims, "to open more clearly the MORAL of the poem" (5.7n). Is her speech "the moral center" of the poem?[26] Or, is she, as the one who gives the Baron his scissors and a rival to Belinda, an interested and untrustworthy party? Is the poem openly didactic in espousing the superiority of "good sense" and "good humour" over "beauty"? Or is the notion of "a clear moral reading" fraught with "difficulty, perhaps ... absurdity"?[27] If Clarissa does speak for Pope, is his lesson a good one, or does it affirm a patriarchy in which women must capitulate to the marriage economy? Perhaps Pope simply uses Clarissa's banal moral truth as the springboard for his poetic acrobatics?

Pope dodges some of these questions through the final gesture of apotheosis. Time turns all locks to gray, but the poet's magic evades time and death by transforming the lock into a heavenly constellation – and transforming the social squabble into a fabled contest. The mock heroic here whisks everyday matters into the protected sphere of the mythical. The work of this subgenre may then be, as Christian Thorne suggests, "to solve at the level of genre ideological problems that can no longer be addressed at the level of argument," combining the mundane and the fabulous. Whether in the anti-sublime of the *Dunciad* or the mini-sublime of the *Rape*, the mock heroic removes Pope from a dangerous public space (Grub Street, Hampton Court) even as he describes that space with intimate knowledge. He can occupy the paradoxical position of being both epic and modern. Through the epic tone he offers a fading "afterimage of traditional, authoritarian ideals" at the very moment when those ideals are being superseded.[28] The *Rape* satirizes the frivolous flights of female affection by consecrating them.

The tension between "mock" and "heroic" in *The Rape of the Lock* thus marks a bifurcation. On the one hand, the secret truths of the heart that it analyzes will become the subject matter of the very genre that Pope dismisses in his 1714 dedication – the novel. On the other hand, the outer shell of the epic will contain ever-more-trivial matters; the heroic couplet becomes a vehicle for parody and light verse, and Pope becomes the godfather of modern camp.[29] After Pope, the eighteenth century sees many more mock epics – "more than 200 titles ending in –*iad*," including *The Scribleriad* (1752), *The Hilliad* (1753), *The Smartiad* (1753), *The Rosciad* (1761), *The Lousiad* (1786), *The Baviad* (1792), and *The Maeviad* (1795) – but they have faded into literary history, often as topical squabbles and jokes.[30]

Battles of the Sexes

The treatment of sex and gender in Augustan verse satire speaks to changing social conditions. The rising wealth and leisure of the middle and upper classes, brought on by global conquest and trade, led to new stereotypes of women as idle, narcissistic consumers (such as Pope's Belinda). Male writers perpetuated the long anti-feminist tradition of Juvenal's notorious sixth satire, even as Augustan decorum (sometimes) replaced the Renaissance vilification of women as fiends and monsters with a patronizing gallantry.[31] Nonetheless, for several decades newly empowered women poets had been able to respond to anti-feminist satire in kind. Beginning in the late seventeenth century, Aphra Behn, Sarah Fyge Egerton, Lady Mary Wortley Montagu, Anne Finch, and others took up the pen to defend their sex. For example, Robert Gould's harsh and obscene *Love Given O're: Or, A Satyr against the Pride, Lust, and Inconstancy of Woman* (1682) launched "a satiric paper war between the sexes" that lasted twenty years; in one skirmish, Egerton's *The Female Advocate* (1686) – written when she was Sarah Fyge, still a teenager – rebuts Gould's charges and levels its own accusations against men.[32] Such female authorship posed a new threat to the privileged position of male writers, and, in reaction to women's exhibition of learning and wit, male satirists and critics linked wit in women to promiscuity and social entropy.[33]

Pope was at the center of many such paper wars. "To a Lady," the second of his *Moral Essays* (1735), proceeds through a series of caricatures of women. The reader of *The Rape of the Lock* recognizes among these the stereotype of the woman as consumer of material goods, concerned more with possessions than with passion:

> She, while her Lover pants upon her breast,
> Can mark the figures on an Indian chest;
> And when she sees her Friend in deep despair,
> Observes how much a Chintz exceeds Mohair.   (167–170)

Pope cloaks his bitterness in gallantry as he praises his friend Martha Blount as a positive counter-example, even crediting her with the thesis of the poem's argument, "Most Women have no Characters at all" (2), and thereby recruiting her to testify against her own sex. The ruse indeed typifies how the new tone of courtesy could reinforce gender roles. Yet it could not disarm women poets such as Anne Ingram, Lady Irwin, whose "Epistle to Mr. Pope" responded by arguing that women's faults result from their exclusion from formal education.

A more heated paper war took place between Pope and Lady Mary Wortley Montagu. Montagu was a neighbor and former friend of Pope's; what soured the relationship is uncertain. One story relates that Montagu burst into laughter when the diminutive, hunchbacked Pope declared his affections; another that, after borrowing bedsheets from Pope, she returned them unwashed.[34] Certainly their politics drifted apart, as Montagu was aligned with the Whig Minister Robert Walpole, the *bête noire* of Pope, Swift, and their circle.

According to Augustan protocols, satire was supposed to attack general types, not individuals, yet Pope regularly indulged harsh personal lampoons; *The Dunciad* (1728) is a virtually Nixonian enemies list. Pope's jabs at Montagu began in that work when he alluded to a financial scandal involving her and a French admirer named Nicolas-François Rémond. The enmity intensified over the next few years as Pope suspected Montagu's involvement in anonymous published satires that attacked him; a 1732 drama, *Mr. Taste, the Poetical Fop*, possibly written by Eliza Haywood, depicted a foolish poet named "Alex Taste" rejected in love by an aristocratic lady. Pope took some mild shots at Montagu in his *Epistle to Bathurst* in 1733, but it was in his imitation of Horace's Satire 2.1 that he drew blood with a couplet later called "unquotable":[35] "From furious *Sappho* scarce a milder Fate, / P-x'd by her Love, or libell'd by her Hate" (85–86). Montagu ("Sappho") had suffered smallpox and had bravely pioneered the practice of inoculation on her own children, but Pope uses her bout of "pox" to suggest syphilis.

Enraged, Montagu appears to have teamed up with another target of Pope's, Lord Hervey, a bisexual whom Pope had repeatedly ridiculed as the effeminate "Lord Fanny." Montagu and Hervey's *Verses Addressed to the Imitator of Horace* are, in the words of Montagu's biographer, "as crude and bludgeoning a lampoon as appeared in the pamphlet wars of the time."[36] They stress the differences between the Roman poet and his modern imitator. Unlike Horace, they claim, Pope writes only raillery, not satire; he possesses "the Rage but not the Talent of Abuse" (28); driven by misanthropy, he pursues the defenseless. They mock Pope's body too. Having suffered tuberculosis of the spine in childhood, Pope stood about four-foot-six; Montagu and Hervey sneer at his "wretched little Carcass" (70) and call him "our own Species in Burlesque" (13). They link his misshapen body to his ineffectual satire, riffing on the old idea, from Hall and Oldham, of the porcupine as symbol of satire:

> When fretful *Porcupine*, with rancorous Will,
> From mounted Back shoots forth a harmless Quill,
> Cool the Spectators stand; and all the while
> Upon the angry little Monster smile.
> Thus 'tis with thee: – whilst impotently safe,
> You strike unwounding, we unhurt can laugh.   (73–78)

Pope is inhuman, his satire impotent, his phallic "quill" powerless. Capable of neither affection nor sex, he is in two senses "No more for loving made than to be lov'd" (49). His crooked back is evidence of his "crooked Mind" (110), and his ugly books of his ugly body. Montagu and Hervey conclude with an Archilochean curse: "as thou hate'st, be hated by Mankind" (109).

The paper war raged for two years. Pope and some friends hit back, but Montagu also had allies: Hervey with his *Letter to a Doctor of Divinity* (1733) and the publisher Curll with *The Poet Finish'd in Prose* (1735), which described Pope as a masturbator who was afraid of being raped by Montagu. Pope, meanwhile, had in 1734 published a second Horatian imitation, of Satire 2.2, deriding Montagu and her husband for parsimony:

> *Avidien*, or his Wife (no matter which,
> For him you'll call a dog, and her a bitch,)
> Sell their presented Partridges, and Fruits,
> And humbly live on rabbits and on roots[.]   (49–52)

The frugal pair consider themselves lucky on finding a banknote or on learning that their son has drowned. In his *Epistle to Dr. Arbuthnot* later that year, Pope turned the brunt of his attack on Hervey in a ruthlessly homophobic caricature. Cast as Sporus, the castrated boy favorite of the Emperor Nero, Hervey takes to an extreme the neither-this-nor-that figure seen in Donne's courtier and Dryden's Zimri:

> Now high, now low, now Master up, now Miss,
> And he himself one vile Antithesis.
> Amphibious Thing! that acting either Part,
> The trifling Head, or the corrupted Heart!
> Fop at the Toilet, Flatt'rer at the Board,
> Now trips a Lady, and now struts a Lord.   (324–329)

The fop, an old satiric target, is here reviled as a sexual changeling. The attack, moreover, proceeds on an axis of class as well as sexuality: whereas Montagu and Hervey in their *Verses* had run down Pope for his "obscure" (20) – that is, middle-class – birth, Pope associates Hervey's aristocratic status with leisure, consumption, and effeminacy.[37] The skirmish can thus be understood as part of a struggle for cultural capital between aristocratic "amateurs" like Montagu and Hervey and professionals like Pope who wrote for a living. In 1735 Pope included further jabs against the filthy "Sappho" in "To a Lady" (24ff.), the whore "Sappho" in his imitation of Donne's second satire (6), and "a famous Lady" in a footnote in his reprinting of the *Dunciad*. Montagu, however, had the last laugh: she had Pope's name painted on the inside of her chamberpot so that well after his death, she could shit on him daily.[38]

If this story is to be trusted, right next to Pope's name on the pot was that of Swift, who was no stranger to scatological warfare. Among Swift's varied works are his so-called scatological poems. Written in the 1730s, poems such as "Cassinus and Peter," "A Beautiful Young Nymph Going to Bed," and "Strephon and Chloe," written in Hudibrastics, offer graphic and arguably misogynistic representations of the body that express and elicit both glee and revulsion. "A Beautiful Young Nymph," like *The Rape of the Lock*, enters the intimate space of the woman's boudoir, but whereas Pope's Belinda retains her glamour when dressing, Swift's Corinna, undressing at the end of her evening, is reduced to grotesquerie. She first takes off her "artificial hair" (10), then her "Chrystal Eye" (11), and soon dismantles her entire body – teeth, breasts, hips – rendering the adjectives of the poem's title thoroughly ironic. Yet the deadpan speaker never drops the fiction that Corinna is a "lovely Goddess" (23) and that he is but a modest observer.

Such ironies are multiplied in "The Lady's Dressing Room," which also enters the boudoir. In this case, however, the woman is absent, represented by the clutter of objects that are the metonymic extension of her body – clothes, combs, and pastes, but also bodily excrescences such as "Sweat, dandruff, powder, lead, and hair" (24). (Compare Belinda's less noxious "Puffs, powders, patches, bibles, billet-doux" (1.138) from the *Rape*.) The catalogue of secretions culminates in the discovery of the chamber pot that conceals Celia's feces, the ultimate emblem of her corporeality. The poem's horrified undoing of female beauty resembles Gulliver's horror at the maids of Brobdingnag, and Celia's magnifying glass provides a view of the blackheads in her skin much like Gulliver's close-up of the thick hairs and moles of the young giantesses.

Just like the falsely modest speaker in "A Beautiful Young Nymph," the speaker in "Dressing Room" tries to disavow his revulsion. To do this, he uses the surrogate figure of the "peeping" (120) voyeur Strephon. Strephon's "strict survey" (7) of the boudoir bears the classic traits of the anal retentive personality, and he becomes giddy when he literally gets his hands on the object of his revulsion:

> Thus finishing his grand survey,
> Disgusted Strephon stole away
> Repeating in his amorous fits,
> "Oh! Celia, Celia, Celia shits!"   (115–118)

Strephon's presence allows the speaker to pretend he doesn't share Strephon's fascination with women's excrescences. The speaker wants to preserve the impossible lie of his own ignorance of women's bodies – to maintain the gallant pose of the admirer of female beauty. Yet the reader sees through this thin fiction, and the poem therefore displays not only secrets of the dressing room but, as Fredric Bogel shows, the *structure* of satire: the use of Strephon shows how satire externalizes illicit desires so that they can be condemned (*DSM* 114–118).

Critics often attribute Swift's attention to women's excremental functions to personal neurosis, although it can equally be seen as the satirist's efforts to disabuse male readers of their own hangups and hypocrisies. Montagu, evidently, took the first view, and she responded to Swift's poem with "The Reasons That Induced Dr. Swift to Write a Poem Called the Lady's Dressing Room," an account of Swift's ostensible sexual failure with a prostitute that led to his attack on Celia. Montagu uses the same meter as Swift, the same tropes, and the same feigned propriety as she too voyeuristically enters a private space.[39] She too reveals a truth about the poetry that derives from a truth about the poet's body. In short, she unmasks Swift's unmasking. His poem, which purports to debunk female beauty, is itself debunked. In this case, however, the secret of the private room is not defecation but impotence:

> The Reverend Lover with surprize
> Peeps in her Bubbys and her Eyes,
> And kisses both and trys – and trys.   (63–65)

The language stalls and repeats its effort, to no avail; the triple rhyme emphasizes the lack of progress. Swift attempts to blame Betty instead of himself – "your damn'd Close stool so near my Nose, / Your Dirty Smock, and Stinking Toes" (70–71) – but Montagu has reduced Swift's satiric power to a symptom of biographical trauma. His male body is as defective as the hunchbacked Pope's is in her *Verses*. Swift's vow to "be reveng'd" (84) through satire is equally impotent. As Montagu wrote in an unpublished couplet that links his poetic and sexual failure:

> Perhaps you have not better Luck in
> The Knack of Rhyming than of –

Thus the whore gets the last word: "I'm glad you'll write, / You'll furnish paper when I shite" (88–89), dragging Swift down with her as she reduces his satire to what Dryden called "relics of the bum." Like Swift, Montagu splits her persona: she assigns the crudest insults to the whore, while her speaker adopts a high-minded tone.

Taken together, these paper wars demonstrate satire's materialist tendency to ground ideas in the physical human body, and to use the sexual and the scatological as an antidote to false idealizations. They also demonstrate satire's inherent tendency toward provocation and debate – the antagonistic orientation of its speech acts, which serve to make (other people's) private business public. Finally, they testify to an increased freedom for women writers to take part in satiric exchange, to enter a public sphere with language both indecorous and witty.

Late Phases: Johnson, Churchill, Byron, Walcott

Verse satire declines in cultural centrality after the deaths of Swift and Pope, and of their favorite political target, Robert Walpole. One recent scholar calls the verse satire of the later eighteenth century "a series of footnotes to the *Dunciad*," and despite the efforts of the canon-busters to call attention to understudied writers, the diminutive Pope still casts a long literary shadow.[40]

One successor, Samuel Johnson, produced two important satires, *London* (1738) and *The Vanity of Human Wishes* (1749), both of which imitate Juvenal: *London* the third satire, *Human Wishes* the tenth. The imitation was a popular subgenre; in it, an original, usually a classical text, is adapted to the formal conventions of English poetry (e.g. heroic couplets), and its references updated with examples from the modern world. Imitation closely resembles poetic translation, which had come to reject slavish fidelity in an effort to make an ancient work relevant to a modern readership, and also parody, which in the eighteenth century did not necessarily connote mockery.[41] Johnson attributes the origin of the imitation to Oldham and Rochester; the latter, in his "Allusion to Horace," modernizes Horace's Satire 1.10, casting himself as the graceful Horace and Dryden as the clumsy Lucilius. Byron's "Hints from Horace," an imitation of his predecessor's *Ars Poetica*, offers a late example. The prominence of the imitation reminds us that, against the Romantic ideal of "originality," eighteenth-century aesthetics valued "invention," which in its root sense means *finding*; the ancients provided an inventory where ideas and tropes could be found.

London displays the stylistic influence of Pope in its sharply cut couplets. Johnson's theme, like Juvenal's, is the danger of urban life (fire, crime, accident); on a deeper level it indicts the corruption and greed that have eroded civic virtue. Many of Juvenal's references are updated easily: as Rome becomes England, Greece becomes France, a pernicious influence on the national character. Johnson's French are talented actors who can be all things to all people, able

> To shake with laughter ere the jest they hear,
> To pour at will the counterfeited tear[.]   (141–142)

Under French influence, London has lost its English character and become "The common shore of Paris and of Rome" (94). (A "common shore" is a sewer – and perhaps also a "common whore.") Dominated by commerce, the city is a place "Where looks are merchandise, and smiles are sold" (178–179); the malign looks and whispers of *The Rape of the Lock* are now converted into currency. Thus Johnson's Thales, just like Juvenal's Umbricius, announces his departure for the country. In other ways, however, Johnson aggressively alters Juvenal's original to modern conditions, particu-larizing Juvenal's complaints into a political attack on Walpole; the market for invective against the prime minister was still robust in 1738. Thales bemoans policy toward Spain, the pro-Walpole *Daily Gazetteer*, taxes, and pensions.[42] Johnson thus ably uses the shadow of Juvenal to have it both ways. He launches a modern partisan attack on the Walpole government, while endow-ing that attack with the *gravitas* of his classical precursor.[43]

The Vanity of Human Wishes, written a decade later, is a more philosophi-cal poem. It announces its panoramic survey of all human affairs with a geographical scope suited to the imperial expansiveness of the age: "Let observation with extensive view, / Survey mankind, from China to Peru" (1–2). The comprehensiveness of the poem is temporal as well, as Johnson retains classical examples from Juvenal but supplements them with new ones from modern history. All human strivings – political power, scholarly learn-ing, military glory, old age, beauty – are shown to end in disappointment. Juvenal's grotesque, scatological detail is gone, and with it the garish color; instead Johnson offers compressed abstraction, and rounds off his historical examples with neat maxims. The conclusion to his account of Charles XII of Sweden, the defeated military hero, has become proverbial: "He left the name, at which the world grew pale, / To point a moral, or adorn a tale" (221–222). In an irony of fate, Charles appalls the world not because of his triumphs but because of his defeat. Some critics have seen tragedy, or "tragical satire," in these examples, and Johnson's bracing vision makes the model of Democritus – invoked unproblematically in Juvenal – a troubling one. Johnson summons the laughing philosopher to provide "instructive mirth" (50), but then wonders whether the present age might not be too bleak even for his "philosophic eye" (64).

Johnson also Christianizes the pagan Juvenal. His title invokes the verses of Ecclesiastes from the Hebrew Bible ("all is vanity"), and his ending enjoins the reader to look heavenward: "Inquirer, cease! petitions yet remain, / Which heaven may hear, nor deem religion vain" (349–350). Such petitions, Howard Weinbrot argues, are spiritual rather than human wishes, and therefore not to be deemed "vain." From the lofty perspective of its opening, the poem had rapidly descended into a "clouded maze of fate" (6), reminiscent of the "Pathless and dangerous wand'ring ways" of Rochester's "Satyr against Reason and Mankind" (57.14). But once he finds religious faith, man is no longer "without a guide" (8).[44] The Stoic Juvenal asked for a sound mind in a sound body; he counsels the reader *not* to put his faith in the fickle deity Fortune.[45] The Christian Johnson, in contrast, insists that "celestial wisdom calms the mind, / And makes the happiness she does not find" (367–368).

Nonetheless, the section advocating religious faith is short, and feels tacked on to its long, pessimistic survey of human endeavors. The bleakness of the satire survives the consolation that the ending offers.[46] For Johnson's satire cannot be confined to any special class of fools or knaves. No one, for example, escapes the ravages of old age:

> everlasting dictates crowd his tongue,
> Perversely grave, or positively wrong;
> The still returning tale, and lingering jest,
> Perplex the fawning niece and pampered guest[.] (279–282)

As with the Struldbrugs in *Gulliver's Travels*, age brings only mounting indignities. Yet the universalism of human vanity produces, nonetheless, a compassion for the poem's subjects. Johnson's satire refuses the sadistic laughter that Pope and Swift exhibit when castigating their targets. Already in *London*, Johnson expressed reticence about satire's cruelty:

> Of all the griefs that harass the distressed,
> Sure the most bitter is a scornful jest;
> Fate never wounds more deep the generous heart,
> Than when a blockhead's insult points the dart. (166–169)

In *Human Wishes*, famous fallen men such as Cardinal Wolsey or Charles XII are extended compassion even as they serve as examples of vain wishing. These are not sketches or caricatures but portraits.

Johnson's stance is often seen as symptomatic of a historical shift in cultural attitudes toward satire. Beginning with Shaftesbury, Addison, and Steele in the early part of the century, dissenting voices question the harshness of the satiric temper, and the second half of the century sees the rise of a "cult of sensibility." The new genre of the novel, with its psychologizing tendencies, undermines the hard, public judgments of the Augustans. Still, the novelists Henry Fielding and Tobias Smollett both wrote verse satire, as did mid-century figures including Christopher Smart, Christopher Antsey, and William Cowper. Satire in these decades offers light entertainment, moral instruction, and attacks on literary rivals, but for the most part it retreats from the front lines of partisan warfare, becoming "a literary performance rather than a practical enterprise" (*PSE* 250). It becomes more self-conscious and uncertain about its own aggression, mellowing into humor.[47]

One exception to the new mellower tone is Charles Churchill, who, allied with the journalist and politician John Wilkes in the 1760s, attacked the Tory prime minister Lord Bute through their radical newspaper *The North Briton*. Churchill and Wilkes engaged in a bare-knuckled paper war with Bute's supporter William Hogarth. Churchill's "Epistle to William Hogarth" (1763) portrays the greatest of caricaturists as a palsied dotard squandering the remains of his genius in petty, malicious attacks. Churchill's own malice, meanwhile, rivals in intensity the bitterest of Pope's broadsides:

> Virtue, with due contempt, saw Hogarth stand,
> The murd'rous pencil in his palsied hand.
> What was the cause of Liberty to him,
> Or what was Honour? Let them sink or swim,
> So he may gratify without control
> The mean resentments of his selfish soul.[48]

Hogarth produced in response "The Bruiser," a satiric drawing of Churchill as a drooling, drunken bear looking on as Hogarth's dog pisses on the *Epistle* (Figure 9); an inset picture shows Hogarth himself as a whip-wielding trainer disciplining both the bear Churchill and the monkey Wilkes. Even in the era of "sentiment," the old Elizabethan tropes of satiric whipping and cursing survive.

Verse satirists of the late eighteenth century are rarely read today, but they were known to their more famous Romantic successors. The satire of William Gifford and Thomas James Mathias, often featured in the Tory journal *The Anti-Jacobin*, assumed a conservative and Juvenalian mode of moralism and invective, while the Whiggish John Wolcot, writing as "Peter Pindar," adopted a more amiable Horatian manner aimed at a broader readership.[49] In the United States, a group of Yale graduates called the Connecticut Wits modeled themselves on the Augustans, and their *Anarchiad* was the first major political satire of the young republic.[50] The emerging Romantic aesthetic of feeling, sincerity, and sublimity, however, often entailed an overt rejection of the Augustans, and Coleridge's description of Pope's writing as "mere metrical good sense and wit" hints at the dramatic shift in taste that was taking place.[51]

Still, satire is more abundant, popular, and important in the Romantic era than is generally credited.[52] It turns away, however, from the classically influenced models of Dryden and Pope to native and popular forms.

Figure 9 William Hogarth (1697–1764), "The Bruiser," 1763.
By permission of the British Museum, London.
   In William Hogarth's late-career attack on Charles Churchill, the
Elizabethan tropes of satire as whipping and cursing persist. Note
Hogarth's dog urinating on Churchill's "Epistle to William Hogarth."

William Blake and Robert Burns use ballads and songs to vent their moral
indignation in harsh attacks on religious hypocrisy and repression; Burns's
"Holy Willie's Prayer" reduces Calvinism to absurdity through the prayers
and confessions of a monologist who thanks God for including him among
the redeemed while blithely excusing his many sexual sins as the consequence
of drunkenness. Percy Shelley's "New National Anthem" provides new lyrics
to "God Save the Queen" to transform it into a radical political critique.
The publisher William Hone and caricaturist George Cruikshank collaborate
on *The Political House that Jack Built* (1819), a political response to the
Peterloo massacre that draws on popular forms including almanacs, advertisements, children's books, and nursery rhymes.[53]
   In keeping with the spirit of the age, Romantic-era satire was often radical
and populist. Paper wars persisted, and vituperative satires against the royal
family thrived, as in Charles Lamb's *The Triumph of the Whale* (1812), which
mocked the obese Prince Regent in tetrameters that draw on children's
rhymes:

> Not a fatter fish than he
> Flounders round the polar sea,
> See his blubbers – at his gills
> What a world of drink he swills,
> From his trunk, as from a spout,
> Which next moment he pours out.[54]

This from the writer hailed by Coleridge as "gentle-hearted Charles." Thus satiric irony and invective coexist with the more familiar visionary side of the Romantic imagination. In a short lyric like "Mock on, mock on Voltaire, Rousseau," Blake can bitterly mock the *philosophes* Voltaire and Rousseau for mocking, but he does so in the name of the spiritual ideal symbolized by the bright tents of the newly redeemed Israelites camped on the shore of the Red Sea.

This same dialectic between satire and utopia, between debunking and idealizing, shapes the verse of the Romantics' greatest satirist, Lord Byron.[55] Byron's allegiance to the great Augustans is famous. His first major work, *English Bards and Scotch Reviewers* (1809), uses Popean couplets to attack the two groups named in his title with a brashness worthy of the Elizabethans: "Prepare for rhyme – I'll publish right or wrong / Fools are my theme, let Satire be my song." But in the mature phase of *Beppo* (1818), *The Vision of Judgment* (1822), and his greatest satiric work, *Don Juan* (1818–1823), he swerves from his precursors with a virtuosic comedic use of *ottava rima* stanzas. *Don Juan* is satiric, but it hardly looks like the genre practiced by Horace and Juvenal, or Dryden and Pope. To be sure, Byron often declares his admiration for these poets rather than his contemporaries:

> Thou shalt believe in Milton, Dryden, Pope;
> Thou shalt not set up Wordsworth, Coleridge, Southey
> Because the first is crazed beyond all hope,
> The second drunk, the third so quaint and mouthy[.]　　(1.205)

But *Don Juan*, which Byron called an "epic satire" (14.99), contains elements of satire, comedy, romance, epic, parody, picaresque, and bildungsroman. Byron may champion the Augustans who were falling out of favor in his day, but the poetic satire he creates is something wholly new.

The most visible feature of this new fusion is its irrepressible comic self-consciousness on all levels: stanza, plot, narration, genre. Byron discovers improbably clever and showy feminine rhymes, enjambs his sentences across lines and stanzas, and mixes lofty poetic diction with tossed-off colloquialism. He closes stanzas with reversals and anti-climaxes. His plot races across every corner of Europe, feeding a reader hungry for melodramatic stories of love and sex, war and danger. Most distinctively, his garrulous and free-associating narrator constantly interrupts the story to describe and display his own haphazard process of composition. Like *A Tale of a Tub* and *Tristram Shandy*, *Don Juan* makes a virtue of its struggle with form. Swift digresses to praise digression; Byron is inconstant on the subject of inconstancy:

> I hate inconstancy; I loathe, detest
> Abhor, condemn, abjure the mortal made
> Of such quicksilver clay that in his breast
> No permanent foundation can be laid.
> Love, constant love, has been my constant guest,
> And yet last night, being at a masquerade,
> I saw the prettiest creature, fresh from Milan,
> Which gave me some sensations like a villain.   (3.209)

With a smile and a wink, the narrator returns from high principle to his devilish desires.

Unlike the seasoned, worldly narrator, the hero, Juan (pronounced to rhyme with "new one"), is not a rake or libertine as in previous treatments of the legend, but a young, beautiful naïf tossed from one adventure to the next. Juan's act of cross-dressing when trapped in a Turkish harem emble-matizes his sexual polymorphousness and comic vulnerability. His heroism in war seems accomplished almost by accident. The book was thus both a scandal and a best-seller: the transgressive content flouted prudish standards of morality, while the transgressive form broke rules of genre, rhyme, narra-tive, and tone.

That tone is predominantly one of energetic irreverence, but its most consistent trait is its variability. Sometimes the satiric barbs are tendentious, as when Byron goes after political figures like King George III, the Duke of Wellington ("Villainton"), and Lord Castlereagh, the foreign secretary. These targeted attacks are part of Byron's general anti-militarist satire, which dis-plays an outraged sense of moral justice. But *Don Juan* shifts its attitude even more often even than its location. Byron indulges romances and fantasies, then exposes their false idealizations. He reminds his reader that his tale is fantasy, yet keeps alive the wish-fulfillment. Indeed the high theatricality of Byron's lyricism shares much with camp, as does the smiling irony that invites the reader to share his pleasure. Byron will debunk one ideal simply to enshrine a new one, as when he scorns military glory but then extols romantic passion:

> If Antony be well remember'd yet,
> 'Tis not his conquests keep his name in fashion,

> But Actium, lost for Cleopatra's eyes,
> Outbalances all Caesar's victories.   (6.4)

Thus the poem can pass from romantic heroism to bitter invective to comic clowning and even to a world-weary resignation – as when, contemplating great cities destroyed in war, the narrator concludes, "the woods shall be our home at last" (8.60).

Such dialectical turnings are everywhere. The narrator's self-defense at the opening of Canto 7 illustrates them well. Answering critics who accuse him of "A tendency to underrate and scoff / At human power and virtue and all that," he responds: "I say no more than has been said in Dante's / Verse and by Solomon and Cervantes" (7.3). He continues the catalogue in the next stanza:

> By Swift, by Machiavel, by Rochefoucault,
> By Fenelon, by Luther, and by Plato;
> By Tillotson, and Wesley, and Rousseau,
> Who knew this life was not worth a potato.   (7.4)

Like Johnson, Byron invokes the bleak vision of Ecclesiastes (thought to be penned by Solomon). But in rhyming the "vanity" of Ecclesiastes with "inanity" and "Christianity," and by rhyming "Plato" with "potato," he draws the reader into the impertinent pleasure he takes in "holding up the nothingness of life" (7.6). Byron's celebration of his own poetic self in all its high theatricality belongs firmly to the Romantic age.

The legacies of formal verse satire after Byron are varied. Among the Victorians, Tennyson famously hated satire, and Matthew Arnold dismissed Dryden and Pope as "classics of our prose."[56] To be sure, important poets display satiric tempers and attitudes in their responses to the social turmoil, inequality, violence, war, revolution, and horror of modern times. Some display heated vituperation; others react with ironic or bitter resignation. But the nineteenth century splits off the serious aims of satire from its levity and wit.[57] After Byron, the poetry of light verse, comic epigram, and humor assumes a self-consciously minor status. Verbally dexterous creations from Lewis Carroll, Gilbert and Sullivan, Dorothy Parker, and Ogden Nash tamp down satiric anger; modern wits, gadflies, and parodists often restrict their purview to the small-scale perils and paradoxes of daily life, offering private commentary to a smiling readership.

As for verse satire in the formal, classical mode, it cannot shake the association with the seventeenth and eighteenth centuries. Satiric couplets thus function as historical allusion, quotation, or deliberate anachronism. T.S. Eliot excised from *The Waste Land* lines that cross-bred Pope's Belinda with Joyce's Leopold Bloom:

> Leaving the bubbling beverage to cool,
> Fresca slips softly to the needful stool,
> Where the pathetic tale of Richardson
> Eases her labour till the deed is done.[58]

Eliot apparently deemed these lines too close to pure parody – out of sync with *The Waste Land*'s more subtle method of literary allusion. Similarly, the heroic couplets of John Shade, part of Vladimir Nabokov's novel *Pale Fire,* suggest through their anachronistic and mannered style the minor status of the fictional poet.

W.H. Auden's "The Unknown Citizen" is not exactly a formal verse satire either. It succeeds by departing from a strict Popean formula, modernizing the meter of the couplet into a rough, prosy line. The mock eulogy describes the life of an unnamed modern man from the impersonal point of view of an emerging bureaucratic state for whom the individual is just a collection of Big Data:

> The Press are convinced that he bought a paper every day
> And that his reactions to advertisements were normal in every way.
> Policies taken out in his name prove that he was fully insured,
> And his Health-card shows he was once in hospital but left it
>   cured.   (14–17)[59]

Derek Walcott's "The Spoiler's Return" is similarly informed rather than limited by the work of the canonical verse satirists. Walcott fuses the style – in places the actual language – of Rochester to the vernacular voice of the Trinidadian calypso singer Theophilus Philip, "The Mighty Spoiler." The Spoiler, returning from the underworld to his hometown as a revenant, casts a satiric and satanic eye on his nation during the calypso contests of Carnival when singers battle for the "monarchy" of the annual festival:

> Catch us in Satan tent, next carnival:
> Lord Rochester, Quevedo, Juvenal,
> Maestro, Martial, Pope, Dryden, Swift, Lord Byron,
> the lords of irony, the Duke of Iron,
> hotly contending for the monarchy
> in couplets or the old re-minor key[.]   (184–189)[60]

Walcott's couplets reinvigorate the forms of the past with a rhythm, a language, and a politics derived from popular music. His catalogue mixes the names of the Western canon with those of the great calypsonians such as Maestro and the Duke of Iron. (Quevedo is the name of both a Spanish satirist

and a Trinidadian singer.) The heroic couplets are rooted in local geography
and dialect, yet unabashedly aspire to a universalism:

> all those who gave earth's pompous carnival
> fatigue, and groaned *"O God, I feel to fall!"*
> all those whose anger for the poor on earth,
> made them weep with a laughter beyond mirth[.]   (190–193)

Walcott reroutes the European tradition to the needs of the modern
Caribbean, and discovers within the "Old Brigade of Satire" (34) fellow
champions of the dispossessed. In this modern verse satire, Juvenalian
anger punctures the pretentions of the vain and the powerful, and finds in
Lucifer's fall a protest against poverty and injustice.

Part III

Introduction: Satire and the Novel

One way of understanding the relationship between satire and the novel has been to see them as two distinct genres, each enjoying a moment of historical dominance. In this understanding, satire gives way to the novel over the course of the eighteenth century as part of a larger shift in sensibility or cultural temperament. For Ronald Paulson, "the novel and satire are convenient poles from which to chart the patterns of change in eighteenth-century literature and criticism" (*SNEE* 3). In his analysis, the hard moral judgment of satiric ridicule is replaced by "an aesthetics of pleasurable response, sympathetic laughter, and comedy," leading to the "disinterestedness of comic laughter in the novel."[1] At the same time, the public, social concerns of satire give way to the novel's exploration of individual psychology. Other critics have offered similar analyses, setting the simplification and compression of satiric narrative against the complexity and expansiveness of the novel; satire's "comedy of correction" against the novel's "comedy of forgiveness"; satire's essayistic analysis against the novel's use of fictional narrative; satire's penchant for fantasy and exaggeration against the novel's interest in the realistic representation of ordinary life.[2] For Frank Palmeri, the static and oppositional narrative structure of satire is supplanted by the novel's assumption of historical development and aim of "reconciling opposed cultural or historical claims."[3] Charles Knight suggests that the shift can be understood in political terms: satire's desire to retain social hierarchies aligns with Tory beliefs, while the novel's exploration of individual consciousness aligns with the individualism of Whiggish politics (*LS* 226).

Such binary analyses, for all their legitimate insight, produce a historical narrative in which satire dwindles to minor status. In this narrative, mid-eighteenth-century novelists such as Henry Fielding and Tobias Smollett show strong satiric tendencies, but the more sentimental works of Laurence Sterne soon push satire aside. In the early nineteenth century, Jane Austen's novels contain moral and social judgments, but these are expressed more delicately than the judgments of Swift and Pope. The Victorian era brings a taste for decency and moderation, and by the 1840s satire has become "unavailable as a free-standing genre," and, with few exceptions, the major novelists turn to comedy.[4] Thackeray's remarks on Fielding illustrate the Victorian aversion to satiric aggression:

> The world does not tolerate now such satire as that of Hogarth and Fielding, and the world no doubt is right in a great part of its squeamishness . . . It is wise that the public modesty should be as prudish as it is; that writers should be forced to chasten their humour, and when it would play with points of life and character which are essentially immoral, that they should be compelled by the general outcry of incensed public propriety, to be silent altogether.[5]

Late-century figures such as Samuel Butler and Oscar Wilde may slough off this Victorian squeamishness, but the modernism that follows is said to favor "irony" over satire, as modernists are deemed too self-critical, and their judgments too unstable, to fit the old model of satire. Only with postmodernism (in this account) does satire re-emerge as a dominant literary phenomenon, and even then it is common for critics to claim that the "black humor" of postmodern fiction is something other than satire, or that postmodern "fabulations" are something other than novels.

It would be a mistake to discard the legitimate insights of this account. The novel does introduce elements lacking from earlier kinds of prose satire. Historical periods, while hardly uniform in their tastes, do vary in their aesthetic norms. Yet for all its utility, this account marginalizes much of the most important satire of the last three hundred years: satiric novels. In such novels, judgment, attack, and censure prove compatible with sympathy and psychological understanding, as do the recursive or unstable ironies that we like to find in twentieth-century and contemporary works. Inquiry, play, provocation, fantasy, skepticism toward cherished ideals – all comfortably exist, indeed thrive, within the novel.

The key theorist of such a compatibilist view of satire and the novel is Mikhail Bakhtin. In his analysis, the novel – especially the British comic novel – offers a dynamic and vital representation of *heteroglossia*, "the social diversity of speech types" (*DI* 263): professional jargons, public discourses, artificial literary styles, class and regional dialects, and so on. Every such language embodies a "verbal-ideological belief system" (*DI* 311), and the novel, sensitive to this variety, becomes "an encyclopedia of all strata and forms of literary language" (*DI* 301). Heteroglossia, moreover, retains a satirical edge since it is above all dogmatic and authoritarian discourses which are "double-voiced," or inflected with subversive accents:

> Heteroglossia is parodic ... aimed sharply and polemically at the official
> languages of its time ... Incorporated languages and socio-ideological
> belief systems are ... unmasked and destroyed as something false,
> hypocritical, greedy, limited, narrowly rationalistic, inadequate to
> reality.   (DI 311–312)

Along with this linguistic variety, the comic novel is a rich source of those
motifs Bakhtin calls the grotesque and carnivalesque (discussed in Chapters 3
and 4): the inversion of social hierarchies, the emphasis on the body's materiality, the debunking of false authorities, the openness or "unfinalizability" of
human experience. Such qualities make the novel fully capable of accommo-
dating satiric attitudes and judgments.

Bakhtin's thought emphasizes optimism and the celebration of human
fallibility. Recently, however, Aaron Matz has identified in satiric novels an
opposing tendency – the shared interest that the novel and satire take in
realism. Matz finds in late-Victorian realism a commitment to close observation that leads to an austere, blunt, even censorious aesthetics. This tradition
partakes less of fantasy than of realism, less of gleeful transgression than of the
bitter recognition of human limitation. It pushes satire not toward comic
celebration but toward tragic resignation. Indeed, realism and satire both
authorize their representations through a claim to truth-telling, showing
things as they are, even if that reality is ugly or unsavory. Yet novelistic
understanding or forgiveness does not disappear from Matz's account,
because the very coldness of realism makes room for sympathy: "If everything
and everyone is to be scorned, then maybe everyone and everything deserves
to be pitied."[6]

In yet a different vein, Kathryn Hume has argued that the contemporary
novel might best be understood through a concept of "diffused satire."
In Hume's analysis, many satiric novels lack the intense affect – generally
anger or indignation – typically associated with satire, yet retain enough
satiric features (irony, critique, cynicism, provocation, analysis, humor, fantasy) to justify our description of them as satires. Satiric novels frequently run
at a "lower emotional temperature" than Juvenalian invective, offering cooler
irony or more meditative critique.[7] Indeed, when the temperature is lowered
enough, satiric novels can offer a bracingly honest skepticism or anti-
humanism. As Wyndham Lewis remarks, "Satire is *cold*, and that is good!"[8]

For these critics and many others, a key question in assessing the novel's
relation to satire is the treatment of feeling. Does it cultivate sentimental
attachment to its characters, hard moral judgments, or critical distance? It has
been argued that Sarah Fielding's novels of the mid-eighteenth century retain

the dark, unsentimental worldview that prevailed earlier in the century, but actively work to show how satire must be informed by compassion – in effect putting sentiment to a satiric purpose.[9] Almost two centuries later, Evelyn Waugh, rejecting Victorian sentimentality, uses coldness and cruelty to extinguish false emotion, but leaves space for a residue of authentic feeling. In contemporary fiction, it has been argued, writers like George Saunders modify the ironic cool of canonical postmodernism by cultivating sympathy in spite of their irony.[10] The relationship between satire and sentiment is thus hardly one of static opposition, but one of complex interrelations, and one that every generation of novelist engages anew.

What makes a novel satiric then? Generally some critical mass of the same features that make other literary and cultural works satiric: aggression, judgment, humor, wit, fantasy, transgression, referentiality, and so on. Like other satires, a satiric novel may range in tone from bawdy irreverence to seething indignation to amused detachment to cold nihilism. The world it represents tends to be one that is debased, unjust, or at least deeply flawed. Its plots often appear aimless, circular, or regressive. Its characters tend to be two-dimensional or cartoonish; even "heroes" of satiric novels are often unheroic, venal, or foolish.

The novel's satiric methods are as varied as those of the poetry, drama, and prose narratives that precede it. A narrator is an obvious source of satire; she can offer direct commentary or inflect the language of others with irony. Sometimes the narrator herself is satirized, and the comic self-exposure of the first-person narrator allows for the layering and multiplication of ironies. Other characters can also serve as satirists in the text; often minor characters serve as walk-on truth-tellers – children work especially well in this role – redescribing the actions and beliefs of the novel's major players. But most of all, novelistic satire is dramatic and structural: novels present characters' behavior and merely imply judgment.

Because of this variety, the chapters to follow do not offer a unitary analysis of a single type called "the satiric novel." Instead, they describe three subgenres, each held together by its own set of family resemblances, lines of influence, and shared interests and techniques. I call these subgenres the *comedy of manners*, the *picaresque*, and the *Menippean novel*, and I describe each one through analyses of important historical examples. The comedy of manners focuses narrowly on an isolated community; the picaresque provides a traveling episodic survey of various facets of society; the Menippean novel satirizes the processes of the human mind, or, more broadly, the suprahuman systems and institutions that dominate modern life. These subgenres are not, I emphasize, "archetypes" rooted in some universal unconscious in the manner of Northrop Frye, nor even discrete categories rooted in crisp logical distinctions. They are, rather, loose historical forms that have developed and changed over time. Their territories overlap. Classificatory judgments will be open for contestation. Some satiric novels may belong to more than one genre – I discuss *White Noise* as both comedy of manners and Menippean novel, *The Pickwick Papers* as Menippean novel and picaresque, *Gentlemen Prefer Blondes* as picaresque and comedy of manners – while others might not fit neatly among any. But employing these terms enables a specificity of analysis and a tracing of resemblances that attempting a unitary account of "satire and the novel" would forbid.

Three chapters addressing three kinds of satiric novel, together with a fourth chapter on popular culture, will, I hope, provide a capacious survey of satire in its modern forms.

Chapter 7

Small Worlds: The Comedy of Manners

The comedy of manners is a term most often applied to a set of plays: the Restoration comedies of William Wycherley, George Etheredge, Aphra Behn, William Congreve, and others, written after the reopening of the English theaters in 1660. Produced in reaction to an era of Puritan repression, featuring female actors on the English stage for the first time, these plays – full of sex, intrigue, and farcical comedy – treat the foolishness of the upper classes and deploy familiar stock types like the rake, the fop, and the cuckold. The dialogue is witty and stylish, and the base motives of the characters clash with the standards of decorum they are obliged at least nominally to obey. These comedies derive from the satirical drama of Jonson and Molière, but they blunt the polemical edge of those earlier works and replace moral indignation with amusement and titillation.

Some critics insist upon distinguishing this stage genre, the *comedy of manners*, from the *novel of manners*, a genre of narrative fiction, not always comic, that reached perfection first in Jane Austen and later in Henry James and Edith Wharton. Novels of manners provide unique qualitative insight into a culture's values by registering what Lionel Trilling called "small actions": nuances of diction, tone, and gesture. But the smallness of these actions can look like pettiness, and pettiness provides fuel for satire. In using the term "comedy of manners" to refer to a type of satiric novel, then, I describe a narrative form which draws on both the dramatic and the novelistic traditions, and which has become a widespread vehicle for social satire.

Understood as a type of satiric novel, the comedy of manners focuses on a closed society, a thin stratum taken from a multilayered socioeconomic world. Its setting, to use the title of one of David Lodge's novels, is a small world, and this smallness, while offering recognizable conventions for readers, constricts the characters' behavior. Jane Austen famously wrote to her nephew that she painted with a fine brush on two inches of ivory, and the novelist of manners is a miniaturist, picking up subtle details and discriminations unobserved by the satirist who works on a vast canvas. While politics can enter into the comedy of manners, its satire is primarily social, with special interest in class, gender, and sexuality. Sometimes it mocks an eccentric aristocracy; more often it dissects the customs of those a rung or two lower on the social ladder. Courtship, marriage, and adultery supply storylines, and satirists of manners tend to agree with Mr. Scogan of Aldous Huxley's *Crome Yellow* that sex is "one of the few permanently and everlastingly amusing subjects that exist."[1] The genre has been especially hospitable to female satirists, allowing them to exercise their intelligence aggressively as they focus their critique on the domestic and erotic realms of experience. The smallness of the society represented can also lure the reader into reading the satire as a *roman à clef* ("novel with a key"), and hunting down real-life prototypes for fictional characters.

The comedy of manners takes as its subject the conventions and unwritten laws of its self-contained world. To use the title of Jean Renoir's great cinematic comedy of manners, it delineates The Rules of the Game. Indeed, from the games of whist that pass the characters' time in Austen's books to the parlor game "Humiliation" that Phillip Swallow introduces to his academic coterie in Lodge's *Changing Places*, games themselves offer handy metaphors for, or sublimations of, the highly structured rituals of social jousting and sexual courtship that these novels analyze. Pierre Bourdieu, articulating how literary works perform a unique kind of sociological analysis, has described the "social field" as "a battlefield which also can be seen as a game." The "trump cards" in this game are "the habitus, that is to say, the acquirements [*sic*], the embodied, assimilated properties such as elegance, ease of manner, beauty and so forth."[2] Trilling similarly described manners as "a culture's hum and buzz of implication ... the whole evanescent context in which its explicit statements are made."[3] A culture's code of manners, in short, is implicit, subtle, and indirect. Characters and readers alike must school themselves in manners, teaching themselves to read social cues. In any given society, moreover, there is more than one system of manners in play, and so culture can be understood as a *clash* of manners or, as Joseph Litvak argues, "a contest of sophistications," defining sophistication as "a creative interposition ... at the level of manners, of propriety versus impropriety." For Litvak, out-sophisticating or outclassing your rival means showing that you can do what she does, only better.[4] The contest of manners thus involves parodic imitation and ironic redescription of the other. The characters themselves must act as successful parodists and ironists in order to triumph in the social game.

When the heroine or hero does triumph – winning wealth, status, or a desirable mate – the novel edges toward comedy; when she or he is defeated, or when the villains go unpunished, as in Mary McCarthy's *The Groves of*

Academe, the novel gets called satire. The distinction is not absolute: happy endings coexist in Austen with pointed critique, bitter ones in Waugh with buffoonery and farce. Regardless of the ending, the genre usually sides with the authentic values of the individual over the restrictive ones of the collective. The social rules to be mastered are held up as superficial; adhering to them produces pretension, snobbery, hypocrisy, and social climbing. This is not to say that individualism is always laudable: comedies of manners, like other kinds of satire, recognize self-interest and self-aggrandizement as basic human motives. Yet for certain favored characters, personal conviction, held in defiance of social norms, can uphold the libidinal prerogatives of the self. The satiric critique of false appearances speaks on behalf of individual emancipation. If manners naturalize ideology, as James Kincaid argues, then the comedy of manners reverses the process, revealing manners as ideological constructs.[5] The genre in this way provides a double vision: an insider's view intimately versed in the rules of the game, and an outsider's anthropological gaze that offers critical distance.[6]

Manners and its cognates – taste, sophistication, class – need not align with mere wealth, and can sometimes stand in opposition to it as criteria for establishing hierarchies. Wealth may pass from old families to new, from landed aristocrats to upstart capitalists, but the more elusive standards of manners are harder to acquire, and in fact may compensate for losses of wealth brought about by socioeconomic upheaval. British philosophical discourses of taste in the eighteenth century, indeed, arose at least partially in response to an influx of wealth in the form of aesthetic objects acquired through global trade; taste could maintain social hierarchies in the face of economic mobility. Simply put, the difference between new money and old money is manners. As Dawn Powell writes in regard to one of her characters' bad manners, "here, like ancestry or race, was something neither money nor power could correct" (39). Sometimes, of course, an author will bless a character with both wealth and manners, but an ill-mannered upstart might be satirized for shameless climbing, or an old-money baron for petty snobbery.

While Jane Austen's three or four families in a country village provide a prototype for the comedy of manners, in theory any closed world will serve. Djuna Barnes's *Ladies Almanack* sends up the lesbian coterie of Natalie Barney's Paris salon; printed and circulated privately, it not only represents a small world but limits its readership to a small circle as well. A recent bestseller, Kevin Kwan's *Crazy Rich Asians*, gently mocks the manners and values of super-rich Chinese expatriates living in Singapore. Much of Woody Allen's oeuvre focuses on love and marital relations among a narrow circle of

New York artists and intellectuals; Robert Altman's *The Player* fuses an insider's satire of Hollywood manners (the language of the pitch, the insistence on particular brands of bottled water) to a noirish thriller; Whit Stillman's *Metropolitan* looks at Manhattan's increasingly marginalized young "UHBs" (urban haute-bourgeoisie) and their very small world of prep schools and debutante balls. *Seinfeld* has been seen as a comedy of manners, identifying and dissecting the unwritten rules surrounding dating and other social interactions among urban thirtysomething singles.

A Fine Brush: *Pride and Prejudice*

Eighteenth-century satire acknowledges and mocks these games of manners and class, of taste and status, of sex and aggression. The parodic conduct guides of Swift and Collier explicitly satirize the unwritten rules governing social relations. *Candide*'s Parisian episodes zero in on the snobberies of urban literary and artistic life, while *The Rape of the Lock* depicts a glittering but hollow upper-class social world. Pope indeed discerns how highly regulated social situations mask a violence that finds expression through furtive glances and malicious whispers: "A third interprets Motions, Looks, and Eyes / At every Word a Reputation dies" (3.15–16). The genre of the novel, however, introduces a new balance of psychological realism and satiric artifice. Thus Jane Austen combines two kinds of characters. Clownish secondary characters, whose prototypes lie in the theater, serve as objects of mockery and correction, while heroic protagonists, who possess complexity and depth, receive sympathy and forgiveness.[7] This combination of flat and round characters, of attention to surfaces and depths, supports Georg Simmel's claim that modernity generates two conflicting tendencies in human character: in breaking old hierarchies, it renders people equal, but as people are liberated from old bonds, they assert their personal uniqueness as a measure of value.[8] Simmel's tension between the human being as individual and the human being as type is the fundamental tension of the comedy of manners – pitting the constraining norms of the social world against the aspiration of the individual for self-realization.

Austen's *Pride and Prejudice* (1813) exemplifies how the novelistic comedy of manners both continues and transforms older modes of narrative satire. Austen's world is small not only in geographical scope but also in plot and theme. It focuses tightly on what Darcy calls a "confined and unvarying society" (29) – the rural landed gentry – and the desire of its young women to find happiness in love and marriage. Its society is so confined and unvarying, in fact, that the relationships of characters over-lap artificially: Darcy's aunt, Lady Catherine, just happens to be the patroness of Elizabeth's cousin, Collins; Darcy's father just happens to have employed Wickham's father. Such stylization, contrived as it may seem, highlights real constraints, calling attention to a closed system of social relations.

It is the ideological smallness of the world that Austen evokes in the ironies of her famous opening sentence: "It is a truth universally acknowledged, that a single man in possession of a good fortune, must be in want of a wife" (3). Mrs. Bennet and the local yentas misrecognize as "truth" what is only their fantasy, mistaking as "universal" what is only contingent. They do so because their small world "acknowledge[s]" no values other than the economically driven pursuit of marriage. In contrast to Mrs. Bennet and her ilk, however, Austen and her reader do recognize that the statement contains fantasy or ideology masquerading as truth, and discern the limits of a universe in which the false belief passes as "universal." In *Pride and Prejudice,* indeed, the invocation of communal opinion is nearly always the occasion for an irony that points beyond the narrow collective view: when Austen writes about the view of "every body" (93, 191), she is invariably noting the self-aggrandizement and parochialism that accompany conforming to settled opinion. The critique of such a communal opinion is a fundamental motif of the comedy of manners.

Austen's narrator is not a voluble stage manager like Fielding's, nor does she revel in linguistic excess like those of Rabelais or Swift.[9] Instead she works through restraint, slipping her satiric knives in quickly and lethally. Describing Collins's engagement to Charlotte Lucas she comments: "In as short a time as Mr. Collins's long speeches would allow, every thing was settled between them to the satisfaction of both" (83). Just a few sentences later Lady Lucas (whose daughter will now inherit the Bennets' estate) is shredded with the swiftest of strokes: "Lady Lucas began directly to calculate with more interest than the matter had ever excited before, how many years longer Mr. Bennet was likely to live" (83). If there is a signature device of Austen's narrator, it is *litotes,* the use of negation to achieve ironic under-statement: "Mr. Collins was not a sensible man, and the deficiency of nature had been but little assisted by education or society" (48). Litotes is the technique of well-mannered satire.[10] Through such polite insult ("not a sensible man," "but little assisted"), *Pride and Prejudice* reproduces and exposes the gap between superficial manners and submerged aggression. Yet the subtlety of the style in no way hobbles Austen's treatment of her knaves and fools; the pompous Collins, the hysterical Mrs. Bennet, the haughty Lady

Catherine, the pedantic Mary, the flighty Lydia are all politely and even fastidiously brutalized.

It is not only Austen's narrator, however, who provides us with critical purchase on her world. Mr. Bennet is a satirist within the text who derives endless "amusement" from the "ignorance and folly" of his wife and younger daughters (155). He enjoys Collins's visit precisely because the man is "as absurd as he had hoped" (47), and even after Lydia's disastrous marriage to Wickham, he can wryly remark, "I defy even Sr. William Lucas himself, to produce a more valuable son-in-law" (214). A man who hates London and retreats from the games, dinners, and dances of Hertfordshire into his private library, Bennet efficiently converts every character's failings into material for his private amusement. As he says to Elizabeth, only half in jest, "For what do we live, but to make sport for our neighbours, and laugh at them in our turn?" (237). Yet Mr. Bennet's amusement is eventually shown to be too easy, his satire too Horatian. He lacks Juvenalian moral outrage, and the mildness of his authority enables Lydia's sexual transgression. Elizabeth, however, is a more complicated satirist. She has "a lively, playful disposition" (9), and like her father, "delight[s] in anything ridiculous" (9). Like Swift and Pope, she insists on the moral rectitude of her laughter, claiming to ridicule only "follies and nonsense" (39); to Darcy, however, she concedes an exhibitionistic side that desires to "say something that will amaze the whole room, and be handed down to posterity with all the eclat of a proverb" (63). Indeed, she is an epigrammatist of Wildean skill and perversity: "I wonder who first discovered the efficacy of poetry in driving away love!" (31). Her contrarian temper also harbors a hint of Swiftian misanthropy: "The more I see the world, the more I am dissatisfied with it" (90–91).

Of all the characters, however, it is Darcy who is said to possess a "satirical eye" (17). That this eye is itself observed by the satirical Elizabeth suggests that the two protagonists exist both inside and outside the social scene, at once observers and observed. Like Pope's Hampton Court, Austen's Hertfordshire is full of silent scheming and sublimated violence. Indeed the tension between what is seen and what is actually said makes the comedy of manners a form of satire particularly hospitable for Foucaultian readings with their thematics of surveillance and subtle discipline. Yet Elizabeth and Darcy observe and discipline their own world as much as they are observed and disciplined by it. The two lovers share a critical perspective on the norms of the whole society, and their own social interaction is therefore far more entertaining than that of the too-nice, plain-vanilla Bingley and Jane. Their flirtation takes the form of edgy dueling. Like those ritual exchanges of insults, from flyting to the dozens, long recognized as satiric speech acts, their verbal sparring contains elements of self-display, danger, hostility, and bonding. They fall in love by acknowledging, in themselves and in each other, aggressive impulses that other characters deny.

The reconciliation of conflict through marriage has led many critics to a reading of the text in which Elizabeth's moral principles and her recognition of Darcy's patrician virtues allow for a happy ending that ratifies the patriarchal social system. The morally deviant are reformed or punished and the good are rewarded. The social order proves flexible enough to accommodate the rebellious characters, but no radical critique is imagined. But feminist criticism has made another reading available, in which female intelligence, wit, and autonomy – culminating in Elizabeth's defiance of Lady Catherine – more radically disrupt the small world's hierarchies of wealth and rank. Mrs. Bennet, whose only business in life is to get her daughters married, may be a risible spokeswoman for the system, but ultimately it is the system itself which is indicted. Charlotte recognizes pragmatically but joylessly that marriage is her only economic option, and Elizabeth herself, sounding a bit like Mandeville, questions the distinction between "the mercenary and the prudent motive" (102) for matrimony. In this view, the object of Austen's satire is not the moral failure of some of the characters, but the system of rules that structures *all* sexual and social relations. The novel's sharpest satire might lie then in a remark of Elizabeth's that usually passes as a joke. "Will you tell me how long you have loved him?" Jane asks near the novel's end; Elizabeth responds, "I believe I must date it from my first seeing his beautiful grounds at Pemberley" (244). Such a reading can begin to recover Austen from the haze of romance in which popular culture has enshrouded her.

Victorian and Modern Manners

Austen provides something like an ideal type of the comedy of manners, but as the genre develops it departs from her model in different ways. A direct Victorian successor is a work like Anthony Trollope's *Barchester Towers*, in which the self-sufficient world of Barchester is contrasted to the world of London that intrudes upon its stability and peace. But more often the British comic novel during the Victorian years expands the social canvas, and the great comic urban realists like Dickens and Thackeray, while still dissecting familial, domestic, and erotic relations, take a more heterogeneous view that encompasses a range of economic strata, a diversity of speech-types, a host of political issues, a multiplicity of plotlines. Class-based manners take their place as merely one of a panoply of satiric targets. Modernism's turn to the examination of consciousness presents another distraction; Marcel Proust's *Remembrance of Things Past* is one of literature's greatest comedies of manners, but because Proust combines his social satire with a revolutionary method of representing mental life, his satire is often overlooked.

While the tight focus and controlled understatement of Austen's comedy can widen into a more heterogeneous comic realism, her mordant commentary on affectation and frivolity can also give way to the stylization, fancy, and play that characterize the camp novel. In the nineteenth century, the country-house conversation novels of Thomas Love Peacock, the nonsense humor and wordplay of Lewis Carroll, the comic operas of Gilbert and Sullivan, and the epigrammatic wit of Oscar Wilde all direct satire at manners, but strong social critique is moderated or concealed by banter and silliness. From Wilde's coattails comes not only the comedy of manners of the twentieth-century stage (Noel Coward, Somerset Maugham) but also the early twentieth-century fiction of Max Beerbohm, Ronald Firbank, E.F. Benson, P.G. Wodehouse, Saki, and others. In these works, rococo prose, long runs of comic dialogue, broad caricatures, and stagey elements of farce create a light comedy whose prevailing affect is an amused indifference. Aristocrats' foibles are seen as ludicrous but largely harmless, and heterosexual romance is depicted as laughably artificial. These works of camp and farce represent a comic tradition on the borders of satire.

The comedy of manners also informs the work of the major British satirists of the modernist period and mid-century including Aldous Huxley, Wyndham Lewis, Evelyn Waugh, George Orwell, Anthony Powell, Ivy Compton-Burnett, and Muriel Spark. Huxley's early novels, modeled on Peacock's country-house fictions, focus on small worlds of artists, bohemians, and intellectuals as they blend social satire of upper-class affectation with intellectual satire of the zany ideas put forth by various eccentrics. Largely benign, Huxley's oddballs serve as vehicles for his cultural criticism, and the wild prognostications of a character like *Crome Yellow*'s Scogan foreshadow the weightier social theory informing *Brave New World* a decade later. Lewis, notable as a theorist as well as a practitioner of satire, also focuses his satire on bad art and bad ideas, associating them with pretentious manners and philistine tastes. While the iconoclastic Lewis would surely chafe at being called a novelist of manners, he embraces the label of satirist. His attacks often target self-contained artistic subcultures: in *Tarr*, the "Bourgeois Bohemians" of Paris's Latin Quarter; in *The Apes of God*, the salons of Bloomsbury and the Sitwells; in *The Revenge for Love*, Oxford-educated Communists who proclaim their ideological purity even as they earn money by painting forgeries or pimping out their wives. Lewis's targets are "apes" because of their second-hand tastes and empty mimicry; they are disdained for their inability to comprehend the degree to which they are automata, slaves to their own compulsions. Lewis uses what he calls an external method – focusing on behavior and appearance rather than interior monologue – to deflate the human pretention to distinctiveness.

The period's most successful reinvention of the comedy of manners, however, are the novels of Waugh. Waugh's version of the genre, like many twentieth-century incarnations, is something of a hybrid; he deploys elements of the picaresque (naïve protagonists, episodic plots, travel) and he satirizes a broad array of modern phenomena including partisan politics, evangelical Christianity, tabloid journalism, birth control, bureaucracy, Bauhaus architecture, cinema, and world war. Still, his novels center on a small English upper-class world, and his technique – consistent with Wyndham Lewis's prescriptions – trains its focus on the externals of manners and social behavior. His broad, energetic comedy deploys Wildean confusions of identity, Carrollian nonsense, and Dickensian caricature, but his overarching assessment of modern society is bleak. Yet Waugh rarely comes across as indignant or preachy, coolly maintaining a pose of amused indifference in the face of the society's follies, cruelties, and injustices. This narratorial detachment, suppressing any impulse toward sanctimony or sentimentality, balances the ludicrous excesses of the characters' behavior. It often seems not only to accept cruelty and violence, but irreverently to enjoy it, even to share its blithe indifference to suffering:

> Then Nina said, "Do be amusing Adam. I can't bear you when you're not amusing."
> Then Adam began to tell her about Simon Balcairn and Margot's party. He described how he had seen Simon being horse-whipped in the middle of the office.
> Nina said, "Yes, that's amusing. Go on like that."[11]

Forging a new solution to the problem of how the novel can manage satiric aggression and skepticism without scuttling sympathy altogether, Waugh offers a cruel humor that feels strikingly contemporary, and offers a model for satirists later in the century confronting even greater horrors.

A Handful of Dust (1934) presents two conflicting codes of manners. Tony Last's code is old-fashioned and nostalgic; his wife Brenda's, modern and materialistic. Although Tony's naïve decency is preferable to Brenda's ruthless self-gratification, he is still foolish, in his trust of his adulterous wife and in his sentimental attachment to his country estate, Hetton Abbey. The physical decay of Hetton suggests the similarly antiquated condition of its aristocratic customs, which include the local parson's long-outdated sermons and the brutal fox hunt in which Tony's son, John Andrew, is accidentally killed. Few besides Tony see anything of worth in these anachronistic traditions. Emblematic of the new tastes and values is Mrs. Beaver the interior decorator, who renovates London apartments with chromium plating and sheepskin carpet, and who is introduced at the start of the novel:

> "Was anyone hurt?"
> "No one I am thankful to say," said Mrs. Beaver, "except two housemaids who lost their heads and jumped through a glass roof into the paved court. They were in no danger. The fire never properly reached the bedrooms I am afraid." (3)

The passage typifies how Waugh uses dialogue rather than narration to achieve his satire. It is left for the reader to understand that Mrs. Beaver doesn't consider the housemaids "anyone," and doesn't care whether they were hurt.

Most of the other characters, from the stupid and parsimonious John Beaver to the self-dramatizing Jenny Abdul-Akbar, are similarly self-serving and vulgar. Brenda's friends ("Polly and Daisy and Angela and all the gang of gossips") enjoy each other's affairs and divorces as the amusing stuff of "drawing-room comedy"; no one asks, in any of this, whether anyone was hurt. The communal voice that Austen represents through the attitudes of Mrs. Bennet and her neighbors here becomes a busily circulating "opinion" that expresses the values of Waugh's small world:

> Opinion was greatly in favour of Brenda's adventure. The morning telephone buzzed with news of her; even people with whom she had the barest acquaintance were delighted to relate that they had seen her and Beaver the evening before at restaurant or cinema. It had been an autumn of very sparse and meagre romance; only the most obvious people had parted or come together, and Brenda was filling a want long felt by those whose simple, vicarious pleasure it was to discuss the subject in bed over the telephone. (74)

Most heartless of all is Brenda herself. When she is told that "John" has died, Brenda initially thinks Jock Grant-Menzies is speaking of her lover, John Beaver, not her son, John Andrew:

> "I've been down at Hetton since the week-end."
> "Hetton?"
> "Don't you remember? John was going hunting today."

> She frowned, not at once taking in what he was saying. "John . . . John Andrew . . . I . . . Oh thank God . . . " Then she burst into tears. (161–162)

Jock, the messenger, is actually one of the more decent characters in the novel, but at the end of the novel he happily marries Brenda despite having witnessed this chilling response to her son's death.

Rather than lecturing the reader in a huff of outrage, or stoking sympathy for the bereaved and betrayed Tony, Waugh foregrounds the inadequacy of the characters' behavior: in Jenny's narcissistic reaction to the death ("What have I done to deserve it?") or Polly's callous one ("That's the end of Tony so far as Brenda is concerned") (157, 165). Tony, meanwhile, persists in his naiveté, unable share the blasé attitude that constitutes a social norm. "Please do not mind too much" (172), Brenda writes politely, while her brother-in-law Reggie upbraids him, "you seem rather to be taking the line of the injured husband" (204). Throughout it all, the narrator himself appears to share – or pretend to share – this same indifference, seeming at times to participate in the gossips' fun, at times to regard it all with disdain. The conclusion injects a note of uncanny horror into the satire, as Tony, fleeing England on a tourist's adventure, ends up lost in Guiana, the prisoner of the ominously named Mr. Todd who forces him daily to read aloud the complete works of Dickens. The episode is at once absurd and terrifying; the jungle's heart of darkness turns out to be the very Dickensian sentimentality and Victorian domesticity that Tony longed for. Brenda marries Jock, Hetton Abbey is turned over for the breeding of foxes, and the extinction of decency is complete.

Twentieth-Century Austen

In the 1930s and 1940s, many of Austen's female successors create variations of the comedy of manners that demonstrate the growing freedom of the woman writer to challenge patriarchal norms. Stella Gibbons's *Cold Comfort Farm* opens with an epigraph from *Mansfield Park*, and features a heroine, Flora Poste, who inherits from Austen a taste for tidiness and comfort. Flora (who shares her initials with *Mansfield Park*'s Fanny Price) aspires to update Austen by writing "a novel as good as *Persuasion* but with a modern setting" (19). That novel may well be *Cold Comfort Farm* (1932), which offers a clash between two sets of manners, Flora's urbane, bourgeois metropolitanism, and the regressive Gothicism of her rural cousins, the Starkadders. In the course of the novel, Flora remakes her cousins' speech, dress, diet, and hygiene, taming their ill-mannered affect and teaching them to regulate their desires. Herself a model of good manners, Flora brings the small world of the rural society into the twentieth century, opening it to the modern world.

Above all, Flora imposes new manners in the realm of sexuality. The society of the Starkadders is so closed that it is inbred. But Flora instructs the servant girl Meriam in birth control (a scene for which the book was banned in Ireland), hires a psychoanalyst to re-direct Judith's lust for her son Seth, and rescues Elfine from the possessive desire of her cousin Urk. As the novel ends, Flora looks upon Elfine's wedding to the local squire and takes pride in the well-mannered scene she has staged:

> There they all were. Enjoying themselves. Having a nice time. And having it in an ordinary human manner. Not having it because they were raping somebody, or beating somebody, or having religious mania or being doomed to silence by a gloomy, earthy pride, or loving the soil with the fierce desire of a lecher, or anything of that sort. (217)

The contest of manners, of course, is one-sided, since the eccentricities of the Starkadders are amusing rather than threatening, and the novel's self-conscious humor produces comic wish-fulfillment rather than unsettling critique. But through its playful parody of the conventions of Gothic fiction, the novel attains satiric force. Flora's bourgeois norms might seem overly regulatory from one vantage, but from another they free the Starkadders from tyrannical authority and outmoded codes of sexual and religious behavior. Still, Flora's own marriage at the end of the novel poses a critical conundrum: in a scene right out of Hollywood, her handsome cousin Charles whisks her away in an airplane. Such a fantasy, however charming, seems to diminish Flora's artistic, sexual, and political agency. But as with *Pride and Prejudice*, a more ironic reading of the wish-fulfillment is possible. For the very perfection of the resolution suggests a satiric comment on the reader's desires – forcing us to acknowledge that the Hollywood ending contains a regressive wish for masculine control.

Ivy Compton-Burnett offers a different variation of Austen, refusing the compromises of the comic plot and taking a less forgiving view of human behavior. Like Austen, Compton-Burnett tends to write about three or four families in a country village, and she examines courtship, marriage, inheritance, and domestic relations among the English rural gentry. Her small world, however, is darker and more claustrophobic, with plots hinging on murder, adultery, and deception. Tyrannical parents exercise their power ruthlessly over children, servants, and other dependents. Characters suffer –

mostly at each other's hands – but cruelty and evil go unpunished. Compton-Burnett's satire indeed has little interest in moral reform or instruction, only in the revelation of human baseness. Her technique is striking: in the manner of Peacock, Firbank, and the early Huxley, the novels are told virtually entirely through dialogue, but the table-talk, while often witty, is just as frequently tense, gossipy, or aggressive. The formalism of the technique, pushed to a deliberately artificial extreme, reproduces at the level of reading the same sense of constriction that social proprieties produce at the level of content.

A House and Its Head (1935) illustrates the concentrated intensity of Compton-Burnett's small world. Again the connection to Austen is explicit: when the despotic patriarch Duncan Edgeworth returns from a trip, his daughter quotes directly from *Mansfield Park*: "My father is come! ... He is in the hall at this moment!" (101). As in *Cold Comfort Farm*, the closeness of Austen's society appears incestuous. When Grant gets engaged to his cousin Nance, Oscar bizarrely congratulates him on having "come near to marrying your sister" (205). Codes of manners provide Duncan with opportunities to terrorize his family, as he forces them to come down to breakfast or attend church. Infantile and omnipotent, he interrogates, scolds, corrects, and berates them. Indeed the dialogue that constitutes the novel is both *about* manners and a *form* of manners. It is about manners in that characters repeatedly explore questions of appearance and reality, discussing whether public behavior reveals or conceals people's private motives. At the same time the dialogue itself is a form of manners, presenting speech acts through which characters attack each other and defend themselves.

The satire of *A House and Its Head*, even more than that of *A Handful of Dust*, adheres to the external method advocated by Lewis. It also catches glints of black humor, as when Grant, on hearing that the infant who has superseded him in the family line is healthy, exclaims, "No flicker of hope!" (148). It uses these techniques to eviscerate sentimental pieties about family, community, and humanity. Religious characters are narcissistic busybodies; community opinion, a cacophony of gossip. The institutions of heterosexual marriage and patrilineal inheritance breed craven self-interest, and the novel repeatedly illustrates Elizabeth Bennet's insight that in marriage the prudent motive and the mercenary cannot be disentangled. Indeed, marriage appears so oppressive a regime that one character notes a "feeling of escape in spinster populations" (266), hinting at a queer angle to the critique. And the characters' willingness to reconstitute this oppressive community, despite the murder of a child, for purely economic reasons suggests that what gets called forgiveness is actually complicity. Like *A Handful of Dust*, the novel concludes with the collective dismissal of a child's death, the re-assertion of a patriarchal will, and a cold recognition of human ruthlessness.

Dawn Powell's novels are perhaps closest to Austen's in their balance of comedy and satire, though they situate their stories of love, sex, and marriage not in the countryside but in the city. Her later books focus on select circles of New York society – both wealthy socialites and the artists and intellectuals with whom they cross paths. Powell, however, broadens her satire to include attention to consumer capitalism, national politics, and a dysfunctional public sphere saturated with print and electronic media. Still, amid the swirl of urban activity and national politics, she trains her attention on personal relations, which are marked by pettiness, deception, and snobbery. *A Time to Be Born* (1942) focuses on a love triangle in which two young women from the same provincial Ohio town, now living in New York, fall for the same man. On one level the moral architecture looks clear and traditional. The unsophisticated heroine, Vicky Haven, serves as a naïf through whose innocent eye the baroque customs and quiet cruelties of New York upper-class social codes are rendered amusing or absurd; Vicky is divested of the aggression that characterizes her author's satire. In contrast, Powell the author delights in savaging Vicky's rival Amanda Keeler (based on the real-life figure Clare Boothe Luce), who has slept her way to wealth and fame by marrying the owner of a media empire. For Amanda sex is merely a means to exercise a will to power: "It was not that she wanted an affair for lust's sake, for she had a genuine distaste for sexual intimacy and hated to sacrifice a facial appointment for a mere frolic in bed; but there were so many things to be gained by trading on sex and she thought so little of the process that she itched to use it as currency once again" (25). The novel's happy ending thus tilts us toward the wish-fulfillment of comedy as Vicky wins Ken Saunders while Amanda suffers the indignity of an abortion and the collapse of her marriage. Yet just as Austen's Elizabeth slyly concedes her own mercenary motives for marriage, so Powell undercuts the satisfaction of the romantic comedy in the closing lines, when Ken reassures Vicky that he will never return to Amanda:

> "Thank you for that, darling," she said gratefully.
>   But she was not at all sure whether he was speaking the truth or what he hoped was the truth.
>   For that matter, neither was Ken. (334)

Like Gibbons at the end of *Cold Comfort Farm*, Powell gives us the happy ending of comedy, but with a satiric twist that directs attention to the shallowness of its wish-fulfillment.

Powell, however, also gestures toward the wider political conditions in which the comedy of manners is set. The bravura opening of *A Time to Be Born* establishes a dichotomy between sexual and national axes of identity, implicitly advocating for the value of private desires in the face of political pressures. Amid the "nightmare" of wartime when "Paris was gone, London was under fire, the Atlantic was now a drop of water between the flame on one side and the waiting dynamite on the other," Powell's narrator intones, "This was a time when writers dared not write of Vicky Haven or of simple young women like her" (3). Yet Powell is daring to write exactly such a story. Vicky's authentic private concerns are thus pitted against Amanda's desire for celebrity; while Vicky cries into her pillow over a lost love, "her old friend . . . rode the world's debacle as if it were her own yacht and saved her tears for Finland and the photographers" (4). Amanda, the female rival-villain, comes to embody not only the age-old vices of greed and sexual rapaciousness but also the inauthenticity of the modern public sphere, a communal voice now enlarged to national scope.

Both at the level of social manners and at the level of mass-mediated public opinion, then, Powell uses the comedy of manners as a vehicle for exposing public morality as a mask for private self-interest. When Dr. Swick, a college president, praises Hitler for driving intellectuals out of Europe into his little school, his facetiousness is hard to gauge. Yet his words clearly indict the Evans media empire – and by implication the real-life media empire of Henry and Clare Boothe Luce – which, churning out high-sounding patriotic discourse, profits from the war far more than Swick's small college. In an age of mass media, Powell's satirical skepticism toward national mythology becomes more necessary than ever because the affective demands made upon us in the name of the nation are so colossal. As another character says, with resignation, "This is war-time. National fantasy is necessary" (183). In siding with Vicky over Amanda, Powell asserts the need for an independent, private space outside of any such national fantasy.

The Campus Novel

In the middle of the twentieth century, a new variety of the comedy of manners arises: the campus novel or academic novel. With the expansion of higher education in the postwar years, more novelists make their living as faculty or writers-in-residence; to many of them the professional world of the college campus appears as closed-off and self-contained as any English country village. Indeed in an ever-modernizing world, the walled-in campus becomes an almost anachronistic instance of formalized, regimented, and quasi-pastoral society. Two foundational works, Mary McCarthy's *The Groves of Academe* (1952) and Kingsley Amis's *Lucky Jim* (1954), provide contrasting examples of the satiric and comic tendencies of the genre. In McCarthy's grim satire, the triumph of the knave Henry Mulcahy over the university president attests to a moral spinelessness in the liberal academic culture that fails to stop him; in Amis's more farcical comedy, the hero happily escapes the petty academic world that frustrates his economic and sexual desires. These novels, along with several others from the 1950s and early 1960s (by C.P. Snow, Randall Jarrell, Vladimir Nabokov, Bernard Malamud, and others) inaugurate a popular and lasting subgenre.

Like other closed societies, academia possesses its own baroque codes of social behavior, its own rules of the game, often its own language. Amis satirizes the uselessness of specialized research when Jim Dixon contemplates his own article, "The Economic Influence of the Developments in Shipbuilding Techniques, 1450 to 1485":

> It was a perfect title, in that it crystallized the article's niggling
> mindlessness, its funereal parade of yawn-enforcing facts, the pseudo-
> light it threw upon non-problems. Dixon had read, or begun to read,
> dozens like it, but his own seemed worse than most in its air of being
> convinced of its own usefulness and significance.[12]

The small world also has its own intellectual fads. *The Groves of Academe*'s Jocelyn College indulges the mid-century vogue for Deweyan progressive education, while David Lodge's *Changing Places* goofs on the 1960s trendiness of Marshall McLuhan with his proclamations of the death of print. In the 1980s Don DeLillo's *White Noise* mocks postmodern theory and cultural studies, presenting a coterie of "New York émigrés" who teach in a department called "American Environments." Murray Siskind, a visiting lecturer in Elvis Studies, and Jack Gladney, the chair of Hitler Studies, debate the trend:

> "I understand the music, I understand the movies, I even see how comic
> books can tell us things. But there are full professors in this place who
> read nothing but cereal boxes."
> "It's the only avant-garde we've got left."   (9–10)

More recently, J.M. Coetzee's *Disgrace*, while not primarily a satire, finds grim laughter in the death of the liberal arts, as a scholar of Romantic poetry is compelled, in the new corporate university, to teach inane courses in "Communications Skills." The replacement of literature departments with such monstrosities as "Professional and Public Writing" programs looms. Indeed, as universities have been corporatized, the campus novel, with its crises of economic security, of love, and of status, increasingly registers the alienation of a broader swathe of white-collar labor, questioning belief in the value of academic work itself.[13]

The campus novel, like other comedies of manners, trades in caricatures and types: pedants, pretenders, snobs, eccentrics, lechers, seductresses, self-promoters. McCarthy's narrator remarks that Jocelyn invariably attracts "a certain number of seasoned non-conformists and dissenters, sexual deviants, feather-bedders, alcoholics, impostors" (84). McCarthy's Henry Mulcahy, a James Joyce scholar, pretentiously carries an ashplant with him in imitation of Joyce's Stephen Dedalus. Amis's Ned Welch forces junior faculty to stay at his house for an "arty weekend" of madrigal-singing and recorder-playing in celebration of "Merrie England." Lodge's Philip Swallow fantasizes about publishing his exam questions as a series of Wittgensteinian aperçus; Morris Zapp aims to write an analysis of Jane Austen so comprehensive that it will "put a definitive stop to the production of any further garbage on the subject."[14] All of these types may be seen as variations on stock comic figures, but in one respect the campus novel continues a more specialized tradition: its egghead professors hark back, past Swift's Academy of Lagado, to the Renaissance humanists' satire of the pedantry of the scholastic theologians lost in mazes of their own thought. A prime example is Nabokov's Charles Kinbote in *Pale Fire*, who transforms his neighbor John Shade's poem into a coded account of Kinbote's own (imaginary) secret past as a Slavic King. Here the campus novel overlaps with the intellectual or epistemological satire of the Menippean novel.

It is the satire of social relations, however, that anchors the academic novel in the tradition of the comedy of manners. Plots about professional survival or advancement intertwine with stories of flirtation, courtship, marriage, adultery, and divorce. Not by accident are the twinned protagonists of *Changing Places* both Austen scholars, and the central turning-point of *Lucky Jim* a ball.[15] Like other small words, academia is rife with social hierarchies and pressures, as evident in Jim Dixon's inability to refuse even the most maddening request from Ned Welch. Department politics, in McCarthy's Jocelyn, are shown to be as petty as the Lilliputians' debates about the height of their heels:

> The experienced parliamentarians quickly learned the trick of party regularity, that is, to vote the opposite of the enemy, whatever the merits of a motion, but this rule was not foolproof against a devious opponent,

> who could suddenly change his position and thrown the whole meeting
> into confusion. (71)

The professors' maneuverings are as Machiavellian as the political schemes of
Queen Anne's court. Academia, moreover, is also a world of tradition, ritual,
and custom, as the opening to *White Noise* shows. Jack Gladney describes,
with a Rabelaisian catalogue, the "day of the station wagons," a September
spectacle when students arrive in cars spilling over with material goods –
clothes, books, dorm accoutrements, sports equipment, electronics, contra-
ceptives, junk food. It is a ritual that, as Gladney points out, bestows "a sense
of renewal, of communal recognition," and, "more than formal liturgies or
laws," establishes their membership in a particular class and even a particular
nation (3–4). Such communal rituals, here defamiliarized by the
outsider–insider Gladney, perform subtle but powerful ideological work in
establishing the boundaries of the small world.

Yet even in the self-contained, pseudo-utopian small world of the campus,
political and historical events intrude, driving the plots and shaping the themes
of the novel. *The Groves of Academe* registers the political pressures of the Red
Scare, as Mulcahy manipulates his way to tenure by pretending to have been
a Communist in the 1930s, forcing the well-meaning university president to
retain him, lest he be seen as capitulating to right-wing pressure. *Lucky Jim*
takes up postwar social mobility and class antagonism by pitting Jim, a humble
newcomer to the academy, against the snobbish Welches, who embody the old
rigid system. In *Changing Places*, the political and sexual turmoil of the 1960s
roils the university culture, and the swapping of spouses implies a satiric
questioning of traditional sexual mores. Philip Roth's *The Human Stain* is set
during the impeachment of Bill Clinton, a moment of puritanical backlash
during which the American media engaged in "an ecstasy of sanctimony." Roth
links this right-wing moralism to a left-wing political correctness in which the
white male has become such a familiar villain that he does not need to be
named. During a eulogy, a lesbian environmentalist dairy farmer rhapsodizes
about an unsullied American landscape:

> We chose this resting place for Faunia because it has been sacred ever
> since the aboriginal peoples bid farewell to their loved ones here.
> The wonderful stories that Faunia told our kids – about the swallows in
> the barn and the crows in the field, about the red-tailed hawks that glide
> in the sky high above our fields – they were the same sort of stories you
> might have heard on this very mountaintop before the ecological balance
> of the Berkshires was first disturbed by the coming of . . .
> The coming of you-know-who.[16]

Zuckerman's cynical "you-know-who" reframes the speaker's ostensibly liberal values as the predictable, rigid code of a conformist society. In both the macrocosm and microcosm, repression and *ressentiment* cloak themselves in the language of morality.

It is fitting that the title of the original campus novel, McCarthy's *Groves of Academe*, alludes to Horace: "I wanted to distinguish crooked from straight, / And to search for truth in the groves of academe."[17] The utopian academic grove becomes the tortuous labyrinth from which the artificer must escape. A visiting poet, dragged into Mulcahy's political machinations, offers a clarity available only to someone from outside the small world:

> Within twenty hours, he perceived, they had succeeded in leading him up the garden path into one of their academic mazes, where a man could wander for eternity, meeting himself in mirrors . . . Possibly they are all very nice, high-minded, scrupulous people with only an occupational tendency toward backbiting and a nervous habit of self-correction . . . but he did not care to catch the bug, which seemed to be endemic in these ivied haunts. (295)

The utopian closed-in space of the rural American small college, far from offering a shelter from the political pressures of national politics, only concentrates and intensifies them. A garden gives way to a maze in which it is impossible to discern crooked from straight.

Widening the Small World: *Babbitt*

On the surface Sinclair Lewis may not look like a satirist of manners. Part of a broad early twentieth-century progressive revolt against capitalist ideology and genteel taste, Lewis practiced a social realism modeled on the work of H.G. Wells (and, via Wells, Charles Dickens), and his novels are more wide-ranging in scope and explicit in their political engagement than are those of a miniaturist like Austen. Yet in their own way they present a small world; *Babbitt*, one of the most influential American satires of the twentieth century, may satirize American business, politics, and religion, but at is core lie the manners of a specific class, a code of behavior as distinct as the customs of Austen's rural gentry or Waugh's fashionable urbanites. Indeed, *Babbitt* usefully demonstrates how the patterns of social satire that are distilled in a more tightly focused version of the comedy of manners can persist, even as the satire widens in setting and plot and its concerns become more explicitly the collective problems of a mass society.

Lewis's novel gave a name to a new social type: the word "Babbitt" came to denote a recognizable class of newly moneyed, philistine small businessmen. Babbitt represents the middle-class white male American in the first half of the century much as John Updike's Rabbit does in the second half. This class is defined not only by its wealth, but also by its tastes, beliefs, and possessions. As Lewis's narrator notes, in a modern Midwestern city, "a family's motor indicated its social rank as precisely as the grades of the peerage determined the rank of an English family" (62). Lewis illustrates the subtle yet rigid stratification of this social world through the silent comparison of two symmetrical dinner parties in Chapter 15; the Babbitts, although crushed by their failure to impress their social superiors, the McKelveys, nonetheless disdain, just as blithely, an overture from the socially inferior Overbrooks. The city of Zenith is introduced grandly as a young metropolis aspiring to join a new global economy, but its outsize ambitions are immediately shrunk to a mock-heroic scale closer to that of a village, and George Babbitt's own inflated self-image is pierced with sharp narratorial irony.

This reduction of the character to a type is both Lewis's satiric method and also his theme. If the wide-ranging satire of the novel converges on one single target, it is "the Standardized American Citizen" (153). In their anti-labor politics, their perfunctory church-going, their happy ignorance of culture, the businessmen of Zenith are as alike as the rapidly built houses that Babbitt makes a living selling. Class-based norms creep into all aspects of Babbitt's personality; his mind is drenched in canned phrases and recycled slogans. Just as Republican senators decide his politics, and Protestant preachers his religious beliefs, so, we are told, "did the large national advertisers fix the surface of his life, fix what he believed to be his individuality" (79). His delight in new products and gadgets, the rituals and conversation of his dinner parties, even his unthinking physical habits like cigar-smoking, all rob him of, rather than bestow him with, distinctiveness. And although Lewis's satiric technique includes heavy narratorial moralizing, he deftly captures Babbitt's sociolinguistic environment – the clichés of advertising and newspapers, the slang of male camaraderie and Rotary Club speeches – and reveals these speech genres as fraught with ideology.

Because Babbitt does not possess the critical apparatus to free himself from these forces of standardization, when he lacks a pre-fabricated opinion, he becomes flustered and inarticulate. His irritability, his resentment of his wife, his complaints of fatigue – all point to an unexpressed dissatisfaction with the constriction of this code of manners. Babbitt's rebellion against this ideological code, whether social (parties with a new bohemian crowd), sexual (the affair with Tanis), or political (sympathy for the socialist Seneca Doane), thus proves short-lived, in part because the disciplinary mechanisms of the small world restore him to his "proper" social role. After he expresses sympathy for striking miners at the Zenith Athletic Club, "Babbitt knew that he was being watched" (262); later he is said to be "afraid of men's eyes and the incessant hiss of whispering" (312). The male social network of Zenith, operating through its clubs, churches, and businesses, proves as efficient in its surveillance as the belles of Pope's Hampton Court or the gossips of Austen's country villages.

Lewis initially holds Babbitt in such contempt that he appears as a fool or a clown rather than a villain or knave, almost Lilliputian in his pettiness. Despite his immoral business dealings and overt racism, he is most memorable for his stupidity and selfishness, his hypocrisy and self-justification. In his failure to transcend the norms of his class, he remains a mere ideological construct. Yet in Babbitt's fantasies of flight, his vision of the "fairy child," and his feeble rebellion, a psychological realism kicks in, summoning pathos for both Babbitt's spiritual constriction and his inability to comprehend his unhappiness. At his nadir, Babbitt begins to see through the ideology of middle-class America, and finds behind it a terrifying void:

> It was coming to him that perhaps all life as he knew it and vigorously practiced it was futile; ... that he hadn't much pleasure out of making money; that it was of doubtful worth to rear children merely that they might rear children who would rear children. (227)

Babbitt's business is not so different from Austen's Mrs. Bennet, whose sole purpose in life is the marriage of her daughters and the empty perpetuation of the social system. The domestic world appears not a refuge from the pressures of capitalism, but as another facet of it. Paul Riesling voices the novel's most explicit condemnation of the middle-class "morality" of monogamy, but the intermittent "bored routine" (75) of the Babbitts' sex life, and more generally the wearying minutiae of marriage and family, undermine any consolatory myth of domestic bliss. *Babbitt* concludes, like *Pride and Prejudice*, with marriages both legitimate (Verona and Ken) and quasi-scandalous (Ted and Eunice), while reuniting George and Myra after George's affair. But while the reconstitution of the existing society may appear comic and reassuring, it masks Babbitt's fear that such unions only reproduce a system whose value and purpose are never understood or even examined.

Chapter 8

Unfortunate Travelers: The Picaresque

The picaresque originates in Golden Age Spain as the name for a fictional autobiography of a *pícaro* – Spanish for rogue or rascal – and his (occasionally her) sundry adventures traveling from place to place. Its expansive plot and social survey of many tiers of society represent a countervailing tendency to the comedy of manners with its tight focus on a closed community. As it evolves, the picaresque plays a key role in the birth of the English novel in the eighteenth century, and assumes varied yet recognizable forms in the nineteenth and twentieth.[1] Its conventions are taken up in non-novelistic works as diverse as the prose fiction *Candide*, the narrative poem *Don Juan* and the mockumentary film *Borat*. It draws upon ancient, medieval, and early modern works, yet proves flexible enough to thrive when the novel becomes the culturally dominant form of fictional prose.

The first modern picaresque is generally held to be *Lazarillo de Tormes* (1554), about a fatherless boy's servitude to a series of masters who are, by turns, cruel, greedy, impoverished, and deceitful. The genre flourishes in subsequent decades, first in Spain with Mateo Alemán's *Guzmán de Alfarache* (1599, 1604) and works by Cervantes and Quevedo, then throughout Europe: in England, Thomas Nashe's *The Unfortunate Traveller* (1594); in Germany, Hans Jakob von Grimmelhausen's *Simplicissimus* (1669); in France, works by Charles Sorel and Paul Scarron, and, most influentially, Alain-René Le Sage's *Gil Blas* (1715–1735).[2] The roots of the picaresque, however, lie in the Roman prose satires of Petronius and especially Apuleius, who supplies a low comic realism achieved through careful attention to private life. The transformation of Apuleius's Lucius into a donkey allows him mutely to witness dimensions of human behavior – domestic, criminal, sexual, scatological – largely off-limits in more decorous registers of literature. In Renaissance humanism, this cheerful, irreverent comedy is joined to a critique of corrupt political and religious institutions, and the modern picaresque takes shape.[3]

The standard translations for *pícaro*, "rogue" and "rascal," have a quaint, even awkward ring, but they capture an innocent quality of the hero, who is typically an amoral outsider but not an outright villain. Usually a bastard, foundling, outcast, or orphan, he is thrown upon his own resources as a youth or a boy. As Virginia Woolf says of Defoe's protagonists, "each of these boys and girls has the world to begin and the battle to fight for himself." The *pícaro* usually attaches himself to a master, creating a comic duo. And although he lives on the edges of the law, his goals are sympathetic because they are universal. He lives, in Woolf's phrase, by a "rule-of-thumb morality," ignoring abstract ethical questions in his efforts to satisfy his basic needs: to acquire food, shelter, or money; to escape mistreatment or punishment; sometimes to attain revenge on a cruel master.[4] An anti-hero, he lives by his wits rather than traditional heroic values like courage. His example exposes as false the portraits of the valiant warriors who populate the epic and the romance.

The picaresque structure is episodic. It strings together a series of small adventure tales and comic scenarios according to the formula of "The Life and Adventures of X." As a fictional autobiography, it is typically told in the first person, offering an account of the narrator's criminal past with a measure of self-justification, incomprehension, or unreliability. "Hear Jack Wilton tell his own tale," invites Nashe's English *pícaro* (254). The episodic structure means that additional stories and adventures can easily – even indefinitely – be added to its plot; hence Ronald Paulson describes it as "all middle," indifferent to beginnings and ends (*SNEE* 25). As Dickens's Mr. Pickwick says to his friends, "The only question is, Where shall we go to next?" (468). When the picaresque plot does conclude, it promises further adventures, as when Huck Finn contemplates lighting out for the territory.[5] Here the contrast to the closure of the comedy of manners is pronounced: the goal is not integration into society, but flight from it.

The openness of form allows a survey of the world in its vast social heterogeneity. The picaresque partakes of Bakhtin's "chronotope of the road" (*DI* 244), a representation of time and space suitable for depicting a diversity of professions, customs, and cultures, crossing boundaries of nation and class. Such variety offers, in Claudio Guillén's words, "a standing invitation to satire," an opportunity to observe and record a panoply of social evils.[6] The world of the road is also ruled by chance: picaresques emphasize the sudden rise and fall of individual fortunes, the unpredictable and unscripted nature of experience (*DI* 128). Capricious Fortune, not all-seeing Providence, is its governing deity. The full titles of picaresque novels (*The Fortunes and Misfortunes of the Famous Moll Flanders, The Luck of Barry Lyndon*) may emphasize this theme, as may the heroes' names (Roderick Random, Felix Krull). "There is no man in the world, of my birth, whose misfortunes can at all be compared to mine," laments Thackeray's Barry Lyndon,[7] while Anita

Loos's *pícara* Lorelei Lee ruminates, "when a girl's life is as full of fate as mine seems to be, there is nothing else to do about it" (21).

A gritty realism distinguishes the picaresque from the more fantastical "imaginary voyage" found in Lucian's *True History* or Swift's *Gulliver's Travels*. The *pícaro* navigates a world permeated with deception, corruption, and criminality – what Bakhtin calls "the underside of real life" (*DI* 128). Indeed, Stendhal's defense of realism in *The Red and the Black* invokes a picaresque symbol in its famous comparison of the novel to a mirror traveling along the highway, reflecting both the blue of the sky and the mud of the road. The picaresque purports to show the world as it is.

The genre partakes of both the comic and the satiric.[8] The satiric side is visible in the injustice of the circumstances that the *pícaro* must navigate. Paulson argues that picaresques extend the basic structure of Horatian and Juvenalian verse satire through space and time. Where the Roman poets list examples of vice and folly taking place in current-day Rome, a travel-adventure plot elaborates each example into a narrative episode, then links these episodes to make a story (*SNEE* 21). But while the picaresque's image of society as cruel and degraded is satiric, its laughter has an affirmative side, embodied in the *pícaro*'s vitality, resiliency, and appetite. While motifs of servitude and punishment advance satiric agendas of moral correction or attack, motifs of disguise, mutability, self-reinvention, and movement emphasize a longing for freedom.

The *pícaro* himself balances elements of the trickster and the naïf. Characters like Lazarillo de Tormes or Huck Finn can appear foolishly innocent when exploited by the vicious or the cunning, but charmingly clever when profiting from others' folly. The *pícaro*'s role can even vary from one episode to another, depending on the relationship in which he finds himself. As a trickster, the *pícaro* possesses some kinship to medieval and Renaissance figures such as Reynard and Panurge, but he is usually motivated less by impishness than by basic needs.[9] When his knavery reaches an extreme, the *pícaro* gives way to an outright criminal or villain; when his foolishness reaches an extreme, he becomes a dunce like Candide. A survivor of the world's brutality, he puts little stock in high ideals or religious doctrines. Above all, the *pícaro* is, like Mr. Pickwick, an "observer of human nature" (26), someone who by virtue of his changing location and outsider status gains a critical purchase on his fellow beings and their society. Often his social insignificance aids him in this role; he observes best when unseen or inconspicuous. Apuleius's Lucius the ass is all-but-invisible since he is assumed to be a dumb animal, as is the lapdog who narrates Charles Gildon's 1709 adaptation of Apuleius, *The New Metamorphosis* (*SNEE* 221); servants, children, and prostitutes are more realistic figures who quietly obtain access to the seamier side of private life. Tobias Smollett's Cadwallader Crabtree overhears private conversations as he feigns deafness; Ralph Ellison's Invisible Man learns many truths because others do not see or recognize him.

As its title suggests, Nashe's *The Unfortunate Traveller* demonstrates the importance of both fortune and travel to the genre. Influenced by criminal biographies, cony-catching pamphlets, and Elizabethan jokebooks such as *Scoggin's Jests*, Nashe's narrative develops from an account of Jack Wilton's mischief as a page in an English military camp to his weightier experiences journeying through Europe as a soldier, servant, lover, and prisoner.[10] Nashe tips his hat to his satiric precursors: in Rotterdam, Jack meets Erasmus and Thomas More, whom he commends for recognizing the world's folly; in Venice he encounters Pietro Aretino, whose literary wit and political courage he extols. There is a gleeful comedy to many of Jack's pranks, but he also levels judgment – for example, against both the foolish Anabaptist soldiers who misinterpret a rainbow as a sign of God's favoritism and the merciless German army that slaughters them. Such violence, rife throughout the book, suggests a capricious world in which no providential plan is visible. Heraclide, raped upon the corpse of her murdered husband, declares, "The only repeal we have from God's undefinite chastisement is to chastise ourselves in this world" (339) before killing herself, while the murderer Cutwolfe blasphemously proclaims, "There is no heaven but revenge" (367). As for travel, the banished earl who saves Jack's life in Italy recites a litany of reasons against it; from Italy the traveler learns only "the art of atheism, the art of epicurising, the art of whoring, the art of poisoning, the art of sodomitry" (345). The darkening tone of this picaresque suggests that to travel is to subject oneself to the cruel vicissitudes of Fortune.

From such early patchworks of sex, violence, crime, and pranking, the picaresque plays a crucial role in the emergence of the novel in eighteenth-century England. English translations of *Don Quixote* and *Gil Blas* were among the best-selling books of the century's early decades,[11] and Defoe, Fielding, and Smollett all deploy picaresque elements including travel, episodic structures, social variety, and an ethos of expediency over moral principle. Smollett argues for the picaresque novel as a form of satire:

> Of all kinds of satire, there is none so entertaining and universally improving, as that which is introduced, as it were occasionally, in the course of an interesting story, which brings every incident home to life, and by representing familiar scenes in an uncommon and amusing point

of view, invests them with all the graces of novelty, while nature is appealed to in every particular.

Anecdote and precept, sympathy and indignation, go hand in hand "to animate the reader against the sordid and vicious disposition of the world."[12] The early English novelists blend the European picaresque with native forms including travel narratives and spiritual autobiographies. In a time of increasing social mobility, the *pícaro*'s "vertical" movement illustrates how birth, wealth, fortune, and character determine one's place in society. As interest in psychology deepens, the inner life of the protagonist becomes a focus. The *pícaro* is no longer simply an agent for surveying the social panorama, and the satiric catalogue of social ills now exists alongside a chronicle of the hero's emotional growth, pushing the form toward the genre of the bildungsroman, or novel of education. The coherence of the overall plot also becomes more important. By 1837, Dickens writes of *The Pickwick Papers* that "every number should be, to a certain extent, complete in itself, and yet the whole twenty numbers, when collected, should form one tolerably harmonious whole" (6). Novels also increasingly exploit the first-person structure of the autobiography. The reflections of the mature narrator on his or her younger self allow critical commentary that highlights past folly. Of course, as often happens in satire, such claims to a moral or spiritual purpose can feel unconvincing when set against the transgressive allure of the stories themselves.[13]

In England the picaresque also blends with the native sensationalistic tradition of criminal biography. Defoe's *Moll Flanders* infuses its autobiographical account of the heroine's adventures as servant, mistress, wife, adulterer, thief, and virtual prostitute with moral reflection, but Defoe's rendering of her character fosters sympathy more than judgment; her life story reveals a world in which Christian principle is in tension with economic necessity, and a woman's security is tied to her sexual availability. Fielding's *Jonathan Wild*, in contrast, chooses a true knave as a protagonist. The narrator's praise for Wild's ruthlessness, like the self-praise of Erasmus's Folly, reads as tongue-in-cheek censure:

> In our hero there was nothing not truly great: He could, without the least abashment, drink a bottle with the man who knew he had the moment before picked his pocket, and, when he had stripped him of everything he had, never desired to do him any further mischief; for he carried good nature to that wonderful and uncommon height that he never did a single injury to man or woman by which he himself did not expect to reap some advantage.[14]

On a strictly topical level, the satire here takes aim at the ruthless "Great Man," Prime Minister Robert Walpole, but on a broader level it indicts a society that holds decency and virtue in contempt. A century later, Thackeray's *Barry Lyndon* (1844), which praises "the old style of Molière and Fielding," takes up this strain of the picaresque, ironically justifying the behavior of the *pícaro*, who has now become an outright villain.[15] Barry Lyndon, outcast, soldier, con-man, rake, and gambler, does criticize his society – most acutely the ruthless practices of the conscription of soldiers – but increasingly he is the object rather than the agent of Thackeray's satire. Still, Barry's unscrupulous self-advancement and tortured self-justification are emblematic of a society where outright gambling is scorned but the deception of businessmen is sanctioned and even admired:

> The broker on the Exchange who bulls and bears, and buys and sells, and dabbles with lying loans, and trades on state secrets, what is he but a gamester? The merchant who deals in tea and tallow, is he any better? His bales of dirty indigo are his dice, his cards come up every year instead of every ten minutes, and the sea is his green table.[16]

Charismatic and self-justifying rogues like Joyce Cary's Gulley Jimson in *The Horse's Mouth* and Anthony Burgess's Alex in *A Clockwork Orange* continue this tradition, discounting goodness as they cultivate greatness.

The Quixote Figure: Fielding and Dickens

Another enduring variation of the *pícaro* is the Quixotean hero. In some ways, of course, Don Quixote is an anti-picaresque figure. Animated by idealism rather than realism, he is not an indigent young servant but a wealthy older master, and his motive is not economic survival but the old-fashioned chivalry of the knight-errant. Lazarillo de Tormes's imagination serves flatly pragmatic ends; Don Quixote's magically re-envisions the world.[17] Still, *Don Quixote* shares with the picaresque the basic form of a traveling, episodic social survey enlivened by low comic gags, motifs of disguise and deception, interpolated tales, quasi-philosophical dialogues, and an anti-romantic perspective fundamental to its satire. But Don Quixote and its successors also illustrate how the novel modifies satiric laughter. Two enduring Quixote fictions, Fielding's *Joseph Andrews* and Charles Dickens's *The Pickwick Papers*, suggest a mellowing of humor from the late sixteenth century to the early nineteenth, even as they demonstrate the versatility of the picaresque as a mode for comic-satiric writing.

Joseph Andrews (1742) was published during what is generally seen as a broad shift in taste, when polite middle-class sensibility was moving away from the harsh, punitive laughter associated with Augustan satire. The Earl of Shaftesbury, Joseph Addison, and Richard Steele advocated an affectionate laughter, based not in Hobbesian superiority or Aristotelian mockery, but in a charitable understanding of human imperfection. Yet despite this vaunted "sentimental turn," the mid-century, as Simon Dickie has shown, retained a taste for sadistic and physical comedy – often at the expense of helpless or abject targets such as cripples, blind men, beggars, the elderly, even rape victims.[18] Smollett's *Roderick Random* (1748) and Fielding's *Tom Jones* (1749) initiated a vogue for a kind of picaresque that Dickie calls "the ramble novel" – episodic comic fiction that recycled familiar slapstick gags and episodes, mostly for the sake of a good laugh. Fielding's apologia for *Joseph Andrews*, his "comic Epic-Poem in Prose" (49), should thus be understood as navigating between a new standard of politeness and a continuing appetite for the crude and the cruel. Fielding disavows sadistic laughter and aligns himself with mild comedy and high-minded satire. Because he "describe[s] not Men, but Manners; not an Individual but a Species," he classifies himself as a "Satirist" rather than a "Libeller" (203). Like Jonson and Swift before him, he claims to attack general human failings with the aim of reform rather than humiliating specific individuals. He disavows the distortions of caricature and burlesque in favor of the more realistic scale of comedy. The object of the comic, for Fielding, is not true "Villainy" but only the "Ridiculous," which arises from human "Affectation," which in turn stems from "Vanity" and "Hypocrisy" (50–52). This is satire based in amusement rather than anger.

Joseph Andrews, in its wandering tour of the roads, inns, homes, and alehouses of rural England, offers a survey in which comic episodes call attention to the moral deficiencies of the novel's characters – a long succession of parsons and innkeepers, squires and servants, lawyers and judges, flirts and fops. An early example occurs when, after Joseph is robbed on the highway and left naked in a ditch, the passengers in a stage-coach find ingenious and self-serving reasons to deny him first a ride and then a coat to cover himself. Only the fear of being held as accessories to his murder spurs them to pick him up. The pettiness of the characters is comic, and the exposure of their moral failings makes the comedy satiric. Such juxtaposition of stated belief and actual behavior is Fielding's dominant technique, though other episodes take a graver tone. Mr. Wilson's narrative of his dissolute years in London and eventual reform is presented as an almost Johnsonian moral fable; the subsequent episode, in which the squire's son gratuitously kills Wilson's daughter's pet dog, indulges a sentimental mode that anticipates Sterne.

Sexual morals are another focus of the novel's satire. In its conception, *Joseph Andrews* is a joke at the expense of Fielding's rival, Samuel Richardson, whose bestselling *Pamela; or, Virtue Rewarded* (1740) sentimentally extolled the virtue of female chastity. By writing about Pamela's equally chaste brother, Joseph, Fielding transforms the melodrama of the virgin threatened with rape into the comedy of a young man so sexually reticent he appears foolish. ("Lady Booby, are you trying to seduce me?") After all, in 1742, a young man seeking to preserve his virginity was more likely to be ridiculed than praised.[19] Joseph's sexual innocence is so extreme as to be unnatural, much like Candide's moral innocence two decades later. Meanwhile, his lustful pursuers, Booby and Slipslop, appear hilariously vain. Fielding may be satirizing *Pamela*'s "lesson" that sexual virtue is rewarded with material success, or simply rejecting Richardson's priggish moralism; in either case, once Fanny appears on the scene, the narrator himself engages in some heavy breathing over the prospect of the lovers consummating their relationship, making chastity appear a social convention rather than a religious virtue. Joseph, for his part, can barely keep his hands off his fiancée, and at one point is described as "fondly meditating on that lovely Creature" (257) in near-masturbatory fashion.

The real Quixote figure of the novel, however, is Parson Adams. Adams reads and is deluded by the classics just as Alonso Quijano reads and is deluded by romances, and his benevolent Christianity is as impractical as Quixote's chivalric code. Like Quixote, Adams is childishly innocent of the world's devious ways; he seeks to right injustices as he travels from inn to inn, always game for physical combat. And while Fielding praises Adams's Christian decency and idealism, the parson, like Quixote, has flaws. Most prominent is pomposity – what Erasmus calls "philautia": he can't resist sermonizing on weighty topics, even though the other characters fall asleep during his speeches. His wisdom proves impractical too. When Fanny is abducted by would-be rapists, Adams can only advise Joseph to refrain from immoderate grief. His advice to the distraught lover is as useless as Pangloss's reassurances that Candide lives in the best of all possible worlds.

Like Quixote, Adams endures one physical humiliation after another. His efforts to right the world's wrongs cause him to be doused with a pan full of hog's blood (144), thrown into the mire of a pig sty (182), attacked by a pack of hounds (242), soaked with the contents of a chamber pot (259), and, in a single evening, mistaken first for Slipslop's would-be rapist and then for Fanny's (323–326). Most egregiously, in the "roasting" scene at the squire's house in Book Three, modeled on the episodes of the Duke and the Duchess in *Don Quixote*, the squire and his friends subject Adams to gratuitous humiliations, and his outraged protests only feed their mirth. The squire, in his sophistication and malice, illustrates what is wrong with the upper classes, but Fielding's slapstick mobilizes our own sadism, which complicates our sympathy for the hapless but clueless clergyman.[20]

Does Fielding then level his judgment against an un-Christian world or against the parson whose idealism equips him so poorly to function in that world? Ultimately, what matters is the gap between the two possibilities. The Quixote fiction balances satire of the hero's idealism and of the world's injustice, promoting dialectical shifts in judgment. The role of the narrator in *Joseph Andrews* tends to support such doubleness. Rather than stabilizing meaning, he undermines his attempts at moralism with irony. He impishly subjects Fanny to one sexual peril after another. Blithely ignoring the reader's concern for her safety, he leaves her in the hands of villains while indulging in a discussion between the poet and the player. In Sternean fashion, he advises the reader "to skip over" (172) an upcoming description of Fanny's physical charms, joking with us about our own desires and fantasies. He undercuts moralistic speeches by calling attention to their tediousness or skipping them altogether. And while the novel's rather contrived happy ending can imply an underlying benignity to the world, it is just as persuasive to say with Michael McKeon that in Fielding's degraded, satiric world, only the active interference of the author can produce such wish-fulfillment.[21]

Almost a century after *Joseph Andrews*, Dickens's *Pickwick Papers* (1837) represents a further mellowing of the Quixote fiction. The book features a traveling hero who undertakes a survey of the nation, "mixing with different varieties and shades of human character" (749). Some episodes resemble pure farce or slapstick, and several interpolated tales shift to a sensational Gothic mode. Others, like the early episode of Winkle's duel, demystify heroic values by showing the cowardice of the mild-mannered duelist in a comic but sympathetic light. The skeptical observation of society remains a steady theme, and particular episodes take up specific targets, with Pickwick and his friends serving mainly to observe or comment wryly. The visit to Eatansville offers a dry satire of party politics, with the Buffs and the Blues representing two polarized yet symmetrical factions, much like the low- and high-heeled parties of Swift's Lilliput:

> [E]verything in Eatanswill was made a party question. If the Buffs proposed to new skylight the market-place, the Blues got up public meetings, and denounced the proceeding; if the Blues proposed the erection of an additional pump in the High Street, the Buffs rose as one man and stood aghast at the enormity. There were Blue shops and Buff

shops, Blue inns and Buff inns – there was a Blue aisle and a Buff aisle in the very church itself. (166)

The episode's satire extends to partisan journalism, campaign events, political speeches, and the manipulation of voters through bribes and dirty tricks. Similarly, the episodes featuring Reverend Stiggins and his temperance association take steady aim at the clergyman's greed, self-righteousness, and hypocrisy – including his missionary work "providing the infant negroes in the West Indies with flannel waistcoats and moral pocket handkerchiefs" (355–356). Dickens defends these attacks in his preface to the 1867 edition, insisting he satirizes not religion but "the cant of religion," and condemning "any class of persons who, in the words of SWIFT, have just enough religion to make them hate, and not enough to make them love, one another" (765). Of course, as with Fielding, Dickens's outspoken effort to contain and stabilize the effects of his own satire signals its capacity to misfire.

The most prominent targets of *The Pickwick Paper* are the law, the courts, and the prison system. Pickwick's ridiculous trial (a source for the even more absurd trial in *Alice in Wonderland* thirty years later) demonstrates many of the flaws of the system: bogus displays of tears; a foolish, distracted judge; the ludicrously sexual interpretations of Pickwick's references to tomato sauce; the erroneous guilty verdict. With his representation of his society's various disciplinary institutions, Dickens extends his satire to an emerging system of bureaucratic or administered capitalism – a target no longer reducible to individual fools or knaves. In this, *The Pickwick Papers,* like much of Dickens's later work, contains elements of not only the picaresque but also the institutional satire of the Menippean novel.

Mr. Pickwick is a reinvention of the Quixote figure for the Victorian age. Parson Adams is saner than Don Quixote, and Mr. Pickwick is saner still; the delusion of the hidalgo is tempered into lovable eccentricity. Pickwick is introduced in a mock-heroic mode – "There sat the man who had traced to their source the mighty ponds of Hampstead, and agitated the scientific world with his Theory of Tittlebats" (16) – and he never quite lives up to the grandeur that the narrator ascribes to him. He also possesses Quixote's basic combination of goodwill and naiveté, which sets him up, like his predecessors, to be the butt of incessant physical comedy. He falls through the ice while skating on a pond, chases in vain after runaway horses, tumbles over a garden wall into a rose bush, gets caught in the middle of a kitchen brawl. Throughout these indignities, Dickens's narrator maintains a detached, philosophical tone that allows us to smile at the hero's suffering: "There are very few moments in a man's existence when he experiences so much

Figure 10 Robert Seymour (1798–1836), "Mr. Pickwick in Chase of His Hat," 1836. The New York Public Library Digital Collections, Henry W. and Albert A. Berg Collection of English and American Literature.
   "There are very few moments in a man's existence when he experiences so much ludicrous distress, or meets with so little charitable commiseration, as when he is in pursuit of his own hat."

ludicrous distress, or meets with so little charitable commiseration, as when he is in pursuit of his own hat" (62) (Figure 10).

Pickwick survives such indignities, but he is prone to indignation when he confronts selfishness, injustice, and bad manners. His dudgeon is comic. After one of Alfred Jingle's transgressions, Pickwick's outrage begins to simmer, while the narrator maintains a balance of mock-heroic teasing and buttoned-up discretion:

> If any dispassionate spectator could have beheld the countenance of the illustrious man, whose name forms the leading feature of the title of this work . . . he would have been almost induced to wonder that the indignant fire which flashed from his eyes did not melt the glasses of his spectacles – so majestic was his wrath. (141–142)

Unlike the battle-ready Quixote and the pugilistic Adams, however, Pickwick's indignation never boils over in rage; he fails even "to call up a sneer" (708). Still, Pickwick eventually becomes enmeshed in the society that he initially plans only to survey. He fully assumes the role of comic knight errant when he tries to rectify Jingle's injustices and takes up arms for middle-class decency: "'Whenever I meet that Jingle again, wherever it is,' said Mr. Pickwick, raising himself in bed, and indenting his pillow with a tremendous blow, 'I'll inflict personal chastisement on him, in addition to the exposure he so richly merits. I will, or my name is not Pickwick'" (228).

With Pickwick himself in the (mock) heroic role of the knight errant, the role of the rogue or trickster is displaced onto the charismatic actor and conman Jingle; later, Bob Sawyer functions as an impish prankster to play off against the straight man Pickwick. Sam Weller, meanwhile, seizes center stage in the role of Sancho Panza, the devoted servant. With steady sang-froid (and a satyr's eye for pretty young women), Sam uses solid common sense to balance his master's impractical idealism. His comfort in negotiating the modern world makes up for Pickwick's cluelessness: both Sam and Pickwick live by Sam's wits. Unlike the soft-hearted Pickwick, the hard-headed Sam is never persuaded by tears: "Tears never yet wound up a clock, or worked a steam ingin" (217). This rejection of sentimentality is part of a general impatience with fakery and fraudulence. Sam's language, too, speaks to his pragmatism. His "Wellerisms" update Sancho's proverbs; these add a witty twist to a plain proverb, often with an unexpected element of violence: "'Business first, pleasure second, as King Richard the Third said when he stabbed the t'other king in the Tower, afore he smothered the babbies'" (329). His malapropisms function similarly. Unlike Mrs. Slipslop's mistakes in *Joseph Andrews*, which demonstrate her intellectual pretensions, Sam's errors expose snobbishness in the language of *others* – "habeas corpus," for example, becomes the more sensible "have-his-carcase." As Dickens's friend John Forster wrote, "Sam Weller and Mr. Pickwick are the Sancho and Quixote of Londoners."[22]

No More Mean Tricks: *Huckleberry Finn*

In moving the picaresque to the American West, Mark Twain's *Adventures of Huckleberry Finn* restores a geographic openness to the genre, which in *The Pickwick Papers* had become limited to a tour of country villages and suburban towns. The size of the American continent and the national mythologies of escape and expansion mesh easily with the picaresque themes of exploration, outsiderhood, and self-reinvention. In adapting the genre to the American setting, Twain also creates a framework for countless American road movies in the century to come – although the raft and the river, not the car and the highway, are Twain's central symbols. Indeed, Twain's Mississippi

River comes to stand for several powerful ideas at once: the majesty of nature, the quest for freedom, the uncertain currents of fate.

Twain wrote to William Dean Howells that he was modeling *Huck Finn* on *Gil Blas*,[23] and the character of Huck returns the *pícaro* to his roots. He is a child, an orphan, and an outsider. In his innocence and limited understanding, he is a classic naïf, but in his methods of survival he is a trickster, constantly inventing new names and histories for himself. His reasoning is prudential rather than principled – and his morality based in experience turns out to be sounder than alternatives based in religion or social tradition. Most of all, his first-person account returns us to a model of the picaresque as autobiography, and Huck's voice and perspective – rich in sensuous detail, colorful idiom, and unconscious insight – infuse the novel and make possible its sharpest ironies.

In its opening chapters, the novel appears as though it might be a Quixote fiction, with Tom Sawyer playing the mad knight's role. It is *Don Quixote*'s belief in enchanters that Tom cites to explain why it is that the Spaniards, Arabs, camels, and elephants he attacks appear to Huck as an innocent Sunday-school picnic (25). Through Tom, Twain rewrites Quixotean delusion as a childhood play – the sane but ludic exercise of imagination – and Twain's opening "Notice" against seeking morals and motives in his work supports Tom's advocacy of imagination for its own sake. However, Tom's games make him a trickster, the perpetrator and not the victim of deceptions and hoaxes.[24] For this reason, Tom's childhood mischief runs up against the hard reality of slavery.

As the plot unfolds, Huck escapes from his role as Tom's Sancho and becomes a purer version of the *pícaro*. His tour of the American West provides a satiric survey of customs and behavior interspersed with episodes of low comedy, cross-dressing, slapstick, and interpolated dialogues and tales. But the novel as a genre has changed in the course of the nineteenth century, and the emergence of the bildungsroman means that Huck's character will not be static or one-dimensional. His growth – his moral and emotional understanding of Jim's humanity and of the evil of slavery – becomes central to the novel's purpose. It is for this reason that the reappearance of Tom the trickster in the novel's final chapters has proved so problematic for readers: Huck seems to regress in following Tom's plans, and the gears of the plot gnash as we shift suddenly from the dangerous encounter with reality back to the sheltered play of childhood games.

The heart of the novel, of course, does not concern Tom. Yet even after Huck has fled, he still measures his ingenuity and cleverness against his idealized image of his friend, variously wishing that Tom were present to help him imagine his way out of a fix, or commending himself for pulling off a stunt as well as Tom could have. But the novel steadily calls into question the ludic pleasure of deception that Tom advocates, most importantly when Huck tricks Jim into believing that Huck's disappearance in the fog had only been a dream. After Jim figures out the truth and rebukes Huck – "all you wuz thinkin 'but wuz how you could make a fool of ole Jim with a lie. Dat truck dah is *trash*" – Huck humbles himself in apology and changes his ways: "I didn't do him no more mean tricks, and I wouldn't done that one if I'd a knowed it would make him feel that way" (95). The moral risks of deception are further dramatized by King and the Duke, who reveal the dark side of roguery, now judged not by Renaissance but by Victorian moral standards. Their malicious deception not only highlights the relative innocence of Huck's shenanigans but also helps to sharpen Huck's moral faculties as he progresses from merely observing their frauds to subverting them.

Huck's tricks take place in the service first of survival and then of altruism. In contrast, Tom's fun in the final chapters is purchased at the cost of delaying Jim's freedom. Many readers have disparaged Twain's ending as a reversion to a simple children's tale that undermines the moral stakes of the novel. Yet Huck's resistance to Tom's Quixotean games suggests that Twain is actually critiquing Tom's actions, exposing the fact that one boy's joke is another man's torment. (Tom's role here, far from innocent, is closer to the Duke and the Duchess than to Quixote himself.) Huck may play along with Tom, but his sympathies are with Jim, who "couldn't see no sense in the most of it" (256). Even when Huck and Jim are on the raft, Jim has no interest in adventure for its own sake, which merely puts his tenuous freedom at risk. For Huck, white and free, the romance of the picaresque supersedes the importance of their mission, but Jim is clear that "he didn't want no more adventures" (86). Thus, when Huck calls Tom "Full of principle" (254), there is no hint of admiration, as there is for the principled stands of Pickwick or Parson Adams; Twain sides fully with Huck's experiential pragmatism.

If Tom is a modified Quixote figure and the Duke and the King are rogues, what is Jim's role? The relationship briefly appears to be a Crusoe–Friday dyad, but the utopian idyll on Jackson's Island is short-lived, and Jim is no more Huck's servant than Huck is Jim's. As they travel, however, they form a comic pair, and while some have found precedents in American stage comedy routines, their conversations function like the discussions, debates, and dialogues in *Don Quixote, Joseph Andrews,* and Diderot's *Jacques le Fataliste,* exploring ideas in a non-dogmatic way. A brilliant example is their discussion of the story of the Judgment of Solomon, in which Jim's "misreading" provides an oblique commentary on the commodification of the human body, one that stems from

Jim's experience as both a father and another person's property. But if Jim is a debating partner, he is even more centrally a father, as Toni Morrison has discerned.[25] Jim in fact functions as both a substitute father and a substitute mother for the orphaned Huck, caring for him and protecting him as neither Tom nor the widow Douglas can or will.

The picaresque formula of *Huck Finn* allows the hero to serve, like Lucius the Ass, Jack Wilton, or Moll Flanders, as a satiric observer of the crimes and follies of society, which in *Huck Finn* turn out to be horrifically violent. The Grangerford-Shepherdson feud, for example, draws a humorous contrast between the minister's "ornery preaching" about "faith, and good works, and free grace" and the men in the pews with their guns between their knees (129). More ambiguous is the speech that Colonel Sherburn gives to the lynch mob; he condemns the mob mentality as cowardly, yet the force of his condemnation is undercut by his own needless killing of the drunkard Boggs. Here Twain's satire slashes at both the arrogance of Southern gentility and the violence and stupidity of the white underclass.[26] The venality of the King and the Duke, meanwhile, provokes Huck to Juvenalian misanthropy; when the men cheat the Wilkses of their inheritance, he complains: "It was enough to make a body ashamed of the human race" (176).

While violence, corruption, and greed are omnipresent in *Huck Finn*, the central target of Twain's satire is racism. Early on, Pap's tirade against the mixed-race college professor in Ohio distills a combination of anti-government, anti-intellectual, and anti-black hatreds that is still at work in American politics today. Yet the primary weapon that Twain uses to attack white supremacy is his representation of Huck's voice. Huck's youth, naiveté, and limited understanding lead him to employ a moral language that is not his own, and so to reach conclusions that reflect the skewed values of Southern Christian culture rather than the superior judgment shared by Twain and his implied reader. As Wayne Booth famously put it, "the narrator claims to be naturally wicked while the author silently praises his virtues ... behind his back."[27] If Erasmus perfected the mode of blame-by-praise, Twain here perfects praise-by-blame. Twain uses this technique throughout the novel, including the climactic moment in which Huck, after wrestling with the "sin" of having helped Jim to escape, writes a note turning in his friend, then has second thoughts:

> "All right then, I'll go to hell" – and tore it up.
> It was awful thoughts, and awful words, but they was said. And I let them stay said; and never thought no more about reforming. I shoved the

whole thing out of my head; and said I would take up wickedness again, which was in my line, being brung up to it, and the other warn't. And for a starter, I would go to work and steal Jim out of slavery again.   (223)

Famous as this moment is, it is only the culmination of a long series of similar ironies in which the language and judgments of Huck's culture clash with his instincts and experiences, causing him to mislabel good as bad and vice versa. Sentences such as "Jim had a wonderful level head, for a nigger" (97) expose the contradiction between a racist education and Huck's natural perception of Jim's humanity; the phrase "for a nigger" may outrage us, but it illustrates how Huck must supplement his plain common sense with a degrading epithet in order to square his experience with his corrupt ideology.

The racism that Twain indicts is inseparable from the Christian culture that economically and ideologically supports it, and Twain's anti-racist satire is enmeshed with his anti-religious satire.[28] When Huck tells Miss Watson that he prefers Hell to Heaven, he is not choosing evil but embracing life over death and freedom over confinement – much as he does thirty chapters later when he decides to "go to hell." The religious ideology that underwrites slavery is, for Twain, part and parcel of a sentimental Southern cavalier culture, and his rejection of this culture lies behind his admiration for the anti-chivalric satire of *Don Quixote*.[29] (It likewise drives his wonderful parody of nineteenth-century sentimental poetry in the "Ode to Stephen Dowling Bots, Dec'd.") Like Sam Weller, Huck sees through false tears, as we learn with the early scene of Pap's tearful but bogus repentance. For Twain, Southern sentimentality, chivalry, and Christianity do not merely fail to counter the evils of racism and slavery, but in fact make those evils possible.

Modernist Naïfs: Loos, Waugh, and West

The early twentieth century produces several memorable reinventions of the picaresque. Lorelei Lee, the flapper heroine of Anita Loos's *Gentlemen Prefer Blondes* (1925), travels from Little Rock to New York City to the great capitals of Europe, satirizing en route the sexual economy that makes the twenties roar. Lorelei begins where Huck Finn left off – in Arkansas. According to Loos, the inspiration for choosing this ostensibly illiterate corner of the United States as Lorelei's birthplace was not Twain but H.L. Mencken; in his 1917 essay "Sahara of the Bozarts," Mencken (punning on "Ozarks" with a Lorelei-like spelling of "beaux arts") depicted the South as a cultural desert, a judgment Loos concurred with in calling the state "the nadir in shortsighted human stupidity" (xl). But *Huck Finn* was Mencken's favorite book, and Loos might thus owe her choice indirectly to Twain. In any case, after being acquitted in the shooting of Mr. Jennings, Lorelei lights out for the territory, which by the 1920s is no longer Oklahoma but Hollywood.

Lorelei is a true *pícara*. Her worldview is charmingly narcissistic, her goals flatly pragmatic, her methods cheerily amoral. She not only attempts murder, but also commits theft, blackmail, and probably adultery, yet she wins the reader's affection with her vitality and optimism. Her freedom from the constraints of guilt and repression are so striking that Freud himself is baffled: "Dr. Froyd said that all I needed was to cultivate a few inhibitions and get some sleep" (90). The diary form of Lorelei's narrative may descend from the sentimental Richardsonian tradition, but her voice, with its colorful idiosyncrasies, owes a debt to Huck, and the self-justifying nature of her account draws on Defoe's fusion of criminal adventure with spiritual autobiography. Her episodic escapades allow her to fashion new identities, and like Moll Flanders, she keeps her birth name a secret. "Lorelei," the name she adopts "to express her personality" (26), is a river-nymph of German folklore, a siren who lures men to their death. The musical syllables hint at beauty (allure) and deception (a lie).

Huck's speech provides authenticity, but Lorelei's suggests performance. Her grammatical mistakes ("a girl like I") illustrate the hypercorrection of the upwardly aspirational autodidact, and her diction absorbs the euphemisms of the society she wants to join. While there is an element of Mrs. Slipslop's pretentiousness in her malapropisms, she also shares Sam Weller's skill in bending elevated vocabulary to the demands of common sense ("Eyefull Tower"), and her indifference to proper spelling suggests a healthy freedom that makes space for unconscious association and Joycean polysemy.

Like Huck, Lorelei combines the roles of naïf and trickster. The most obvious jokes in the novel are about Lorelei's ignorance – of spelling and grammar, of history and literature, of mathematics and geography. In France she surmises that someone named Louis XVI "used to be in the anteek furniture business" (62); she is unimpressed with a Whistler painting because her father was a good whistler himself. These solecisms place her in a line of unlettered American characters that includes not only Huck but also a series of "rubes" created by vernacular humorists such as Ring Lardner, simpletons whose errors provoke amiable laughter rather than outright derision.[30] Yet if Lorelei's ignorance is mocked, she is nobody's fool when it comes to the manipulation of wealthy men. Her ability to promise and withhold is an art of delaying fulfillment, and the slang meaning of a prostitute's "trick" hovers in the background whenever Lorelei converts her sexual allure into diamonds or other gifts. She flatters Beekman by playing on his vanity, and wins Henry's mother away from Miss Chapman's influence with false compliments. As soon as she gets what she wants, she coldly moves on to the next target. Her diary is a trick as well. This ostensibly confessional mode serves to conceal as much as it reveals – leaving the reader uncertain, for example, as to whether Lorelei is rewarding generous men with sex or merely luring them with a lie.[31] Like Oscar Wilde's Gwendolyn, Lorelei knows that a diary exists not only to be written but also to be read.

Lorelei's sidekick, Dorothy, is her Sancho. Where Lorelei's language is full of euphemism and refinement, Dorothy's is forthright and salty: "Dorothy speaks their own languadge to unrefined people better than a refined girl like I" (59). Dorothy, brunette and sharp-tongued, is a stand-in for Loos herself, and even lunches with Loos's friend Mencken. But while Dorothy utters terrific one-liners, Lorelei rejects invective as a mode of satire too direct and ill-mannered. She instead aspires to refinement, and attempts to put on the manners that she believes society demands.

Critics agree that *Gentlemen* contains satire, but exactly what the novel satirizes is less certain. In its representation of ruthless social climbing, hollow courtship rituals, and class snobbery, it shares targets and methods with the comedy of manners. In Lorelei's often admiring accounts of self-improvement and positive thinking, Loos laughs at the inanity of these 1920s fads. And her embrace of the decade's ethos of conspicuous consumption – "shopping really seems to be what Paris is principaly for" (63) – can be read as Loos's satiric judgment; Faye Hammill argues that Loos uses "the classic satiric method" of having a naïve narrator praise what the knowing author censures.[32]

But simple inversion of praise to blame cannot fully account for the operations of satire in *Gentlemen*. Lorelei's hedonism may be mocked, but it comes off better than the Puritan moralizing that shadows it. Loos jokes about the killjoy Henry Spoffard:

> So Mr. Spoffard spends all of his time looking at things that spoil peoples morals. So Mr. Spoffard really must have very very strong morals or else all the things that spoil other peoples morals would spoil his morals. But they do not seem to spoil Mr. Spoffards morals. (78)

Not only Henry but all the men rendered pliable by Lorelei's beauty are satiric targets just as deserving as the legacy-hunters of *Volpone*. For that matter, so are the women; fussy Margaret Dumont types, they serve as sexless, humorless agents of repression. Some readers see capitalism rather than Puritanism as Loos's main target, unwittingly endorsing the view of the "Soviet authorities," who, Loos jokes, took the novel "as evidence of the exploitation of helpless female blondes by predatory magnates of the Capitalistic System" (xxxviii–xxxix). Others defend Lorelei's acquisitiveness for debunking the false idealization of sexuality, an idealization that obscures the economic basis of modern sexual relations; for them, Lorelei articulates an important truth when she says, "Kissing your hand may make you feel very very good but a diamond and safire bracelet lasts forever" (55). All of these positions recognize that *Gentlemen* never condemns Lorelei outright, and that her position as unreliable "authoress" of her own narrative ensures a play of ironies that prevents the reader's judgment and sympathy from becoming fixed.

Evelyn Waugh's Paul Pennyfeather, the protagonist of *Decline and Fall* (1928), is another naïf, but he lacks Lorelei's cunning. As his "terribly funny" (6) Dickensian surname implies, Pennyfeather is a lightweight character, and throughout his misadventures as student, schoolteacher, lover, and prisoner, he acts as a decent but innocent fool. Waugh's narrator calls him "the shadow that has flitted about this narrative under the name of Paul Pennyfeather" (162), someone who cannot "fill the important part of hero for which he was originally cast" (163). In choosing such an insubstantial character, Waugh detaches the picaresque from the bildungsroman and returns the protagonist to the role of the innocent. An orphan and an outcast (thrown out of Oxford), "someone of no importance" (6), Paul becomes a passive observer of the madness and immorality of the modern world.

Sometimes Paul's mild reasonableness serves as a backdrop for the outrageousness of more "dynamic" (283) characters such as the pedophile Grimes, the depressive Prendergast, the criminal Philbrick; Grimes in particular, described as "a life force" and "of the immortals" (276), is an alternative *pícaro* who shares the vitality and resiliency of the Renaissance prototype. The lightweight Pennyfeather, in contrast, seems exceptionally vulnerable to the winds of fortune. Such a passive protagonist makes possible Waugh's narrative technique of casually describing vices, horrors, and outrages – whether small (a Welsh bandleader trying to pimp out his sister at Llanabba Hall's athletic games) or large (the demise and eventual death of young Tangent, accidentally shot in the foot by a starter's gun at those same games). The result is a picture of modern Britain in which just about everything seems to be wrong, but it is presented for our amusement first and our judgment only secondarily.

The lunacies that Paul observes include specific ideas and trends associated with modernity. The architect Otto Silenus believes that "[t]he only perfect building must be the factory, because that is built to house machines, not men" (159). The prison reformer Sir Wilfred Lucas-Dockery holds that "all crime is due to the repressed desire for aesthetic expression" (226). Margot Beste-Chetwynde embodies the materialism and narcissism of the modern woman, and speaks in "the high invariable voice that may be heard in any Ritz Hotel from New York to Buda-Pesth" (95). (Margot has probably crossed paths with Lorelei Lee in these hotels.) Yet the old institutions and structures fare no better than the modern fads. The novel opens with Oxford's elite "Bollinger Club" happily stoning a fox to death with champagne bottles, and it goes on to indict public schools, aristocrats, and the "whole code of ready-made honour that is the still small voice, trained to command, of the Englishman all the world over" (252). Tradition and modernity are equally disdained.

The modern world in *Decline and Fall* has "lost its reason" (165), and it seems to cry out for someone to analyze its ills. But the analyses that the novel offers come from such peculiar characters that we can't know whether they represent the author's judgment or the kind of modern thinking that he wants us to be wary of. The crackpot *avant-gardiste* Silenus deems that "All ill comes from man ... Man is never beautiful; he is never happy except when he becomes the channel for the distribution of mechanical forces" (160). Grimes, contemplating his upcoming marriage, condemns domesticity with a similarly impersonal view of the species: "As individuals we simply do not exist. We are just potential home builders, beavers and ants" (133–134). And Prendergast has never been the same since the onset of his Doubts: "*I couldn't understand why God had made the world at all*" (38) – doubts which resonate through the whole novel. Whether Waugh is endorsing or lamenting these ideas, they surely suggest the picaresque theme of a world "where Fortune rules in the absence of Providence."[33]

Paul is ultimately not only the observer of this indifferent cosmos but also, from the moment he is targeted by the Bollinger Club, its victim. On the brink of his marriage to Margot, a joyous Paul raises a glass to "Fortune . . . a much-maligned lady!" (211), and in the next moment is arrested for his unwitting complicity in Margot's international prostitution ring. His trial, like Mr. Pickwick's, is a farce; he lands, like Pickwick, in prison. Yet society is so rotten that Paul's time spent in solitary confinement ironically proves pleasurable, as he savors his freedom from the wearying concerns of his social class. But even this respite is merely another accident, another turn of Fortune's wheel. Thus Silenus's final soliloquy compares life to "the big wheel at Luna Park" (282) appropriately refiguring the ancient trope of the *rota fortunae* as a modern commercial amusement.

The title *Decline and Fall* alludes to Edward Gibbon's *Decline and Fall of the Roman Empire*, and the allusions suggest a national allegory: another great empire is now in decline. Nathanael West's *A Cool Million* (1934) makes similar use of the picaresque, offering a hero as passive as Paul and even stupider than Lorelei. West models his treatment of Depression-era America on *Candide*, but he combines Voltaire with Horatio Alger, the nineteenth-century master of the "young adult series," who wrote dozens of rags-to-riches novels about poor boys attaining wealth through honesty and industry. In West's parodic rendition, Alger's gospel of success becomes as absurd as Leibniz's theodicy or Richardson's virtue rewarded. The stupidity of West's hero, Lemuel Pitkin – named after Lemuel Gulliver – is laughable. His "incurable optimism" (84) makes him prey to ruthless moneylenders, sly con-artists, brutal policemen, money-grubbing lawyers, exploitive employers, communist operatives, violent Indians, and, above all, a fascist demagogue – the ex-president Shagpoke Whipple. Lacking any critical perspective on his society, Lem can only be its victim.

Like other *pícaro*s, Lem is fatherless. Urged to "Go out into the world and win your way" (73), he is tossed about by Fortune: imprisoned twice, beaten and robbed, and maimed so often that he becomes a patchwork of false body parts. The casually brutal treatment that Lem suffers is matched by what Betty Prail undergoes. A modern-day Cunegonde, Betty is repeatedly beaten, abducted, sold, and raped. As in Voltaire, however, the deliberate thinness of the characters destabilizes the reader's reaction to the violence, which hovers between laughter and horror. Near the end of the novel, Lem is working as a vaudeville "stooge," enduring beatings onstage for laughs:

> To be perfectly just, from a certain point of view, not a very civilized one it must be admitted, there was much to laugh at in our hero's appearance. Instead of merely having no hair like a man prematurely bald, the gray bone of his skull showed plainly where he had been scalped by Chief Satinpenny. Then, too, his wooden leg had been carved with initials, twined hearts and other innocent insignia by mischievous boys. (172)

The reader also finds Lem laughable "from a certain point of view," and West sets the cruel laughter of slapstick in direct conflict with the claims of human compassion. The result is skepticism toward both satiric laughter and senti-mental identification.

Whipple, the master to whom the *pícaro* attaches himself, is also Lem's Pangloss, and a spokeman for an ideology of American exceptionalism. In Whipple's America, the wheel of Fortune will always turn to affirm the American Dream:

Here a man is a millionaire and a pauper the next, but no one thinks the worse of him. The wheel will turn, for that is the nature of wheels ... Office boys still marry their employers' daughters. Shipping clerks are still becoming presidents of railroads. Why the other day, I read where an elevator operator won a hundred thousand dollars in a sweepstake and was made a partner in a brokerage company.   (98)

In his cliché-ridden speeches, America "is the land of opportunity" (74), any misfortune is due to a conspiracy of "Jewish international bankers and Bolshevik labor unions" (111), and political power is gained by stoking a combination of sexual, racial, and ethnic phobias: "Your sweethearts and wives will become the common property of foreigners to maul and mouth at their leisure" (169).

Alongside the explicitly political satire, *A Cool Million* critiques the society of spectacle that West observed in 1930s America.[34] The narrative dwells on the commodities and costumes, such as the coonskin caps of Whipple's National Revolutionary Party, which serve as props in the spectacle of America's ideology. The most outrageous example of such a spectacle is Wu Fong's whorehouse, described in creepily lavish detail, in which each girl possesses a room and a costume conforming to a different regional cliché ("Pennsylvania Dutch, Old South, Log Cabin Pioneer, Victorian New York," and so on (126)). Sexual acquisitiveness here combines with a Disneyfied national history and consumerist marketing. Later Lem himself becomes a spectacle when he sells his body for exhibition as the artifact of another bogus history, "the last man to have been scalped by the Indians" (159). West suggests that such false narratives of national identity, which tie politics to myth and fantasy, are central to the appeal of fascism.[35]

Among the novel's most complex satiric devices is its narrator's voice. West wrote that "Alger is to America as Homer was to the Greeks,"[36] and he borrows from his predecessor not only basic plot elements but Alger's tone and even language lifted verbatim from Alger's books. (*A Cool Million* illustrates Bourdieu's insight that simply repeating an existing work in a new context can serve as parody.) West's narrator, in his wooden, over-polite tone, directly addresses the reader in order to draw moral lessons, but the novel's events do not permit the proper moral to be drawn. The narrator in fact promulgates views that West clearly rejects: "it is lamentable but a fact ... that the inferior races greatly desire the women of their superiors. This is why the Negroes rape so many white women in our southern states" (93). By having the narrator espouse such vile ideas, West locates racism not in the views of a particular speaker but in the American Dream ideology implicit in Alger's fiction.

Most disturbingly, the fictional world of the novel turns out to be one in which Whipple's right-wing conspiracy theories are borne out: Communists and Wall Street bankers really are working to defeat Whipple and his Revolutionary Party. In his final speech, Lem declares "there are times when even clowns must grow serious" (177). Yet he is assassinated at that moment in a Fieldingesque interruption: no serious speech here. Instead the last words go to the stodgy narrator who proclaims Lem's martyrdom. Even in death, he says, Lem testifies to "the right of every American boy to go into the world and there receive fair play and a chance to make his fortune by industry and probity without being laughed at or conspired against by sophisticated aliens" (179). We can laugh at this language as fascist kitsch, but it still triumphs in the world of *A Cool Million*.

After Modernism: The Picaresque-esque

The twentieth-century picaresque develops in a variety of directions, some more clearly satirical than others. In the aftermath of World War I, Jaroslav Hašek, in *The Good Soldier Švjek*, and Louis-Ferdinand Céline, in *Journey to the End of the Night*, choose – like Nashe, Grimmelhausen, and Thackeray – to make the *pícaro* a soldier and the picaresque a vehicle for the satire of war. They expose war as an experience of large-scale, random violence and disorder, and anti-heroic resourcefulness or even madness wins out over honor and courage as a means for survival.[37] Both Hašek and Céline served as sources for Joseph Heller's *Catch-22*, and for the flourishing anti-war satire of the 1960s.

The *pícaro* also plays a critical role in African-American satire. The trickster has a long history in African and African-American folklore, including the Br'er Rabbit stories popularized by the Southern (white) writer Joel Chandler Harris; the indirection and craftiness of the trickster has been seen as an adaptation to a racist power structure that forecloses straightforward paths to success. The dying words of the narrator's grandfather in Ellison's *Invisible Man* may be taken as a set of instructions to the African-American trickster (although Ellison's protagonist is uncertain about their wisdom): "I want you to overcome 'em with yeses, undermine 'em with grins, agree 'em to death and destruction, let 'em swoller you till they vomit or bust wide open."[38] Even protagonists of works that may not follow the episodic structure of the picaresque – *Black No More*'s Max Disher, *Mumbo-Jumbo*'s PaPa LaBas – bear traits of the *pícaro* such as an emphasis on prudence over principle and a protean capacity for self-reinvention. Exposing the venality of his society, capable of both moral instruction and disruptive mischief, "the black *pícaro*," writes Darryl Dickson-Carr, "is the quintessential African American satiric figure."[39]

Postwar Jewish-American comic fiction similarly relies on a figure with roots in folk culture, the *schlemiel*, a hapless comic fool or failure. Jewish authors from Saul Bellow and Philip Roth to Sam Lipsyte and Gary Shetyngart, as well as writer-performers like Woody Allen, Larry David, and Louis CK, find in the schlemiel an anti-hero who stands outside of mainstream Christian norms of masculinity and success.[40] Although the butt of jokes and the victim of bad fortune, the schlemiel "puts reality, and not his own actions into question"[41] because his marginalization, dislocation, and suffering make an ethical claim on the reader. The schlemiel has affinities with other weak or vulnerable comic heroes such as Chaplin's Little Tramp or the "Little Man" of James Thurber's humor pieces, and non-Jewish novelists like Thomas Pynchon and Kurt Vonnegut create schlemiel-*pícaros* in figures like Benny Profane of *V.* (1963) and Billy Pilgrim of *Slaughterhouse-Five* (1969).

The mid-century sees a surge in novels that various critics have claimed for the picaresque tradition including Ellison's *Invisible Man* (1952), Bellow's *The Adventures of Augie March* (1953), Thomas Mann's *Confessions of Felix Krull* (1954), Iris Murdoch's *Under the Net* (1954), J.P. Donleavy's *The Ginger Man* (1955), Günter Grass's *The Tin Drum* (1959), and John Kennedy Toole's *A Confederacy of Dunces* (1980; written in the early 1960s). These works vary in tone but all possess at least some hallmarks of the picaresque – the narrative of dislocation, the outsider anti-hero, the gap between morality and prudence, the episodic structure, the combination of innocence and trickery, the vitality and selfishness. In these "picaresque-esque" novels, the hero's outsider status resonates with the mid-century's existentialist themes of alienation and dislocation – themes which on a deeper level reflect social, political, and racial discontent. To be sure, some of these works, such as *Augie March* and *Invisible Man*, relinquish the merely episodic progress of the picaresque to the more progressive story of education that marks the bildungsroman. But even for these narrator-heroes, education is a process of disillusion, a series of hard lessons in the ironies of fate. Two notable postmodern novels, John Barth's *Sot-Weed Factor* (1960) and Thomas Pynchon's *Mason & Dixon* (1997), self-consciously invoke the historical form of the picaresque with eighteenth-century diction, a colonial American setting, and a pseudo-Fieldingesque style. Seeking a historical form appropriate to their materials, they redeploy the genre to retell and subvert foundational narratives of American history.

A recent example of the picaresque is the Sacha Baron Cohen film *Borat: Cultural Learnings of America for Make Benefit Glorious Nation of Kazakhstan*

(2006). A fusion of fictional narrative and real documentary, *Borat* assembles a cross-country road trip from a series of discrete episodes. The fictional character's motivation is a simple desire "to get a taste of life here in the United States," but the motives of Baron Cohen the writer-actor combine lunatic clowning with pointed political-cultural critique. In other words, Borat is a naïf, while Baron Cohen is a trickster. Overlaid on this picaresque adventure is a romantic quest: Borat falls in love with Pamela Anderson's *Baywatch* character C.J., who becomes his Dulcinea del Toboso; when Anderson's homemade sex-tape reveals the virginal C.J. to be sexually experienced, the romantic illusion is shattered and C.J. reverts to "Pamela Anderson" in another doubling of roles between character and actor. (Ken Davitian fills the Sancho Panza role of Azamat Bagatov, short and round next to the tall, lean Borat.)

The film's fish-out-of-water gags play on Borat's innocence. Like Lorelei, he mangles pronunciation, diction, and grammar. The viewer laughs at his ignorance of American social customs, technology, and standards of luxury, as when he mistakes a wood-paneled elevator for his hotel room. And although incest, rape, and prostitution are represented as normal in Borat's homeland of "Kazakhstan" (the scenes were filmed in Romania, and the sexual customs are Cohen's invention), Borat in other ways is a sexual innocent: "Are you telling me that the man who tried to put rubber fist in my anus was homosexual?" he asks former presidential candidate Alan Keyes in astonishment. As one critic remarks, this ignorance marks him as "a primitive figure of unreason."[42] Yet the viewer laughs equally at those whom Baron Cohen tricks. The film mocks Americans reduced to awkwardness or speechlessness when confronted with Borat's violations of taboos relating to language, sexuality, or bodily functions; these real people are all-too-ready to believe his behavior typical of a vaguely Eastern "other."[43] Such "real" pranks or hoaxes are embedded in the fictional frame of Borat's American odyssey.

At certain moments, the film clearly aims to expose offensive sociopolitical attitudes by coaxing Americans to echo Borat's outrageous views. At Borat's provocation, a rodeo director endorses the idea of hanging homosexuals; frat boys espouse the belief that women should be slaves; a gun-shop owner advises Borat as to which weapons are best for killing Jews. The rodeo audience cheers when Borat declares Kazakhstan an American ally, just a few years after the American invasion of Iraq (Figure 11):

> We support your war of terror! May we show our support to our boys in
> Iraq! May U.S. of A. kill every single terrorist! May George Bush drink

Figure 11 Sacha Baron Cohen as Borat butchering the American national anthem at a rodeo. *Borat: Cultural Learnings of America for Make Benefit Glorious Nation of Kazakhstan* © 2006, Twentieth Century Fox. All Rights Reserved. Courtesy of Twentieth Century Fox. Movie viewers laugh at the Southerners who cheer on Borat as he calls on George W. Bush to "drink the blood of every single man, woman, and child of Iraq."

the blood of every single man woman and child of Iraq! May you destroy their country so that for the next thousand years not even a single lizard will survive in their desert!

This liberal satire on right-wing attitudes, however, is complicated by Cohen's own use of stereotypes. Borat and Azamat themselves are amalgams of traits associated with clichés of Russians, Slavs, Muslims, Armenians, and Jews. In Baron Cohen's pranks, certain Americans, usually Southerners, are themselves caricatured as primitive and backwards "others"; in its wild irrationalism, the real Pentecostal revival that Borat attends bears an eerie resemblance to the fictional "running of the Jew" held in Borat's hometown.[44] Even when the participants acquit themselves rather decently – as when a driving instructor refuses to let Borat goad him into homophobic or misogynistic statements – the forced politeness and condescension make the participants the objects of laughter. They are simply not in on the joke. The film breaks down the divide between the civilized West and the unciv-ilized East, but reconstitutes it as a divide between urbane viewers and unsophisticated rednecks and meatheads. Near its opening, *Borat* features a comedy class in which Borat and the teacher debate whether one can laugh at mental retardation, arguing the limits of satiric cruelty. The entire film, it turns out, thematizes this very question as it repeatedly forces the viewer to witness scenes that are simultaneously painfully awkward and outrageously funny.

Chapter 9

The Menippean Novel

The Menippean novel is the loosest category of satiric novel that I identify because it brings together three strains of satire that might be treated discretely but which often cohabit: (1) an intellectual or philosophical satire directed at an excessively systematic mind; (2) the self-conscious unmasking of the conventions of the realist novel; and (3) a critical attack on the bureaucratic and ideological institutions of modernity. Highlighting one or another of these tendencies, critics have offered alternative terminologies ("anatomy," "encyclopedic narrative," "metafiction," "mega-novel," "systems novel"), but the term "Menippean novel," coined by Charles Knight, has the virtue of acknowledging the form's roots in Menippean satire while affirming its identity as a novel, and hence a modern genre.

The first strain, intellectual satire, gives precedence to ideas over characters, structures of knowledge over human relationships. It originates in classical and Renaissance parody of discursive genres such as dialogues, symposia, and encomia; it continues with pre-novelistic characters like Swift's Projectors or Voltaire's Pangloss who lose touch with reality in their maniacal pursuit of knowledge or adherence to abstract ideas. Menippean novels further this tradition, treating philosophical propositions jokingly or ironically, and imbuing fictional scenarios with wild fantasy. They often aspire to encyclopedic knowledge, but by presenting their intellectual content through self-absorbed or delusory characters, they ironize such totalizing aspirations and even appear skeptical of knowledge itself (*LS* 220).

The second strain of the Menippean novel exhibits its metafictional or self-conscious tendency. Metafiction overtly displays its own status as an imaginative or narrative construct, undermining the novel's long-held investments in realism. Through its play with aesthetic form, it critiques the ideologically laden conventions that novelistic storytelling and realist representation leave unquestioned. Metafiction begins with the beginning of the novel: *Don Quixote* launches the genre by questioning the nature and methods of representation itself.

213

The third and final strain is the critique of those new institutions organizing life in the modern world. Steven Weisenburger uses the term "degenerative satire" to describe postwar American fiction that seeks to disturb rather than consolidate received norms and truths. These works respond to a new and unique historical situation:

> Its historical context is no longer bourgeois society . . . Instead it conditions (note: not its target) involve a contemporary mega-bureaucracy and its blindly progressive "information society," including . . . the "fast-image" world of advertising, politics, electronic media, and the like.[1]

Unlike satire that focuses on individual vices within bourgeois society, such as the comedy of manners, degenerative satire turns its attention to institutions and systems like multinational corporations, governmental bureaucracies, and extensive infrastructure or technological networks. They function in a society characterized by an electronically mediated public sphere; the uncontrolled dissemination of images and information; the development of capitalism into a "late" or "postindustrial" form; the permeation of nature by culture, technology, and simulacrum; the intensified surveillance and discipline of the individual; and the general diminution of human agency in the face of all these trends. And while such themes are commonly taken as hallmarks of a postmodern moment, institutional satire emerges well before the Cold War, notably in the works of Charles Dickens, who might be said to detect a nascent postmodernity in industrial England.

The three "strains" of the Menippean novel share what Weisenburger calls a "suspicion of all structures, including structures of perceiving, representing, and transforming."[2] The overarching theme of the Menippean novel is, in other words, epistemological skepticism – toward human efforts at knowledge, the distortions of representation, and the institutions of late capitalism. Its characters and readers often find themselves in the position of Thomas Pynchon's Ronald Cherrycoke in *Gravity's Rainbow*: "often he thinks the sheer volume of information pouring in through his fingers will saturate, burn him out" (150). In this sense, the Menippean novel offers a satirical rendering of what Jean-François Lyotard calls a "report on knowledge."[3] It offers that satirical rendering through a familiar cluster of techniques. It exploits heteroglossia, the novel's capacity to represent and ironize the multiple ideological viewpoints embodied in a society's diversity of speech forms. It gravitates toward carnivalesque themes, subverting any dogmatic view of the world via the representation of the grotesque body, the mixing of discourses, and the provocation of laughter. Its tone often tilts toward ludic fantasy and antic comedy, but its plots and themes can be pessimistic and grim. It flaunts its use of flat characters, dismantling literary character as one more artificial convention in a corrective to humanistic pieties about the uniqueness of the individual, or a recognition of the frailty of the human subject in the face of massive systemic forces.[4]

Zigzaggery and Circumlocution: Sterne and Dickens

Laurence Sterne claimed that he wrote *Tristram Shandy* (1759–1767) in "the hopes of doing the world good by ridiculing what I thought deserving of it" (*PSE* 281), but its prevailing mood of high-spirited silliness punctuated by bursts of sentimentality has led many to deny it the label of satire.[5] Sterne's mockery of his characters' weaknesses is tempered by tenderness, while anger, disgust, and moral judgment are scarce. Still, even though his cheery humor may distinguish him from Juvenal or Swift, it hardly disqualifies him as a satirist, and Sterne occupies a crucial space in the transition from pre-novelistic prose satire to contemporary satiric fiction. *Tristram Shandy* continues the tradition of "learned wit" inherited from *Gargantua and Pantagruel* and *Anatomy of Melancholy*, as well more recent precursors like *The Memoirs of Martinus Scriblerus* and *A Tale of a Tub*.[6] Its satire is directed against what critics have variously called "epistemological overconfidence," "the unbridled mind," or the "massively solipsistic individual" (*PSE*, 281; *FS*, 250; *LS* 220).

The prime examples of such unbridled minds are the "speculative" and "systematical" (1.21.91) Walter Shandy with his pedantic immersion in books, the tender-hearted uncle Toby with his "hobby-horse" of recreating the siege of Namur, and Tristram himself, with his quixotic attempt to write the novel that bears his name. Therefore instead of the "Life and Adventures" formula of the popular Fielding–Smollett picaresque, Sterne gives us Tristram's "Life and *Opinions*." Opinions abound in the novel: Tristram's, Walter's, Toby's, their interlocutors', and those of the innumerable classical, medieval, and modern authorities whom they cite in treatises and debates. In the tradition of parodic dialogue, these debates end up stalled, interrupted, or derailed, stranding the reader in a maze of argument and counter-argument. When Tristram bewails the circularity of knowledge – "Shall we for ever make new books, as apothecaries make new mixtures, by pouring only out of one vessel into another?" (5.1.339) – even his fear that he merely recycles old writing is itself lifted from Burton. Elsewhere Tristram speaks of the Goths' "wise custom of debating every thing of importance to their state, twice, that is, –

once drunk, and once sober" (6.17.420), and such a carnivalesque approach to the divagations of the mind aptly describes Sterne's method.

The novel, however, satirizes not only the writing of opinions but also the writing of a life. If the book looks back to Menippean satire, it also looks forward to the novel as a genre with kinship to biography. Its skepticism extends from arcane scholarly debates to the autobiographer's ambition of containing a single life in a coherent narrative. The story's refracted chronology, its "transverse zig-zaggery" (3.3.173), mocks the very possibility of a linear account, which, in removing digressions from a life story, would pluck out the heart of its mystery: "Digressions, incontestably, are the sunshine; – they are the life, the soul of reading; – take them out of this book for instance, – you might as well take the book along with them" (1.22.95). Without digression, there simply is no story. Tristram attempts to begin literally "ab Ovo" (1.4.38), but discovers the arbitrariness of marking any beginning at all. Spinning off tales within tales, he reaches his dedication only in chapter eight, his preface in book three, his birth in book four. Soon he has spent a full year chronicling a single day of his existence:

> at this rate I should just live 364 times faster than I should write – It must follow, an' please your worships, that the more I write, the more I shall have to write – and consequently, the more your worships read, the more your worships shall have to read.   (4.13.286)

The time-frames of living, writing, and reading are incommensurate. Narrative cannot contain life, nor can the mind contain reality.

Tristram Shandy is conscious of itself not only as a narrative but also as a novel and as a book. Sterne reminds the reader of the conventions of the genre of the novel, of the materiality of the printed page, and of the reader's solitary navigation of its chapters. (As Walter Benjamin observes, the novel comes into being with print, and its "birthplace" is "the solitary individual."[7]) A solid black page commemorates Yorick's death; a blank page invites the reader to draw his own image of the alluring Widow Wadman (6.38.451). From the pages of asterisks and dashes to Trim's curved flourish to the visual diagrams of the plot itself, *Tristram Shandy* repeatedly foregrounds its nature as a printed artifact. Similarly, the teasing references to the identity of "dear Jenny," the instruction to "Madam reader" to reread the previous chapter, and the dedication put up for public sale make us conscious of the artifice of the novel, the reader's ability to move back and forth within a printed text, and the book's status as a commodity. Above all, the flouting of novelistic conventions asserts the mind's freedom from arbitrary constraints. As Tristram asks, "is a man to follow rules – or rules to follow him?" (4.10.282).

Yet the interruptive method also suggests a pattern of male sexual failure. Walter views sexual intercourse as a chore as mechanical as the monthly winding of the clock; Toby, wounded in the groin, does not know the "right end of a woman from the wrong" (2.7.121). At the beginning of the novel, Mrs. Shandy interrupts her husband during intercourse, "scatter[ing]" Tristram's "animal spirits" and laying a foundation "for a thousand weaknesses both of body and mind" (1.2.36, 37). At the end of the novel, Walter is still discussing biological conception when Obadiah interrupts, relating yet another story of sexual failure, that of the Shandy family bull. In between are numerous hints of impotence and castration, most notably the mangling of baby Tristram's nose and his accidental circumcision. When Tristram notes that "nothing was well hung in our family" (5.17.369), he is speaking of more than the window sash.

The male characters' private obsessions, their hobby-horses, ultimately obstruct the recognition of the autonomy of others on which intercourse depends. Walter is a pedant, trapped in his own mind, his own books, his own rules. His plans for Tristram's "geniture, nose, and name" are frustrated one after the next. The kind-hearted Toby, temperamentally Walter's opposite, also retreats into simulacrum, creating with his siege of Namur a walled-in playland where he can re-enact the causes of his own unmanning. Toby's bowling green is an all-male world, and its pleasures are masturbatory: "Never did lover post down to a beloved mistress with more heat and expectation, than my uncle Toby did, to enjoy this self-same thing in private" (2.5.118). These self-contained spaces wall off the Shandy men from intercourse with the world. Thus Walter teases Toby about his hobby-horse, Tristram teases Walter for his "infinitude of oddities" (5.24.374), and Sterne teases Tristram for his obsessive attempt to write his life. Ultimately, Sterne's gentle satire insists that the openness of life will win out over the linearity of narrative, the play of language over the stability of representation, and the unruly body over the mechanistic clockwork of systems.

If *Tristram Shandy* has been shunted to the margins of the satiric canon because of its tenderness, the novels of Dickens are often excluded entirely. Received wisdom has it that Dickens's novels are comic rather than satiric because they promote "regimes of decency and moderation," foster a sentimental connection with readers, and affirm the socioeconomic status quo.[8] If satire exists in Dickens at all, it is localized in the derisory representation of isolated characters or institutions. Yet the targets of Dickens's satire resist the efforts at containment that his novels try to impose. In *Bleak House*, for example, the operations of Chancery Court "far exceed the architecture in which it is apparently circumscribed." In particular the lawsuit of Jarndyce and Jarndyce, "so complicated that no man alive knows what it means," works itself into every corner of the plot and of the larger society, like the pervasive fog whose lavish description opens the novel.[9]

Thus although satire coexists in Dickens alongside a variety of non-satiric modes, his fiction steadily critiques those institutions that arise as part of "the emerging bureaucratic, managerial, or administered form of capitalism."[10] George Orwell indeed claimed that "Dickens attacked English institutions with a ferocity that has never since been approached."[11] Dickens depicts with real hatred those institutions that discipline and punish the wayward individual – the prison, the workhouse, the factory, the school – yet his most penetrating satire is directed at the even more expansive systems of law and government that underwrite them. Sometimes the critique is expressed simply as indignation at injustice or compassion for the abused; often it works through satiric humor and irony. Dickens imbues with comedy his representation of the apparatus of bureaucracy, the tedious life of clerks, the language of obfuscation and circumlocution, the legalities that obstruct rather than serve the cause of justice. The ordinary citizen must always get past clerks and secretaries before gaining access to the great men who occupy the seats of power. The law always cloaks its injustice in terms of necessity, and its outrageous madness in a bland tone of reasonableness.

This critique is already prominent in *The Pickwick Papers*, where the picaresque survey gives way to the Kafkaesque drama of Pickwick's trial and punishment. Dickens's description of law offices evokes unintelligible bureaucratic processes:

> These sequestered nooks are the public offices of the legal profession,
> where writs are issued, judgments signed, declarations filed, and
> numerous other ingenious machines put in motion for the torture and
> torment of His Majesty's liege subjects, and the comfort and emolument
> of the practitioners of the law.   (402)

The series of plurals (writs, judgments, declarations, machines) implies an endless business of pushing paper (the novel's title acquires new relevance), while bitter authorial judgment ("torture and torment") creeps into the sonorities of the prose. The plot of the novel bears out this representation of the law as a malign and uncontainable process, and the real villains turn out to be neither the lawyers Dodson and Fogg nor the conmen Jingle and Trotter but the cynicism of the law itself.

The *loci classici* of Dickens's institutional satire are found in his late novels, *Little Dorrit* and *Bleak House*. In *Little Dorrit*, the bureau called the Circumlocution Office is described as "containing the whole science of government" and "having something to do with everything" (87, 88). Dickens employs an arsenal of satiric weapons against it including ironic praise (the office is a "glorious establishment" operating on a "sublime principle" (87)) and touches of black comedy ("Numbers of people were lost in the Circumlocution Office" (89)). This vast engine of inefficiency requires a prose style adequate to it, and Dickens ramps up his rhetoric to a mock-heroic level:

> The Circumlocution Office was (as everybody knows without being told) the most important Department under Government. No public business of any kind could possibly be done at any time without the acquiescence of the Circumlocution Office. Its finger was in the largest public pie, and in the smallest public tart. It was equally impossible to do the plainest right and to undo the plainest wrong without the express authority of the Circumlocution Office. If another Gunpowder Plot had been discovered half an hour before the lighting of the match, nobody would have been justified in saving the parliament until there had been half a score of boards, half a bushel of minutes, several sacks of official memoranda, and a family-vault full of ungrammatical correspondence, on the part of the Circumlocution Office. (87)

The clumsy name of the office repeats ponderously through the paragraph, which ends where it began, enacting the circumlocution it describes. The superlatives indicate the range of its power, while the final sentence compiles near-synonyms to conjure a massive material presence of paper. And the satire works also at the level of the scene: the reader oscillates between amusement and frustration as Arthur Clennam is passed from one bureaucrat to another through the labyrinth of offices. In *Tristram Shandy*, the mind gets lost in mazes of its own creation; in *Little Dorrit*, a sane mind can go mad in the mazes society has built.

These bureaucratic mazes are mazes of language: documents, forms, writs, memoranda, correspondence. Yet language is not only the target but also the *site* of Dickens's satire. Dickens is constantly staging the clash and contest, the mixing and mongrelization, of different languages and the worldviews that they embody. This variety accounts for the oft-praised vitality of Dickens's prose. His inflated rhetoric produces pleasure in both the production and the unmasking of its grandiosity. A mere chapter title like "telescopic philanthropy," used in *Bleak House* to describe Mrs. Jellyby's concern with children in Africa at the expense of her own family, employs a needless periphrasis to signal a position of amused detachment. Dickens excels at what Bakhtin calls "parodic stylizations" of public discourse, as in Bakhtin's example from *Little Dorrit*:

> The conference was held at four or five o'clock in the afternoon, when all the region of Harley Street, Cavendish Square, was resonant of carriage-wheels and double-knocks. It had reached this point when Mr Merdle came home from his daily occupation of causing the British name to be more and more respected in all parts of the civilised globe capable of the appreciation of world-wide commercial enterprise and gigantic combinations of skill and capital.   (331)

As the language shifts mid-paragraph from a neutral description to the clichéd phrasings of an admiring public, the satire captures the hyperbole of public sentiment. Amused yet condemnatory, Dickens's language exposes the inadequacy of a worldview that belongs less to any individual than to a national ideology.

Fantasy, False Learning, and the Kingdom of the Mind

With the rise of realism, the overtly metafictional tendencies of the novel recede.[12] Yet elements of the Menippean novel persist in a range of works. What has been called the camp novel offers gentle social satire that has affinities with the comedy of manners (see Chapter 7), but also draws on the fantastical invention of Lucian, the whimsical side of Swift, and the intellectual games of *Tristram Shandy*. The dialogue novels of Thomas Love Peacock feature characters who, like the idle, loquacious men in Shandy Hall, do little but exchange opinions. Lewis Carroll's *Alice* books string together logical and verbal riddles in a spirit of play and parodic instruction. Max Beerbohm's *Zuleika Dobson* includes a heavy dose of whimsy and fantasy – pearl earrings that change color, busts of emperors that sweat, the ghosts of Chopin and George Sand, a first-person narrator blessed with omniscience by the Greek gods – told in a self-consciously lush voice better described as mock-romantic than mock-epic. In *The Flower Beneath the Foot*, Ronald Firbank decorates his text with reminders of the materiality of the printed page including footnotes, scraps of songs, foreign phrases, onomatopoeic spelling, exclamation points, capital letters, and printed crucifixes in the tradition of Sterne's Dr. Slop. Virginia Woolf's *Orlando* narrates the hero(ine)'s fantastical change of sex through Sternean devices including a stodgy biographer-narrator, illustrations, photographs, and a blank space in the text, staging a carnivalesque parody of masculinist biography.[13]

Other works emphasize the philosophical or encyclopedic side of the genre more than the whimsical, though even here the characters' efforts at learning are more often frustrated than fulfilled. Carlyle's *Sartor Resartus* purports to elucidate the life and opinions of the obscure (fictional) German thinker Diogenes Teufelsdröckh, author of a digressive scientific treatise on clothing. The "encyclopedic narrative" of Melville's *Moby-Dick* has Menippean affinities in its digressive discourses on cetology, cartography, etymology, and epistemology itself, and in the way that it counteracts Ahab's monomania with the wayward narrative and skeptical voice of Ishmael.[14] Flaubert's *Bouvard et Pécuchet* deploys a cold, unflinching representation of its heroes' absurdities to satirize their misguided attempt at encyclopedic learning, and indeed to decry the vanity of all accumulated human knowledge.[15] The *ficciones* of Borges imagine libraries in which all the books have already been written, encyclopedias so exhaustive that they supplant reality, and pedants like Pierre Menard who undertake absurd (indeed Quixotic) tasks like rewriting Cervantes's masterpiece word for word.

The major novelists of Irish modernism display a particular affinity for the Menippean novel. Joyce called *Ulysses* his "chaffering allincluding most farraginous chronicle," and today critics tend to regard the book's Homeric correspondences as a playful conceit rather than a mythopoeic system.[16] Nearly every chapter contains Menippean elements: the catalogue of rhetorical tropes in "Aeolus," the philosophical dialogue of "Scylla and Charybdis," the gigantic Rabelaisian lists of "Cyclops," the literary heteroglossia of "Oxen of the Sun," Bloom's farcical trial in "Circe" (with its debt to *Alice* and *Pickwick*), the comic circumlocution of "Eumaeus," the parodic scientific discourse of "Ithaca." But while *Ulysses* remains a human comedy, Joyce's immediate successors, Flann O'Brien and Samuel Beckett, complete the turn against what Hugh Kenner called "humanist dogma" and make comedy from epistemological rather than ethical conflicts.[17]

O'Brien's *At Swim-Two-Birds* enacts a Sternean deconstruction of narrative conventions, nesting stories within stories and then violating the ontological integrity of the fictional worlds it creates. Dickensian circumlocution, genre parodies, and faux-philosophical disputation constitute the narrator's hobbyhorse, his solipsistic, masturbatory retreat to "the kingdom of [his] mind." O'Brien's narrator offers the Menippean notion that "The modern novel should be largely a work of reference," or indeed "a self-evident sham to which the reader could regulate at will the degree of his credulity."[18] Meanwhile, the narrator of *The Third Policeman* is obsessed with the ideas of DeSelby, a crackpot philosopher whose work is discussed in long footnotes. DeSelby's chief virtue is that reading him convinces you that you are "not, of all nincompoops, the greatest," and his most important work consists of "two thousand sheets of foolscap closely hand-written on both sides" of which "not one word" is legible.[19]

Beckett's protagonists similarly live in the "little world" of the mind, preoccupied with their private intellectual systems.[20] The episodes of the biscuits in *Murphy* and the sucking stones in *Molloy*, in which the narrators proceed through the exhaustive rehearsal of mathematical permutations, satirize the mind's rationality by showing how it devolves into obsessive compulsion. In *Murphy*, Beckett plays Shandean games with the text, referring the reader ahead to "section six," introducing Celia as a list of body parts and measurements, presenting in notation Murphy's entire game of chess with the schizophrenic patient Endon. In *Molloy*, meanwhile, Beckett stages the absurdity of philosophical thinking, in the theological arcana that occupy Moran, or in Molloy's ruminations on the anus:

> We underestimate this little hole, it seems to me, we call it the arsehole and affect to despise it. But is it not rather the true portal of our being and the celebrated mouth no more than the kitchen-door. Nothing goes in, or so little, that is not rejected on the spot.[21]

Molloy's observation, like much of his thought, hovers between bathroom humor and genuine insight into our nature as embodied beings. His principle of composition, meanwhile, is a more despairing version of Tristram's: "And if I failed to mention this detail in its proper place, it is because you cannot mention everything in its proper place, you must choose, between the things not worth mentioning, and those even less so."[22] Such a narrative denies itself even a justification for existence.

Huge Amounts of Data: Postmodern American Fiction

Moving from Irish late modernists to American postmodernists may feel like moving from Erasmus and More to Rabelais and Cervantes, as philosophical puzzles and rumination give way to high-energy comedy, verbal profusion, and explicit engagement with world-historical events. Yet as much as their Irish precursors, American postmodernists take up the traditions of Menippean satire. Brian McHale goes so far as to claim that "postmodern fiction is the heir of Menippean satire and its most recent historical avatar."[23] Postmodern American satires bring together Sterne's play with narrative and Dickens's satire of impersonal modern institutions. They feature flat characters, fantastical events, and markers of their own fictionality. They marshal the Bakhtinian themes of the grotesque and the carnivalesque, and treat violence, suffering, and death with black humor. Their size and scope appear as a necessary response to the massive systems they confront, and they often push the reader to a point of overload, where she can no longer process the information proffered.[24]

A full critical survey of American postmodern satire could include John Barth, William Gaddis, William Gass, Terry Southern, Kurt Vonnegut, and many others; indeed, much of the postwar culture is animated by satirical energies. It should also be noted that the postmodern Menippean novel is not an exclusively American phenomenon, even though it arrived in the UK somewhat later, and the major British writers of postmodern satire – Martin Amis, Julian Barnes, Angela Carter, Salman Rushdie – tend to be born in the 1940s (whereas the Americans listed above were all born in the 1920s and 1930s). My treatment of the postmodern novel here centers on five novels, which together provide an overview of the moment in which the Menippean novel emerged as a cultural dominant.

Perhaps more than any other work, Joseph Heller's *Catch-22* (1961) first gave shape to the anti-institutional, anti-bureaucratic satire of the Cold War years. Though written about World War II, the novel anticipated the rebellious spirit of the 1960s and became a best-seller after Mike Nichols's 1970 film adaptation premiered during the Vietnam War. Heller's mockery of the vapid rhetoric of wartime patriotism continues an old tradition, but his satire on the bureaucracy that runs the war – what Eisenhower called the military-industrial complex – speaks specifically to his age. The book's title refers to a policy, a piece of bureaucratic writing, and the word "catch-22" has become shorthand for any situation in which administrative decisions are paradoxically foreclosed. In the novel, the catch stipulates that a pilot must be certified as crazy to be excused from flying, but anyone who asks to be excused is by definition sane and therefore required to fly. It thus stands in for the malfunctioning of all bureaucracy – the nonsense, circumlocution, and madness that permeates the structure of military command, the thinking of the pilots, even the romantic relationships the men find themselves in. Like Arthur Clennam in Dickens's Circumlocution Office, the hero Yossarian functions as a principled innocent confronting a mad bureaucracy with feeble common sense. Yossarian's wish to stop flying – to value his own survival above a hollow patriotism – appears wholly rational. He says to Major Major:

> "Let somebody else get killed."
> "But suppose everybody on our side felt that way?"
> "Then I'd certainly be a damned fool to feel any other way. Wouldn't I?" (103)

So much for categorical imperatives.

In every chapter, on nearly every page, one finds examples of tautology, paradox, and circumlocution. Heller harnesses the wordplay, farce, and nonsense jokes of Lewis Carroll, Evelyn Waugh, and the Marx Brothers to an attack on the vast organizational complex of the military and the ideology that it promulgates: "'Men,' Colonel Cargill began in Yossarian's squadron, measuring his pauses carefully, 'You're American officers. The officers of no other army in the world can make that statement'" (27). The novel's looping, almost Sternean temporal structure suits these themes, enacting for the reader the deferral, confusion, and déjà vu that the characters experience. The paradoxes, moreover, extend beyond the war operation, as the novel takes passing shots at the inverted logic of tax law, agricultural subsidies, and Cold War loyalty oaths. Milo's bombing of his own camp indicts the logic of capitalism itself, as loyalty to his syndicate trumps loyalty to his fellow pilots.

Bureaucracy in the novel is an epistemological quagmire in which the effort to clarify rules and policies leads only to the production of further rules and policies themselves in need of clarification, as "simple communications swell prodigiously into huge manuscripts" (92). Colonel Cathcart admits frankly that paperwork matters more than lives: "It's not that I'm being sentimental or anything. I don't give a damn about the men or the airplane. It's just that it looks so lousy on the report. How am I going to cover up something like this in the report?" (138). References to reports, memoranda, directives, regulations, and writing pervade the text. General Dreedle and General Peckem engage in "hectic jurisdictional dispute[s]" by issuing contradictory memoranda, ultimately adjudicated by ex-PFC Wintergreen, a mail clerk who "is probably the most influential man in the whole theater of operations" because "he has access to a mimeograph" (302). The system itself is thus at the mercy of lost pages, misdelivered letters, typographical mistakes, computer errors. Because his name is on the flight roster of a crashed plane, Doc Daneeka's physical existence cannot disprove his death. A computer mistakes a Harvard cetologist for a doctor and "shanghais him into the Medical Corps" (15), where he tries to discuss *Moby-Dick* with a dying officer. Peckhem's memoranda accidentally put Scheisskopf "in charge of everything" (391), while "an IBM computer with a sense of humor" promotes Major Major to the rank of Major, in which capacity he is afraid and ashamed to wield authority. He literalizes the fact that bureaucracy is, in Hannah Arendt's Dickensian phrase, the rule of Nobody: "In a fully developed bureaucracy there is nobody left with whom one could argue ... [W]here all are equally powerless we have a tyranny without a tyrant."[25] Just as there is no tyrant, so the catch-22 policy turns out not to exist; the mere belief in its presence allows it to function.

It is because power in *Catch-22* is revealed as centerless that the military leaders are represented as buffoons rather than villains. The generals are post-Freudian clowns, motivated by personal rivalries, neurotic anxieties, petty obsessions, infantile frustrations. They appear petty because they are so much smaller and weaker than the impersonal system through which power is diffused. In this representation of the absurdity of military bureaucracy, *Catch-22* not only anticipates anti-war film satires like *Dr. Strangelove* and *M*A*S*H*, but also "makes legible the double and self-contradictory speech upon which the logic of cold war discourse depended."[26]

It might be argued that satire like this actually accommodates us to the amusing absurdity of the rule of Nobody. Yet Heller ultimately shifts the tone of his satire away from comedy. The brutal and grotesque scenes of death – Kid Sampson's, Snowden's, the maid Michaela's – counter the frivolity with horror. Snowden's death, during which his "insides slithered down to the floor in a soggy pile and just kept dripping out" (439), removes all comedy from the reduction of a living being to a mass of tissue. When Aarfy blithely rapes and murders Michaela, his self-defense invokes the same circular logic used throughout the novel, but now we are too close to the situation to laugh. Throughout Chapter 39, appropriately set in Rome itself, Heller reasserts a moral dimension to the satire, rising to Juvenalian indignation. Yet the most significant protest against the outrages of war might be the novel's own representation of writing. Yossarian begins the book by deliberately making mischief when assigned to censor letters. Later, Major Major disavows his power by signing his name "Washington Irving" in "an act of impulsive frivolity and rebellion for which he knew afterward he would be punished severely" (92). It is in this spirit that one should understand the vitality of Heller's own prose, his long, energetic, spiraling sentences, which raise a protest by insisting with every flourish that this novel is something other than a bureaucratic report.

Ishmael Reed's *Mumbo Jumbo* (1972) satirizes an institution even more diffuse and far-reaching than the military-industrial complex, taking aim at "Civilization As We Know It" (4). The novel exposes the dominant, Eurocentric understanding of high culture as a racial ideology dependent on the repression of the contributions of Africans and other non-European peoples. It achieves this exposure through a disruption of the act of reading combined with a mock-encyclopedism that playfully rewrites Western history. It uses a relatively small detective story – the efforts of PaPa LaBas to solve a string of murders and locate a missing text – to describe the outbreak of the plague called Jes Grew and the efforts of a secret society, the Atonist Path, to arrest its spread. Yet the plot (like Jes Grew itself) ramifies further, wrapping itself around a history of the United States in the 1910s and 1920s and eventually a mythological account of Jes Grew's origins in ancient Egypt. PaPa LaBas serves as a trickster[27] – a satirist within the text and a primary source of the diasporic perspective that destabilizes the authority of European culture. He is rumored to be a descendant of a Nigerian oracle, or, alternatively, "the reincarnation of the famed Moor of Summerland himself, the Black gypsy who according to Sufi Lit. sicked the Witches on Europe" (23). This fantasized background alludes to the putative origins of satire in cursing, to the magical power of satire to destroy one's enemies.

Jes Grew, whose manifestations include ragtime, jazz, blues, dance, and slang, is represented as an environmental or public health phenomenon, a plague, or more precisely an "anti-plague" that "enliven[s]" (6) the body of the host instead of weakening it. It is less a system than an anti-system, since it disrupts rather than reinforcing the monotheistic, monological order. The Eurocentric or Atonist worldview, on the other hand, is indeed a system, one which rigidly structures thought and power. The Atonist mind seeks "to interpret the world by a single loa. Somewhat like filling a milk bottle with an ocean" (24); Atonists invoke "universal" principles "as a way of measuring every 1 by their ideals" (133). Nathan Brown rebukes Hinkle Von Vampton for such a false universalism: "when people like you, Mr. Von Vampton, say 'The Negro Experience' you are saying that all Negroes experience the world the same way" (117). The Atonist Path is imperialistic, as the subplot of the US invasion of Haiti reveals, and sexually repressive, as seen in its opposition to the "bumping and grinding" (13) and "Wiggle and Wobble" (17) of Jes Grew. It is also bureaucratic and utilitarian: Set, the original Atonist, is "the deity of the modern clerk, always tabulating" and may even have "invented taxes" (162). Framing history as a continuous conflict between Jes Grew and the Atonist Path, Reed casts human experience as an ongoing struggle between freedom and repression.

Mumbo Jumbo is itself a manifestation of the anti-plague. It carnivalizes erudition and high culture by mixing genres, languages, and media. It imports into the literary novel elements of gangster movies, detective novels, and comic books. (Reed dedicates it to the cartoonist George Herriman, creator of *Krazy Kat*, whose African heritage was made public only in 1971). It integrates African diasporic traditions into its treatment of its story, and freely blends history and fiction. The overarching effect of this carnivalization is comic and ironic. By juxtaposing interpretive frames of reference, *Mumbo Jumbo* overturns inherited understandings of history and culture. Time and again the novel redescribes people, institutions, and cultural phenomena in new languages or from new points of view. Art museums become detention centers, "Dungeons for the treasures from Africa, South America and Asia" (15), and the "theft" of artworks becomes reclamation and repatriation. Western figures of myth and legend are redescribed in terms from non-European cultures: Faust is "a *bokor* adept at card tricks" (90); Dionysus, the god from Nysa (164); the rosary, a "Sufi invention" (115); Christ, a "minor geek" (171), "a *bokor*, a sorcerer, an early Faust" who raises Lazarus as a Vodou bokor raises a zombie (170). Reed similarly uses anachronism and slang to ironize the stories of Isis and Osiris, and of Moses. Set's "legislators and their wives" are compared to "a Billy Graham audience at Oakland Coliseum" (173), while Moses is described at one point as going "into the kitchen and munch[ing] on some cereal that had been left in some ritual bowls" (180). In desacralizing the ancient myths, Reed suggests that all such foundation narratives are factitious.

Mumbo Jumbo revels in the Sternean possibilities of the printed text. Reed includes in his novel epigraphs, definitions, footnotes, news articles, headlines, graphs, photographs, drawings, and advertisements. The title and copyright pages do not appear until after the first chapter, and some of the details of the novel's mystery are revealed in a reproduced hand-written letter. These many "paratexts" frequently hint at political critique, but the lack of explicit connection between text and paratext leaves interpretation open. For example, a graph of "U.S. Bombing Tonnage in Three Wars" (163), set in the middle of PaPa LaBas's account of Set and Osiris, implies but does not articulate a link between ethnocentric accounts of culture and American aggression abroad (Figure 12). The Shandean footnotes, scholarly quotations, references, and bibliography also remind us that for all its lively humor and improbable plotting, *Mumbo Jumbo* is an erudite work of scholarship, a fiction-discourse hybrid that draws upon research in history, mythology, psychoanalysis, and the esoterica of various religions and cults. The novel's scholarship, however, is best understood not as a comprehensive history of culture but as a satire of encyclopedic learning. Its attack on the Atonist view of culture, after all, is precisely an attack on a monological, ethnocentric view. The conspiracy theories and origin stories are clearly unserious, and Reed has fun riffing on some of the more lunatic ideas scholars have put forth, such as spaceships landing in Teotihuacán. Reed's Freudian fable of how sibling rivalry between Set and Osiris spawns violence and repression asks to be understood as comic myth – a satiric intervention into our understanding of culture. Indeed, the novel never provides the authoritative written text that both LaBas and the Wallflower Order are seeking.

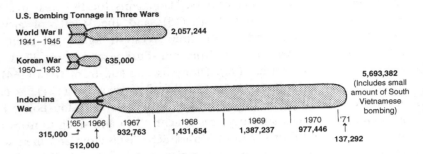

Figure 12 "US Bombing Tonnage in Three Wars." © 1971, the *New York Times*. Reprinted in *Mumbo Jumbo* by Ishmael Reed. © 1972. Reprinted with the permission of the *New York Times* and by Scribner, a division of Simon & Shuster, Inc. All rights reserved.

Ishmael Reed's images and illustrations often hint at political critique without making explicit connections between text and paratext.

Instead of authoritative, encyclopedic texts, Reed offers an image of art as "amusing lampoons" (96). Hamid displays in his headquarters carved African sculptures, "grotesque, laughable wooden ivory and bronze cartoons":

> They depict Whites who went into Africa seeking skins, ivory, spices, feathers and furs. The subjects are represented giving bribes, drinking gin, leading manacled slaves, wearing curious, outlandish hats and holding umbrellas. Their chalk-faces appear silly, ridiculous . . . What side-splitting, bellyaching, satirical ways these ancient craftsmen brought to their art! (96–97)

Contemplating these works, LaBas observes, following Baudelaire, that Christ never laughed. Unlike humorless African-American social realism or dour Marxist dogma, the carvings embody a jubilant aesthetic of exaggeration and lampoon that "represent[s] the genius of Afro satire" (97).

For many critics, Thomas Pynchon's *Gravity's Rainbow* (1973) remains the high-water mark of American postmodernism, a novel at once representative and transcendent of its era in the manner of Joyce's *Ulysses* or Melville's *Moby-Dick*. Like those works, and like Rushdie's *Midnight's Children* a decade later, its encyclopedic aspirations, symbolic patterning, and sheer size put it in proximity with epic and historical allegory. Satire, after all, may strive – as do Juvenal's satires, Dryden's *Absalom and Achitophel*, and even *Joseph Andrews*, Fielding's "comic epic poem in prose" – for the epic's grandiloquence of tone, significance of theme, or breadth of scope. Yet *Gravity's Rainbow* simultaneously subjects narrative and character to the forces of digression, incompleteness, and whimsy. Pynchon's readers must therefore ask whether the events of the novel cohere in deep mythic or allegorical patterns, or whether they scatter into a profusion of random details. As the novel's protagonist, American serviceman Tyrone Slothrop thinks, "Either They have put him here for a reason, or he's just here" (434). Both options, the paranoid, encyclopedic masterplot and the denial of all connection, are equally disquieting.

Gravity's Rainbow describes Slothrop's quasi-picaresque "Progress" (25) through Europe during the closing months of World War II as he seeks a mysterious V-2 rocket numbered 00000, which contains a "Schwarzgerät" (292) (black device) made of a plastic, Imipolex G, that was (probably) used in behavioral experiments on the infant Slothrop; at the same time, he is fleeing vague corporate and governmental interests using him for their own purposes. This plot – "The schlemiel against the impersonal efficiency of information systems and international cartels"[28] – is rendered orders of magnitude more complex by a proliferation of characters, scenes, subplots, digressions, fantasies, flashbacks, and drug-induced hallucinations. The novel thus fuses the anti-narrative tendency of *Tristram Shandy* (whose narrator-hero shares much more than his initials with Tyrone Slothrop) with a Dickensian satire on the institutions that govern modern life – including intelligence agencies, chemical-pharmaceutical conglomerates, and the amorphous system of what Foucault called knowledge-production. It absorbs both Heller's satire on the bureaucracy of the emergent military-industrial complex and Reed's articulation of encyclopedic world-historical conspiracy theories. "Check out Ishmael Reed," Pynchon's narrator tells us after a digression on the Masonic affiliations of Benjamin Franklin, David Livingstone, and Mikhail Bakunin, "He knows more about it than you'll ever find here" (588).

The novel's plotting is fundamentally satiric in its subversion of the quest-romance and replacement of continuity with rupture.[29] This regressive plotting is symptomatic of a Cold War world in which technological advances paradoxically hurtle humanity backwards toward destruction. As with plot, so with character: Slothrop's identity, his ontological status within Pynchon's fiction, begins to "to thin" (509) and is finally (echoing *Tristram Shandy*) "Scattered" (712), unlikely to be found again. As for style, the constant shifts into song lyrics and poetry – bawdy limericks, vaudeville numbers, drinking songs, occasionally blank verse or a sonnet – give it the "prosimetric" combination characteristic of ancient Menippean satire. Often these songs burst onto the page in a mood of spirited clowning reminiscent of Joyce's Buck Mulligan, with his "Ballad of Joking Jesus," or the musical-comedy-variety formats of the Marx Brothers and Monty Python. Technical description of rocket science shifts to highbrow literary allusion and then to a whimsical humor that produces, among innumerable oddities, a rampaging Giant Adenoid, a conversation between skin proteins, a Russian dope fiend turned Frank Sinatra impersonator, and a mock epic of a sentient, immortal, politically rebellious lightbulb. Yet what appears to be the exercise of a wayward spirit of play may reverberate with hidden purpose: to take one favorite example, in naming a Boston law firm "Salitieri, Poore, Nash, De Brutus, and Short" (588), Pynchon, by punning on Hobbes' description of human life in a state of nature, intimates that despite our scientific progress, the war of all against all remains our basic condition.

Among the more outrageous episodes of *Gravity's Rainbow* are the ones treating sex and defecation, human activities belonging to what Bakhtin called the material bodily lower stratum. The scatological scenes range in tone from Rabelaisian play (Slothrop's hallucinated dive down a toilet in search of his harmonica) to Swiftian disgust (Pudding's non-hallucinated ingestion of the feces of his dominatrix), while sex scenes like the orgy of aristocrats on the *Anubis* partying amid the wreckage of war hark back to the decadence of Petronius. But, notwithstanding a mitigating aura of camp, the novel tends to present sex as pedophilia, sadomasochism, and an unloving homosexuality, most garishly in the figure of the Nazi officer Captain Blicero who launches the missile at the novel's conclusion with his lover Gottfried inside. Life-giving sexual instincts have been corrupted into instruments of domination and death.

The mechanization of the human being thus includes the mechanization of human sexuality, and the corresponding sexualization of (military) machines. Slothrop himself is "immachinated" when as an infant he is "sold to IG Farben like a side of beef" (286) and conditioned to respond sexually to Imipolex G. Slothrop considers his condition:

> His erection hums from a certain distance, like an instrument installed, wired by Them into his body as a colonial outpost here in our raw and clamorous world, another office representing Their white Metropolis far away. (285)

The simile connects his body with technology and imperialism, throwing in an allusion to Fritz Lang's 1927 dystopian film, *Metropolis*, whose themes anticipate Pynchon's. The mechanization of sexuality is everywhere in the novel; even the rocket limericks joke about intercourse between human being and weapon. This mechanization is part of a yet larger cluster of forces – capitalism, imperialism, racism, and murderous parental impulses. These processes are shown to have historical roots in the German conquest of the Hereros of Southwest Africa and in the Puritanism of the early American settlers, who sorted populations into the chosen ("elites") and the damned ("preterites"). Certain individuals (especially scientists such as Jamf, Pointsman, and, extra-textually, Wernher von Braun) and corporations embody domination in their amoral pursuit of instrumental knowledge or wealth, but ultimately Pynchon's satire takes aim at the very direction of world historical development, a suprahuman force that infiltrates the human psyche: "The Man has a branch office in each of our brains . . . each local rep has a cover known as the Ego, and their mission in this world is Bad Shit" (712–723).

The novel's setting, the transition from wartime to "the bright new Postwar" (80), suggests that Pynchon sees these years as a historical turning point. The end of World War II holds out hope for a Weberian "routinization of charisma" (325) that eliminates the "the Führer-principle" (81), that is, the charismatic, cultic appeal of dictators. But the new routinized, "cartelized" (164) order is one in which the victors are eager to coopt Nazi rocket science for the next phase of their imperial ambitions. In this "Interregnum" (295), Slothrop wonders whether some anarchist alternative is possible: "there might be a route back . . . maybe for a little while all the fences are down, one road as good as another, the whole space of the Zone cleared, depolarized . . . without elect, without preterite, without even nationality to fuck it up" (556); here, as elsewhere – Roger and Jessica attending Christmas services in Kent, or, much later, Roger furiously pissing on the executives assembled in Mossmoon's office – the novel offers glimmers of resistance against the (post)modern world. But the anarchy of the Zone is hardly a utopia, filled as it is with impoverished refugees and exploited children.

One should therefore doubt whether Pynchon's levity is anything more than a weak counterforce to the gravity of the postwar situation. It may even be part of the problem, as Pynchon's readers may feel trapped inside the author's own hobby-horse, his own private manias and references. The novel itself can resemble "an information system that threatens its readers' freedom."[30] On the other hand, Slothrop may achieve a paradoxical freedom in escaping "Them" by scattering, and Pynchon's scattershot humor may at least disrupt the cause and effect that bureaucrat-scientists like Pointsman insist upon. Indeed, for a society bent on suicide, hope may reside only in Shandean digression. As Joseph Ombindi tries to convince Oberst Enzian of the value of a tribal suicide for the Hereros, Enzian recognizes the appeal of a "renunciation of the things of this world." Yet he realizes that as soon as one attempts to list everything to be renounced, "by Godel's Theorem there is bound to be some item around that one has omitted from the list," leading the list-maker to inevitable corrections, repetitions, and additions, so "that the 'suicide' ... might have to be postponed indefinitely!" (320). If the over-powering death-drive of the novel can be counteracted, it is through incompleteness and digression.

The final section of Pynchon's magnum opus ends with an epigraph from Richard Nixon, and Nixon may or may not be the Richard M. Zhlubb in whose Los Angeles movie theater Blicero's missile lands at the novel's close. But while Nixon is a marginal presence in Pynchon's work, he is central to Robert Coover's *The Public Burning* (1977). The novel tells the story of the 1953 execution of Julius and Ethel Rosenberg, American Jews convicted of passing nuclear secrets to the Soviet Union. The novel makes no pretense of offering an accurate or even plausible historical account, intermixing reality and fantasy in a wild, sometimes hallucinatory narrative meant to distill symbolic rather than literal truths about the killings. Defying historical fact, Coover relocates the "public burning" of the convicted spies from Sing Sing Prison to Times Square, "the ritual center of the Western World" (205). These modern autos-da-fé take place at the culmination of a gala spectacle attended by a procession of politicians, entertainers, religious leaders, sports figures, Disney characters, and assorted American icons, and witnessed by a delirious bloodthirsty crowd. Orchestrating the mad carnival is a cartoon "Superhero" (263), Uncle Sam (he of military recruiting posters), for whom the executions are part of "a irrepressible conflict betwixt opposin' and endurin' forces!" (418) – a struggle against his nemesis, The Phantom, the shadowy agent of Communism and all things un-American.

Although Coover satirizes particular politicians (most obviously the then-vice-president Richard Nixon), his real target is the anti-Communist hysteria that put the Rosenbergs to death and orphaned their sons. More broadly still, he unmasks what has been called the "American civil religion," the ideology that encompasses American exceptionalism, manifest destiny, white supremacy, laissez-faire capitalism, and other national myths.[31] This ideology, for all its many guises, is plainly recognizable in the slogans that the novel holds up for scrutiny, such as the Times Square sign that boasts, "America the Hope of the World" (44), but is changed by the Phantom to declare America the dope, rope, rape, rake, fake, fate, hate, bile, pile, pule, puke, juke, and joke of the world. In focusing on the symbolism of national events like the execution, Coover discloses how this civil religion, rooted in unconscious fantasies, takes hold through public discourse, mass entertainments, and political pageantry.

Coover might be said to be updating the satire of *Babbitt*, with its attacks on Rotary Clubs and evangelist preachers, but his mode is not Lewis's realism with its focus on the daily routines of the middle-American business class. Instead his Menippean novel works on a vast canvas, treating world events and public language with a frenzied comic tone, mixing voices, styles, and genres. Chapters alternate between third-person and first-person narration, balancing objective and subjective accounts, occasionally supplementing them with "intermezzi" or interludes – a collage of Eisenhower's speeches, a stage play, an operetta – that add still other perspectives to the collage.

The third-person chapters offer a hyped-up newsreel account of historical events. Their narration assimilates the language of billboards, protest signs, graffiti, newspaper editorials, even the Rosenbergs' private letters, subjecting all to ironic "double-voicing." It includes the jocular, folksy, vaguely Western, and often crude language of Uncle Sam, who sounds by turns like a revivalist preacher, a stump-speech orator, and a carnival barker. It also incorporates the language of the "Poet Laureate" TIME, a personification of the national news magazine, whose prose Coover arranges in the form of ballads or short poems in order to indicate the ideological work that the mass media performs. (In contrast, Dawn Powell's satire of *Time* in *A Time to Be Born* also sees the magazine as promulgating an uncritical patriotism, but her comedy of manners focuses on the personal failures of Henry and Clare Boothe Luce.) Coover's polyphony of voices creates what he intended to be "a text that would seem to have been written by the whole nation,"[32] stuffed with the clichés of a national mythology, but vibrating with ironic skepticism.

The first-person chapters are narrated by Nixon, and deploy the old-fashioned satiric device of an unreliable narrator who in his self-justification unwittingly discloses his failings. Coover's technique resembles that of Mark Twain's *King Leopold's Soliloquy* (1905), in which the Belgian king's defense of his atrocities in Central Africa simultaneously belittles and indicts the monarch. Coover's pitch-perfect impersonation of Nixon reveals both the vice-president's comic grandiosity ("Washington had got the obelisk, Jefferson the dome and circle, Lincoln the cube, what was there left for me? I wondered. The pyramid maybe." (328)) and his skewed sense of victimization ("Why is it, I wondered, that people think of *me* as the cagy and devious one?" (289)). Nixon comes across as a slapstick clown, a bumbler who suffers innumerable minor humiliations – stepping in horseshit, walking into a concrete wall, failing to hit a golf ball squarely. Reduced from the "Fighting Quaker" to the "Farting Quacker," from the epic role of "Aeneas" to the satiric one of "Anus," he becomes so pathetic, indeed, that he wins a measure of sympathy from the reader.

Above all, Nixon is obsessed with the Rosenbergs' sex life. Like *Catch-22*, *The Public Burning* reduces the fearsome authority figure to a Freudian cartoon, a mess of insecurities and neuroses. The novel, indeed, repeatedly connects patriotism and imperialism to unhealthily violent sexuality, through the orgiastic Times Square mob, and most notoriously, through the final scene of Uncle Sam's homosexual rape of Nixon. ("It felt like he was trying to shove the whole goddamn Washington Monument up my ass!" (658), Nixon complains.) It is only through rape that the Vice-President is "incarnated" with the spirit of America. The scene depicts, as Tom LeClair argues, an America mastered by its own ideological constructs.[33]

The public burning of the Rosenbergs ultimately promotes national cohesion by sacrificing symbolic ritual scapegoats, in this case Communist New York Jews. As Uncle Sam tells Nixon, "It ain't easy holdin' a community together ... and a lotta people gotta get killt tryin' to pretend it is" (657). The comic tone of the narration reflects the gleeful but ultimately violent hatreds of the American populace, the mob tendency that Alvin Kernan identifies as a central satiric trope in works from *The Dunciad* to Nathanael West's *The Day of the Locust*.[34] At the same time, no fair-minded reader will deny the sadistic pleasure Coover himself takes in the satiric attack on Nixon's body. Yet Coover, like Heller, also modulates from this satiric glee to a darker grotesque mode. The scene of Ethel's execution lurches from carnivalesque to horror as the crowd and reader witness "a sudden harsh metallic rattle." In coldly descriptive prose, the narrator notes that "Ethel leaps against the straps," and the crowd smells an "odor of burning meat." Then

> Ethel Rosenberg's body, held only at head, groin, and one leg, is whipped like a sail in a high wind, flapping out at the people like one of those trick images in a 3-D movie, making them scream and duck and pray for deliverance. (638)

This gruesome reminder of the vulnerability of the human body, transformed from a living being to "burning meat," at once fantastical and all-too-real, testifies to the violence embedded in national ideals.

Don DeLillo's *White Noise* (1985) is representative of a later phase of postmodern fiction, one that lacks the showy self-conscious play or formal radicalism of Reed, Pynchon, and Coover, yet maintains a focus on the systems and institutions of contemporary society, and on the way that understanding of those systems and institutions eludes our epistemological grasp. The novel can on one level be analyzed as a comedy of manners, a satire of middle America in the vein of Sinclair Lewis updated for the decades of cable TV, the shopping mall, and the "blended" family, or, as we saw in Chapter 7, a campus novel that mocks academic manners and trends during the years of cultural studies and French theory. Yet, as Jack Gladney concedes, his world is not the insulated "small world" that the name College-on-the-Hill connotes. Jack struggles to accept that he is vulnerable to the same catastrophic dislocation that regularly besets the poor in other parts of the nation or the globe – at least on TV:

> I'm a college professor. Did you ever see a college professor rowing a boat down his own street in one of those TV floods? We live in a neat and pleasant town near a college with a quaint name. These things don't happen in places like Blacksmith.   (114)

Jack here begins to articulate what the novel impresses upon us all along: Jack and his family are tiny figures in a vast, dangerous, unknowable world.

Knowing the world is a central problem in *White Noise*. As *Tristram Shandy* wreaks havoc with the philosophy of Locke, so the postmodern theory batted around between Jack and various interlocutors is comic fodder for DeLillo as he questions the very grounds for knowledge. Sheathed in irony, these bits of armchair theorizing are frequently silly yet stubbornly persuasive. An early dialogue with Heinrich about whether it is raining devolves into a morass of skepticism, at which point Jack declares: "A victory for uncertainty, randomness, and chaos ... The sophists and the hairsplitters enjoy their finest hour" (24). While Jack's interlocutors – Heinrich, Stompanado, Murray Siskind – revel in postmodern uncertainty, Jack plays the anxious innocent, and the reader laughs uneasily at his desire for clear truths in a world that refuses to grant them.

All this brainy theorizing attempts to analyze the ways that experience is determined by the systemic forces of postmodern society. During the airborne toxic event, Jack observes that "They seem to have things under control," but quickly realizes that he has no idea who "they" are, who actually is "in charge" (147) of public safety. Even the mundane act of checking a bank balance is satirically presented as a wrenching emotional engagement with "the system" in which an expected result produces "Waves of relief and gratitude":

> The system had blessed my life. I felt its support and approval.
> The system hardware, the mainframe sitting in a locked room in some distant city ... we were in accord, at least for now. The networks, the circuits, the streams, the harmonies.   (46)

There is just enough mock-epic exaggeration here to make the reader smile, even as she recognizes, with Jack, the authority of machines, the importance of digitized information, and the geographic dispersal and invisibility of the "system" itself.

Throughout *White Noise*, the displacement of reality by simulacrum affords muted comedy, from the barn that is photographed because it is America's most photographed barn to the nuns who pretend to believe in God so that no one else has to. Even nature can't be regarded as authentic; Heinrich observes "something ominous in the modern sunset" (61). Simulacrum, technology, and bureaucracy also create paradoxes reminiscent of *Catch-22*. Official records override experienced reality, as when Jack, like Heller's Doc Daneeka, recalls that he is "technically dead" (158). Jack's blood test may or may not reveal the presence of a particular toxin. His doctor tells him:

> "We have true elevations and false elevations. This is all you have to know."
> "Exactly how elevated is my potassium?"
> "It has gone through the roof, evidently."
> "What might this be a sign of?"
> "It could mean nothing, it could mean a very great deal indeed."
> "How great?"
> "Now we are getting into semantics." (260)

Yet the prevailing affect here is different from Heller's jubilant nonsense. Instead of Marx Brothers-style lunacy, *White Noise* recovers in the postmodern condition an archaic sense of dread or awe – ultimately, a fear of death – that persists in spite of our capacities for irony.

Many of the systems and networks that govern Jack's life are chemical or technological. The pharmaceutical industry infiltrates the characters' bodies with synthetic compounds, while the airborne toxic event threatens a death that "would penetrate, seep into the genes, show itself in bodies not yet born" (116). For Heinrich, the human will is merely "a question of brain chemistry, signals going back and forth, electrical energy in the cortex" (45). The shelter of the family home is penetrated by the "white noise" of technology, by the disembodied voices of TV and radio, by "huge amounts of data flowing through the house" (101), by "radiation that surrounds us every day" (174), "a primal force in the American home" (51). Even death is imagined as "Electrical noise . . . Uniform, white" (198). Jack lives in an age in which threats of plane crashes, environmental contamination, mass murder, and other catastrophes have become familiar. Passing comments allude to a multitude of real historical threats to human life: AIDS, Three Mile Island, India's Union Carbide disaster, the thalidomide crisis.

Frequently the satire in *White Noise* works through double-voiced discourse, as DeLillo underscores the linguistic symptoms of postmodernity. The radio first describes the chemical cloud as a "feathery plume" (111), then as a "black billowing cloud" (113), finally as "an airborne toxic event" (117), each phrase an attempt to contain the danger by naming it. But the proliferating jargon is actually a symptom of the anxiety it seeks to tame, and Heinrich enunciates the terms "in a clipped and foreboding manner, syllable by syllable, as if he sensed the threat in state-created terminology" (117). The "airborne toxic event," in fact, is only the most prominent example of a pervasive technical jargon that is always reproduced with ironic accents – the recurring names of commercial products, the corporate-speak of letters from the bank, even mention of Wilder's "system of sensory analysis" (167). Jack himself points out the strangeness of such language when he describes a TV reporter's account of a serial killer: "Digging would continue through the night, he said, and the station would cut back to the scene as soon as developments warranted. He made it sound like a lover's promise" (222). Or again: when visiting a medical center for his tests, Jack asks, "Why would such a place be called Autumn Harvest Farms? Was this an attempt to balance the heartlessness of their gleaming precision equipment? Would a quaint name fool us into thinking we live in pre-cancerous times?" (275).

But while Jack can point out the absurdity of the language that surrounds him, he still fails (as we all fail) to understand the system that he must trust in spite of its evident fragility and malfunctioning. *White Noise* presents this condition of unknowing as both eerie and funny. At the start of the novel, Jack reports, "The smoke alarm went off in the hallway upstairs, either to let us know the battery had just died or because the house was on fire" (8): the technologically mediated environment produces unreadable signs, suspending the family between the mundane and the catastrophic. The same uncertainty occurs during the evacuation as the car's gas gauge "quiver[s] on E," and the family debates whether "There's always extra" (126) – pointing out how poorly we understand the technological systems on which we rely. Jack has recently noted that "In a crisis the true facts are whatever other people say they are. No one's knowledge is less secure than your own" (120), but this epistemological insecurity is by now a norm; rumors and scraps of information routinely stand in for genuine understanding of a world too large to comprehend. At moments, Jack does manage to attain a wider perspective on his world, as when he discerns "an epic quality" in the evacuating crowd of "trudging people" that makes it appear "part of some ancient destiny, connected in doom and ruin to a whole history of people trekking across wasted landscapes" (121). Yet even as Jack sounds this note of grandeur, his ironic overtones imbue the description with satire, reducing the epic procession to a parade of fools.

In recent decades, the cartoonish humor of Pynchon, the ironic cool of DeLillo, and the showy heteroglossia of Rushdie have come under attack. Broadsides by David Foster Wallace against "irony" and by James Wood against "hysterical realism" have seemed to signal a turn away from the cynicism (for Wallace) or whimsy (for Wood) characteristic of postmodern satire. For Wallace, "TV's institutionalization of hip irony" has coopted the political force of so-called first-wave postmodern satire, rendering it "not liberating but enfeebling."[35] For Wood, the stimulation of information and caricature has replaced convincing human drama: "Bright lights are taken as evidence of habitation."[36] For both, the problem is a lack of seriousness, and in the twenty-first century many novelists have sought, following Wallace's injunction, a "new sincerity" or "postironic" stance, through which they might reassert commitments to particular values or ideals.[37] Yet contemporary writers born in the 1960s and 1970s – Paul Beatty, Mohsin Hamid, Sam Lipsyte, George Saunders, Will Self, Zadie Smith, even Wallace himself – have hardly abandoned satire. Like many before them, they combine irony and commitment, skepticism and sympathy, as they draw on the resources of postmodernism, and indeed of the Menippean novel in general, to satirize the conditions of their world: global capitalism, ideologies of race and gender, conspicuous consumption, the mechanization of the body, and the infiltration of these and other impersonal forces into our most intimate being.

New Maps of Hell: The Dystopia

A final kind of satiric novel, enormously popular today, is the dystopia. Like the encyclopedic satires of postmodernism, the dystopia originates in Menippean satire. It derives, however, specifically from the imaginary voyages of *Utopia* and *Gulliver's Travels*. Its basic trope is to imagine a fully realized alternative world in order to stage a series of satiric contrasts with the society of the here-and-now. In this it resembles its parent-genre, the utopia. But whereas the utopia mounts its critique by holding up an ideal by which to measure the deficiencies of the real world, the dystopia extrapolates existing tendencies to a point of absurdity or horror in order to direct attention to present-day ills.[38] And while the dystopia maintains the Menippean tradition of intellectual satire in its mockery of utopian ideas and projects, its satire is primarily political. This political satire, moreover, extends into the economic, social, cultural, and sexual realms, since the dominant dystopian formula assumes a world in which every dimension of life has become colonized and managed by the state. The dystopia thus offers what Kingsley Amis called "new maps of hell."

Some of the most well-known dystopias – Yvgeney Zamyatin's *We*, Sinclair Lewis's *It Can't Happen Here*, George Orwell's *Nineteen Eighty-Four*, Margaret Atwood's *The Handmaid's Tale* – offer clear examples of satire divorced from comedy (though not from irony, which is embedded in the very idea of dystopia). Feelings of fear and horror crowd out amusement, pushing the dystopia to the borders of social criticism, the novel of ideas, or political fable. Today's dystopian young adult novels, comic books, and Hollywood blockbusters are primarily adventures and romances, with only a residue of satirical critique retained to supply an air of profundity. Some dystopias, however, do rely on comic invention. A subtype that Amis dubbed the "comic inferno" introduces an array of new technologies and social practices with a satiric aim.[39] In Aldous Huxley's *Brave New World* (1932), mass cloning, popular entertainments, engineered narcotics, caste hierarchy, sanctioned childhood sex play, and enforced adult promiscuity all ludicrously exaggerate existing phenomena from the 1920s and 1930s. In Terry Gilliam's film *Brazil* (1985), the excesses of the modern bureaucratic state are taken to fantastic extremes when Robert DeNiro's Harry Tuttle literally disappears in a storm of paperwork. Gary Shteyngart's *Super Sad True Love Story* (2010) depicts a post-9/11, post-Lehman Brothers, post-Internet-porn America where fascism is on the rise under the Orwellian name of the Bipartisan Party; ubiquitous "credit poles" display the financial health of passing pedestrians whose mobile devices they scan; and these same mobile devices, through instantaneous crowdsourcing, display the relative "fuckability" of all the customers in a bar. Even when the dystopia's tone is not explicitly jokey, high levels of fantasy situate it firmly in Menippean tradition: Samuel Butler's *Erewhon* describes an imaginary voyage akin to those of Gulliver and Hythlodaeus, while H.G. Wells's *The Time Machine* imagines a fantastic world removed from us temporally rather than spatially. George Schuyler's *Black No More* uses a single technological innovation – a machine that changes skin color – as a springboard for a wild transformation of American society, while a beast fable like *Animal Farm* enacts its satire on Soviet Communism with a whimsical humor derived from dressing up farm animals in the roles of historical personages, grafting weighty political themes onto a children's story like *Charlotte's Web*. All demonstrate the satiric elements of fantasy and invention underlying dystopia.

Dystopias might be grouped into two broad types: totalitarian and anarchic. In the totalitarian dystopia of Huxley, Orwell, and Atwood, the state extends its control over the individual beyond mere obedience, taking hold of the inner life. A dissident comes to recognize that the system is evil. Private acts of defiance – Orwell's Winston Smith or Atwood's Offred recording thoughts in a diary, Huxley's Bernard Marx contemplating the moonlit sea in silence – lead to larger rebellions, usually culminating in the dissident's defeat by the state. The anarchic dystopia, in contrast, reflects on what happens to the human being cut loose from the restraints and comforts of civilization, in a state of nature often brought on by nuclear war or environmental disaster. Huxley's *Ape and Essence*, William Golding's *Lord of the Flies*, J.G. Ballard's *The Drowned World*, and Cormac McCarthy's *The Road* owe a debt to quest narratives and Crusoe-like survival stories, but they can retain satiric functions of warning against contemporary developments and debunking falsely benign views of human nature.

In both utopia and dystopia, setting, rather than plot or character, is the key feature. But while the utopian islands of Prospero, Crusoe, and Gulliver exist at a spatial remove from the here-and-now, the modern dystopia is likely to imagine a world removed from us in time. The near-future setting of the dystopia emphasizes historicity; the imagined world is one somehow arrived at from our own, and its collective future is shaped by scientific and technological changes, not just political and cultural ones. This emphasis on historicity also reveals the dystopia as a cousin to the modest proposal: the modest proposal is a mini-dystopia, which puts forth a putatively minor policy suggestion and adumbrates the nightmarish near-future it would create.

Satire has always shadowed utopia. In Aristophanes' *Birds* the utopian aspiration may critique contemporary Athens, but its realization is mocked as Cloudcuckooland. More's *Utopia* gives rise to what has been called the first anti-utopia, Hall's *Mundus Alter et Idem*.[40] The fourth book of *Gulliver's Travels* is both utopia and dystopia since it undermines the desirability of the Houyhnhnms' society even as that society is used to critique contemporary England. Thus while the nineteenth century sees a boom in utopian thinking – given literary form in works such as Edward Bellamy's *Looking Backward 2000–1887* (1888) and William Morris's *News from Nowhere* (1890) – the era also produces anti-utopian novels including Nathaniel Hawthorne's *Blithedale Romance* (1852), Mark Twain's *A Connecticut Yankee in King Arthur's Court* (1889), and Joseph Conrad's *The Secret Agent* (1907) that mock utopian communities or schemes and give shape to the dangers lurking beneath utopian desires.

The dystopia proper, however, takes its satire a step further than such anti-utopias, imagining an entire world that conceives of itself as a utopia but turns out to be a nightmare. It is popularly understood as a response to

Communism and fascism, and to the unprecedented horrors of systematic repression, violence, and genocide that they perpetrated. Yet dystopia's first satiric targets were not the mid-century totalitarian states but wider trends fundamental to social and technological "progress" (and often taken up by postmodern satire): rationalization, industrialization, standardization, utilitarianism, bureaucracy, mass surveillance. The satiric force of dystopia indeed rests in its recognition of continuity between the forces of modernization that are supposed to usher in utopia and the forces of dehumanization that make it horrific. It represents, in Irving Howe's phrase, "Not progress denied but progress realized."[41] Thus the basic condition of Orwell's Oceania is paradox, or "doublespeak," an ideological condition under which opposite values become indistinguishable: "War is peace. Freedom is slavery. Ignorance is strength."[42]

The decades leading up to World War I see a range of proto-dystopias including Butler's *Erewhon* (1872), Wells's *The Time Machine* (1895), and E.M. Forster's "The Machine Stops" (1909), in which the human being grows so dependent upon the machine that she becomes a machine. *Erewhon* represents machines as organisms subject to the forces of evolution and inextricably embedded in the human ecosystem, redescribing Victorian technophilia as slavery to mechanical masters, and liberal humanism as narrow anthropocentrism. Darwin casts a similar shadow over *The Time Machine*, in which the class antagonism of industrial capitalism has become, in the year 802,701, a divide between two species: the effete, vegetarian Eloi (descended from the aristocracy) and the carnivorous Morlocks (descended from the proletariat) who literally feed on them. In Forster's "The Machine Stops," finally, all human existence has become subject to one great Machine, which becomes a divinity to the people it rules. In a science fiction version of Plato's Allegory of the Cave, people dwell in underground cells with little or no direct contact with nature or other human bodies, interacting only with simulacra.

Jack London's *The Iron Heel* (1908) inaugurates a different variety of dystopia, the alternative history. It offers a counterfactual account of a socialist revolution crushed by a cabal of capitalist oligarchs. Tracts of Marxist dogma thinly disguised as dinner conversation render the book closer to social criticism than satire, yet the novel opens the way for a strain of antifascist alternative histories that include Schuyler's *Black No More* (1931), Lewis's *It Can't Happen Here* (1935), and West's *A Cool Million* (1934), as well as Philip Roth's more recent *The Plot Against America* (2004). Rather than depicting a fully achieved dystopia, this variety of near-future fiction focuses on the nation in the process of political transformation.

Zamyatin's *We* (1921) and Huxley's *Brave New World* (1932) mark the arrival of the dystopian novel in its most familiar form; the reigns of Hitler and especially Stalin lead to Orwell's *Nineteen Eighty-Four* (1949), which establishes the dystopia's cultural ubiquity. Certain features recur in these works and across the genre. Society is organized into hierarchical groups and castes. Ruling elites manipulate the masses by stirring up violent human passions for their own political ends – in Orwell's Hate Week, Huxley's orgies and feelies, Atwood's Particicution rituals. Political conformity is enforced through mass media. High art and independent thought are discouraged; books are banned or burned. A particular preoccupation of Orwell's is the degradation of language. Oceania's Newspeak, a streamlined version of English, eliminates expressiveness, limits dissent, and covers over brutality, all in the name of efficiency. Orwell cites Nazi and Soviet coinages – *Gestapo, Comintern, Agitprop*, even *Nazi* itself – as precedent for his own invention. As he writes elsewhere, "Political language . . . is designed to make lies sound truthful and murder respectable, and to give an appearance of solidity to pure wind."[43]

In many ways *Brave New World* and *Nineteen Eighty-Four* have come to represent opposite poles in the spectrum of dystopian possibilities. Orwell targets Soviet Russia first of all, and Big Brother is Stalin as surely as *Animal Farm*'s Napoleon is Lenin. The icon of *Brave New World*, in contrast, is Henry Ford, a titan of American capitalism, and Huxley's World State mixes capitalist mass-production with Wellsian social engineering in a vision that can actually be described as a triumph of a technocratic neoliberalism.[44] Orwell's Cold War satire sees a world divided into warring superstates; Huxley's Depression-era satire sees a single, unified World State. Orwell's society is built on material deprivation and torture, while Huxley's rests on easy pleasures and material satisfactions – jazz, sports, films, drugs, sex. Orwell's vision suggests that our leaders will enslave us; Huxley's, that we will enslave ourselves.

Dystopias also pay particular attention to an array of themes that Foucault called biopolitical: the regulation of sex and reproduction, health and illness, life and death. Social engineering is supplemented by biological engineering and eugenics,[45] and dystopias envision radical changes in sexual norms and practices, whether in the repressive vein of Orwell's Oceania with its intent to abolish the orgasm, or in the permissive vein of Huxley's World-State with its compulsory promiscuity. The institutions of marriage and the family are often transformed, as in *The Handmaid's Tale* where the state of Gilead creates a caste of female sexual slaves. Dystopias imagine the management of death (often through euthanasia) and food production (sometimes entailing cannibalism), and apartheid-like divisions of populations. All of these features stem from an overarching attack on a modernity that destroys individual freedom, dignity, love, and truth in the name of an ostensibly greater collective "good."

As the genre develops, these basic themes are assimilated to new social concerns. The core problem of Anthony Burgess's *A Clockwork Orange* (1962) is urban crime, especially rape, which the novel loosely links to the rise of the bureaucratic welfare state and the alienation of its youth; the state's solution, to biochemically deprive the hero of free will, is even worse, since it replaces an anarchic condition with a totalitarian one. In works such as J.G. Ballard's novel *High-Rise* (1975) or Paul Verhoeven's action film *Robocop* (1987), the central dystopian condition becomes capitalism's remaking of the human environment and its division of society into haves and have-nots. In response to Reaganism and the growing political power of the religious right, Atwood's *Handmaid's Tale* (1985) recasts the Orwellian state as a homophobic, patriarchal theocracy.

Will Self's phantasmagoric comedy *Great Apes* (1997) is not quite a dystopia, but creates an alternate universe in which evolved, literate chimpanzees have become the dominant species, and humans a brutish cousin confined to zoos and reserves; like Swift in *Gulliver's Travels*, Self uses a primate society with radically alien family structures, sexual practices, and modes of communication as "a satirical trope" to unmask humanity's pretention to a special place in the natural order.[46] Kazuo Ishiguro's *Never Let Me Go* (2005) returns to Huxley with its interest in bioengineering, imagining a group of human clones who have been raised in order to have their vital organs harvested. Most recently, Michel Houellebecq's *Submission* (2015) envisions the rise of an Islamic theocracy in France under the Muslim Brotherhood; while Houellebecq's fantasy invites charges of reactionary Islamophobia, his satire attempts to think past not only *Nineteen Eighty-Four*'s Cold War nightmare but also *Brave New World*'s neoliberal one. Houellebecq's narrator accepts with cynical resignation that Enlightenment values can prevail for only a small, passing episode in the long and mostly unhappy narrative of human history. Houellebecq's vision, among the grimmest and most unforgiving offered by the dystopian novel today, reminds us that satire retains the power not only to amuse but also to unnerve.

Chapter 10

Satire and Popular Culture since 1900

The poems, plays, novels, and other prose works surveyed in the nine previous chapters represent a small fraction of the satiric works that human beings have produced. While some of these works – Roman verses read on street corners, dramas performed on the Jacobean stage, pamphlets debated in eighteenth-century coffeehouses, formal verse satire printed in journals like *The North Briton* and *The Anti-Jacobin* – can justly be considered as the popular forms of their time, they are commonly read today as artifacts of high culture. But satire as it exists in popular culture – in journalism, cartooning, print culture, film, television, digital media, and elsewhere – often makes no pretense to aesthetic greatness and seeks no audience beyond the present. Such popular works, indeed, can possess a responsiveness to their historical moment that makes them particularly hospitable to satiric judgment and commentary. Of course, no clear, bright line separates high art and popular culture. Many satiric novelists – Mark Twain, George Schuyler, Flann O'Brien (Brian O'Nolan), to name only a few – write satiric journalism. Others draw upon popular forms in fashioning their literary voices: it would be hard to imagine Philip Roth's Alexander Portnoy without the example of Lenny Bruce, or Paul Beatty's "Me" without Richard Pryor.

This chapter's final brief look at satire in popular culture does not aspire to be a comprehensive survey. Because it begins in the twentieth century, it omits the longer history of satire in popular culture. In the eighteenth and nineteenth centuries, many kinds of popular performance (pantomime, music hall, stage comedy) had been tinged with satire, while the tradition of graphic and periodical satire was especially rich. The lively print culture of Augustan England spawned a "golden age" of satiric prints that lasted through the early decades of the next century. But public taste and morality grew more conservative, and the bawdiness and radicalism of periodical satire softened. The British weekly *Punch*, along with many imitators, emerged to offer milder satire aimed at a moderate middle-class readership.[1] With new, inexpensive methods of production and distribution, comic periodicals thrived, but they shifted from rough-edged political radicalism to respectable light entertainment.[2] There were of course exceptions, and late-century examples of journalistic writing – George Bernard Shaw's criticism in the UK or the humor pieces of Mark Twain and Ambrose Bierce in the United States – helped to initiate a rebellion in public taste. This rebellion was taken up in the next century by a new generation of satirists seeking freedom from repressive social codes.

Even restricting itself to the last hundred-odd years, this chapter can only cover a sample of representative satires. It selects a few key historical moments that hint at the variety of forms that satire has assumed in response to changing social, technological, and historical conditions. Yet in each of these moments a different genre or medium emerges which becomes signally characteristic of the satire of its time. I examine early twentieth-century satire through the journalism of H.L. Mencken and Dorothy Parker, two figures associated with the "smart magazines" of American's new urban public sphere; mid-century satire through the darkly comic and countercultural (anti-)war films of Stanley Kubrick and Robert Altman; and twenty-first-century satire through the mockumentary and parodic TV news programs that circulate through cable television, the Internet, and social media. In an epilogue, I examine the public discussion and debate surrounding the murder of the writers, editors, and cartoonists at the satiric French magazine *Charlie Hebdo*, and what these debates say about satire today.

Modernist Print Culture: Mencken, Parker, and the Smart Magazines

The artistic revolution known as modernism occurred in the early twentieth century alongside a broader shift in society – in popular entertainment, social relations, gender roles, political discourse, and everyday behavior. Literary satire was part of this shift: novels, plays, and poems chronicled and precipitated sociocultural changes by making sport of both the old pieties and the new fashions. Within a multifaceted print culture that included newspapers, magazines, and best-sellers, one notable venue for satire was the American smart magazine. Smart magazines – *The Smart Set*, *Vanity Fair*, *The New Yorker*, *The American Mercury*, *Esquire* – mixed literature, reviews, humor, gossip, and politics. These publications lacked the readership of mass-circulation weeklies such as *Time*, yet they were disproportionately influential in their appeal to a subculture of young, educated city-dwellers. Harold Ross's 1925 proposal for *The New Yorker* describes their tone:

> The New Yorker will be a reflection in word and picture of metropolitan life. It will be human. Its general tenor will be one of gaiety, wit and satire, but it will be more than a jester. It will be what is commonly called sophisticated, in that it will assume a reasonable degree of enlightenment on the part of its readers. It will hate bunk.[3]

Although the smart magazines struck a light and even frothy tone, they embraced the age's new social and sexual freedoms, and modeled a worldly, amused response to changing behavior. Scorning "bunk," they indirectly advanced a polemic against everything puritanical and provincial – those values embodied in the imaginary reader whom Ross represented as "the little old lady in Dubuque." The smart magazines thus provided a cultural-aesthetic pedagogy that worked both positively, by offering readers models of sophistication, and negatively, by showing them what to laugh at, in others and in themselves.

Within this new subculture, the *New Yorker* cartoon became a signature genre. As Iain Topliss has shown, in sketching ephemeral moments from everyday life, these cartoons – unlike the political cartoons of the daily papers – practice social satire. They capture quirky new experiences situated "at the very edge of semantic availability," not yet available to theoretical understanding.[4] Peter Arno, one of the magazine's leading cartoonists, chronicled New York City's speakeasies, nightclubs, bars, and ballrooms – sites of leisure, consumption, and flirtation – juxtaposing a hedonistic youth culture of flappers, dandies, and bohemians against a stodgy older generation of businessmen and stockbrokers. Through his cartooning, Arno himself assumes the role of the dandy; he becomes, as Topliss says, a roving painter of modern life who scorns Victorian seriousness and duty. Along with other cartoonists, essayists, and humorists of the magazine's early years (E.B. White, James Thurber, Robert Benchley), he conjures for the middle-class reader a fantasy of almost aristocratic freedom, satirizing the old ethos of productivity and self-discipline.[5] The work of Arno and his fellow cartoonists, every bit as much as the novels of F. Scott Fitzgerald, has shaped the image of the 1920s that has endured in the popular imagination.

Ross's model for *The New Yorker* was *The Smart Set*, edited by H.L. Mencken and George Jean Nathan. As a columnist, reporter, reviewer, and editor, Mencken was possibly his era's most influential taste-maker. The enemy of repressive traditions and beliefs, he belongs with LaRochefoucauld and Shaw as what George Test calls an "iconoclast," a subspecies of satirist who openly flouts all orthodoxies (*SSA* 221–222). Confrontational, cynical, sometimes misanthropic, the iconoclast's preferred mode is full-throated invective; he does not uphold communal norms but attacks them. Yet for all his directness, the iconoclast is a *persona*, a character fashioned through voice and performance. Essays, reviews, speeches, interviews, and even conversational witticisms help to shape his public personality. During the very years that Hollywood was inventing modern celebrity – commodifying personality itself – Mencken fashioned himself as both a critic of the culture and a public figure within it.

Mencken himself extols the anarchic spirit of the iconoclast in a 1924 essay, refusing to offer any new gods to replace the idols he smashes:

> The liberation of the human mind has never been furthered by ... learned dunderheads; it has been furthered by gay fellows who heaved dead cats into sanctuaries and then went roistering down the highways of the world, proving to all men that doubt, after all, was safe – that the god in the sanctuary was finite in his power, and hence a fraud. One horse-laugh is worth ten thousand syllogisms.[6]

Mencken here describes the *practice* of satire. Irreverent provocation is needed to expose fraudulent orthodoxies. This critical gesture (cat-heaving) works on the level not of the intellect but of the gut (the horse-laugh), yet its intuitive intelligence outstrips the pedantry of the "learned dunderheads" who support established authorities and norms.

Mencken famously defined Puritanism as "the haunting fear that someone, somewhere, may be happy," and this quip encapsulates his satiric agenda. As a columnist for the *Baltimore Sun*, he declared his purpose "to combat, chiefly by ridicule, American piety, stupidity, tin-pot morality, cheap chauvinism in all their forms."[7] These included the fussy, genteel tradition in American letters; the strictures of preachers and prohibitionists; the irrationalism of religion; and the self-satisfied ignorance of the business class, which he called the "booboisie" or, after Sinclair Lewis's character, the "Babbittry." Mencken's politics were all over the map: pro-German and inexcusably sympathetic to Hitler in the early 1930s, he also supported women's suffrage, anti-lynching laws, and the acceptance of Jewish refugees. As a shaper of public tastes, though, his impact was strongest in cultural matters. Satirical novelists including Lewis, Anita Loos, George Schuyler, and Aldous Huxley all testified to the inspiration they took from Mencken's brash style and glee in challenging received opinion. Richard Wright recalled his first reading of Mencken as a thunderbolt:

> I was jarred and shocked by the style, the clear, clean, sweeping sentences ... I pictured the man as a raging demon ... Yes, this man was fighting, fighting with words. He was using words as a weapon, using them as one would use a club.[8]

Mencken in fact made American taste itself more satiric. As editor of *The Smart Set* and *The American Mercury*, he promoted and published authors who defied reigning standards of gentility. *The Smart Set* was an avowedly light magazine, influenced by Aubrey Beardsley's defunct *Yellow Book* in England (1894–1897), which appealed to young readers through an insouciant, clever tone. Like *The New Yorker*, it promoted modern attitudes about gender, sex, and morality, contrasting them to those held by a doltish American public in the hinterlands. Its motto was "One Civilized Reader is Worth a Thousand Boneheads."[9] Like the similarly tempered Wyndham Lewis in England, Mencken believed the greatest satire to be non-moral, and his magazine aimed to delight, not to instruct.

With his move to *The American Mercury* in 1924, however, Mencken sought a venue with more intellectual heft and political content. Yet the new magazine retained the truculence of the old; in the first issue, Mencken and Nathan declared their intention "to carry on steady artillery practice against every variety of artistic pedant and mountebank."[10] Mencken continued to find young, brainy readers, and *American Mercury* became the top-selling magazine at the Harvard and Columbia college bookstores. At the same time, by syndicating his newspaper column and publishing discount paperbacks sold at drugstores, Mencken cultivated other methods to spread his views.[11] By the late 1920s, his tastes were so pervasive among a certain class that in *The Sun Also Rises* Hemingway's Jake Barnes could scoff, "So many young men get their likes and dislikes from Mencken."[12]

Mencken's style is aggressive, sardonic, and anti-academic. He balances pungent diction with self-consciously grand oratory, crude epithet with learned reference. He sprinkles his sentences with recherché words, slang, foreign phrases, neologisms – any fuel he can find to make his prose crackle. His writing draws on an abiding love–hate relationship with American vernacular. He detests its looseness and crassness, which he mocks in his parodic "Declaration of Independence in American":

> All we got to say on this proposition is this: first, me and you is as good as anybody else, and maybe a damn sight better; second, nobody ain't got no right to take away none of our rights; third, every man has got a right to live, to come and go as he pleases, and to have a good time whichever way he likes, so long as he don't interfere with nobody else.[13]

Bad as this prose is, it pales next to the oratory of President Harding, which Mencken derides as "Gamalielese" after the President's biblical middle name:

[H]e writes the worst English I have ever encountered. It reminds me of a string of wet sponges; it reminds me of tattered washing on the line; it reminds me of stale bean-soup, of college yells, of dogs barking idiotically through endless nights. It is so bad that a sort of grandeur creeps into it.

Harding's "sonorous nonsense," aspiring to profundity, substitutes grandiose and often incorrect words for simple, direct ones.[14] Yet Mencken also rejects the prim and fastidious. His own prose draws on the vernacular tradition of Mark Twain, Ambrose Bierce, and Ring Lardner for an earthiness that gives it a feel of authenticity.

If Harding epitomized for Mencken the idiocy of the Babbittry, four-time presidential candidate William Jennings Bryan embodied the religious fundamentalism of what Mencken named the Bible Belt. In 1925, five days after the Scopes Trial, in which Bryan defended creationism, the aging orator died. Mencken's merciless obituary begins with mischievous blame-by-praise which depicts Bryan as backwards and filthy: "The man felt at home in such simple and Christian scenes. He liked people who sweated freely, and were not debauched by the refinements of the toilet." Soon the statesman is reduced to a "peasant come home to the barnyard," a physical grotesque with "a vague, unpleasant manginess about his appearance." If such mockery appears brutal for a man so recently dead, Mencken soon reveals Bryan as not a fool but a demagogue. Bryan may be "preposterous" but he is anything but "harmless":

The evil that men do lives after them. Bryan, in his malice, started something that it will not be easy to stop. In ten thousand country towns his old heelers, the evangelical pastors, are propagating his gospel, and everywhere the yokels are ready for it.[15]

Mixing the high sentence of Shakespeare with colloquial words like "heelers" and "yokels," Mencken accuses Bryan of dumbing down the entire political culture. Mencken himself, meanwhile, may have roughed up public discourse, but he aimed to make it more discriminating.

If Mencken's ornery iconoclasm derives from Twain and Shaw, Dorothy Parker's sophisticated wit descends from a line of dandies including Byron and Wilde, with A.E. Housman and Edna St. Vincent Millay as the major influences on her poetry. Parker worked in many short forms – light verse, short stories, book reviews – but like Wilde she became famous most of all for her spoken wit. Her quips address changing sexual mores ("If all the girls at the Yale Prom were laid end to end, I wouldn't be a bit surprised") and occasionally politics (on being told that the taciturn Calvin Coolidge had died: "How could they tell?").[16] As a young theater critic at *Vanity Fair*, she met many of the journalists, critics, and playwrights who formed the core of the famous Algonquin Round Table. The writers of this circle – including George S. Kaufman, Alexander Woolcott, Robert Benchley, F.P.A. (Franklin Pierce Adams), and Marc Connelly – soon came to epitomize wit in the American imagination. Tourists would gather at the Algonquin Hotel in midtown Manhattan to "overhear" their very public performance of ostensibly private banter, and choice *bon mots* would circulate to a wider audience through gossip columns – sometimes written by the Algonquinites themselves.[17] Their wit became the focus for further wit, as Anita Loos's Lorelei Lee mocked their fame: "[E]very genius who eats his luncheon at the Algonquin Hotel is always writing that that is the place where all the great literary geniuses eat their luncheon" (138). In contrast to the rough humor of vaudeville that drew on ethnic styles and stereotypes, the verbal nimbleness of the Round Table promoted laughter as an expression of refined detachment. And as the female mainstay of the male-dominated circle, Parker presented herself as a woman wise to the ways of the city, intelligent and witty enough to navigate those new social and sexual codes that promised liberation yet often delivered heartbreak. She thus became "simultaneously a subject, a producer, and . . . an icon of modern culture."[18]

It was Mencken who published Parker's first piece of fiction in *The Smart Set* in 1922. "Such a Pretty Little Picture" satirizes the new suburban bourgeoisie by presenting a young husband crushed by the twin forces of modern capitalism, which chains him to his advertising job, and modern marriage, which subordinates him to a domineering mate. Like Lewis's Babbitt or Thurber's Walter Mitty (or Eliot's J. Alfred Prufrock), he can escape only through daydream. A 1927 *New Yorker* story, "Arrangement in Black and White," satirizes the patronizing racism of a white liberal fawning over a famous black singer at an upscale cocktail party, giving a hint at Parker's lifelong commitment to racial equality. (She left her estate to the NAACP.) These and other early stories offer a comedy of manners, registering the absurdities and contradictions forced upon people – especially women – by social life.

Even more memorable than Parker's stories were her reviews of other people's fiction. Writing as "Constant Reader" in *The New Yorker,* she crafted a persona that combined touches of vulnerability with biting wit: "This is not a book to be tossed aside lightly. It should be thrown with great force"; "The reading of *Dawn* is a strain upon many parts, but the worst wear and tear fall on the forearms."[19] Like Mencken, she establishes her sophistication by what she rejects, and she articulates a standard of taste impatient with the pretentious and the sentimental. Her review of A.A. Milne, for example, concludes with revulsion at Winnie the Pooh's baby-talk: "And it is that word 'hummy,' my darlings, that marks the place in *The House at Pooh Corner* in which Tonstant Weader Fwowed up" (513). The tenderness Milne reaches for is false; Parker exposes it with parodic imitation.

Parker's sophistication is predicated on knowingness – knowing how to distinguish false sentiment from true, but also knowing enough not to be impressed by artsy experimenting. Constant Reader knows in advance how the Dashiell Hammett mystery will end, and what the reviewers will say about the new Hemingway. Sexual transgression cannot faze her. Reviewing a play about Elizabeth Barrett Browning, she rolls her eyes at the depiction of the poet's father as a sexual predator: "isn't it late in the day to drag up incest? He was bad enough just plain, without making him fancy" (482). As Jessica Burstein has shown, the anti-sentimental tastes that Parker shares with her fellow *New Yorker* writers is part of a larger dynamic of sophistication in which the dandy's world-weary "failure to engage" actually constitutes a form of judgment. Parker's been-there-done-that jadedness illustrates Pierre Bourdieu's analysis of taste as a game in which the key move is to distinguish yourself; as soon as others adopt your taste, you must change to stay a step ahead of the crowd.[20] Thus Constant Reader mocks the swell of young writers who scurry to "luncheons, teas, and banquets," "bubbling away" about all the fun they are having (507, 505). The gossipy accounts they publish, under semi-clever titles like "Jottings on a Cuff," indict them as sorry imitators of Parker's *New Yorker* colleagues. In this "jolly brotherhood" of hip journalists, Constant Reader discerns "the sweet and reassuring sense of superiority" characteristic of the pretender. She concludes, cuttingly: "For, being literary folk, they are licensed to be most awfully snooty about the Babbitts" (507). Parker does not just laugh with Mencken at the booboisie; she laughs at the laughers. The result is what Burstein calls a "wobble between hicks and sophisticates" in which metropolitanism is exposed as merely a special case of provincialism.[21] Decades later, the cartoonist Saul Steinberg exploited this wobble in perhaps the *New Yorker*'s most famous cover, "A View of the World from Ninth Avenue," which reveals the ironically limited vision available from the skyscraper in the center of the metropolis.[22]

Parker's light verse, with its polysyllabic rhymes, metrical precision, and linguistic virtuosity, presents a woman savvy to the modern world's new rules of love.[23] She deploys the forms, diction, and tropes of old-fashioned love poetry with just enough irony to craft a modern persona. Often her poems work by establishing a familiar romantic image, then undercutting it. In "Unfortunate Coincidence," the orgasmic and overblown adjectives of the second and fourth lines are undone by the sixth line's terse instruction in reality: "By the time you swear you're his, / Shivering and sighing, / And he vows his passion is / Infinite, undying – / Lady, make a note of this: / One of you is lying" (96). Parker's technique of compression similarly displays her knowingness; her tight epigrams imply that the boring details don't matter since she's heard it all before.

Parker's sophistication also means that she recognizes the seriality of her love affairs.[24] Passions and heartbreaks come and go in a cycle as steady and familiar as the changing seasons, and each new love turns out to be merely the latest in a series. "Resumé," maybe her most famous poem, brings together these qualities of virtuosity, compression, and indifference to novelty. A catalogue of suicide methods profiles a woman who has had her heart broken over and over:

> Razors pain you;
> Rivers are damp;
> Acids stain you;
> And drugs cause cramp.
> Guns aren't lawful;
> Nooses give;
> Gas smells awful;
> You might as well live.   (99)

The worldly speaker ticks off suicide methods along with the (amusingly illogical) arguments against them, but all this variety collapses into similarity. The voice turns out to be so experienced that even life and death are interchangeable. Parker's satire thus critiques modern love – something must be wrong if a woman knows suicide this well – yet salvages from love's wreckage the resources she needs for survival: sophistication and wit.

The Postwar Satire Boom

If Parker's blasé treatment of suicide exemplifies the smart sensibility of satire in the years after World War I, Tom Lehrer's song "We Will All Go Together When We Go" (1959) epitomizes the gallows humor typical of satire after World War II. Lehrer's cabaret number urges celebration of an imminent nuclear extermination for the simple reason that it leaves behind no grief-stricken mourners:

> We will all go together when we go.
> Every Hottentot and every Eskimo.
> When the air becomes uranious,

We will all go simultaneous.
. . . Yes we all will go together when we go.[25]

Lehrer bridges Jazz Age and Cold War satire. His witty rhymes – "There will be no more misery / When the world is our rotisserie" – continue the light verse, satire-as-entertainment tradition that Parker shares with popular lyricists such as W.S. Gilbert and Cole Porter. Like Parker, Lehrer appealed to an intellectual counterpublic: he began performing at parties while a math student at Harvard, and he sold his self-produced first album at Cambridge newsstands. "We Will All Go Together" also partakes of Parker's dark humor, yet, as befits the new nuclear age, it addresses not individual but collective suicide. The song's basic conceit is representative of the era's satire: it combines eros on the level of form with thanatos on the level of content.

Lehrer was only one figure in a transatlantic resurgence of satire after World War II sometimes called the "satire boom." Cultural historians have increasingly located the origins of the 1960s counterculture in 1950s humor, and have understood "sick" jokes, "black" comedy, and radical satire to arise from a nexus of social, political, and technological changes. Just as English satire of the Augustan period flourished in a culture of coffeehouses, theaters, and salons, supported by an explosive growth in print, so satire in the early Cold War saturated popular culture through new modes of writing, image-making, and performance, supported by new social spaces and technologies. It arose from a generational rebellion against the staid conformity of mainstream entertainment, and was enabled by new frankness in language and openness about sex. But it also reacted to the political conditions of the Cold War, especially the existential paradox that technological innovation had led the human race to the brink of self-extermination.[26]

In 1952, William Shawn took over the editorship of Harold Ross's *New Yorker*, moving satire to its back pages as he turned the magazine into the nation's leading venue for well-crafted fiction. That same year, however, the cartoonist Harvey Kurtzman founded *Mad*, whose zany parodies skewered American icons like the Lone Ranger and Superman, eviscerating the heroic American ideology they represented. With its appeal to adolescent male readers, *Mad* purveyed a comic-Jewish mockery of mainstream culture that reached an entire generation of budding satirists; the graphic novelist Art Spiegelman asserts that it did more to inspire the counterculture of the Vietnam era than pot or LSD.[27] In the same years, Walt Kelley's comic strip "Pogo," running in the *New York Star*, injected satire into the newspapers' funny papers with attacks on Eisenhower and Joe McCarthy, offering a pop-culture beast fable not so different in method from George Orwell's *Animal*

Farm.[28] Soon Jules Feiffer and Gary Trudeau were offering satiric comics aimed at adults.

Perhaps the most radical satirical periodical of the era was *The Realist*, founded in 1958 by *Mad* alumnus Paul Krassner as a kind of *Mad* for grownups. Its outrages and obscenities included Krassner's (fictional) 1967 reporting of Jackie Kennedy's account of Lyndon Johnson performing necrophilia on her assassinated husband:

> That man was crouching over the corpse, no longer chuckling but breathing hard and moving his body rhythmically. At first I thought he must be performing some mysterious symbolic rite he'd learned from Mexicans or Indians as a boy. And then I realized – there is only one way to say this – he was literally fucking my husband in the throat. In the bullet wound in the front of his throat.[29]

In what one critic has called "the most notorious parodic text . . . issued from the underground press," Krassner fused a politically defiant critique of William Manchester's "official" history of the assassination with a parodic pornography that plays on Kennedy's own status as sex symbol and participates in the very sensationalism it sends up.[30]

Stand-up comedy underwent a similar transformation. Mort Sahl and Lenny Bruce rejected the established mode of performance in which clownish jokesters dressed like bandleaders and recycled each other's shtick. Sahl, Bruce, and their followers cultivated individual styles and wrote material that was transgressive both politically (going after figures like McCarthy and J. Edgar Hoover) and culturally (speaking with candor and often vulgarity about sex). Nightclubs, meanwhile, replaced resorts and casinos as performance spaces: Sahl rose to prominence performing for students and hipsters at San Francisco's hungry i, which soon became ground zero for the new satire. As one historian has written, "What the Algonquin Round Table was to American humor in 1935, the hungry i wall was to American comedy in 1955."[31]

If the new stand-up comedy began in dives and clubs, it spread through new technologies. Television talk shows introduced the acts of comic performers to millions, as did the LP, created in 1948. In the UK, meanwhile, the comic ensemble Beyond the Fringe revolutionized popular culture almost overnight. Made up of young Oxford and Cambridge alumni, Beyond the Fringe took its name from the Edinburgh International Festival of performing arts, which had spawned its own "Fringe Festival" of comic entertainments. Going beyond this fringe, the new sketch comedy dispensed with "décor, dancing, and all the other irrelevant dum-de-da of conventional revue" in favor of skits that were witty, transgressive, and often political. It leaped from Edinburgh to Cambridge to London. Deploying the silliness, the intelligence, and the freedom from censorship of undergraduate comedy, this new satire was, in the phrase of comedian-turned-playwright Alan Bennett, "private humour going public."[32] By 1961 this wave of brainy satire had spawned a magazine, *Private Eye* (influenced by *Mad* and the Ross-era *New Yorker*), and a nightclub, the Establishment (hailed as England's answer to the hungry i).[33] In 1962 the UK satire boom reached a zenith with the seminal fake-news program *That Was the Week That Was*, or *TW3*, soon followed by an American version that included musical contributions from Lehrer.

The satire boom mixed low clowning with smart college comedy: Beyond the Fringe had theaters laughing at its mimicry of Oxford philosophers, while Chicago's Compass Players and Second City drew inspiration from the avant-garde theater of Brecht and Ionesco.[34] In the United States the Harvard *Lampoon* turned its attention to a wider national culture; its graduates went on to found the *National Lampoon* in the 1970s and *Spy* in the 1980s, and to write *The Simpsons* in the 1990s. The legacy of these groups was powerful: Second City and Beyond the Fringe inspired Monty Python and *Saturday Night Live*; Mort Sahl and Lenny Bruce made possible the satiric stand-up of Dick Gregory, Richard Pryor, George Carlin, and others. Even if popular culture in subsequent decades usually regressed to a middlebrow mean, the satire boom in both the United States and the UK significantly loosened restrictions on ridiculing politicians and public figures, while making space for popular forms of comedy to be more intelligent, crude, political, and indeed satirical.[35]

But while satire flourished in magazines, stand-up, and sketch comedy of the postwar years, the most emblematic satires from the era are films. By the 1960s, the weakening of the old studio system and the rise of international cinema had positioned film squarely at the crossroads of mass entertainment and high art, allowing ambitious auteurs to reach large audiences with innovative films addressing social and political issues. The new taste for black humor and the loosening of taboos led to startling transgressions such as Mel Brooks's *The Producers* (1968), which defied the belief that the Holocaust was beyond the reach of satire. Its signature number, "Springtime for Hitler," ridiculed the Third Reich by travestying fascism's dependence on stagecraft, deploying a Jewish comic idiom "far less redolent of self-hatred than of self-love."[36]

Most emblematic of the era however, were a number of iconic satiric war films that directly addressed the geopolitical concerns of the early Cold War. True, satiric treatments of war were not new; the Marx Brothers' *Duck Soup*

(1933) spoofs nationalism, propaganda, and the pettiness of dictators, while Charlie Chaplin's *The Great Dictator* (1940) burlesques the expansionist ambitions of Hitler ("Adenoid Hynkel") by showing the dictator dancing dreamily to the violins of a Wagner prelude while batting about an inflatable globe. But in their critique of an entire system of military bureaucracy, technology, and foreign policy thinking, two films, Stanley Kubrick's *Dr. Strangelove* (1964) and Robert Altman's *M*A*S*H* (1970), represent something new to the screen and to the culture as a whole.

Dr. Strangelove, adapted in collaboration with the novelist Terry Southern, is an ironic celebration of nuclear apocalypse in the vein of Lehrer's song or certain Beyond the Fringe sketches, expanding a grim one-off joke into a comprehensive satire of the paradoxical logic underlying Cold War ideology. Kubrick originally imagined the film as a serious thriller in the vein of the recent *Fail Safe*, but realized that the material rendered the traditional boundaries of genre obsolete. As Margot Henriksen puts it, the comic absurdity of the scenario "became the message and the method" of the film, whose satiric tone challenged "the cherished seriousness and rationality of America's nuclear ethos."[37] Plot, dialogue, and cinematography converge to reveal an inhuman system in which technology, language, and bureaucracy prove immune to the modest powers of human reason. The black-and-white film's coldly formal visual style juxtaposes the claustrophobia of the bomber, crowded with instruments and switches, with the cavernous and shadowy War Room, with its chilly halo of artificial light. Set off against the frozen Arctic landscape, the airmen tasked with dropping the bomb appear vulnerable, and they carry out their mission in the manner of the heroes of old American war films, to the patriotic soundtrack of "When Johnny Comes Marching Home." But while these dutiful airmen seem characters from a bygone past, the military and civilian leaders in the War Room represent an insane future, characterized by squabbling, indecision, and slapstick wrestling. Situated between the men in the air and their leadership underground is the ground-level space of the military base, strangely depopulated, where the sane Mandrake vainly tries to prevent the apocalypse.

Elements of farce, slapstick, and burlesque gain political force from the extremity of a historically unprecedented narrative situation. When the ineffectual President Muffley calls the drunken Premier Kissov to alert him to the imminent nuclear attack, the one-sided phone conversation uses a deadpan stand-up device that had been popularized by Bob Newhart. Muffley's tone shifts as he goes from trying to break the news of the attack to soothing the hurt feelings of his childlike counterpart:

One of our base commanders he had a sort of – well, he went a little
funny in the head, you know, just a little . . . funny, and, uh, he went and
did a silly thing . . . Well, I'll tell you what he did. He ordered his planes
to attack your country – . . . Well let me finish, Dimitri. Let me finish,
Dimitri . . . Well, listen, how do you think *I* feel about it, Dmitri? Can you
imagine how I feel about it, Dimitri? . . . Why do you think I'm calling
you? Just to say hello? . . . Of course I like to speak to you. Of course I like
to say hello.

The grim sense of mission in the B-52 is similarly undercut by quick visual
gags like the centerfold posing with a strategically positioned copy of *Foreign
Affairs* or Kong's tossed-off quip that "a fella could have a pretty good weekend in Vegas" with the items in the airmen's survival kits. The old-style
military virtues and preparation of the airmen may once have served
a purpose, but they have no place in the new intercontinental theater of
technology-driven warfare.[38]

But the film does more than expose the fictions of old war stories. It opens
with a crawl of text: "It is the stated position of the US Air Force that their
safeguards would prevent such events as are depicted in this film." This
disclaimer carries enormous irony, since the film patently challenges this
"stated position." *Dr. Strangelove* challenges not merely war but also the
burgeoning military-industrial complex, a system that has exceeded human
scale and control. As in *Catch-22*, the verbal paradoxes found in Lewis Carroll
or the Marx Brothers are now seen as symptomatic of a nonsensical public
discourse surrounding war. Turgidson's fear of a "mineshaft gap" spoofs John
F. Kennedy's rhetoric of a "missile gap." A billboard proclaims, in Orwellian
doublespeak, "Peace Is Our Profession" as American soldiers exchange gun-
fire in front of it. In the film's most famous line, Muffley admonishes
Turgidson and Sadeski, "Gentlemen, you can't fight in here! This is the War
Room!"

Turgidson's own language satirizes the speech of politicians and generals.
He is comically tentative in condemning Ripper's renegade action, and speaks
in preposterous euphemisms. The policy that has empowered the renegade
general to launch the initial nuclear strike becomes a "retaliatory safeguard,"
while an all-out attack will result in "modest and acceptable civilian casualties," by which Turgidson means "no more than 10 or 20 million, tops."
The very discussion of how many millions of deaths constitute "acceptable
casualties" indicts the entire rational-utilitarian calculus underlying Cold War
foreign policy. Like Swift's Modest Proposer, Turgidson doesn't understand
that number-crunching means nothing when the entire premise of the debate
is mad. As in *Catch-22* or *The Public Burning*, the military and political leaders

are not knaves but fools – psychotics, neurotics, obsessives, sex-fiends. Their buffoonery suggests that the film's satire transcends any critique of individuals. The system itself has gone haywire.

As both the movie's title and subtitle suggest, *Dr. Strangelove or: How I Learned to Stop Worrying and Love the Bomb*, like *Gravity's Rainbow* after it, exposes an erotic investment in the fantasies of military domination and nuclear annihilation. From the opening shots of one plane refueling another to the final shot of Major Kong straddling the nuclear warhead as he plummets earthward, the cartoonish phallic images show that military technology has become a fetish. The characters' lewd Dickensian names (Merkin Muffley, Buck Turgidson, DeSadeski, Jack D. Ripper) are no more subtle, suggesting (respectively) emasculation, arousal, sadism, and misogynistic sexual violence. The most explicit connection between sexual pathology and nuclear war, however, is articulated by the "obviously ... psychotic" Ripper, who explains his reasons for launching the attack: "I can no longer sit back and allow Communist infiltration, Communist indoctrination, Communist subversion, and the international Communist conspiracy to sap and impurify all of our precious bodily fluids." Ripper's fantasy of a Communist fluoridation plot turns out to be a displacement of a deeper sexual phobia, expressed in Ripper's refusal to let women drain him of his semen:

> I first became aware of it, Mandrake, during the physical act of love. Yes, a, uh, a profound sense of fatigue, feeling of emptiness followed me ... Loss of essence. I can assure you it has not recurred, Mandrake. Women sense my power, and they seek the life essence. I do not avoid women, Mandrake, but I do deny them my essence.

For Ripper, Purity of Essence means Peace on Earth, while sexual contact correspondingly means impotence or castration. And if Ripper expresses the phobic side of the Cold War's strange love, Strangelove himself represents its id, its celebratory fusion of sex and violence. Emerging late in the movie, seemingly from the shadows, Strangelove is a virtual cyborg whose involuntary twitches, Nazi salutes, and address of Muffley as "Mein Führer" reveal a lack of basic human naturalness. It is he who gleefully anticipates the apocalypse with the fantasy of an underground sex colony with a ratio of ten women to every man: "I hasten to add that since each man will be required to do prodigious service along these lines, the women will have to be selected for their sexual characteristics, which will have to be of a highly stimulating nature." Walter Benjamin, in assessing F.T. Marinetti's proto-fascist call for a poetry of war, remarked that humanity's "self-alienation has reached such a degree that it can experience its own destruction as an aesthetic pleasure of the first order."[39] The Nazi scientist Strangelove experiences that pleasure; the film analyzes it.

Robert Altman's *M*A*S*H* (1970), from a screenplay by Ring Lardner, Jr., does not address the nuclear threat like *Strangelove*, but rather the fiasco of American military intervention in Asia. The film is nominally set in Korea, but the context of reception was the Vietnam War, and the opening shot of the military helicopter would have resonated powerfully with the images of the war that Americans were watching nightly on TV. The reference to the ongoing fighting was in fact so obvious that 20th Century Fox insisted on opening with the quotations from MacArthur and Eisenhower to establish the Korean setting.[40] Yet just as Kubrick ironizes his opening disclaimer about the stated position of the US Air Force, so Altman ironizes these epigraphs. The heroic tone of MacArthur's heroic farewell address, already rendered suspect by appearing at the end of a ruminative and elegiac title sequence, loses any remaining authority when juxtaposed to the single sentence from Eisenhower, "I will go to Korea" – a 1952 campaign slogan that probably hints at MacArthur's calamitous (and virtually treasonous) insubordination to Truman. The subplot of Ho-Jon's effort to avoid conscription alludes to Americans' rising resistance to the draft,[41] while the use of kitschy Japanese versions of American pop songs speaks to the servicemen's experience of cultural dislocation.

Despite this political subtext, however, the movie's satire is mainly cultural, and both its commercial success and the controversy that it caused stem from its reception in an American society that was increasingly anti-war and anti-authoritarian. The critique of American foreign policy remains implicit, but the movie openly mocks religion, the sentimentalization of war, and the bureaucratic apparatus of the military-industrial complex. As free-spirited jokers, Hawkeye, Trapper John, and Duke score a series of victories over oppressive authorities. The religious Burns and Houlihan are mocked for their piety and hypocrisy when they undress each other while invoking God's will. Duke hands Ho-Jon a porn magazine to replace the Bible that Burns has given him. The film, meanwhile, desentimentalizes war not through traditional battle episodes but by the blood-soaked surgery scenes. Here the doctors' cool, casual wit appears as an aspect of their courage and realism (Figure 13). When Duke needs Dago's assistance, he pulls the chaplain away from administering last rites, saying, "This man's still alive and that man's dead. And that's a fact." The reality of saving lives outweighs the fiction of the afterlife. In this regard the film does not so much dislodge old models of manly heroism as relocate them in the figure of the doctor as rebel-outsider.

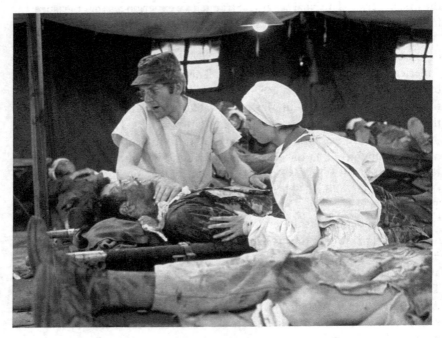

Figure 13 The Surgery in *M*A*S*H*. © 1970, Twentieth Century Fox. All Rights Reserved. Courtesy of Twentieth Century Fox.

In *M*A*S*H*, the doctors' cool, casual wit appears as an aspect of their courage and realism, de-sentimentalizing war but retaining a space for heroism.

The satire of military bureaucracy and incompetence owes a debt to *Catch-22* and *Dr. Strangelove*. *Strangelove*-style jokes about military doublespeak, such as General Hammond's claim that football is "one of the best ways we've got to keep the American way of life going here in Asia," point to the underlying paradox of the American mission, but also contribute to a representation of authority as rigid and clownish. The ineffectual Colonel Blake, sipping champagne in bed with a naked nurse while Houlihan thunders on about her humiliation, offers another example. *Catch-22* also provides models for important minor characters such as the meek, crisis-ridden chaplain Dago and the low-ranking but ultra-competent factotum Radar. Altman's recurrent use of absurdist and often ineptly delivered public-address announcements furthers the representation of the military base as the site of disorder, nonsense, and miscommunication rather than traditional military efficiency. Bureaucratic language has lost touch with reality, and the meaning of the acronym of the movie's title is never explained in the film.

Altman's improvisatory, impressionist style contributes to the de-romanticizing of war. The *vérité* elements – the overlapping dialogue, the moving camera, the unbalanced framing, the sudden transitions – establish everyday life in the presence of death, randomness and incoherence eroding discipline and hierarchy, accident winning out over plot. At the same time this unstructuredness opens the film to an antic energy that descends from the Marx Brothers (especially the anti-war satire of *Duck Soup* and the football sequences of *Horse Feathers*). Hawkeye and Trapper John are college-educated, golf-playing, martini-sipping versions of the leering, wisecracking Groucho, and they temper his mania with smart 1960s cool. When, during sex, Lieutenant Dish reminds Hawkeye that he has a wife, Hawkeye's non-sense-logic is pure Groucho: "If my wife were here, I'd be with her."

Yet while Hawkeye and Trapper may appeal to the audience in their rejection of repressive sexual strictures, the sexual politics of the movie come across today as misogynistic: privileged men engage in the repeated sexual humiliation of women for entertainment. Women's professional abil-ities are dismissed; Hawkeye and Trapper John tell the nurses in the Japanese hospital they need "at least one nurse who knows how to work in close without getting her tits in the way" so that they can get their golf game in by the end of the day. Indeed, the irreverence of the protagonists often slides into a sadism that the audience is encouraged to enjoy: as often happens in satire, once a kind of license is unleashed, it can hardly be contained and deployed for only respectable purposes.

The "suicide" of Painless Waldowski, however, complicates things. It may be an adolescent joke to serve up Dish to the preternaturally endowed Painless in order to restore his sexual confidence, but both Painless's nickname and his planned suicide refer to the lyrics of the theme song, which is reprised on camera at the scene of the suicide by a black serviceman. Indeed, the treat-ment of Painless's death-wish by his friends also picks up on the tone of the opening sequence, which delicately combines stoic acceptance and ironic detachment. (To say that suicide "brings on many changes" is an under-statement taken to the point of denial; compare Parker's "Resumé.") Painless, who has diagnosed himself as a latent homosexual because of a bout of impotence, occupies the uncertain position of the post-Freudian male recog-nizing an end to his privilege and power. The macho antics of his friends may succeed in "resurrecting" the Pole, but they only mask the more profound emasculation brought on by modern, mechanized war. This is in fact the place of the individual subject in the opening sequence – a small, nameless, incapacitated victim at the mercy of the rescue helicopter. The plaintive theme song, with its desperate stoicism, becomes almost a lullaby.

The rebellion and defiance of *Strangelove*'s laughter is replaced in *M*A*S*H* by small acts of self-protection and resignation, despite the nominally happy ending of the homecoming. In a parallel shift, the high spirits of Tom Lehrer's 1959 march "We Will All Go Together" are supplanted by resentment and bitterness in Randy Newman's 1972 shuffle "Political Science." Newman's song, with its gritty musical idiom and New Orleans rag-band instrumentation, expresses the 1970s' white male resentment – the voice of a once-triumphant superpower brought low by the debacle of Vietnam. Unappreciated by allies, the American speaker of "Political Science" is a Trump voter *avant la lettre* – or what used to be called a Nixon voter. He wants to reassert dominance through the phallic aggression of dropping "the big one":

> We give them money, but are they grateful?
> No, they're spiteful and they're hateful.
> They don't respect us, so let's surprise them.
> We'll drop the big one and pulverize them.[42]

Unlike 1959, it is no longer "we" who are being incinerated but only "they" – and NATO allies are obliterated along with enemies ("Boom goes London / Boom Paree / More room for you / More room for me"). The worn-out citizen's indifference to mass death gives his destructive fantasy the form of an impulsive experiment, indeed a modest proposal: "Let's drop the big one and see what happens." Like Lehrer, Kubrick, and Altman, Newman turns nuclear incineration into black comedy, but irreverence and mischief have been replaced by the low heat of a misanthropic bitterness.

Satiric News

The Vietnam-era mood of anger, frustration, and malaise captured by *M*A*S*H* and "Political Science" finds further expression a few years later in Sidney Lumet's *Network* (1976), a film which, like *M*A*S*H*, begins with the threat of a suicide. By 1976, "the American people are," in the words of the character Diana Christiansen, "turning sullen." A populace "clobbered on all sides by Vietnam, Watergate, the inflation, the depression," disappointed by the failed sex-and-drugs utopianism of the 1960s, needs "somebody to articulate their rage for them." That someone is news anchor Howard Beale, who snaps after being fired because of low ratings and promises to kill himself on live TV. Ironically, his ratings spike, and cynical executives repackage him as "a latter-day prophet denouncing the hypocrisies of our time." Part madman, part truth-teller, Beale's authenticity becomes a spectacle unto itself, and his viewers repeat his primal scream, "I'm mad as hell and I'm not going to take this anymore!"

Network satirizes the way that television degrades politics, transforming it into commerce, entertainment, and spectacle. Beale's Juvenalian indignation initially promises progressive mobilization but soon begins to smack of fascism; in any case, its power is coopted as his cry is reduced to a TV tagline. When Beale attempts to expose a secret deal of his corporate employers, CCA chairman Arthur Jensen tames the insurrection not by threat but by persuasion. In a speech that could well occur in a postmodern Menippean novel, Jensen offers a cynical account of the inevitable triumph of global capital and convinces Beale that human dignity is an outmoded myth:

> There are no nations. There are no peoples. There are no Russians. There are no Arabs. There are no third worlds. There is no West. There is only one holistic system of systems, one vast and immane, interwoven, interacting, multivariate, multinational dominion of dollars.

Although old-school news producer Max Schumacher longs to preserve high-minded standards of news reporting and values like "simple human decency," he also must eventually recognize his cause as a sentimental cliché. The conflict between Max and his lover Diana (described as "television incarnate") is like that between Huxley's John the Savage and Mustapha Mond in *Brave New World*: the author's heart might side with one character's old-fashioned humanism, but the evolution of society seems to lead ineluctably to the cold utilitarianism of the future.

The black comedy of *Network* – Beale becomes the first news anchor killed because of low ratings – holds little hope for a public sphere dominated by electronic media, owned by corporate interests, subject to unforgiving markets. Moreover, its focus on the fusion of news, media, and spectacle identifies a cluster of issues that will concern TV and film satire over the next several decades. Satire of course takes on many topics during these years, but the emergence of daily parodic TV news is one of the most singular developments of contemporary popular satire. Jon Stewart's *The Daily Show* and Stephen Colbert's *The Colbert Report* (whose runs ended in 2015 and 2014) offered the most visible examples of such fake news in the twenty-first-century United States, but they are part of a larger set of shows, films, performances, sketches, hoaxes, pranks, and other kinds of "interactive satire" in many countries disseminated through a variety of media, technologies, and platforms that take up the satiric agenda set forth in *Network*.[43] These include satiric journalism and punditry, comic talk shows, polemical documentaries, parodic web-based newspapers, and the various kinds of publicity stunts that Amber Day has called "culture jamming."[44]

The history of fake TV news goes back at least to the 1960s satire boom, when *TW3* inaugurated the genre of the weekly fake news show, and Peter Cook impersonated Prime Minister Harold Macmillan for Beyond the Fringe. In the late 1960s, *The Smothers Brothers Comedy Hour* followed with controversial critique of the Vietnam War; in 1975 *Saturday Night Live* debuted with its still-running "Weekend Update" segment, which spoofed the style, tone, and conventions of news broadcasts. From Chevy Chase's Gerald Ford through Alec Baldwin's Donald Trump, *SNL* also popularized the kind political caricature that Cook had begun, the mocking impersonation of a political leader, helping to launch a subgenre of "embodied parody" that has become a staple of TV and stage comedy.

While comedians were mocking politics, politicians, and the news business, documentary film was morphing into hybrid genres that undermined the authority of the visual conventions by which film and television purported to convey the truth about the world. Woody Allen, first in *Take the Money and Run* (1969), then more fully in *Zelig* (1983), comically deployed documentary devices such as interviews, still photographs, "found" footage, newspaper headlines, and voice-over within a fictional narrative frame. Albert Brooks's mock-documentary *Real Life* (1979) parodied the popular PBS documentary *An American Family*, by filming "not only the life of a real family, but of the real people who came to film that family, and the effect they had on each other"; it exposes the documentary form as anything but a neutral and unobtrusive process as the filmmaker throws into chaos the life of the family he purports to chronicle.[45] With Rob Reiner's *This Is Spiñal Tap* (1984) and the films of Christopher Guest, the mockumentary went mainstream; these works offered light satire while expanding documentary techniques into fictional filmmaking. Recent programs like *The Office* casually import the techniques and visual style of documentary and reality TV into the sitcom.

A different sort of hybrid is Michael Moore's *Roger & Me* (1989), which details the effects of a General Motors plant closing on Moore's hometown of Flint, Michigan. Moore does not fictionalize, but he departs from traditional documentary tone and style by creating grim, sometimes poignant comedy from a variety of pathetic characters and situations. Moore's polemical guerilla filmmaking deliberately dispenses with any pretense of neutrality and implicitly asks whether those standards can even hold in the larger public sphere.[46] Sacha Baron Cohen's characters from *Da Ali G Show* (2000) combine a fictional interviewer – Baron Cohen playing the role of Ali G, Borat, or

Bruno – with real interviewees in front of a real camera in a form that sits at the crossroads of prank, hoax, and satire. In *Borat* (2006) and *Who Is America?* (2018), the fictional character's interviews and stunts expose the distasteful views of actual politicians and ordinary people.

The explosion of parodic news today was also made possible by a new irreverence in the TV comedy of the 1990s. In the 1970s, a few shows attempted political satire, but the reassuring frame of the sitcom blunted their edge, and *All in the Family*'s bigoted curmudgeon Archie Bunker ("crusty but benign," to use a phrase from *Network*) became a hero to the very working-class conservatives whom he was intended to satirize.[47] But in the 1980s David Letterman remade the staid form of Johnny Carson's late-night routines by offering "snark as the . . . antidote to the Reagan era's cant";[48] in the 1990s, *Seinfeld* and *The Simpsons* scorned the anodyne humor of *The Cosby Show* and *Cheers*. *Seinfeld*'s motto of "No hugging, no learning" marked a new ironic sensibility for a top-ranked sitcom, while *The Simpsons* nested aggressive satire in various realms of life – politics, economics, religion – within the ultimately reassuring frame of a dysfunctional but loving suburban family. The success of *The Simpsons*, more than any other show, opened a market for irreverent animation, clever comedy, and television satire in general.[49]

The boom in fake TV news also arose from broader changes in the overall media environment. In the 1980s, cable news channels changed the nature of the news cycle itself, saturating the public sphere with day-long political talk; soon right-wing talk radio (Rush Limbaugh in 1988) and TV (Fox News in 1996) began to use news programming for nakedly partisan propaganda. The initial response on the left came not from journalists, however, but from humorists, who fashioned themselves as comic pundits. Bill Maher launched his talk show *Politically Incorrect* in 1993; in 1996, *Saturday Night Live* writer (and later US senator) Al Franken's book *Rush Limbaugh Is a Big Fat Idiot* parodied the insult-ridden style of Limbaugh's best-sellers.

With the rise of the World Wide Web (early 1990s), Facebook (2004), Twitter (2006), and the iPhone (2007), the media environment altered further. Constantly updated blogs and feeds, and an ever-more-plugged-in public, made news and commentary available instantaneously. Broadcasting was replaced by "narrowcasting" – a multiplicity of news outlets serving a public splintered into demographic niches. In today's media environment, people increasingly watch news "clips," both real and fictional, outside of the initial broadcast context, coming upon them through social media feeds, emails, and interlinked websites. With the "TV program" transformed into "digital content," sketch comedy and parodic news gain an advantage over longer narrative forms that are less easily cut and spliced.[50] Thus Colbert's 2006 address to the Washington press corps initially aired on the little-watched C-Span, but it reached approximately 2.7 million viewers in its first forty-eight hours on YouTube. Today in 2018, the webpage of the *Washington Post* is likely to feature a "story" that is simply a link to a clip of a sketch that itself is a spoof of a press conference held earlier in the week. *Saturday Night Live*, a show that thrived on the riskiness of uncensored live broadcast, now survives by being cut, spliced, posted, circulated, and re-watched on Sunday morning.

A final set of events that enabled the rise of the daily fake news show was the terrorist attacks of September 11, 2001. As noted in Chapter 2, the horror of the attacks led many journalists and intellectuals to renounce the irreverent spirit of the 1990s, declaring – even calling for – a death of irony. Political leaders discouraged dissent, and the news media largely abdicated its role of criticizing those in power. Yet irony didn't die. On September 15, the cover of *Private Eye* depicted an aide informing George W. Bush of the attacks with the words, "It's Armageddon, Sir," and the president responding, "Armageddon outahere!" (Figure 14). On October 3, America's *The Onion*, a Wisconsin college humor magazine that had recently gone national, declared, "A Shattered Nation Longs to Care about Stupid Bullshit Again," spoofing the rash of commentary that consecrated Americans' sudden moral serious-ness. A subsequent headline went further, announcing the imminent show-down between Osama bin Laden and George W. Bush: "Privileged Children of Millionaires Square off on World Stage." The article drew unnerving equivalences between the two wealthy scions of oil families who both had discovered religion in midlife after dissolute, misspent youth and several failures in business ventures sponsored by wealthy family members and friends.[51]

Even more than *Private Eye* and *The Onion*, however, the fake news shows of Jon Stewart, Stephen Colbert, and their successors – Trevor Noah, Samantha Bee, John Oliver, Seth Myers – have proved to be the signature satiric form of the early twenty-first century. *The Daily Show*, which Stewart took over in 1999, and its spin-off, *The Colbert Report*, launched in 2005, functioned simultaneously as sources of the news, satiric commentaries upon it, and parodies of the way that it is covered.[52] Stewart offered direct com-mentary on various falsehoods, hypocrisies, and outrages from the recent news cycle, but his position was less that of the traditional newscaster than of the viewer's surrogate.[53] He paused or replayed news clips so that he could "talk back" to politicians, anchors, reporters, and pundits – seizing their authority on behalf of his audience. His tone was one of amused detachment,

Figure 14 "Bush Takes Charge," *Private Eye*, Issue 1037, Sept. 21, 2001. Reproduced by kind permission of *Private Eye* magazine www.private-eye.co.uk. Photo credit: Paul J. Richards/AFP.

By September 15, 2011, the satirical British magazine *Private Eye* was demonstrating that despite proclamations to the contrary, irony and dissent were alive and well.

and he mixed eye-rolls and smirks with bursts of heated indignation. He signaled his position as satirist by periodically puncturing the aura of seriousness with slang, vulgarity, joking, or other informal discourse.[54] Colbert's method was different. He created a persona clearly distinct from his real-world self, modeled not on a traditional newscaster but a pundit (specifically the now-disgraced Bill O'Reilly). With Swiftian mimicry, he inhabited the O'Reilly persona, exaggerating the fallacies of O'Reilly's arguments and hamming up the bluster and narcissism of his style to achieve a *reductio ad absurdum*. Whereas Stewart pointed out the hypocrisy of the right, Colbert embodied it. He effectively demonstrated how easy it was to be a loudmouth pundit, demystifying the authority of the TV personality.

Both shows attacked not only politicians but also the manufacture of the news itself as spectacle: the predictable storylines, the partisan talking points, the entire taken-for-granted visual and rhetorical vocabulary that buttresses the authority of television news. As Colbert himself noted, "Our game is to make fun of the newsmakers but we also make fun of the news style."[55] Stewart borrowed the visual and tonal conventions of the TV anchor seated at desk, looking directly into the camera, but he conflated the conventions of the evening news broadcast with those of the late-night talk show and the old TV variety show, such as a panoramic shot of the TV studio. The effect was to puncture the aura of seriousness that usually surrounded the consumption of the news.[56] Colbert's visual style, meanwhile, mimicked that of O'Reilly and similar "opinion" shows. The opening sequence featured a computer-generated eagle swooping through the frame while the host wielded an American flag like a weapon; the set, the graphics, even the structure of the show with recurring segments like "The Wørd," directly parodied O'Reilly's.

In mocking pundits, however, Stewart and Colbert became pundits themselves. Both men famously ventured "outside" their shows – Stewart in exposing the bad faith of CNN's *Crossfire* and CNBC'S *Mad Money*, Colbert in his address at the 2006 White House Correspondents' Dinner, when he attacked not only President Bush, who was seated next to him, but the Washington press corps, a group of journalists notoriously cozy with the politicians they report on. (Just as the ostensibly liberal press rallied to Bush's defense in 2006, so again in 2018 they rushed to the side of Donald Trump's press secretary Sarah Sanders after her rough treatment from comedian Michelle Wolf.) Stewart's 2004 exchange with Tucker Carlson on *Crossfire* illustrates the ambiguity of his position as a pundit claiming not to be a pundit. Stewart pointed out that talk-show host Carlson is no more serious than a comedian:

STEWART: Now, this is theater. It's obvious. How old are you?
CARLSON: Thirty-five.
STEWART: And you wear a bow tie.[57]

But while Stewart's exposure of *Crossfire* as theater can hardly be disputed, Carlson's response – attacking Stewart for partisan journalism – has merit too. Stewart claimed he was merely an "unserious" entertainer, but he appeared on *Crossfire* asking to be taken seriously as a media critic. Stewart wanted it both ways: to be part of the punditry and yet a critic of it.

Satirists like Stewart and Colbert claim to remain committed to an ideal of the public sphere governed by logic, rationality, and consensus, played out in the print and electronic media. Because this ideal presumes a respect for objective truth, the deceptions of politicians and the news industry became a primary target of their satire. In October 2005, Franken published *The Truth with Jokes*, a satiric account of the recent presidential election, implying in his title that he could combine an accurate account of facts with non-serious jokes, and that the audience could distinguish the two. That same month, *The Colbert Report*'s debut introduced the neologism *truthiness*, a concept based not on reason but intuition:

> What about Iraq? If you "think" about it, maybe there are a few missing pieces to the rationale for war, but doesn't taking Saddam out *feel* like the right thing? Right here, right here in the gut. 'Cause that's where the truth comes from, ladies and gentlemen, the gut. Do you know you have more nerve endings in your stomach than in your head? Look it up. Now somebody's gonna say, "I did look that up and it's wrong." Well mister that's because you looked it up in a book. Next time try looking it up in your gut.[58]

By substituting "truthiness" for "truth," Colbert implied, the Bush administration and its supporters sold the war to the public with lies. Against Bush's "truthiness," Colbert implicitly endorsed truth itself.

Some analysts therefore claimed that satirists like Stewart and Colbert promoted a healthier, more informed, more truthful public sphere in which savvy viewers understood their ironies and distilled their truth from their jokes.[59] When *The Daily Show* contrasted video footage of a sitting president's statements with footage of contradictory positions he took as a candidate, as it did in its split-screen "Bush vs. Bush" debate of 2003, it performed the traditional journalistic function of broadening public discussion and holding leaders accountable for their words.[60] Yet although their politics may be more appealing to liberal viewers than those of the politicians they criticize, Stewart and Colbert themselves relied, as satirists, on an appeal to the gut through laughter. (Recall Mencken's horse laugh.) In decrying the failures of the news business, Stewart and Colbert uncomfortably resembled *Network*'s Howard Beale exhorting his TV audience not to watch TV; they are TV pundits pointing out the problem of TV punditry. They are caught in the same paradox of immanent critique as the eighteenth-century pamphleteers who condemned the print culture of their time through the medium of print.

Just as the relationship of the satirist to the public sphere proves contradictory, so does the relationship of the audience to the political world. It is frequently objected that parodic news programs, like the conservative shows they mock, speak only to their own splinter of the wider public and merely reinforce entrenched partisan beliefs. Satire becomes the Swiftian glass in which self-satisfied young liberals behold everyone's face but their own. In contrast, many academic scholars of parodic news shows argue that these shows not only hold politicians accountable, but also, through their unique disruption of genres, transform a passive audience of viewers into an active counterpublic – a group of citizens, strangers to one another, loosely allied in political dissent, able to consume and disseminate satirical content. Then again, if satiric TV news can mobilize progressive communities of viewers, the same process must be equally possible among those with contrary agendas. Like Howard Beale's cry, the critique of the mediated public sphere and the political energy of counterpublics can be coopted by the system, turned into empty amusement. Even more darkly, they can be harnessed by demagogues who, while claiming to voice legitimate grievances, rouse armies of Internet trolls to promote the destruction of the very norms and institutions that ensure the basic freedoms of contemporary democracies.

Donald Trump rose to power in 2016 with a combination of new media and old, Twitter posts and mass rallies. A political career that began with zany fabrications about Barack Obama's identity took flight with a variety of exaggerations, lies, and conspiracy theories. The persistent old-school fact-checking of the *New York Times* and the *Washington Post* halted his ascent no more than did the steady satiric assaults from Comedy Central, *Saturday Night Live*, and HBO. Perhaps Trump's own clownishness had inoculated him to satire: his followers already laughed at him, and his campaign staff defended his wildest outrages by claiming he was speaking ironically, or jokingly, or satirically. ("Just words, folks," Trump said in one presidential debate.) Perhaps no insult could hurt him because he had already degraded public discourse so severely; by treating long-held norms of civility and rationality as political double-talk, he rendered serious discussion a joke. Perhaps he stoked a misogyny and racism so heated that all the corrections, fact-checkings, scoldings, challenges, jokes, and insults that tried to hold him to account only confirmed for his supporters what they admired in him: that he was malicious, dangerous, and accountable to no one.

When the 2016 election began, satiric news from the left seemed triumphant, and its service to democracy in correcting the errors and oversights of the right-wing and mainstream press appeared invaluable. Yet just a few weeks after the election, pundits were wringing their hands as they tried to assess the impact of fake news stories, Internet rumors, Fox News propaganda, Breitbart conspiracy theories, Wikileaks, and Russian interference on public opinion. The election seemed to close a chapter in the history of satire, marking a point at which the transgressive performances of Stewart and Colbert, having grown increasingly tame during the Obama years, had become fully absorbed into the machinery of partisan debate, and parodic news had become just one more variety of political talk. As if to recognize the end of this chapter, on December 1, 2016, *The New York Times* reviewed a new oral history of *The Daily Show*. The review was titled, "When Fake News Was Funny."[61]

Charlie Hebdo, Satire and the Enlightenment

On January 7, 2015, two men wearing masks and bearing Kalashnikov assault rifles entered the office building of the French satirical weekly *Charlie Hebdo* and proceeded to massacre twelve people including cartoonists, editors, writers, copy editors, police officers, and a maintenance worker. Another police officer was killed on January 8, and four Jewish civilians were murdered at a kosher supermarket on January 9. During the murders, the killers, Saïd and Chérif Kouachi, reportedly shouted, "We have avenged the prophet Muhammad." They themselves were eventually killed by French law enforcement, along with a third gunman, Amedy Coulibaly, in two separate raids.

The *Charlie Hebdo* killings were part of a larger pattern of rising terrorist violence across Western Europe, but they also culminated a series of attacks and threats made specifically in response to the magazine's publication of cartoons depicting Muhammad, whose representation, according to some strict interpretations of Islam, is in itself blasphemous. In 2007 the magazine had republished drawings that, when first printed in Denmark's newspaper *Jyllands-Posten,* had set off demonstrations worldwide. In November 2011, the *Charlie Hebdo* offices were firebombed in response to a "Charia Hebdo" issue that put a cheerful Muhammad on the cover declaring, "100 lashes if you have not died laughing." In 2013, the magazine's editor-in-chief, Stéphane "Charb" Charbonnier – one of the January 2015 victims – had been placed by al-Qaeda alongside Salman Rushdie and the Somali-Dutch feminist Ayaan Hirsi Ali on a "Wanted: Dead or Alive" list. But the murderousness of the 2015 attack produced unprecedented public outrage. In France, and throughout Western democracies, politicians, religious leaders, writers, artists, and millions of ordinary citizens took to the streets in vigils and demonstrations, culminating in a rally of about two million people, including forty world leaders, on January 11 in Paris. The sentence "je suis Charlie" spread worldwide on t-shirts, Facebook posts, and email signatures, serving as a slogan of political liberty and a declaration of solidarity with the victims (Figure 15).

This feeling of solidarity, and the belated recognition of the risks that the satirists of *Charlie Hebdo* took in insisting on their freedom to publish and to

Figure 15 "Je suis Charlie." Photo credit: Frederic Lafargue/Polaris.
Demonstration in support of the murdered satirists of *Charlie Hebdo*.

provoke, found formal expression when PEN America, a writers' organization
dedicated to "unit[ing] writers and their allies to celebrate creative expression
and defend the liberties that make it possible," honored the *Charlie* victims
with its Toni and James C. Goodale Freedom of Expression Courage Award.[1]
However, what was expected to be a rallying point for free expression erupted
into controversy, as a number of PEN members protested the award on the
grounds that *Charlie Hebdo* was a racist publication. Prominent writers,
cartoonists, and columnists weighed in on both sides in a hot-tempered and
wide-ranging debate that called into question the very nature of satire and its
role in a multicultural, democratic society.

A few voices equated *Charlie Hebdo* with "hate speech" and advocated
curtailing its legal rights to free expression, but the more serious objections to
the award never denied the satirists' right to publish, the horror of the
murders, or the responsibility of a free society to defend artists from terror-
istic violence. Instead, the protests centered on whether the slain satirists
merited recognition in the form of an award from a major human rights
organization. If, as the protesters claimed, *Charlie Hebdo* was a racist,
Islamophobic magazine, how could one justify giving it any award? In its
defense, PEN America maintained that the award was being granted not as

praise for the content of the magazine, but as recognition of the courage the satirists displayed in insisting on their right to publish in the face of death threats. PEN's bestowal of the award, it explained, did not entail an endorsement of the magazine's views. Others, however, took up a more robust line of defense, claiming not simply that *Charlie* was *not* racist but that it was actively *anti*-racist – a voice for liberty and equality. The award thus exposed a political fault line between two groups of writers, artists, and intellectuals, both of which claimed to espouse progressive principles. How could this be?

The answer, of course, is that people interpreted the cartoons differently. Interpretation, intention, irony, meaning, authorship, caricature, and satire suddenly became topics whose relevance reached far beyond the seminar room. One side looked at the cartoons and saw crude caricatures that traded in old, harmful, and unfunny stereotypes. The other saw a buoyant juvenile rebelliousness in the spirit of counterculture periodicals like *Mad* and *The Realist*. Those who condemned *Charlie Hebdo* pointed to Muhammad's prominent hooked nose, as well to other offensive images published in the magazine. *Charlie*'s defenders read those images as parodic racist imagery coming from the left – much like the 2008 Barry Blitt *New Yorker* cover that represented Barack Obama as a turbaned Kenyan and Michelle as an Angela Davis-style black militant. *Charlie*'s accusers interpreted the Muhammad cartoons as taking aim at France's downtrodden Arab immigrant population, while supporters interpreted them as sallies against the tyrannical fundamentalism of terrorists and their sponsors. One side saw the cartoons as "hitting down," picking on the victims of imperialism and oppression; the other saw them as "hitting up," taking on powerful and violent forces of reaction. Both claimed to speak on behalf of the powerless.

The differing interpretations resulted at least in part from the different contexts in which people framed their readings of the cartoons, and from different understandings of satire's nature and its history. *Charlie*'s attackers viewed satire as a conservative mode used to enforce traditional norms by marginalizing the weak and the deviant. For them, the most salient historical precedent for *Charlie* was the caricature of Jews by the German tabloid *Der Stürmer* in the 1930s; in this view, caricature's reduction and dehumanization constitutes "a refusal to understand otherness."[2] *Charlie*'s defenders, on the other hand, called attention to the magazine's record of fighting racism and Islamophobia in France, its commitment to the rights of Muslims, its stance against Israeli military action in Gaza, and its support from the anti-racist organization SOS Racisme and from French-Arab intellectuals such as Kamel Daoud. They noted that the victims included *Charlie*'s Algerian-French copy editor, Mustapha Ourrad, and the survivors included the Moroccan-born columnist Zineb El Rhazoui. Finally, they offered their own theory and history of satire. Instead of invoking *Der Stürmer* and right-wing caricature, they cited the long history of French anti-clerical and anti-authoritarian satire, the tradition of Rabelais, Voltaire, and Daumier. They pointed out the magazine's origins in the 1968 student and labor protests and in the counterculture of the 1960s. (Its name comes from *Peanuts'* Charlie Brown.) With this history and this context, satire becomes a liberal rather than a conservative force.

In choosing one interpretation, frame of reference, or historical account over another, political sympathies and solidarities come into play. Those who called *Charlie* racist saw only empty self-congratulation in the January marches and the *je suis Charlie* slogan, an affirmation of the readiness of the West to create a bugbear of radical Islam in order to affirm its own bourgeois values. For them the magazine spoke for a white, conservative, xenophobic establishment whose political vision they rejected. *Charlie*'s defenders, meanwhile, tended to feel that it is not only legitimate but also necessary to reject the imposition of religious strictures on non-believers. They would be likely, indeed, to be sympathetic to any artwork or argument, whether sophomoric or sophisticated, that chips away at the power of irrationalism and dogmatism. They insisted on separating fundamentalist violence from the Muslim faith it presumed to speak for. They invoked Stéphane Charbonnier's own theory of satire: his aim, he said, was to "banalize" Islam, to render it mundane just as centuries of French satire had removed the aura of untouchability from Catholicism.

The opposing sides, however, shared one thing: a desire to stabilize the meaning of the satire. In the debates about the *Charlie* cartoons, context, history, and irony were almost always invoked to limit or contain how the magazine might be read. *Charlie Hebdo* was either racist or it was anti-racist. Yet of all literary and artistic modes, satire is especially provocative, volatile, and prone to controversy. Caricature in particular, as the psychoanalytic critic Ernst Kris suggested years ago, "is a play with the magic power of the image," and unless the ego recognizes belief in that magic and controls it, caricature will not appear as "a joke but rather a dangerous practice."[3] Indeed, religious strictures against representation, including the very strictures against the representation of Muhammad that *Charlie Hebdo* defied, have roots in this ancient belief in the destructive power of satire.

In activating this primitive kind of magical thinking, the *Charlie Hebdo* satirists revealed a rift within contemporary liberalism itself, one that is widening in Western politics as liberalism is confronted, both from without and within, with resurgent forms of nationalism, fundamentalism, and reaction. The political future of Western democracies now seems hazier than it has for some time. *Charlie Hebdo*'s defenders stood for an Enlightenment version of liberalism: secular, rational, individualist. *Charlie*'s accusers, in contrast, favored a liberalism sometimes called (however imprecisely) identity politics or cultural relativism; indeed, for some time a portion of the left has been abandoning values such as reason, science, cosmopolitanism, free speech, and individual rights.[4] As the debate over *Charlie Hebdo* revealed, the cultural and political role of satire in these debates is not an incidental or secondary matter, but an utterly central one. To put it another way, the question, "Were the *Charlie* covers racist?" turned out to be a surrogate for the older and more vexing question: "What is Enlightenment?" That question, in turn, might prompt another, the question that began this book: "What is satire?"

Notes

What Is Satire?

1. Samuel Johnson, *A Dictionary of the New English Language*, ed. E.L. McAdam and George Milne (Mineola: Dover, 2005), p. 357. *Google Books*. Web.
2. *The Onion Book of Known Knowledge: A Definitive Encyclopaedia of Existing Information* (New York: Little, Brown and Company, 2013), p. 174.
3. Because of Rochester's reputation as a rake, printers often attributed bawdy poems to him in order to increase sales, making attribution particularly difficult. Harold Love, "Introduction," *The Works of John Wilmot, Earl of Rochester*, ed. Harold Love (New York: Oxford, 1999), p. xxvi.
4. Love, "Explanatory Notes," *Works*, pp. 414, 476, 416.
5. Claude Rawson, *Satire and Sentiment 1660–1830* (New York: Cambridge University Press, 1994), pp. 3–4.
6. Paul Davis, "Introduction," in John Wilmot, *Earl of Rochester, Selected Poems*, ed. Davis (New York: Oxford University Press, 2013), p. 3.
7. Ralph Verney, quoted by Love, "Explanatory Notes," *Works*, p. 420.
8. James Grantham Turner, *Libertines and Radicals in Early Modern London: Sexuality, Politics, and Early Modern Culture 1630–1685* (New York: Cambridge University Press, 2002), p. 219.
9. Salman Rushdie, *Joseph Anton: A Memoir* (New York: Random House, 2012), pp. 43, 124, 396.
10. Salman Rushdie, *The Satanic Verses* (1988. New York: Random House, 2008), p. 109.
11. Rushdie, *Joseph Anton*, p. 124.
12. Pete Wells, "As Not Seen on TV," *New York Times*, November 12, 2012, D4. Web.
13. Quoted in Joshua Wolford, "That Hilarious Guy Fieri Restaurant Review Has over 45,000 Facebook Shares," *Web Pro News*, November 16, 2012, Web; see also Katie Baker, "Guy Fieri Battles Scathing New York Times Review by Pete Wells," *Daily Beast*, November 16, 2012, Web; J. Bryan Lowder, "Postcards from Camp," *Slate*, April 8, 2013, Web.
14. A lipogram is a work that omits a particular letter entirely. George Perec's novel *La Disparition* avoids all use of the letter *e*; *Les Revenentes* uses no vowels except for *e*.

15. Harry Levin, *Playboys and Killjoys: An Essay on the Theory and Practice of Comedy* (New York: Oxford University Press, 1987), pp. 199–200.
16. Howard D. Weinbrot, *Menippean Satire Reconsidered: From Antiquity to the Eighteenth Century* (Baltimore: Johns Hopkins University Press, 2005), pp. 1–6.
17. Alastair Fowler, *Kinds of Literature: An Introduction to the Theory of Genres and Modes* (Cambridge, MA: Harvard University Press, 1982), p. 107.
18. Jonathan Greenberg, *Modernism, Satire, and the Novel* (New York: Cambridge University Press, 2011), pp. 2, 9, 13.
19. Linda Hutcheon, *Irony's Edge: The Theory and Politics of Irony* (New York: Routledge, 1995), p. 5.
20. Steven E. Jones, *Shelley's Satire: Violence, Exhortation, and Authority* (DeKalb, IL: Northern Illinois University Press, 1994), p. 8.
21. Jürgen Habermas, *The Structural Transformation of the Public Sphere: An Inquiry into a Category of Bourgeois Society* (Cambridge, MA: Massachusetts Institute of Technology Press, 1989); Michael Warner, *Publics and Counterpublics* (New York: Zone Books, 2002).
22. Randal Johnson, "Editor's Introduction," in Pierre Bourdieu, *The Field of Cultural Production*, ed. Johnson, trans. Richard Nice et al. (New York: Columbia University Press, 1993), p. 2.
23. Alvin Kernan, *The Cankered Muse: Satire of the English Renaissance* (New Haven: Yale University Press, 1959), pp. 54–62.
24. Kathryn Hume, "Diffused Satire in Contemporary American Fiction," *Modern Philology* 105.2 (2007), p. 303.
25. Cf. *FS*, iv; Alvin Kernan, *The Plot of Satire* (New Haven: Yale University Press, 1965), p. 9.
26. Edward W. Rosenheim, *Swift and the Satirist's Art* (Chicago: University of Chicago Press, 1963), p. 31.
27. Hume, "Diffused Satire," p. 305
28. David Worcester, *The Art of Satire* (New York: Russell & Russell, 1960), p. 38. For longer syntheses of the canonical view, see *DSM*, pp. 1–4; Steven Weisenburger, *Fables of Subversion: Satire and the American Novel, 1930–1980* (Athens: University of Georgia Press, 1995) pp. 14–22.
29. Ezra Pound, "The Serious Artist," *Literary Essays* (New York: New Directions, 1968), p. 45.
30. Patricia Meyer Spacks, "Some Reflections on Satire," in *Satire: Modern Essays in Criticism*, ed. Ronald Paulson (Englewood Cliffs: Prentice-Hall, 1971), p. 363.
31. W.H. Auden, "Notes on the Comic," *The Dyer's Hand and Other Essays* (New York: Random House, 1962), p. 385.
32. Kernan, *Plot*, p. 13.
33. Leonard Feinberg, *Introduction to Satire* (Ames: Iowa State University Press, 1967), p. 11.

34. Robert Hume, "'Satire' in the Reign of Charles II," *Modern Philology* 102 (2005), p. 361.
35. See Pope's "Imitations of Horace, Epistle 2.1"; Swift's "Verses on the Death of Dr. Swift."
36. P.K. Elkin, *The Augustan Defence of Satire* (Oxford: Clarendon Press, 1973), p. 3.
37. *Manhattan*, directed by Woody Allen, written by Woody Allen and Marshall Brickman (United Artists, 1979).
38. Kenneth Burke, *Attitudes Towards History* (Berkeley, CA: University of California Press, 1987), p. 49.
39. William Hazlitt, "The Pleasure of Hating," *Selected Writings* (New York: Penguin, 1985), p. 399.
40. Wyndham Lewis, *Men Without Art* (New York: Russell & Russell, 1964), p. 108.
41. Sherman Alexie, "Evolution," *The Business of Fancydancing: Stories and Poems* (New York: Hanging Loose Press, 1992), p. 48.
42. Aaron Matz, *Satire in an Age of Realism* (New York: Cambridge University Press, 2010).
43. Lewis, *Men Without Art*, p. 226.
44. Mohsin Hamid, *How to Get Filthy Rich in Rising Asia* (New York: Riverhead, 2014), p. 196.
45. Rawson, *Satire and Sentiment*, p. 5.
46. Dawn Powell, *The Diaries of Dawn Powell: 1931–1962*, ed. Tim Page (South Royalton, VT: Steerforth, 1999), p. 75.
47. Stanley Fish, *How to Write a Sentence: And How to Read One* (New York: Harper, 2011), p. 3.
48. Sigmund Freud, *Jokes and Their Relation to the Unconscious*, trans. James Strachey (New York: Norton, 1989), pp. 174–75.
49. George Schuyler, *Black No More: Being an Account of the Strange and Wonderful Workings of Science in the Land of the Free, A.D. 1933–1940* (Boston: Northeastern University Press, 1989), pp. 90, 93, 101–02.
50. Evelyn Waugh, *The Essays, Articles, and Reviews of Evelyn Waugh*, ed. Donat Gallagher (Boston: Little, Brown and Company, 1983), p. 73.
51. Niall Rudd, "Notes," *The Satires of Horace and Persius* (Harmondsworth: Penguin), p. 163.
52. William Butler Yeats, "Swift's Epitaph," *The Collected Poems of W.B. Yeats*, ed. Richard Finneran (New York: Scribner, 1996), p. 246.
53. https://twitter.com/simon_schama/status/552805450350362625.
54. Derek Walcott, *The Fortunate Traveler* (New York: Farrar, Strauss, and Giroux, 1981), p. 60.
55. Freud, *Jokes*, p. 178.
56. Percy Bysshe Shelley, "Sonnet: England in 1819," *Complete Works of Percy Bysshe Shelley*, Vol. 3 (New York: Gordian Press, 1965), p. 293.
57. Italo Calvino, *The Uses of Literature: Essays*, trans. Patrick Creagh (New York: Harcourt, 1986), p. 64.

What Isn't Satire?

1. W.H. Auden, "Introduction," *Selected Poetry and Prose of George Gordon Lord Byron* (New York: New American Library, 1966), p. xi; Wayne Booth, *A Rhetoric of Irony* (Chicago: University of Chicago Press, 1974), p. 30; Vladimir Nabokov, *Strong Opinions* (New York: McGraw Hill, 1975), p. 75.
2. Levin, *Playboys and Killjoys*; Walter Sorrel, *Facets of Comedy* (New York: Grosset & Dunlap, 1972).
3. Ruby Cohn, *Samuel Beckett: The Comic Gamut* (New Brunswick: Rutgers University Press, 1962), p. 8.
4. James Wood, *The Irresponsible Self: On Laughter and the Novel* (New York: Farrar, Strauss, and Giroux, 2004), pp. 3–19.
5. Samuel Beckett, *Watt* (New York: Grove, 1959), p. 48.
6. Evelyn Waugh, *Vile Bodies* (Boston: Little, Brown and Company, 1930), p. 314.
7. Slavoj Žižek, *First as Tragedy, then as Farce* (London: Verso, 2009) p. 50.
8. For irony as "transideological," Hutcheon, *Irony's Edge*, p. 9; for jokes as "multiaccented," James English, *Comic Transactions: Literature, Humor, and the Politics of Community in Twentieth-Century Britain* (Ithaca: Cornell University Press, 1994), p. 17.
9. Kernan, *Plot*, p. 82.
10. William Blake, "The Little Black Boy," *The Complete Poetry and Prose of William Blake*, ed. David V. Erdman (New York: Doubleday, 1988), p. 9.
11. David Foster Wallace, "E Unibus Pluram: Television and U.S. Fiction," *The Review of Contemporary Fiction* 13.2 (1993): 151–194.
12. Peters Sloterdijk, *Critique of Cynical Reason*, trans. Michael Eldred (Minneapolis: University of Minnesota Press, 1987).
13. Richard Rorty, *Contingency, Irony, and Solidarity* (New York: Cambridge University Press, 1989), p. 73.
14. Matthew Stratton, *The Politics of Irony in American Modernism* (New York: Fordham University Press, 2014), pp. 10, 17. See also Lee Konstantinou, *Cool Characters: Irony and American Fiction* (Cambridge, MA: Harvard University Press, 2016).
15. Hutcheon, *Irony's Edge*, p. 30.
16. English, *Comic Transactions*, pp. 31–66, esp. 34–36.
17. Kernan, *Plot*, p. 82.
18. Stratton, *Politics*, p. 11.
19. Kernan, *Plot*, p. 90.
20. Booth, *Rhetoric*, pp. 105–120, pp. 3–7.
21. Hutcheon, *Irony's Edge*, pp. 12–13, 12.
22. Darryl Dickson-Carr, *African American Satire: The Sacredly Profane Novel* (Columbia, MO: University of Missouri Press, 2001), p. 25

23. Harry's Bar and American Grill, *The Best of Bad Hemingway* (San Diego: Harcourt, 1989).
24. Simon Dentith, *Parody* (New York: Routledge, 2000), pp. 7, 7–8, 8.
25. Dan Harries, *Film Parody* (London: British Film Institute, 2000), p. 9.
26. Wendy Cope, "A Nursery Rhyme," *Making Cocoa for Kingsley Amis* (London: Faber & Faber, 1986), p. 18.
27. Genette classifies parody and pastiche as "playful" and travesty and caricature as their "satirical" counterparts. Gerard Genette, *Palimpsests: Literature in the Second Degree* (Lincoln: University of Nebraska Press, 1997), pp. 27–28.
28. Louis Menand, "Parodies Lost," *The New Yorker*, September 20, 2010, pp. 107–110.
29. Dentith, *Parody*, p. 9.
30. *Blazing Saddles*, directed by Mel Brooks, written by Mel Brooks, Andrew Bergman, Richard Pryor, Norman Steinberg, and Al Uger (Warner Brothers, 1974).
31. Kenneth Koch, "Variation on a Theme by William Carlos Williams," *Thank You and Other Poems* (New York: Grove, 1962), p. 68.
32. Bourdieu, *Field*, p. 31.
33. Quoted in Leon Weiseltier, "Washington Diarist," *The New Republic*, December 3, 2008.
34. Apuleius, *The Golden Ass*, trans. Jack Lindsay (Bloomington: Indiana University Press, 1962), p. 126.
35. *Monty Python's Life of Brian*, directed by Terry Jones, written by Graham Chapman, John Cleese, Terry Gilliam, Eric Idle, Terry Jones, and Michael Palin (Cinema International/Orion/Warner Brothers, 1979).
36. Bevis Hillier, *Cartoons and Caricatures* (London: Studio Vista, 1970), p. 34.
37. Ronald Paulson, *Representations of Revolution: 1789–1820* (New Haven: Yale University Press, 1983), p. 181.
38. "Cartoon," *Oxford English Dictionary*. Web.
39. E.M. Forster, *Aspects of the Novel* (New York: Harcourt, 1955), p. 67.
40. Forster, *Aspects*, p. 71.
41. Jay Clayton, *Charles Dickens in Cyberspace: The Afterlife of the Nineteenth Century in Postmodern Culture* (New York: Oxford University Press, 2003), p. 149.
42. Forster, *Aspects*, p. 71.
43. William Hazlitt, *Lectures on the English Comic Writers and Fugitive Writings* (London: Dent, 1963), pp. 43, 76.
44. Lewis, *Men Without Art*, p. 113.
45. Angus Fletcher, *Allegory: The Theory of a Symbolic Mode* (Ithaca: Cornell University Press, 1964), pp. 2, 3, 8, 325, 358.
46. Jayne Elizabeth Lewis, *The English Fable: Aesop and Literary Culture 1651–1740* (New York: Cambridge University Press, 1996), p. 9.

47. Frank Palmeri, "The Autocritique of Fables," *Humans and Other in Eighteenth-Century British Culture: Representation, Hybridity, Ethics*, ed. Frank Palmeri (Burlington: Ashgate, 2006), p. 83.
48. Feinberg, *Introduction to Satire*, p. 52.
49. Aldous Huxley, *Crome Yellow* (Chicago: Dalkey Archive Press, 2001), p. 121.
50. Lawrence Manley, *Literature and Culture in Early Modern London* (New York: Cambridge University Press, 1995), p. 410.
51. Blake, "Proverbs of Hell," *Complete Poetry and Prose*, p. 35.
52. David Barnett, "The Indefinable Charm of Satirical Dictionaries," *The Guardian*, March 1, 2011. Web.
53. Rushdie, *Satanic Verses*, p. 100.
54. Harold Love, *English Clandestine Satire, 1660–1704: Popular Culture, Entertainment and Information in the Early Modern Period* (New York: Oxford University Press, 2009), p. 9.
55. Christopher Hitchens, *The Missionary Position: Mother Theresa in Theory and Practice* (London: Verso, 1995), p. 59.
56. William Powhida, "Dear Jeff Koons," 2011, graphite, colored pencil, and watercolor, williampowhida.com/wordpress/page/9.
57. Ezra Pound, "Hugh Selwyn Mauberley," *Selected Poems of Ezra Pound* (New York: New Directions, 1957), p. 64.
58. Elijah Wald, *The Dozens: A History of Rap's Mama* (New York: Oxford University Press, 2012), p. 126.
59. Mark Polizotti, "Introduction: Laughter in the Dark," *Anthology of Black Humor*, ed. Andre Breton (San Francisco: City Lights, 1997), p. vi.
60. Breton, *Anthology*, pp. xix, xvii, 3, xvi–xvii.
61. Bruce Jay Friedman, quoted in Charles Harris, *Contemporary American Novelists of the Absurd* (New Haven: College and University Presses, 1971), p. 19.
62. Margot A. Henriksen, *Dr. Strangelove's America: Society and Culture in the Atomic Age* (Berkeley: University of California Press, 1997), p. 245.
63. Quoted in Polizotti, "Introduction," *Anthology*, p. xviii.
64. Susan Sontag, *Against Interpretation: And Other Essays* (New York: Farrar, Strauss, and Giroux, 1966), pp. 279, 280, 278.
65. Booth, *Rhetoric*, p. 28; Warner, *Publics*, p. 56.
66. Sontag, *Against Interpretation*, p. 280.
67. Christopher Isherwood, *The World in the Evening* (New York: Farrar, Strauss, and Giroux, 2103), p. 110; Sontag, *Against Interpretation*, p. 288; cf. Robert Kiernan, *Frivolity Unbound: Six Masters of the Camp Novel* (New York: Continuum, 1990).
68. David Galef and Harold Galef, "What Was Camp?" *Studies in Popular Culture* 13.2 (1991), pp. 16, 18.

Classical Origins

1. Homer, *The Iliad*, trans. Robert Fagles (New York: Viking, 1990), pp. 106, 107.
2. William S. Anderson, *Essays on Roman Satire* (Princeton: Princeton University Press, 1982), p. 35; cf. *AS*, pp. 30–40.
3. Thomas Jemielity, "Ancient Biblical Satire," *CS*, pp. 15–30. On Yahweh's laughter, see Wood, *Irresponsible Self*, p. 7.
4. Edith Hall, "Introduction: Aristophanic Laughter across the Centuries," *Aristophanes in Performance, 421 BC–AD 2007: Peace, Birds and Frogs* (London: University of Oxford Press, 2007), p. 1.
5. Jeffrey Henderson, "Introduction," *Three Plays by Aristophanes: Staging Women* (New York: Routledge, 2010), pp. 37–38.
6. William Arrowsmith, "The Birds," *Aristophanes: Three Comedies* (Ann Arbor: University of Michigan Press, 1969), p. 5.
7. Michael Silk, *Aristophanes and the Definition of Comedy* (New York: Oxford University Press, 2000), pp. 102, 119, 35.
8. Henderson, "Introduction," pp. 13–14.
9. Lois Spatz, *Aristophanes* (Boston: Twayne, 1978), p. 95.
10. Douglas M. McDowell, *Aristophanes and Athens: An Introduction to the Plays* (Oxford: Oxford University Press, 1995), pp. 240–241.
11. Spatz, *Aristophanes*, p. 92.
12. Alan Sommerstein, "Introduction," in Aristophanes, *Lysistrata and Other Plays*, ed. Sommerstein (New York: Penguin, 2002) p. 133.
13. Mary C. Randolph, "The Structural Design of the Formal Verse Satire," *Philological Quarterly* 21 (1942), p. 373.
14. For a sustained argument against the Horatian/Juvenalian distinction, see *DSM*, pp. 30–31.
15. Anderson, *Essays*, pp. 32–33.
16. Kirk Freudenburg, *Satires of Rome: Threatening Poses from Lucilius to Juvenal* (Cambridge: Cambridge University Press, 2001), pp. 75ff.
17. Freudenburg, *Satires of Rome*, p. 32.
18. Rudd, "Introduction," *The Satires*, p. xix.
19. Anderson, *Essays*, p. 39.
20. "Burns' Heir," *The Simpsons*, season 5, episode 18, written by Jace Richdale, April 14, 1994.
21. Freudenburg, *Satires of Rome*, p. 17.
22. Peter Green, "Introduction," in Juvenal, *The Sixteen Satires*, ed. Green, p. xxix.
23. On Juvenal and empire, see Victoria Rimmel, "The Poor Man's Feast," *The Cambridge Companion to Roman Satire*, ed. Kirk Freudenburg (New York: Cambridge University Press, 2005), p. 84.
24. Anderson, *Essays*, p. 278. Cf. Rimmel, "Feast," p. 86.

25. "Pee," *South Park*, season 13, episode 14, written by Trey Parker, November 18, 2009.
26. Anderson, *Essays*, p. 310.
27. Quintilian, *Institutio Oratoria X–XII*, trans. H.E. Butler (Cambridge, MA: Harvard University Press, 1961), p. 55.
28. Joel C. Relihan, *Ancient Menippean Satire* (Baltimore: Johns Hopkins University Press, 1993), p. 12.
29. Quoted in W. Scott Blanchard, *Scholars' Bedlam: Menippean Satire in the Renaissance* (Lewisburg: Bucknell University Press, 1995), pp. 33–34.
30. Relihan, *Ancient*, p. 32.
31. Weinbrot, *Menippean*, p. 1.
32. Relihan, *Ancient*, p. 29.
33. Weinbrot, *Menippean*, pp. 67, 63. Cf. Relihan, *Ancient*, p. 17.
34. Izaak Walton, *The Compleat Angler* (London: Macmillan, 1925), p. 11; see Weinbrot, *Menippean*, p. 43.
35. Lucian, "Icaromenippus, an Aerial Expedition," *The Works of Lucian of Samosata*, Vol. III, trans. H.W. Fowler and F.G. Fowler (London: Oxford University Press, 1949), p. 142.
36. Lucian, "Icaromenippus," p. 137.
37. Lionel Casson, "Introduction," *Selected Satires of Lucian* (New York: Norton, 1968) p. xv.
38. *Monty Python's The Meaning of Life*, directed by Terry Jones, written by Graham Chapman, John Cleese, Terry Gilliam, Eric Idle, Terry Jones, and Michael Palin (Universal Pictures, 1983).
39. Lucian, "Icaromenippus."
40. Paul L. MacKendrick, "*The Great Gatsby* and Trimalchio," *Classical Journal* 45.7 (1950), p. 307.
41. Weinbrot, *Menippean*, p. 43.
42. Frank Palmeri, *Satire in Narrative: Petronius, Swift, Gibbon, Melville, and Pynchon* (Austin: University of Texas Press, 1990), p. 37.
43. Palmeri, *Satire in Narrative*, p. 22.
44. Charles Knight, "Listening to Encolpius: Modes of Confusion in the Satyricon," *University of Toronto Quarterly*, 58.3 (1989), p. 340.
45. Erich Auerbach, *Mimesis: The Representation of Reality in Western Literature* (Princeton: Princeton University Press, 1953), p. 30.
46. Tim Whitemarsh, "Class," *The Cambridge Companion to the Greek and Roman Novel*, ed. Tim Whitmarsh (New York: Cambridge University Press, 2008), p. 80.

Renaissance Satire: Rogues, Clowns, Fools, Satyrs

1. Kernan, *Cankered Muse*, p. 58.
2. Manley, *Literature and Culture*, p. 28.

3. On the anatomy as subtype, see Blanchard, *Scholars' Bedlam*, p. 28.
4. Walter Kaiser, *Praisers of Folly: Erasmsus, Rabelais, Shakespeare* (Cambridge, MA: Harvard University Press, 1963), p. 103.
5. Bernd Renner, "From Satura to Satyre: François Rabelais and the Renaissance Appropriation of a Genre," *Renaissance Quarterly* 67.2 (2014), p. 380. On *Momus*, see Blanchard, "Renaissance Prose," *CS*, p. 125.
6. I owe this idea to Naomi Liebler.
7. Kaiser, *Praisers of Folly*, p. 37.
8. Stephen Greenblatt, *The Swerve: How the World Became Modern* (New York: Norton, 2011), p. 227.
9. J.M. Coetzee, *Giving Offense: Essays on Censorship* (Chicago: University of Chicago Press, 1996), pp. 93–100.
10. Fredric Jameson, *Archaeologies of the Future: The Desire Called Utopia and Other Science Fictions* (New York: Verso, 2005), p. 23.
11. Robert C. Elliott, *The Shape of Utopia: Studies in a Literary Genre* (Chicago: University of Chicago Press, 1970), p. 22. I follow Manley, *Literature and Culture*, in invoking Hall here.
12. Greenblatt, *The Swerve*, p. 230.
13. Stephen Greenblatt, *Renaissance Self-Fashioning: From More to Shakespeare* (Chicago: University of Chicago Press, 1980), p. 15.
14. Greenblatt, *Renaissance Self-Fashioning*, p. 37.
15. Walter Benjamin, "Theses on the Philosophy of History," *Illuminations*, trans. Harry Zohn (New York: Schocken, 1968), p. 256.
16. Kaiser, *Praisers of Folly*, pp. 104, 278; Carlos Fuentes, *The Buried Mirror: Reflections on Spain in the New World* (Boston: Houghton Mifflin, 1992), p. 176. On Cervantes's humanism, Anthony Cascardi, *Cervantes, Literature, and the Discourse of Politics* (Toronto: University of Toronto Press, 2014), p. 12.
17. Blanchard, *Scholars' Bedlam*, p. 92
18. On Picrochole as Charles V, see Edwin M. Duval, "Rabelais and French Renaissance Satire," *CS*, p. 75; on Janotus de Bragmardo as Béda, see M.A. Screech, "Notes," *Gargantua and Pantagruel*, trans. M.A. Screech (New York: Penguin, 2006), p. 262.
19. Renner, "From Satura to Satyre," p. 399.
20. Blanchard, *Scholars' Bedlam*, p. 34. Cf. Eric MacPhail, "Lists," *The Rabelais Encyclopedia*, ed. Elizabeth Chesney Zegura (Westport: Greenwood Press, 2004), pp. 145–146.
21. On Panurge as satyr in the tradition of Till Eulenspiegel, see Renner, "From Satura to Satyre," p. 388. On Panurge's satanic qualities, see François Rigolot, "Rabelais, Misogyny, and Christian Charity: Biblical Intertextuality and the Renaissance Crisis of Exemplarity," *PMLA* 109.2 (1994), pp. 225–237.
22. Blanchard, *Scholars' Bedlam*, p. 96.

23. Walter Reed, *An Exemplary History of the Novel: The Quixotic Versus the Picaresque* (Chicago: University of Chicago Press, 1981), p. 124.
24. Erasmus, *The Education of a Christian Prince*, trans. Neil M. Cheshire and Michael J. Heath, ed. Lisa Jardine (New York: Cambridge University Press, 1997) p. 61; cf. Cascardi, *Cervantes, Literature*, p. 21.
25. Milan Kundera, *The Curtain: An Essay in Seven Parts* (New York: HarperCollins, 2006), p. 8.
26. Cascardi, *Cervantes, Literature*, p. 244.
27. Fuentes, *Buried Mirror*, p. 177.
28. Michel Foucault, *Madness and Civilization: A History of Insanity in the Age of Reason*, trans. Richard Howard (New York: Vintage, 1988), p. 29.
29. Alonso Fernandez de Avellaneda had, between the publications of Cervantes's two books, published his own sequel and therefore Cervantes's *Quixote* must, in Book Two, repeatedly assert the reality of his own adventures and the inauthenticity of those recounted by Avellaneda.
30. Joseph Hall, "Prologue, Satires: Book I," *The Works of Joseph Hall, with Some Account of his Life and Sufferings* (Oxford: D.A. Talboys, 1839), p. 156. *Google Books*. Web.
31. Raman Selden, *English Verse Satire 1590–1765* (London: George Allen & Unwin, 1978), pp. 46, 49.
32. Kernan, *Cankered Muse*, pp. 1, 44.
33. I owe this reference to David Currell.
34. Kernan, *Cankered Muse*, pp. 81, 81.
35. Kernan, *Cankered Muse*, pp. 1, 44, 45.
36. Manley, *Literature and Culture*, p. 373.
37. Selden, *English Verse Satire*, p. 46.
38. Manley, *Literature and Culture*, p. 390.
39. John Marston, "Prologue, Book III," *The Scourge of Villanie*, quoted in Kernan, *Cankered Muse*, p. 96.
40. Hall, "Satire III," *The Works of Joseph Hall*, p. 263.
41. Selden, *English Verse Satire*, p. 52.
42. Kernan, *Cankered Muse*, p. 115.
43. Feinberg, *Introduction to Satire*, pp. 72–73. On Combe and his Romantic successors, see Marcus Wood, *Radical Satire and Print Culture 1790–1822* (Oxford: Clarendon Press, 1994), pp. 265–266.
44. See James S. Baumlin, "Generic Context of Elizabethan Satire: Rhetoric, Poetic Theory, and Imitation," *Renaissance Genres: Essays on Theory, History, and Interpretation*, ed. Barbara Kiefer Lewalski (Cambridge, MA: Harvard University Press, 1986); Heather Dubrow, "'No Man Is an Island': Donne's Satires and Satiric Tradition," *SEL: Studies in English Literature* 19 (1979), pp. 71–83; Selden, *English Verse Satire*, pp. 59–61.
45. Kernan, *Cankered Muse*, p. 8.
46. Manley, *Literature and Culture*, p. 394.

47. Manley, *Literature and Culture*, p. 385.
48. Quoted in Richard McCabe, "Elizabethan Satire and the Bishops' Ban of 1599," *The Yearbook of English Studies* 11 (1981), p. 188.
49. McCabe, "Elizabethan Satire," p. 192.
50. Andrew McRae, *Literature, Satire, and the Early Stuart State* (New York: Cambridge University Press, 2009), p. 29.
51. Ben Jonson, "Poetaster," *The Complete Plays of Ben Jonson* (London: Dent, 1925), p. 302.
52. Robert B. Pierce, "Ben Jonson's Horace and Horace's Ben Jonson," *Studies in Philology* 78 (1981), p. 23.
53. Ben Jonson, "Every Man Out of His Humour," *The Complete Plays*, p. 61.
54. Jonson, "The Poetaster," p. 306.
55. Douglas Duncan, *Ben Jonson and the Lucianic Tradition* (New York: Cambridge University Press, 1979), p. 152.
56. Brian Gibbons, *Jacobean City Comedy* (Cambridge, MA: Harvard University Press, 1968), p. 26.
57. Ben Jonson, "Every Man Out of His Humour," p. 62.
58. Anne Barton, *Ben Jonson, Dramatist* (New York: Cambridge University Press, 1984), pp. 113–14.
59. Gibbons, *Jacobean City Comedy*, pp. 24, 11, 17.
60. Kernan, *Cankered Muse*, p. 190.
61. Oliver Hennessey, "Jonson's Joyless Economy: Theorizing Motivation and Pleasure in *Volpone*," *English Literary Renaissance* (2008), p. 83.
62. Gibbons, *Jacobean City Comedy*, p. 30.

Enlightenment Satire: The Prose Tradition

1. On the problems with "Tory," see *SCR*, p. 151; with "Scriblerian," see *PSE*, p. 335; with "Augustan," see Margaret Anne Doody, *The Daring Muse: Augustan Poetry Reconsidered* (New York: Cambridge University Press, 1985), pp. 1–3, and *PSE*, p. 289.
2. J. Paul Hunter, *Before Novels: The Cultural Contexts of Eighteenth Century Fiction* (New York: Norton, 1990), p. 170; Claude Rawson, *Gulliver and the Gentle Reader* (Boston: Routledge & Kegan Paul, 1973), p. 5.
3. Aaron Santesso, "The New Atlantis and Varronian Satire," *Philological Quarterly*, 79.2 (2000), pp. 177–204.
4. M. Dorothy George, *Hogarth to Cruikshank: Social Change in Graphic Satire* (New York: Walker and Company, 1967), p. 13.
5. Habermas, *Structural Transformation*, pp. 58–67.
6. Hunter, *Before Novels*, p. 171.

7. Catherine Gallagher, *Nobody's Story: The Vanishing Acts of Women Writers in the Marketplace, 1670–1820* (Berkeley: University of California Press, 1995), pp. 94, 93.

8. John Richetti, *The Life of Daniel Defoe* (Malden: Wiley-Blackwell, 2005), p. 44.

9. Claude Rawson, *God, Gulliver, and Genocide: Barbarism and the European Imagination 1492–1945* (New York: Oxford University Press, 2001), p. 185.

10. Paul Alkon, "Defoe's Argument in 'The Shortest Way with the Dissenters,'" *Modern Philology* 73.4 (1976), p. S19.

11. Booth, *Rhetoric*, pp. 105, 133.

12. Rawson, *God, Gulliver, and Genocide*, pp. 187, 79.

13. George Wittkowsky, "Swift's Modest Proposal: The Biography of an Early Georgian Pamphlet," *Journal of the History of Ideas* 4.1 (1943), p. 88.

14. Christian Thorne, *The Dialectic of Counter-Enlightenment* (Cambridge, MA: Harvard University Press, 2010), p. 235.

15. Quoted in Bernard Mandeville, "A Vindication of the Book," in *The Fable of the Bees: Or Private Vices, Publick Benefits* (New York: Penguin, 1989), p. 388.

16. Shelley Burtt, *Virtue Transformed: Political Argument in England 1688–1740* (New York: Cambridge University Press, 1992), p. 140.

17. Mary Wortley Montagu, quoted in Kathleen Williams, ed., *Swift: The Critical Heritage* (New York: Routledge and Kegan Paul, 1970), p. 65.

18. Rosenheim, *Swift*, pp. 90–91.

19. John Traugott, "The Yahoo in the Doll's House: *Gulliver's Travels*, the Children's Classic," *The Yearbook of English Studies* 14 (1984), pp. 127–150.

20. James L. Clifford, "Gulliver's Fourth Voyage: 'Hard' and 'Soft' Schools of Interpretation," *Quick Springs of Sense: Studies in the Eighteenth Century*, ed. Larry S. Champion (Athens, GA: University of Georgia Press, 1974), pp. 33–49.

21. Rawson, *God, Gulliver, and Genocide*, p. 262

22. Srinivas Aravamudan, *Enlightenment Orientalism: Resisting the Rise of the Novel* (Chicago: University of Chicago Press, 2011), pp. 79, 17–20.

23. Carey McIntosh, *The Choice of Life: Samuel Johnson and the World of Fiction* (New Haven: Yale University Press, 1973), p. 211.

24. Paul Fussell, *Samuel Johnson and the Life of Writing* (New York: Harcourt, 1971), p. 221.

25. W. Jackson Bate, "Johnson and Satire *Manqué*," *Eighteenth Century Studies Presented in Memory of Donald F. Hyde*, ed. W.H. Bond (New York: Grolier Club, 1970), p. 150.

26. David Hume, *A Treatise of Human Nature*, ed. L.A. Selby-Bigge (Oxford: Clarendon Press, 1985), p. 269.

27. Auerbach, *Mimesis*, p. 411.

Verse Satire from Rochester to Byron

1. David Nokes, *Raillery and Rage: A Study of Eighteenth Century Satire* (New York: St. Martin's, 1987), p. 1.
2. William Bowman Piper, *The Heroic Couplet* (Cleveland: Case Western Reserve, 1969), p. 26.
3. Piper, *Heroic Couplet*, pp. 23–24; Doody, *Daring Muse*, p. 233; J. Paul Hunter, "Formalism and History: Binarism and the Anglophone Couplet," *MLQ: Modern Language Quarterly* 61.1 (2000), p. 113.
4. Hunter, "Formalism and History," p. 121. See also Doody, *Daring Muse*.
5. Selden, *English Verse Satire*, p. 72
6. Doody, *Daring Muse*, p. 55, ch. 2 *passim*.
7. Doody, *Daring Muse*, pp. 32, 34.
8. Hume "'Satire' in the Reign of Charles II," p. 345.
9. Selden, *English Verse Satire*, p. 90.
10. John Harold Wilson, *The Court Wits of the Restoration: An Introduction* (Princeton: Princeton University Press, 1948), pp. 8, 25.
11. Love, *English Clandestine Satire*, p. 29.
12. Wilson, *The Court Wits*, p. 16.
13. John Sheffield, Earl of Mulgrave, and John Dryden, "From 'An Essay on Satire,'" *Rochester: Selected Poems*, ed. Paul Davis (Oxford: Oxford University Press, 2013), p. 73.
14. Love, *English Clandestine Satire*, p. 42.
15. Laura Brown, *Fables of Modernity: Literature and Culture in the English Eighteenth Century* (Ithaca: Cornell University Press), pp. 34, 35.
16. On the epistle, see Howard D. Weinbrot, *The Formal Strain: Studies in Augustan Imitation and Satire* (Chicago: University of Chicago Press, 1969), pp. 129, 137.
17. Claude Rawson, "War and the Epic Mania in England and France: Milton, Boileau, Prior, and English Mock-Heroic," *Review of English Studies* 64.265 (2013), p. 433; Rawson, "Mock-Heroic and English Poetry," *The Cambridge Companion to the Epic*, ed. Catherine Bates (New York: Cambridge University Press, 2010), p. 169.
18. Howard D. Weinbrot, *Eighteenth-Century Satire: Essays on Text and Context from Dryden to Peter Pindar* (Cambridge: Cambridge University Press, 1988), p. 107.
19. Selden, *English Verse Satire*, p. 106.
20. On Dryden's debt to Milton, David Currell, "Epic Satire: Structures of Heroic Mockery in Early Modern English Literature," unpublished Ph. D. dissertation (2012).
21. Weinbrot, *Eighteenth-Century Satire*, p. 87.

22. Brown, *Fables*, pp. 137, 143; Valerie Rumbold, *Women's Place in Pope's World* (New York: Cambridge University Press, 1989), p. 167.

23. Brown, *Fables*, p. 149.

24. Joseph Spence, *Anecdotes, Observations, and Characters of Books and Men* (London: W. Scott, 1890), p. 131. *Internet Archive*. Web.

25. On the lapdog as sexual toy, see Felicity A. Nussbaum, *The Brink of All We Hate: English Satires on Women 1660–1750* (Lexington: University Press of Kentucky, 1984), p. 141.

26. Weinbrot, *Eighteenth-Century Satire*, p. 117.

27. Rumbold, *Women's Place*, p. 70.

28. Thorne, *Dialectic*, p. 256.

29. Sontag, *Against Interpretation*, p. 280.

30. Ritchie Robertson, *Mock-Epic Poetry from Pope to Heine* (New York: Oxford University Press, 2009), p. 99.

31. Rumbold, *Women's Place*, p. 1; Nussbaum, *Brink*, p. 162.

32. Nussbaum, *Brink*, p. 30. On Gould, pp. 25–30; on Egerton, pp. 31–34.

33. Nussbaum, *Brink*, p. 148.

34. Robert Halsband, *The Life of Lady Mary Wortley Montagu* (New York: Oxford University Press, 1960), pp. 131–132.

35. Review of *Lord Hervey's Memoirs*, *The Quarterly Review* 82 (1848), p. 508. *Google Books*. Web.

36. Halsband, *The Life*, p. 142.

37. George E. Haggerty, *Men in Love: Masculinity and Sexuality in the Eighteenth Century* (New York: Columbia University Press, 1999), p. 71.

38. Simon Dickie, *Cruelty and Laughter: Forgotten Comic Literature and the Unsentimental Eighteenth Century* (Chicago: University of Chicago Press, 2011), p. 41.

39. Robert Halsband and Isobel Grundy, "Notes," in Mary Wortley Montagu, *Essays and Poems and Simplicity, a Comedy*, ed. Halsband and Grundy (Oxford: Clarendon Press, 1977), p. 273.

40. Robertson, *Mock-Epic Poetry*, p. 99.

41. Weinbrot, *Formal Strain*, esp. pp. 25–29.

42. Lawrence Lipking, *Samuel Johnson: The Life of an Author* (Cambridge, MA: Harvard University Press, 1998), p. 70; Weinbrot, *Formal Strain*, p. 173.

43. Lipking, *Samuel Johnson*, p. 70.

44. Weinbrot, *Eighteenth-Century Satire*, p. 182, cf. *Formal Strain*, pp. 210–217.

45. Leo Damrosch, *Samuel Johnson and the Tragic Sense* (Princeton: Princeton University Press, 1972), p. 153.

46. Damrosch, *Samuel Johnson*, p. 152.

47. Thomas Lockwood, *Post-Augustan Satire: Charles Churchill and Satirical Poetry 1750–1800* (Seattle: University of Washington Press, 1979), p. 175.

48. Charles Churchill, "Epistle to William Hogarth," *Poems of C. Churchill* (London: Dryden Leach, 1763), p. 146. *Internet Archive*. Web.

49. Gary Dyer, *British Satire and the Politics of Style, 1789–1832* (New York: Cambridge University Press, 2006), esp. pp. 21–38.

50. James Engel, "Satiric Spirits of the Later Eighteenth Century: Johnson to Crabbe," *CS*, p. 239.

51. Steven E. Jones, *Satire and Romanticism* (New York: St. Martin's, 2000), pp. 3, 5; Samuel Taylor Coleridge, *Notes and Lectures Upon Shakespeare and Some of the Old Poets and Dramatists: With Other Literary Remains of S. T. Coleridge*, Volume 2 (London: W. Pickering, 1849), p. 241. *Google Books*. Web. Cf. Lockwood, *Post-Augustan*, p. 171.

52. Jones, *Shelley's Satire*; Dyer, *British Satire*.

53. Wood, *Radical Satire and Print Culture 1790–1822*, p. 215 ff.

54. Quoted in Dyer, *British Satire*, p. 16.

55. Frederick L. Beaty, *Byron the Satirist* (DeKalb, IL: Northern Illinois University Press, 1985), p. 5.

56. Matthew Arnold, "The Study of Poetry," *Essays in Criticism* (Boston: Allyn and Bacon, 1896), p. 23. *Internet Archive*. Web.

57. John Hollander, "Rev. of Not Much Fun: The Lost Poems of Dorothy Parker," *Yale Review* 85.1 (1997), p. 157.

58. T.S. Eliot, *The Waste Land: A Facsimile and Transcript of the Original Drafts*, ed. Valerie Eliot (New York: Harcourt, 1971), p. 39.

59. W.H. Auden, *Collected Poems* (New York: Random House, 1976), p. 201.

60. Walcott, *Fortunate Traveler*, p. 60.

Introduction: Satire and the Novel

1. Ronald Paulson, *Don Quixote in England: The Aesthetics of Laughter* (Baltimore: Johns Hopkins University Press, 1998), pp. xii, xv.

2. Matthew Hodgart, *Satire* (New York: McGraw-Hill, 1969), p. 214; Wood, *Irresponsible Self*, p. 11; *LS*, p. 206.

3. Palmeri, *Satire in Narrative*, p. 13.

4. Frank Palmeri, "Cruikshank, Thackeray, and the Victorian Eclipse of Satire," *Studies in English* Literature, *1500–1900* 44.4 (2004), p. 753.

5. William Makepeace Thackeray, "Fielding's Works," *Critical Papers in Literature* (London: Macmillan, 1904), p. 204. *Google Books*. Web.

6. Matz, *Satire in an Age of Realism*, p. 23.

7. Hume, "Diffused Satire," p. 305.

8. Lewis, *Men Without Art*, p. 121.

9. Sara Gadeken, "Sarah Fielding and the Salic Law of Wit," *Studies in English* Literature, *1500–1900* 42.3 (2002), pp. 541–550.

10. Layne Neeper, "'To Soften the Heart': George Saunders, Postmodern Satire, and Empathy," *Studies in American Humor* 2.2 (2016), pp. 280–299.

Small Worlds: The Comedy of Manners

1. Huxley, *Crome Yellow*, p. 73.
2. Bourdieu, *Field*, p. 150.
3. Lionel Trilling, "Manners, Morals, and the Novel," *The Liberal Imagination: Essays on Literature and Society* (New York: Viking, 1950), p. 194.
4. Joseph Litvak, *Strange Gourmets: Sophistication, Theory, and the Novel* (Durham: Duke University Press, 1997), pp. 5, 14; see also Faye Hammill, *Sophistication: A Literary and Cultural History* (Liverpool: Liverpool University Press, 2010).
5. James R. Kincaid, "Anthony Trollope's Unmannerly Novel," *Reading and Writing Women's Lives: A Study of the Novel of Manners*, ed. Barbara Brothers and Bege K. Bowers (Ann Arbor: UMI Research, 1990), pp. 87–93.
6. David Galef, "Forster, Ford, and the New Novel of Manners," *The Columbia History of the British Novel*, ed. John Richetti et al. (New York: Columbia University Press, 1994), p. 819.
7. Wood, *Irresponsible Self*, p. 14.
8. Georg Simmel, "The Metropolis and Mental Life," *On Individual and Social Forms* (Chicago: University of Chicago Press, 1971), p. 339.
9. Rawson, *Satire and Sentiment*, p. 287.
10. English, *Comic Transactions*, p. 55.
11. Waugh, *Vile Bodies*, pp. 121–122.
12. Kingsley Amis, *Lucky Jim* (New York: Penguin, 1992), p. 14.
13. Jeffrey J. Williams, "The Rise of the Academic Novel," *American Literary History* 24.3 (2012), pp. 561–589.
14. David Lodge, *Changing Places: A Tale of Two Campuses* (New York: Penguin, 1985), p. 44.
15. David Lodge, "Introduction," in Amis, *Lucky Jim*, p. viii.
16. Philip Roth, *The Human Stain* (New York: Houghton Mifflin, 2000) p. 286.
17. The Latin reads, "*scilicet ut vellem curvo dinoscere rectum / atque inter silvas academi quaerere verum.*" Epistle 2.2, 44–45.

Unfortunate Travelers: The Picaresque

1. Robert Alter, *Rogue's Progress: Studies in the Picaresque Novel* (Cambridge, MA: Harvard University Press, 1964), p. ix.
2. Simon Dickie, "Picaresque and Rogue Fiction," *The Oxford History of the Novel in English*, Vol. 1, ed. Thomas Keymer (New York: Oxford University Press, forthcoming), n.p.
3. Reed, *Exemplary History*, pp. 43–44.
4. Virginia Woolf, "Defoe," *The Common Reader: First Series* (New York: Harcourt, Brace, and World, 1925), p. 92.
5. Reed, *Exemplary History*, p. 57.

6. Claudio Guillén, *Literature as System: Essays toward the Theory of Literary History* (Princeton: Princeton University Press, 1971), p. 83.
7. William Makepeace Thackeray, *The Memoirs of Mr. Barry Lyndon, Esq.* (New York: Oxford University Press, 1984), p. 89.
8. Libby Murphy, *The Art of Survival: France and the Great War Picaresque* (New Haven: Yale University Press, 2016) pp. 12–13.
9. Reed, *Exemplary History*, pp. 45–46.
10. Dickie, "Picaresque and Rogue Fiction," n.p.
11. Simon Dickie, "Tobias Smollett and the Ramble Novel," *The Oxford History of the Novel in English: Vol. 2*, ed. Simon Garside and Karen O'Brien (New York: Oxford University Press, 2015), p. 93.
12. Tobias Smollett, *The Adventures of Roderick Random* (New York: Oxford University Press, 2008), p. xxxiii.
13. Michael McKeon, *The Origins of the English Novel, 1600–1740* (Baltimore: Johns Hopkins University Press, 1987) p. 98.
14. Henry Fielding, *The Life of Mr. Jonathan Wild the Great* (New York: Signet, 1962), p. 53.
15. Thackeray, *Barry Lyndon*, p. 310.
16. Thackeray, *Barry Lyndon*, p. 129.
17. Alter, *Rogue's Progress*, p. 109.
18. Dickie, *Cruelty and Laughter, passim.*
19. Martin Battestin, "Introduction," in Henry Fielding, *Joseph Andrews and Shamela*, ed. Battestin (Boston: Houghton Mifflin, 1961) p. xxxi.
20. Dickie, *Cruelty and Laughter*, p. 160
21. McKeon, *Origins*, p. 407.
22. John Forster, *The Life of Charles Dickens*, Ch. 6. Project Gutenberg. Web.
23. "To W. D. Howells," *The Adventures of Huckleberry Finn* by Mark Twain, ed. Thomas Cooley (New York: Norton, 1999), p. 299.
24. Alexander Welsh, *Reflections on the Hero as Quixote* (Princeton: Princeton University Press, 1981), p. 96.
25. Toni Morrison, "Introduction," in Twain, *Huckleberry Finn*, ed. Cooley, p. 388.
26. Arthur G. Pettit, *Mark Twain and the South* (Lexington: University Press of Kentucky, 1974), pp. 87–88.
27. Wayne C. Booth, *The Rhetoric of Fiction* (Chicago: University of Chicago Press, 1961), p. 159.
28. David L. Smith, "Huck, Jim, and American Racial Discourse," in Twain, *Huckleberry Finn*, ed. Cooley, p. 371.
29. Mark Twain, *Mississippi Writings: Tom Sawyer, Life on the Mississippi, Huckleberry Finn, Pudd'nhead Wilson* (New York: Library of America, 1982), p. 502.

30. Daniel Tracy, "From Vernacular Humor to Middlebrow Modernism: *Gentlemen Prefer Blondes* and the Creation of Literary Value," *Arizona Quarterly* 66.1 (2010), p. 127.

31. Susan Hegeman, "Taking Blondes Seriously," *American Literary History* 7.3 (1995), p. 534.

32. Faye Hammill, "'One of the Few Books that Doesn't Stink': The Intellectuals, the Masses and *Gentlemen Prefer Blondes*," *Critical Survey* 17.3 (2005), p. 41.

33. Jeffrey M. Heath, *The Picturesque Prison: Evelyn Waugh and His Writing* (Montreal: McGill-Queens University Press, 1983), p. 295.

34. Rita Barnard, *The Great Depression and the Culture of Abundance: Kenneth Fearing, Nathanael West, and Mass Culture in the 1930s* (New York: Cambridge University Press, 1995), p. 140.

35. Jonathan Veitch, *American Superrealism: Nathanael West and the Politics of Representation in the 1930s* (Madison: University of Wisconsin Press, 1997), p. 91.

36. Quoted in Veitch, *American Superrealism*, p. 94.

37. Murphy, *Art of Survival*, p. xiii.

38. Ralph Ellison, *Invisible Man* (New York: Random House, 1995), p. 16.

39. Dickson-Carr, *African American Satire*, p. 36.

40. Ruth Wisse, *No Joke: Making Jewish Humor* (Princeton: Princeton University Press, 2013), p. 237.

41. Menachem Feuer and Andrew Schmitz, "Hup! Hup! We Must Tumble: Toward an Ethical Reading of the Schlemiel," *MFS: Modern Fiction Studies* 54.1 (2008), p. 971.

42. Leshu Torchin, "Cultural Learnings of Borat Make for Benefit Glorious Study of Documentary," *Film and History* 38 (2008), p. 55

43. Nicholas D. Nace, "Interactive Satire: The Reality of Fiction," *Teaching Modern British and American Satire*, ed. Evan Davis and Nicholas D. Nace (New York: Modern Language Association, forthcoming) n.p.

44. Torchin, "Cultural Learnings," p. 58.

The Menippean Novel

1. Weisenburger, *Fables*, p. 6.

2. Weisenburger, *Fables*, p. 5

3. Jean-François Lytoard, *The Postmodern Condition: A Report on Knowledge*, trans. Geoffrey Bennington and Brian Massumi (Minneapolis: University of Minnesota Press, 1984).

4. Ian Gregson, *Character and Satire in Postwar Fiction* (New York: Continuum, 2008), pp. 4–5, 153.

5. Elkin, *Augustan Defence*, p. 189; Weinbrot, *Menippean Satire*, p. 9.

6. D.W. Jefferson, "Tristram Shandy and the Tradition of Learned Wit," *Essays in Criticism* 1.3 (1951), pp. 225–248.

7. Benjamin, "The Storyteller," *Illuminations*, 87.

8. Palmeri, "Narrative Satire in the Nineteenth Century," *CS*, p. 352.

9. D.A. Miller, *The Novel and the Police* (Berkeley: University of California Press, 1988), p. 60; Charles Dickens, *Bleak House* (Garden City, NY: Doubleday, 1953), p. 3.

10. Clayton, *Charles Dickens*, p. 148.

11. George Orwell, *A Collection of Essays* (Garden City, NY: Doubleday, 1954), p. 56.

12. Robert Alter, *Partial Magic: The Novel as a Self-Conscious Genre* (Berkeley: University of California Press, 1975), p. 89.

13. Maria DiBattista, "Introduction," in Virginia Woolf, *Orlando*, ed. DiBattista (New York: Harcourt, 2006), p. lxi.

14. Edward Mendelson, "Encyclopedic Narrative: From Dante to Pynchon," *MLN* 91.6 (1976), p. 1269. On Melville and Sterne's similaries, Carole Fabricant, "*Tristram Shandy* and *Moby-Dick*: A Cock and Bull Story and a Tale of a Tub," *Journal of Narrative Technique* 7.1 (1977), pp. 57–69.

15. Matz, *Satire in an Age of Realism*, p. 170.

16. James Joyce, *Ulysses* (New York: Random House, 1986), p. 345.

17. Hugh Kenner, *Samuel Beckett: A Critical Study* (Berkeley: University of California Press, 1968), p. 37. Cf. M. Keith Booker, *Flann O'Brien, Bakhtin, and Menippean Satire* (Syracuse: Syracuse University Press, 1995).

18. Flann O'Brien, *At Swim-Two-Birds* (Normal, IL: Dalkey Archive, 1998), pp. 6, 33.

19. Flann O'Brien, *The Third Policeman* (Normal, IL: Dalkey Archive, 1999), pp. 92, 145.

20. Samuel Beckett, *Murphy* (New York: Grove Wiedenfeld, 1957), p. 178.

21. Samuel Beckett, *Molloy, Malone Dies, The Unnamable: Three Novels by Samuel Beckett* (New York: Grove, 1958), p. 80.

22. Beckett, *Molloy*, p. 41.

23. Brian McHale, *Postmodernist Fiction* (New York: Routledge, 1987), p. 172.

24. Tom LeClair, *The Art of Excess: Mastery in Contemporary American Fiction* (Urbana: University of Illinois Press), p. 14.

25. Hannah Arendt, *On Violence* (Boston: Houghton Mifflin Harcourt, 1970), p. 81.

26. Alan Nadel, *Containment Culture: American Narrative, Postmodernism, and the Atomic Age* (Durham: Duke University Press, 1995), p. 182.

27. Henry Louis Gates, *Signifying Monkey: A Theory of Afro-American Literary Criticism* (New York: Oxford University Press, 1988), p. 255.

28. Leo Bersani, *The Culture of Redemption* (Cambridge, MA: Harvard University Press, 1990), pp. 181–182.

29. Michael Seidel, "The Satiric Plots of *Gravity's Rainbow*," *Pynchon: A Collection of Critical Essays*, ed. Edward Mendelson (Englewood, NJ: Prentice-Hall, 1978), pp. 193–194.

30. Bersani, *Culture of Redemption*, p. 198.

31. Jackson Cope, *Robert Coover's Fictions* (Baltimore: Johns Hopkins University Press, 1986), p. 94.

32. LeClair, *Art of Excess*, p. 110.

33. LeClair, *Art of Excess*, p. 121.

34. Kernan, *Plot*, p. 65.

35. Wallace, "E Unibus Pluram," pp. 181, 183.

36. Wood, *Irresponsible Self*, p. 180.

37. Konstantinou, *Cool Characters*, p. 38.

38. Tom Moylan, *Scraps on Untainted Sky: Science Fiction, Utopia, Dystopia* (New York: Perseus Books, 2000), p. 138; Jameson, *Archaeologies*, p. 198.

39. Kingsley Amis, *New Maps of Hell: A Survey of Science Fiction* (Princeton: Princeton University Press, 1960), pp. 120, 155.

40. Krishan Kumar, *Utopia and Anti-Utopia in Modern Times* (Oxford: Basil Blackwell, 1987), p. 105.

41. Irving Howe, "The Fiction of Anti-Utopia," *The New Republic*, April 23, 1962, p. 14.

42. George Orwell, *Nineteen Eighty-Four* (New York: Penguin, 2003), p. 106.

43. Orwell, *Collection*, p. 177.

44. Keith Leslie Johnson, "Ethics in the Late Anthropocene," *Brave New World: Contexts and Legacies*, ed. Jonathan Greenberg and Nathan Waddell (London: Palgrave, 2016), p. 170.

45. Gregory Claeys, "The Origins of Dystopia: Wells, Huxley, and Orwell," *The Cambridge Companion to Utopian Literature*, ed. Gregory Claeys (New York: Cambridge University Press, 2011), p. 109.

46. Will Self, *Great Apes* (New York: Grove, 1997), p. 404.

Satire and Popular Culture since 1900

1. Craig Howes, "Comic/Satiric Periodicals," *The Routledge Handbook to Nineteenth-Century British Periodicals and Newspapers*, ed. Alexis Easley et al. (New York: Routledge, 2016), p. 323. Cf. Richard D. Altick, "Nineteenth Century English Periodicals," *The Newberry Library Bulletin* 9 (1952), pp. 255–264. *The Newberry Library*. Web. www.newberry.org.

2. Palmeri, "Cruikshank, Thackeray," p. 771.

3. Quoted in Ben Yagoda, *About Town: The New Yorker and the World It Made* (New York: Scribner's, 2000), p. 38.

4. Raymond Williams, quoted in Iain Topliss, *The Comic Worlds of Peter Arno, William Steig, Charles Addams, and Saul Steinberg* (Baltimore: Johns Hopkins University Press, 2005), p. 7.

5. Topliss, *Comic Worlds*, esp. pp. 39–44.

6. H.L. Mencken, "From a Critic's Notebook," *Prejudices: Fourth, Fifth, and Sixth Series* (New York: Library of America, 2010), pp. 80–81.

7. Quoted in Marion Rodgers, *Mencken: The American Iconoclast* (New York: Oxford University Press, 2005), pp. 1, 122.

8. Richard Wright, *Black Boy* (New York: Harper, 2015), p. 284.

9. See Sharon Hamilton, "American Manners," *The Oxford Critical and Cultural History of American Magazines*, Vol. 2, ed. Peter Brooker and Andrew Thacker (New York: Oxford University Press, 2012), pp. 224–248; Faye Hammill and Karen Leick, "Modernism and the Quality Magazines," in *Critical and Cultural History*, ed. Brooker and Thacker, pp. 176–196; David Earle, *Re-Covering Modernism: Pulps, Paperbacks, and the Prejudice of Form* (Burlington, VT: Ashgate, 2009).

10. Quoted in Hammill and Leick, "Quality Magazines," p. 183

11. Rodgers, *Mencken*, pp. 3, 184.

12. Ernest Hemingway, *The Sun Also Rises* (New York: Scribner, 2006), p. 49.

13. H.L. Mencken, *A Mencken Chrestomathy* (New York: Random, 1982), p. 584. First published in the 1920 edition of *The American Language*.

14. H.L. Mencken, "Gamalielese," *On Politics: A Carnival of Buncombe*, ed. Malcolm Moos (Baltimore: Johns Hopkins University Press, 2006), p. 42.

15. Mencken, "In Memoriam: W.J.B." *Prejudices: Fourth, Fifth, and Sixth Series*, pp. 214–215, 216, 217, 219.

16. Both attributions are ubiquitous, though I can find original sources for neither. Even if spurious, they have become part of the Parker persona.

17. Nina Miller, *Making Love Modern: The Intimate Public Worlds of New York's Literary Women* (New York: Oxford University Press, 1999), p. 89.

18. Miller, *Making Love Modern*, p. 4.

19. Dorothy Parker, "Reading and Writing," *New Yorker*, September 15, 1928, *The New Yorker Digital Archive*. Web.

20. Jessica Burstein, "A Few Words about Dubuque: Modernism, Sentimentalism, and the Blasé," *American Literary History* 14.2 (2002), p. 236; on Bourdieu, p. 234.

21. Burstein, "A Few Words," p. 240.

22. See Topliss, *The Comic Worlds*, p. 188.

23. John Hollander, "Dorothy Parker and the Art of Light Verse," *Yale Review* 85.1 (1997), pp. 157–158.

24. On compression and seriality as techniques of sophistication, see Burstein, "A Few Words," pp. 237ff.

25. Tom Lehrer, "We Will All Go Together When We Go," *An Evening Wasted with Tom Lehrer* (Cambridge, MA: Lehrer Records, 1959).

26. Steven Kercher, *Revel with a Cause: Liberal Satire in Postwar America* (Chicago: University of Chicago Press, 2006).

27. James D. Bloom, *The Comic Jewish Shaping of Modern America* (Westport, CT: Praeger, 2003), p. 49.

28. Kercher, *Revel*, pp. 63, 145.

29. Paul Krassner, "The Parts that Were Left Out of the Kennedy Book," *The Realist* 74 (May 1967), p. 18.

30. Art Simon, *Dangerous Knowledge: The JFK Assassination in Art and Film* (Philadelphia: Temple University Press, 1996), p. 64.

31. Gerald Nachman, *Seriously Funny: The Rebel Comedians of the 1950s and 1960s* (New York: Pantheon, 2003), p. 10.

32. Jonathan Miller, Alan Bennett, both quoted in Humphrey Carpenter, *A Great Silly Grin: The British Satire Boom of the 1960s* (New York: Public Affairs, 2002), p. 97.

33. Quoted in Carpenter, *Great Silly Grin*, p. 131; on Ross's *New Yorker*, p. 49; on *Mad*, p. 156. Cf. Kercher, *Revel*, p. 183.

34. Kercher, *Revel*, p. 120.

35. Stephen Wragg, "Comedy, Politics and Permissiveness: The 'Satire Boom' and its Inheritance," *Contemporary Politics* 8.4 (2002), pp. 319–334.

36. J. Hoberman, "When the Nazis Became Nudniks," *The New York Times*, April 15, 2001.

37. Henriksen, *Dr. Strangelove's America*, p. 318.

38. Robert Brustein, "Out of This World," *The New York Review of Books*, February 6, 1964.

39. Walter Benjamin, "The Work of Art in the Age of Mechanical Reproduction," *Illuminations*, p. 242.

40. Helene Keyssar, *Robert Altman's America* (New York: Oxford University Press, 1991), p. 57.

41. Keyssar, *Robert Altman's*, p. 58.

42. Randy Newman, "Political Science," *Sail Away* (New York: Reprise Records, 1972).

43. Nace, "Interactive Satire," n.p.

44. Amber Day, *Satire and Dissent: Interventions in Contemporary Debate* (Bloomington: Indiana University Press, 2011), p. 7.

45. *Real Life*, directed Albert Brooks, written by Albert Brooks, Monica Johnson, and Harry Shearer (Paramount Pictures, 1979).

46. Day, *Satire and Dissent*, p. 107.

47. David Marc, "Foreword," *Satire TV: Politics and Debate in the Post-Network Era*, ed. Jonathan Gray, Jeffrey P. Jones, and Ethan Thompson (New York: NYU Press, 2009), p. x.

48. Tom Carson, "The Legacy of David Letterman, Icon of the Grizzled Generation," Rev. of *Letterman: The Last Giant of Late Night* by Jason Zinoman, *The New York Times*, April 10, 2017.

49. Jonathan Gray, Jeffrey P. Jones, and Ethan Thompson, "The State of Satire, the Satire of the State," in *Satire TV*, ed. Gray, Jones, and Thompson, pp. 23–24.

50. Geoffrey Baym, *From Cronkite to Colbert: The Evolution of Broadcast News* (New York: Oxford University Press, 2009), p. 147.

51. "Bush Takes Charge," *Private Eye* 1037, September 21, 2001; "A Shattered Nation Longs to Care about Stupid Bullshit Again," *The Onion* 37.35, October 3, 2001; "Privileged Children of Millionaires Square off on World Stage," *The Onion* 37.38, October 24, 2001.

52. Sophia McClennen, *America According to Colbert: Satire as Public Pedagogy* (New York: Palgrave, 2011), p. 85.

53. Day, *Satire and Dissent*, p. 75.

54. Day, *Satire and Dissent*, pp. 71–72, 58; McClennen, *America*, p. 89.

55. McClennen, *America*, p. 99.

56. Baym, *Cronkite to Colbert*, p. 104.

57. *Crossfire.* "Jon Stewart." CNN. October 19, 2004. *YouTube.* Web. www.youtube.com/watch?t=601&v=aFQFB5YpDZE.

58. *The Colbert Report.* "The Word: Truthiness." Comedy Central. October 17, 2005. Web. www.cc.com/video-clips.

59. Baym, Cronkite to Colbert, p. 110; Day, *Satire and Dissent*, p. 73.

60. *The Daily Show.* "Bush versus Bush." Comedy Central. April 28, 2003. Web. www.cc.com/video-clips.

61. John Koblin, "When Fake News Was Funny," *The New York Times*, December 1, 2016. Web.

Charlie Hebdo, Satire and the Enlightenment

1. "About Us," *Pen America*. Web. https://pen.org/about.

2. Gregson, *Character and Satire*, p. 165.

3. Ernst Kris, *Psychoanalytic Explorations in Art* (New York: International Universities Press, 1952), p. 201. Kris's study exerted a major influence on Robert C. Elliott's foundational study of satire and violence, *The Power of Satire*.

4. Stephen Eric Bronner, *Reclaiming the Enlightenment: Toward a Politics of Radical Engagement* (New York: Columbia University Press, 2006), p. 1.

Editions Cited

For primary works from which I quote frequently, I cite the following editions using parenthetical references. In most cases, parenthetical references indicate page numbers; in other cases, I specify whether they refer to volumes, chapters, cantos, or lines.

Aristophanes. "Lysistrata." *Three Plays by Aristophanes: Staging Women.* Jeffrey Henderson, trans. and ed. New York: Routledge, 2010.

Austen, Jane. *Pride and Prejudice.* New York: Norton, 2001.

Byron, George Gordon. Lord. *Don Juan.* Boston: Houghton Mifflin, 1958. Stanza and canto.

Cervantes, Miguel de. *Don Quixote.* Edith Grossman, trans. New York: HarperCollins, 2003. Book, chapter, and page.

Collier, Jane. *An Essay on the Art of Ingeniously Tormenting.* Katherine A. Craik, ed. Oxford: Oxford University Press, 2006.

Compton-Burnett, Ivy. *A House and Its Head.* New York: New York Review of Books, 2001.

Coover, Robert. *The Public Burning.* New York: Bantam, 1978.

Defoe, Daniel. "The Shortest Way with the Dissenters." *Selected Writings of Daniel Defoe.* New York: Cambridge University Press, 1975.

DeLillo, Don. *White Noise.* New York: Penguin, 1985.

Dickens, Charles. *Little Dorrit.* New York: Oxford University Press, 1982.
The Posthumous Papers of the Pickwick Club. New York: Penguin, 1999.

Donne, John. *The Complete English Poems of John Donne.* C.A. Patrides, ed. London: Dent, 1985. Satire and line. For modernization of spelling and punctuation, I have consulted *Selected Poems of John Donne.* Ilona Bell, ed. New York: Penguin, 2006.

Dryden, John. *Absalom and Achitophel* and *Mac Flecknoe. The Works of John Dryden, Vol. II: Poems 1681–1684.* H.T. Swedenberg, ed. Berkeley: University of California Press, 1972. Line.
"A Discourse Concerning the Original and Progress of Satire," and "Postscript to the Reader," *Essays of John Dryden, Vol. II.* W.P. Ker ed. New York: Russell & Russell, 1961.
"An Essay of Dramatic Poesy," *Essays of John Dryden, Vol. I.* W.P. Ker, ed. New York: Russell & Russell, 1961.

Erasmus, Desiderius. *The Praise of Folly*. Robert M. Adams, trans. and ed. New York: Norton, 1989.

Fielding, Henry. *Joseph Andrews* and *Shamela*. New York: Penguin, 1999.

Gibbons, Stella. *Cold Comfort Farm*. New York: Penguin, 2006.

Heller, Joseph. *Catch-22*. New York: Simon & Schuster, 2011.

Horace. *The Satires of Horace and Persius*. Niall Rudd, trans. and ed. New York: Penguin, 2005. Book, satire, and line.

Johnson, Samuel. *Selected Poetry and Prose*. Frank Brady and W.K. Wimsatt, eds. Berkeley: University of California Press, 1977. For *The History of Rasselas, Prince of Abyssinia*, chapter and page. For "London" and "The Vanity of Human Wishes," line.

Jonson, Ben. "Volpone." *Volpone and Other Plays*. Michael Jamieson, ed. New York: Penguin, 2004.

Juvenal. *The Sixteen Satires*. Peter Green trans. and ed. New York: Penguin, 3rd edn, 2004. Satire and line.

Lewis, Sinclair. *Babbitt*. New York: Oxford University Press, 2010.

Loos, Anita. *Gentlemen Prefer Blondes and But Gentlemen Marry Brunettes*. New York: Penguin, 1998.

Lucian. *Selected Satires of Lucian*. Lionel Casson, trans. and ed. New York: Norton, 1968.

Mandeville, Bernard. *The Fable of the Bees: Or Private Vices, Publick Benefits*. Philip Harth, ed. New York: Penguin, 1989.

McCarthy, Mary. *The Groves of Academe*. New York: Harcourt Books, 2002.

Montagu, Lady Mary Wortley. "Verses Addressed to the Imitator of the First Satire of the Second Book of Horace," *Essays and Poems and* Simplicity, a *Comedy*. Robert Halsband and Isobel Grundy, eds. Oxford: Clarendon Press, 1977. Line.

More, Thomas. *Utopia*. Robert M. Adams, trans. and ed. New York: Norton, 2010.

Nashe, Thomas. *The Unfortunate Traveller and Other Works*. J.B. Steane, ed. New York: Penguin, 1985.

Parker, Dorothy. *The Portable Dorothy Parker*. Marion Meade, ed. New York: Penguin, 2006.

Persius. *The Satires of Horace and Persius*. Niall Rudd trans. and ed. New York: Penguin, 2005. Satire and line.

Petronius. *The Satyricon*. P.G. Walsh, trans. and ed. New York: Oxford University Press, 2009.

Pope, Alexander. *The Poems of Alexander Pope: A Reduced Version of the Twickenham Text*. John Butt, ed. New Haven: Yale University Press, 1963. Line and, where relevant, page, canto, book, or epistle. Includes all cited writings of Pope.

Powell, Dawn. *A Time to Be Born*. South Royalton, VT: Steerforth Press, 1996.

Pynchon, Thomas. *Gravity's Rainbow*. New York: Penguin, 1973.

Rabelais, François. *Gargantua and Pantagruel*. M. A. Screech, trans. and ed. New York: Penguin, 2006. Book, chapter, and page.

Reed, Ishmael. *Mumbo Jumbo*. New York: Scribner's, 1996.

Rochester, John Wilmot, Earl of. *The Works of John Wilmot, Earl of Rochester.* Harold Love, ed. New York: Oxford, 1999. Page and line. For modernization and minor editorial modifications, *Selected Poems* by John Wilmot, Earl of Rochester. Paul Davis, ed. New York: Oxford University Press, 2013.

Sterne, Laurence. *The Life and Opinions of Tristram Shandy.* New York: Penguin, 1967. Book, chapter, and page.

Swift, Jonathan. *The Essential Writings of Jonathan Swift.* Claude Rawson and Ian Higgins, eds. New York: Norton, 2010. Page. Includes all cited writings of Swift except *Gulliver's Travels.*

Gulliver's Travels: Based on the 1726 Edition. Albert Rivero, ed. New York: Norton, 2002. Book, chapter, and page.

Twain, Mark. *The Adventures of Huckleberry Finn: A Norton Critical Edition.* Thomas Cooley, ed. New York: Norton, 1999.

Voltaire. *Candide: or Optimism.* Robert M. Adams, trans. and ed. New York: Norton, 1991. Chapter and page.

Waugh, Evelyn. *A Handful of Dust.* Boston: Little, Brown, 1934.

Decline and Fall. Boston, Little, Brown, 1928.

West, Nathanael. *A Cool Million* and *The Dream Life of Balso Snell.* New York: Farrar, Strauss, Giroux, 1996.

Films Cited

I quote from the following films.

Borat: Cultural Learnings of America for Make Benefit Glorious Nation of Kazakhstan. Directed by Larry Charles. Written by Sacha Baron Cohen, Peter Baynham, Anthony Hines, and Dan Mazer. 20th Century Fox, 2006.

Dr. Strangelove. Directed by Stanley Kubrick. Written by Stanley Kubrick, Terry Southern, and Peter George, from the novel *Red Alert* by Peter George. Columbia Pictures, 1964.

M*A*S*H. Directed by Robert Altman. Written by Ring Lardner, Jr. from the novel by Richard Hooker. 20th Century Fox, 1970.

Network. Directed by Peter Lumet. Written by Paddy Chayefsky. MGM/UA, 1976.

Index

Cambridge Introductions to Literature

Authors

Margaret Atwood Heidi Macpherson

Jane Austen (second edition) Janet Todd

Samuel Beckett Ronan McDonald

Walter Benjamin David Ferris

Lord Byron Richard Lansdown

Chaucer Alastair Minnis

Chekhov James N. Loehlin

J. M. Coetzee Dominic Head

Samuel Taylor Coleridge John Worthen

Joseph Conrad John Peters

Jacques Derrida Leslie Hill

Charles Dickens Jon Mee

Emily Dickinson Wendy Martin

George Eliot Nancy Henry

T. S. Eliot John Xiros Cooper

William Faulkner Theresa M. Towner

F. Scott Fitzgerald Kirk Curnutt

Michel Foucault Lisa Downing

Robert Frost Robert Faggen

Gabriel Garcia Marquez Gerald Martin

Nathaniel Hawthorne Leland S. Person

Zora Neale Hurston Lovalerie King

James Joyce Eric Bulson

Kafka Carolin Duttlinger

Thomas Mann Todd Kontje

Christopher Marlowe Tom Rutter

Herman Melville Kevin J. Hayes

Milton Stephen B. Dobranski

George Orwell John Rodden and John Rossi

Sylvia Plath Jo Gill

Edgar Allan Poe Benjamin F. Fisher

Ezra Pound Ira Nadel

Marcel Proust Adam Watt

Jean Rhys Elaine Savory

Edward Said Conor McCarthy

Shakespeare Emma Smith

Shakespeare's Comedies Penny Gay

Shakespeare's History Plays Warren Chernaik

Shakespeare's Poetry Michael Schoenfeldt

Shakespeare's Tragedies Janette Dillon

Tom Stoppard William W. Demastes

Harriet Beecher Stowe Sarah Robbins

Mark Twain Peter Messent

Edith Wharton Pamela Knights

Walt Whitman M. Jimmie Killingsworth

Virginia Woolf Jane Goldman

William Wordsworth Emma Mason

W. B. Yeats David Holdeman

Topics

American Literary Realism Phillip Barrish

The American Short Story Martin Scofield

Anglo-Saxon Literature Hugh Magennis

British Poetry, 1945–2010 Eric Falci

Contemporary American Fiction Stacey Olster